31 Days Before Your
CCNA Routing & Switching Exam

A Day-By-Day Review Guide for the ICND1/CCENT (100-105), ICND2 (200-105), and CCNA (200-125) Certification Exam

Allan Johnson

Cisco Press • 800 East 96th Street • Indianapolis, Indiana 46240 USA

31 Days Before Your CCNA Routing & Switching Exam

Allan Johnson

Copyright © 2017 Cisco Systems, Inc.

Published by:
Cisco Press
800 East 96th Street
Indianapolis, IN 46240 USA

Printed in the United States of America

1   17

Library of Congress Control Number: 2017932351

ISBN-13: 978-1-58720-590-3

ISBN-10: 1-58720-590-4

Warning and Disclaimer

This book is designed to provide information about exam topics for the Cisco Certified Networking Associate (CCNA) Certification. Every effort has been made to make this book as complete and as accurate as possible, but no warranty or fitness is implied.

The information is provided on an "as is" basis. The authors, Cisco Press, and Cisco Systems, Inc. shall have neither liability nor responsibility to any person or entity with respect to any loss or damages arising from the information contained in this book or from the use of the discs or programs that may accompany it.

The opinions expressed in this book belong to the author and are not necessarily those of Cisco Systems, Inc.

Trademark Acknowledgments

All terms mentioned in this book that are known to be trademarks or service marks have been appropriately capitalized. Cisco Press or Cisco Systems, Inc., cannot attest to the accuracy of this information. Use of a term in this book should not be regarded as affecting the validity of any trademark or service mark.

Special Sales

For information about buying this title in bulk quantities, or for special sales opportunities (which may include electronic versions; custom cover designs; and content particular to your business, training goals, marketing focus, or branding interests), please contact our corporate sales department at corpsales@pearsoned.com or (800) 382-3419.

For government sales inquiries, please contact governmentsales@pearsoned.com.

For questions about sales outside the U.S., please contact intlcs@pearson.com.

Feedback Information

At Cisco Press, our goal is to create in-depth technical books of the highest quality and value. Each book is crafted with care and precision, undergoing rigorous development that involves the unique expertise of members from the professional technical community.

Readers' feedback is a natural continuation of this process. If you have any comments regarding how we could improve the quality of this book, or otherwise alter it to better suit your needs, you can contact us through email at feedback@ciscopress.com. Please make sure to include the book title and ISBN in your message.

We greatly appreciate your assistance.

Editor-in-Chief	Mark Taub
Alliances Manager, Cisco Press	Ron Fligge
Executive Editor	Mary Beth Ray
Managing Editor	Sandra Schroeder
Development Editor	Ellie Bru
Senior Project Editor	Tonya Simpson
Copy Editor	Krista Hansing Editorial Services, Inc.
Technical Editor(s)	Rick McDonald
Editorial Assistant	Vanessa Evans
Cover Designer	Ockomon Haus
Composition	CodeMantra
Indexer	Erika Millen
Proofreader	Larry Sulky

·ı|ı.ı|ı.
CISCO.

Americas Headquarters	Asia Pacific Headquarters	Europe Headquarters
Cisco Systems, Inc.	Cisco Systems (USA) Pte. Ltd.	Cisco Systems International BV
San Jose, CA	Singapore	Amsterdam, The Netherlands

Cisco has more than 200 offices worldwide. Addresses, phone numbers, and fax numbers are listed on the Cisco Website at **www.cisco.com/go/offices.**

CCDE, CCENT, Cisco Eos, Cisco HealthPresence, the Cisco logo, Cisco Lumin, Cisco Nexus, Cisco StadiumVision, Cisco TelePresence, Cisco WebEx, DCE, and Welcome to the Human Network are trademarks; Changing the Way We Work, Live, Play, and Learn and Cisco Store are service marks; and Access Registrar, Aironet, AsyncOS, Bringing the Meeting To You, Catalyst, CCDA, CCDP, CCIE, CCIP, CCNA, CCNP, CCSP, CCVP, Cisco, the Cisco Certified Internetwork Expert logo, Cisco IOS, Cisco Press, Cisco Systems, Cisco Systems Capital, the Cisco Systems logo, Cisco Unity, Collaboration Without Limitation, EtherFast, EtherSwitch, Event Center, Fast Step, Follow Me Browsing, FormShare, GigaDrive, HomeLink, Internet Quotient, IOS, iPhone, iQuick Study, IronPort, the IronPort logo, LightStream, Linksys, MediaTone, MeetingPlace, MeetingPlace Chime Sound, MGX, Networkers, Networking Academy, Network Registrar, PCNow, PIX, PowerPanels, ProConnect, ScriptShare, SenderBase, SMARTnet, Spectrum Expert, StackWise, The Fastest Way to Increase Your Internet Quotient, TransPath, WebEx, and the WebEx logo are registered trademarks of Cisco Systems, Inc. and/or its affiliates in the United States and certain other countries.

All other trademarks mentioned in this document or website are the property of their respective owners. The use of the word partner does not imply a partnership relationship between Cisco and any other company. (0812R)

About the Author

Allan Johnson entered the academic world in 1999 after 10 years as a business owner/operator to follow his passion for teaching. He holds both an MBA and an M.Ed. in Occupational Training and Development. Allan taught CCNA courses at the high school level for 7 years and has taught both CCNA and CCNP courses at Del Mar College in Corpus Christi, Texas. In 2003, Allan began to commit much of his time and energy to the CCNA Instructional Support Team, providing services to Networking Academy instructors worldwide and creating training materials. He now works full time for Cisco Networking Academy as a Learning Systems Developer.

About the Technical Reviewer

Rick McDonald teaches computer and networking courses via distance from the University of Alaska–Fairbanks campus, where he is a Professor of Information Systems. He holds a BA in English and an M.Ed. in Educational Technology from Gonzaga University in Spokane, Washington. His current academic focus is developing methods for delivering hands-on training in Alaska using web-based teaching tools.

Dedications

For my wife, Becky. Thank you for all your support during this crazy whirlwind of a year. You are the stabilizing force that keeps me grounded.

Acknowledgments

As a technical author, I rely heavily on my technical editor; Rick McDonald had my back for this work. Thankfully, when Mary Beth Ray contacted him, he was willing and able to do the arduous review work necessary to make sure that you get a book that is both technically accurate and unambiguous.

Wendell Odom's *Cisco CCNA Routing and Switching 200-125 Official Cert Guide and Network Simulator Library* was one of my main sources. These two books and the accompanying simulator activities have the breadth and depth needed to master the CCNA exam topics.

The Cisco Network Academy authors for the online curriculum and series of Companion Guides take the reader deeper, past the CCNA exam topics, with the ultimate goal of preparing the student not only for CCNA certification, but for more advanced college-level technology courses and degrees as well. Thank you especially to Rick Graziani, Bob Vachon, Dan Alberghetti, Cheryl Schmidt, Rodrigo Floriano, Suk-Yi Pennock, Dave Holzinger, Jane Gibbons, Allan Reid, Jane Brooke, Martin Benson, and the rest of the ACE team. Their excellent treatment of the material is reflected throughout this book.

Mary Beth Ray, executive editor, amazes me with her ability to juggle multiple projects simultaneously, steering each from beginning to end. I can always count on her to make the tough decisions. Thank you, Mary Beth, for bringing this project to me.

Thank you to the professional and thorough review of this work by development editor Ellie Bru, project editor Tonya Simpson, and copy editor Krista Hansing. Their combined efforts ensure that what I authored is ready for publication.

And to the rest of the Pearson family who contributes in countless ways to bring a book to the reader, thank you for all your hard work.

Contents at a Glance

Contents

Icons Used in This Book

 Router

 Wireless Router

 Wireless Access Point

 Hub

 Hub (alternate)

 Multilayer Switch

 Switch

 ATM Switch Relay Switch

 WAN Switch

 PBX Switch

 Cisco ASA

 Router with Firewall

 PIX Firewall

 Firewall

 VPN Concentrator

 DSLAM

 CSU/DSU

 Access Server

 Voice-Enabled Access Server

 Modem

 IP Phone

 Phone

 Server

 IP/TV Broadcast Server

 Network Management Server

 Web Server

 Laptop

PC

Network Cloud

Ethernet Connection

Serial Line Connection

Wireless Connection

Command Syntax Conventions

The conventions used to present command syntax in this book are the same conventions used in the IOS Command Reference. The Command Reference describes these conventions as follows:

- **Boldface** indicates commands and keywords that are entered literally as shown. In actual configuration examples and output (not general command syntax), boldface indicates commands that are manually input by the user (such as a **show** command).

- *Italic* indicates arguments for which you supply actual values.

- Vertical bars (|) separate alternative, mutually exclusive elements.

- Square brackets ([ ]) indicate an optional element.

- Braces ({ }) indicate a required choice.

- Braces within brackets ([{ }]) indicate a required choice within an optional element.

Reader Services

Register your copy at www.ciscopress.com/title/9781587205903 for convenient access to downloads, updates, and corrections as they become available. To start the registration process, go to www.ciscopress.com/register and log in or create an account*. Enter the product ISBN 9781587205903 and click Submit. When the process is complete, you will find any available bonus content under Registered Products.

*Be sure to check the box that you would like to hear from us to receive exclusive discounts on future editions of this product.

Introduction

If you're reading this introduction, you've probably already spent a considerable amount of time and energy pursuing your CCNA certification. You're taking one of two paths. Either you are planning on taking the two exams, Interconnecting Cisco Network Devices, Part 1 (ICND1 100-105) and ICND2 200-105, or you are planning on taking the full Cisco Certified Network Associate Exam (CCNA 200-125). Regardless of how you got to this point in your travels through your CCNA studies, *31 Days Before Your CCNA Routing & Switching Exam* most likely represents the last leg of your journey on your way to the destination: to become a Cisco Certified Network Associate. However, if you are like me, you might be reading this book at the *beginning* of your studies. If so, this book provides an excellent overview of the material you must now spend a great deal of time studying and practicing. But I must warn you: unless you are extremely well versed in networking technologies and have considerable experience configuring and troubleshooting Cisco routers and switches, this book will *not* serve you well as the sole resource for your exam preparations. Therefore, let me spend some time discussing my recommendations for study resources.

Study Resources

Cisco Press and Pearson IT Certification offer an abundance of CCNA-related books to serve as your primary source for learning how to install, configure, operate, and troubleshoot small to medium-size routed and switched networks.

Safari Books Online

All the resources I reference in the book are available with a subscription to Safari Books Online (https://www.safaribooksonline.com). If you don't have an account, you can try it free for ten days.

Primary Resources

First on the list must be Wendell Odom's *CCNA Routing and Switching 200-125 Official Cert Guide and Network Simulator Library* (ISBN: 9781587206108). If you do not buy any other books, buy this one. Wendell's method of teaching, combined with his technical expertise and down-to-earth style, is unsurpassed in our industry. As you read through his books, you sense that he is sitting right there next to you walking you through the material. The practice exams and study materials on the DVD in the back of the book, plus the online resources, are worth the price of the book. There is no better resource on the market for a CCNA candidate.

If you are a Cisco Networking Academy student, you are blessed with access to the online version of the CCNA Routing and Switching curriculum and the wildly popular Packet Tracer network simulator. The Cisco Network Academy curriculum has four courses. To learn more about CCNA Routing and Switching courses and to find an Academy near you, visit http://www.netacad.com.

However, if you are not an Academy student but want to benefit from the extensive authoring done for these courses, you can buy any or all of CCNA Routing and Switching Companion Guides (CGs) and Labs & Study Guides (LSGs) of the Academy's popular online curriculum. Although you will not have access to the Packet Tracer files, you will have access to the tireless work of an outstanding team of Cisco Academy instructors dedicated to providing students with comprehensive and engaging CCNA preparation course material. The titles and ISBNs for the CCNA Routing and Switching CGs and LSGs follow:

- *Introduction to Networks v6 Companion Guide* (ISBN: 9781587133602)

- *Introduction to Networks v6 Labs & Study Guide* (ISBN: 9781587133619)

- *Routing and Switching Essentials v6 Companion Guide* (ISBN: 9781587134289)

- *Routing and Switching Essentials v6 Labs & Study Guide* (ISBN: 9781587134265)

- *Scaling Networks v6 Companion Guide* (ISBN: 9781587134340)

- *Scaling Networks v6 Labs & Study Guide* (ISBN: 9781587134333)

- *Connecting Networks v6 Companion Guide* (ISBN: 9781587134326)

- *Connecting Networks v6 Labs & Study Guide* (ISBN: 9781587134296)

You can find these books at http://www.ciscopress.com by clicking the Cisco Networking Academy link.

Supplemental Resources

In addition to the book you hold in your hands, I recommend three supplemental resources to augment your final 31 days of review and preparation.

First is Scott Empson's very popular *CCNA Routing and Switching Portable Command Guide* (ISBN: 9781587205880). This guide is much more than just a listing of commands and what they do. Yes, it summarizes all the CCNA certification-level IOS commands, keywords, command arguments, and associated prompts. But it also provides you with tips and examples of how to apply the commands to real-world scenarios. Configuration examples throughout the book provide you with a better understanding of how these commands are used in simple network designs.

Second, Kevin Wallace's *CCNA Routing and Switching 200-125 Premium Edition Complete Video Course* (ISBN: 9780134580708) is a comprehensive training course that brings Cisco CCNA exam topics to life through the use of real-world demonstrations, animations, live instruction, and configurations, making learning these foundational networking topics easy and fun. Kevin's engaging style and love for the technology is infectious. The course contains more than 25 hours of instruction in more than 300 videos. The course also includes excellent practice tests.

Third, Wendell Odom and Sean Wilkins have created more than 400 structured labs that are available in the *CCNA Routing and Switching 200-125 Network Simulator* (ISBN: 9780789757760). These simulations map precisely to chapters in Wendell's book, but they are also a great practice resource for anyone.

The Cisco Learning Network

Finally, if you have not done so already, you should register with The Cisco Learning Network at https://learningnetwork.cisco.com. Sponsored by Cisco, The Cisco Learning Network is a free social learning network where IT professionals can engage in the common pursuit of enhancing and advancing their IT careers. Here you can find many resources to help you prepare for your CCNA exam, in addition to a community of like-minded people ready to answer your questions, help you with your struggles, and share in your triumphs.

So which resources should you buy? The answer to that question depends largely on how deep your pockets are or how much you like books. If you're like me, you must have it all! I admit it; my bookcase is a testament to my Cisco "geekness." But if you are on a budget, choose one of the primary study resources and one of the supplemental resources (such as Wendell Odom's certification library and Scott Empson's command guide). Whatever you choose, you will be in good hands. Any or all of these authors will serve you well.

Goals and Methods

The main goal of this book is to provide you with a clear and succinct review of the CCNA objectives. Each day's exam topics are grouped into a common conceptual framework and use the following format:

- A title for the day that concisely states the overall topic

- A list of one or more CCNA 200-125 exam topics to be reviewed

- A "Key Topics" section to introduce the review material and quickly orient you to the day's focus

- An extensive review section consisting of short paragraphs, lists, tables, examples, and graphics

- A "Study Resources" section to give you a quick reference for locating more in-depth treatment of the day's topics

The book counts down starting with Day 31 and continues through exam day to provide post-test information. Inside this book is also a calendar and checklist that you can tear out and use during your exam preparation.

Use the calendar to enter each actual date beside the countdown day and the exact day, time, and location of your CCNA exam. The calendar provides a visual for the time you can dedicate to each CCNA exam topic.

The checklist highlights important tasks and deadlines leading up to your exam. Use it to help you map out your studies.

Who Should Read This Book?

The audience for this book is anyone finishing preparation for taking the CCNA 200-125 exam. A secondary audience is anyone needing a refresher review of CCNA exam topics—possibly before attempting to recertify or sit for another certification for which the CCNA is a prerequisite.

Getting to Know the CCNA 200-125 Exam

For the current certifications (announced in May 2016), Cisco created the ICND1 (100-105) and ICND2 (200-105) exams, along with the CCNA (200-125) exam. To become CCENT certified, you need to pass just the ICND1 exam. To become CCNA Routing and Switching certified, you must pass both the ICND1 and ICND2 exams, or just the CCNA exam. The CCNA exam simply covers all the topics on the ICND1 and ICND2 exams, giving you two options for gaining your CCNA Routing and Switching certification. The two-exam path gives people with less experience a chance to study for a smaller set of topics at one time. The one-exam option provides a more cost-effective certification path for those who want to prepare for all the topics at once. This book focuses on the entire list of topics published for the CCNA 200-125 exam.

Currently for the CCNA exam, you are allowed 90 minutes to answer 50–60 questions. Use the following steps to access a tutorial at home that demonstrates the exam environment before you go to take the exam:

Step 1.   Visit http://www.vue.com/cisco.

Step 2.   Look for a link to the certification tutorial. Currently, it appears on the right side of the web page under the heading "Related Links."

Step 3.   Click the Certification Tutorial link.

When you get to the testing center and check in, the proctor verifies your identity, gives you some general instructions, and then takes you into a quiet room containing a PC. When you're at the PC, you have a few things to do before the timer starts on your exam. For instance, you can take the tutorial to get accustomed to the PC and the testing engine. Every time I sit for an exam, I go through the tutorial even though I know how the test engine works. It helps me settle my nerves and get focused. Anyone who has user-level skills in getting around a PC should have no problems with the testing environment.

When you start the exam, you are asked a series of questions. Each question is presented one at a time and must be answered before moving on to the next question. The exam engine does not let you go back and change your answer. The exam questions can be in one of the following formats:

- Multiple choice
- Fill in the blank
- Drag and drop
- Testlet
- Simlet
- Simulation

The multiple-choice format simply requires that you point and click a circle or check box next to the correct answer(s). Cisco traditionally tells you how many answers you need to choose, and the testing software prevents you from choosing too many or too few.

Fill-in-the-blank questions usually require you only to type numbers. However, if words are requested, the case does not matter unless the answer is a command that is case sensitive (such as passwords and device names, when configuring authentication).

Drag-and-drop questions require you to click and hold, move a button or icon to another area, and release the mouse button to place the object somewhere else—usually in a list. For some questions, to get the question correct, you might need to put a list of five things in the proper order.

Testlets contain one general scenario and several multiple-choice questions about the scenario. These are ideal if you are confident in your knowledge of the scenario's content because you can leverage your strength over multiple questions.

A simlet is similar to a testlet, in that you are given a scenario with several multiple-choice questions. However, a simlet uses a network simulator to allow you access to a simulation of the command line of Cisco IOS Software. You can then use **show** commands to examine a network's current behavior and answer the question.

A simulation also uses a network simulator, but you are given a task to accomplish, such as implementing a network solution or troubleshooting an existing network implementation. You do this by configuring one or more routers and switches. The exam then grades the question based on the configuration you changed or added. A newer form of the simulation question is the GUI-based simulation, which simulates a graphical interface such as that found on a Linksys router or the Cisco Security Device Manager.

What Topics Are Covered on the CCNA Exam

Table I-1 summarizes the seven domains of the CCNA 200-125 exam:

Table I-1   CCNA 200-125 Exam Domains and Weightings

Domain	% of Examination
1.0 Network Fundamentals	15%
2.0 LAN Switching Technologies	21%
3.0 Routing Technologies	23%
4.0 WAN Technologies	10%
5.0 Infrastructure Services	10%
6.0 Infrastructure Security	11%
7.0 Infrastructure Management	10%

Although Cisco outlines general exam topics, not all topics might appear on the CCNA exam; likewise, topics that are not specifically listed might appear on the exam. The exam topics that Cisco provides and this book covers are a general framework for exam preparation. Be sure to check Cisco's website for the latest exam topics.

Registering for the CCNA 200-125 Exam

If you are starting your *31 Days Before Your CCNA Routing & Switching Exam* today, register for the exam right now. In my testing experience, there is no better motivator than a scheduled test date staring me in the face. I'm willing to bet the same holds true for you. Don't worry about unforeseen circumstances. You can cancel your exam registration for a full refund up to 24 hours before taking the exam. So if you're ready, gather the following information in Table I-1 and register right now!

- Legal name
- Social Security or passport number
- Company name
- Valid email address
- Method of payment

You can schedule your exam at any time by visiting www.pearsonvue.com/cisco/. I recommend that you schedule it for 31 days from now. The process and available test times vary based on the local testing center you choose.

Remember, there is no better motivation for study than an actual test date. *Sign up today*.

Digital Study Guide

Cisco Press offers this book in an online digital format that includes enhancements such as interactive activities and Check Your Understanding questions, plus Packet Tracer activities and a full-length exam.

> *31 Days Before Your CCNA Routing & Switching Exam Digital Study Guide* is available for a discount for anyone who purchases this book. Details about redeeming this offer are found in the back of the book.

- **Read** the complete text of the book on any web browser that supports HTML5, including mobile.

- **Reinforce** key concepts with more than 31 dynamic and interactive hands-on exercises, and see the results with the click of a button. Also included are more than 25 Packet Tracer activities.

- **Test** your understanding of the material at the end of each day with more than 300 fully interactive online quiz questions. You also get a full-length final quiz of 60 questions that mimic the type of questions you will see in the CCNA Routing and Switching Composite certification exam.

To get your copy of Packet Tracer software, go to the companion website for instructions. To access this companion website, follow these steps:

Step 1. Go to http://www.ciscopress.com/register and log in or create a new account.

Step 2. Enter the ISBN 9781587205903.

Step 3. Answer the challenge question as proof of purchase.

Step 4. Click the Access Bonus Content link in the Registered Products section of your account page, to be taken to the page where your downloadable content is available.

This book contains references to the Digital Study Guide enhancements that look like this:

Activity: Identify the Encapsulation Layer

Refer to the Digital Study Guide to complete this activity.

Packet Tracer Activity: Configure Routing Protocol Authentication

Refer to the Digital Study Guide to access the PKA file for this activity. You must have Packet Tracer software to run this activity.

Check Your Understanding

Refer to the Digital Study Guide to take a 10-question quiz covering the content of this day.

When you are at these points in the Digital Study Guide, you can start the enhancement.

Networking Models, Devices, and Components

CCNA 200-125 Exam Topics

- Compare and contrast OSI and TCP/IP models

- Compare and contrast TCP and UDP protocols

- Describe the impact of infrastructure components in an enterprise network

- Compare and contrast collapsed core and three-tier architectures

- Compare and contrast network topologies

- Select the appropriate cabling type based on implementation requirements

Key Points

Both the Open Systems Interconnection (OSI) and Transmission Control Protocol/Internet Protocol (TCP/IP) networking models are important conceptual frameworks for understanding networks. Today we review the layers and functions of each model, along with the process of data flow from source to destination. We also spend some time on the Transmission Control Protocol (TCP) and the User Datagram Protocol (UDP). Then we wrap up the day with a look at devices used in today's networks, the media used to interconnect those devices, and the different types of network topologies.

NOTE: This day might seem a bit long. However, you need to be very familiar with all of this content. Scan the day, focusing on areas where you feel less confident in your knowledge.

The OSI and TCP/IP Models

To understand how communication occurs across the network, you can use layered models as a framework for representing and explaining networking concepts and technologies. Layered models, such as the TCP/IP and OSI models, support interoperability between competing vendor product lines.

The OSI model principally serves as a tool for explaining networking concepts and troubleshooting. However, the protocols of the TCP/IP suite are the rules by which networks now operate. Because both models are important, you should be well versed in each model's layers and know how the models map to each other. Figure 31-1 summarizes the two models.

Figure 31-1   OSI and TCP/IP Models

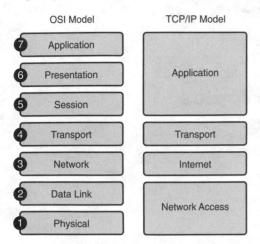

Using two models can be confusing; however, these simple guidelines might help:

- When discussing layers of a model, we are usually referring to the OSI model.

- When discussing protocols, we are usually referring to the TCP/IP model.

The next sections quickly review the OSI layers and the TCP/IP protocols.

OSI Layers

Table 31-1 summarizes the layers of the OSI model and provides a brief functional description.

Table 31-1   OSI Model Layers and Functions

Layer	Functional Description
Application (7)	Refers to interfaces between network and application software. Also includes authentication services.
Presentation (6)	Defines the format and organization of data. Includes encryption.
Session (5)	Establishes and maintains end-to-end bidirectional flows between endpoints. Includes managing transaction flows.
Transport (4)	Provides a variety of services between two host computers, including connection establishment and termination, flow control, error recovery, and segmentation of large data blocks into smaller parts for transmission.
Network (3)	Refers to logical addressing, routing, and path determination.
Data link (2)	Formats data into frames appropriate for transmission onto some physical medium. Defines rules for when the medium can be used. Defines the means by which to recognize transmission errors.
Physical (1)	Defines the electrical, optical, cabling, connectors, and procedural details required for transmitting bits, represented as some form of energy passing over a physical medium.

The following mnemonic phrase, in which the first letter represents the layer (*A* stands for · *Application*), can help in memorizing the name and order of the layers from top to bottom:

All People Seem To Need Data Processing

TCP/IP Layers and Protocols

The TCP/IP model defines four categories of functions that must occur for communications to succeed. Most protocol models describe a vendor-specific protocol stack. However, because the TCP/IP model is an open standard, one company does not control the definition of the model.

Table 31-2 summarizes the TCP/IP layers, their functions, and the most common protocols.

Table 31-2   TCP/IP Layer Functions

TCP/IP Layer	Function	Example Protocols
Application	Represents data to the user and controls dialogue	DNS, Telnet, SMTP, POP3, IMAP, DHCP, HTTP, FTP, SNMP
Transport	Supports communication between diverse devices across diverse networks	TCP, UDP
Internet	Determines the best path through the network	IP, ARP, ICMP
Network access	Controls the hardware devices and media that make up the network	Ethernet, Frame Relay

In the coming days, we review these protocols in more detail. For now, a brief description of the main TCP/IP protocols follows:

- **Domain Name System (DNS):** Provides the IP address of a website or domain name so that a host can connect to it

- **Telnet:** Enables administrators to log in to a host from a remote location

- **Simple Mail Transfer Protocol (SMTP), Post Office Protocol (POP3), and Internet Message Access Protocol (IMAP):** Facilitates sending email messages between clients and servers

- **Dynamic Host Configuration Protocol (DHCP):** Assigns IP addressing to requesting clients

- **Hypertext Transfer Protocol (HTTP):** Transfers information between web clients and web servers

- **File Transfer Protocol (FTP):** Facilitates the download and upload of files between an FTP client and FTP server

- **Simple Network Management Protocol (SNMP):** Enables network management systems to monitor devices attached to the network

   Transmission Control Protocol (TCP): Supports virtual connections between hosts on the network to provide reliable delivery of data

- **User Datagram Protocol (UDP):** Supports faster, unreliable delivery of lightweight or time-sensitive data

- **Internet Protocol (IP):** Provides a unique global address to computers for communicating over the network

- **Address Resolution Protocol (ARP):** Finds a host's hardware address when only the IP address is known

- **Internet Control Message Protocol (ICMP):** Sends error and control messages, including reachability to another host and availability of services

- **Ethernet:** Serves as the most popular LAN standard for framing and preparing data for transmission onto the media

 Activity: Order the Layers of the OSI and TCP/IP Models

Refer to the Digital Study Guide to complete this activity.

Protocol Data Units and Encapsulation

As application data is passed down the protocol stack on its way to be transmitted across the network media, various protocols add information to it at each level. This is commonly known as the *encapsulation process*. The data structure at any given layer is called a *protocol data unit (PDU)*. Table 31-3 lists the PDUs at each layer of the OSI model.

Table 31-3   PDUs at Each Layer of the OSI Model

OSI Layer	PDU
Application	Data
Presentation	Data
Session	Data
Transport	Segment
Network	Packet
Data link	Frame
Physical	Bits

The following steps summarize the communication process from any source to any destination:

1. Data is created at the application layer of the originating source device.

2. As the data passes down the protocol stack in the source device, it is segmented and encapsulated.

3. The data is generated onto the media at the network access layer of the stack.

4. The data is transported through the internetwork, which consists of media and any intermediary devices.

5. The destination device receives the data at the network access layer.

6. As the data passes up the stack in the destination device, it is decapsulated and reassembled.

7. The data is passed to the destination application at the application layer of the destination device.

The TCP/IP Application Layer

The application layer of the TCP/IP model provides an interface between software such as a web browser and the network itself. The process of requesting and receiving a web page works like this:

1. An HTTP request is sent, including an instruction to "get" a file (which is often a website's home page).

2. An HTTP response is sent from the web server with a code in the header, usually either 200 (request succeeded and information is returned in response) or 404 (page not found).

The HTTP request and the HTTP response are encapsulated in headers. The content of the headers allows the application layers on each end device to communicate. Regardless of the application layer protocol (HTTP, FTP, DNS, and so on), all use the same general process for communicating between application layers on the end devices.

The TCP/IP Transport Layer

The transport layer, through TCP, provides a mechanism to guarantee delivery of data across the network. TCP supports error recovery to the application layer through the use of basic acknowledgment logic. Adding to the process for requesting a web page, TCP operation works like this:

1. The web client sends an HTTP request for a specific web server down to the transport layer.

2. TCP encapsulates the HTTP request with a TCP header and includes the destination port number for HTTP.

3. Lower layers process and send the request to the web server.

4. The web server receives HTTP requests and sends a TCP acknowledgment back to the requesting web client.

5. The web server sends the HTTP response down to the transport layer.

6. TCP encapsulates the HTTP data with a TCP header.

7. Lower layers process and send the response to the requesting web client.

8. The requesting web client sends an acknowledgment back to the web server.

If data is lost at any point during this process, TCP must recover the data. HTTP at the application layer does not get involved in error recovery.

In addition to TCP, the transport layer provides UDP, a connectionless, unreliable protocol for sending data that does not require or need error recovery. Table 31-4 lists the main features that the transport protocols support. Both TCP and UDP support the first function; only TCP supports the rest.

Table 31-4   TCP/IP Transport Layer Features

Function	Description
Multiplexing using ports	Function that enables receiving hosts to choose the correct application for which the data is destined, based on the destination port number.
Error recovery (reliability)	Process of numbering and acknowledging data with Sequence and Acknowledgment header fields.
Flow control using windowing	Process that uses a sliding window size that the two end devices dynamically agree upon at various points during the virtual connection. The window size, represented in bytes, is the maximum amount of data the source will send before receiving an acknowledgment from the destination.
Connection establishment and termination	Process used to initialize port numbers and Sequence and Acknowledgment fields.
Ordered data transfer and data segmentation	A continuous stream of bytes from an upper-layer process that is "segmented" for transmission and delivered to upper-layer processes at the receiving device, with the bytes in the same order.

TCP Header

TCP provides error recovery, but to do so, it consumes more bandwidth and uses more processing cycles than UDP. TCP and UDP rely on IP for end-to-end delivery. TCP is concerned with providing services to the applications of the sending and receiving computers. To provide all these services, TCP uses a variety of fields in its header (see Figure 31-2).

Figure 31-2   TCP Header

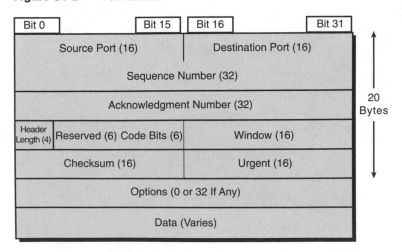

Port Numbers

The first two fields of the TCP header—the source and destination ports—are also part of the UDP header that appears later in Figure 31-7. Port numbers provide TCP (and UDP) with a way to multiplex multiple applications on the same computer. Web browsers now support multiple tabs or pages. Each time you open a new tab and request another web page, TCP assigns a different source port number and sometimes multiple port numbers. For example, you might have five web pages open. TCP almost always assigns destination port 80 for all five sessions. However, the source port for each is different. This is how TCP (and UDP) multiplexes the conversation so that the web browser knows in which tab to display the data.

TCP and UDP usually dynamically assign the source ports, starting at 1024 up to a maximum of 65535. Port numbers below 1024 are reserved for well-known applications. Table 31-5 lists several popular applications and their well-known port numbers.

Table 31-5   Popular Applications and Their Well-Known Port Numbers

Port Number	Protocol	Application
20	TCP	FTP data
21	TCP	FTP control
22	TCP	SSH
23	TCP	Telnet
25	TCP	SMTP
53	UDP, TCP	DNS
67, 68	UDP	DHCP
69	UDP	TFTP
80	TCP	HTTP (WWW)
110	TCP	POP3
161	UDP	SNMP
443	TCP	HTTPS (SSL)
16384–32767	UDP	RTP-based voice (VoIP) and video

Error Recovery

Also known as *reliability*, TCP provides error recovery during data transfer sessions between two end devices that have established a connection. The Sequence and Acknowledgment fields in the TCP header track every byte of data transfer and ensure that missing bytes are retransmitted.

In Figure 31-3, the Acknowledgment field sent by the web client (4000) implies the next byte to be received; this is called *positive acknowledgment*.

Figure 31-3   TCP Acknowledgment Without Errors

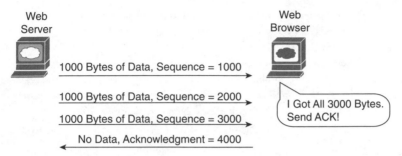

Figure 31-4 depicts the same scenario, except now with some errors. The second TCP segment was lost in transmission. Therefore, the web client replies with an ACK field set to 2000. This is called a positive acknowledgment with retransmission (PAR) because the web client is requesting that some of the data be retransmitted. The web server will now resend data starting at segment 2000. In this way, lost data is recovered.

Figure 31-4   TCP Acknowledgment with Errors

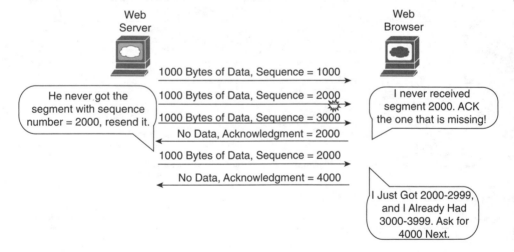

Although not shown, the web server also sets a retransmission timer and awaits acknowledgment, just in case the acknowledgment is lost or all transmitted segments are lost. If that timer expires, the web server sends all segments again.

Flow Control

TCP handles flow control through a process called *windowing*. The two end devices negotiate the window size when initially establishing the connection; then they dynamically renegotiate window size during the life of the connection, increasing its size until it reaches the maximum window size of 65,535 bytes or until errors occur. Window size is specified in the Window field of the TCP header. After sending the amount of data specified in the window size, the source must receive an acknowledgment before sending the next window size of data.

Connection Establishment and Termination

Connection establishment is the process of initializing sequence and acknowledgment fields and agreeing on port numbers and window size. The three-way connection establishment phase shown in Figure 31-5 must occur before data transfer can proceed.

Figure 31-5   TCP Connection Establishment

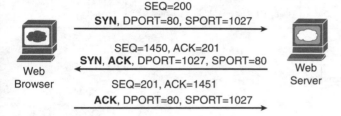

In the figure, DPORT and SPORT are the destination and source ports. SEQ is the sequence number. In bold are SYN and ACK, with each representing a 1-bit flag in the TCP header used to signal connection establishment. TCP initializes the Sequence Number and Acknowledgment Number fields to any number that fits into the 4-byte fields. The initial Sequence Number is a random 32-bit number generated with each new transmission. The Acknowledgment Number is received back and increments the sender's sequence number by 1.

When data transfer is complete, a four-way termination sequence occurs that uses an additional flag, called the FIN bit (see Figure 31-6).

Figure 31-6   TCP Connection Termination

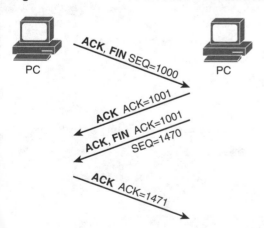

UDP

TCP establishes and terminates connections between endpoints, whereas UDP does not. Therefore, UDP is called a *connectionless protocol*. It provides no reliability, no windowing, and no reordering of the data. However, UDP does provide data transfer and multiplexing using port numbers, and it does so with fewer bytes of overhead and less processing than TCP. Applications that use UDP can trade the possibility of some data loss for less delay, such as VoIP. Figure 31-7 compares the two headers.

Figure 31-7   TCP and UDP Headers

2	2	4	4	4 bits	6 bits	6 bits	2	2	2	3	1
Source Port	Dest. Port	Sequence Number	Ack. Number	Offset	Reserved	Flags	Window Size	Checksum	Urgent	Options	PAD

TCP Header

2	2	2	2
Source Port	Dest. Port	Length	Checksum

UDP Header

* Unless Specified, Lengths Shown
  Are the Numbers of Bytes

 Activity: Identify the TCP and UDP Characteristics

Refer to the Digital Study Guide to complete this activity.

The TCP/IP Internet Layer

The Internet layer of the TCP/IP model and its Internet Protocol (IP) define addresses so that each host computer can have a different IP address. In addition, the Internet layer defines the process of routing so that routers can determine the best path to send packets to the destination. Continuing with the web page example, IP addresses the data as it passes from the transport layer to the Internet layer:

1. The web client sends an HTTP request.

2. TCP encapsulates the HTTP request.

3. IP encapsulates the transport segment into a packet, adding source and destination addresses.

4. Lower layers process and send the request to the web server.

5. The web server receives HTTP requests and sends a TCP acknowledgment back to the requesting web client.

6. The web server sends the HTTP response down to the transport layer.

7. TCP encapsulates the HTTP data.

8. IP encapsulates the transport segment into a packet, adding source and destination addresses.

9. Lower layers process and send the response to the requesting web client.

10. The requesting web client sends an acknowledgment back to the web server.

The operation of IP includes not only addressing, but also the process of routing the data from source to destination. IP is further discussed and reviewed in the upcoming days.

The TCP/IP Network Access Layer

IP depends on the network access layer to deliver IP packets across a physical network. Therefore, the network access layer defines the protocols and hardware required to deliver data across some physical network by specifying exactly how to physically connect a networked device to the physical media over which data can be transmitted.

The network access layer includes many protocols to deal with the different types of media that data can cross on its way from source device to destination device. For example, data might need to travel first on an Ethernet link and then cross a Point-to-Point (PPP) link, then a Frame Relay link, then a Multiprotocol Label Switching (MPLS) link, and then finally an Ethernet link to reach the destination. At each transition from one media type to another, the network access layer provides the protocols, cabling standards, headers, and trailers to send data across the physical network.

Many times, a local link address is needed to transfer data from one hop to the next. For example, in an Ethernet LAN, Media Access Control (MAC) addresses are used between the sending device and its local gateway router. At the gateway router (depending on the needs of the outbound interface), the Ethernet header might be replaced with an MPLS label. The label serves the same purpose as MAC addresses in Ethernet: to get the data across the link from one hop to the next so that the data can continue its journey to the destination. Some protocols, such as PPP, do not need a link address because only one other device on the link can receive the data.

With the network access layer, we can now finalize our web page example. The following greatly simplifies and summarizes the process of requesting and sending a web page:

1. The web client sends an HTTP request.

2. TCP encapsulates the HTTP request.

3. IP encapsulates the transport segment into a packet, adding source and destination addresses.

4. The network access layer encapsulates the packet in a frame, addressing it for the local link.

5. The network access layer sends the frame as bits on the media.

6. Intermediary devices process the bits at the network access and Internet layers and then forward the data toward the destination.

7. The web server receives the bits on the physical interface and sends them up through the network access and Internet layers.

8. The web server sends a TCP acknowledgment back to the requesting web client.

9. The web server sends the HTTP response down to the transport layer.

10. TCP encapsulates the HTTP data.

11. IP encapsulates the transport segment into a packet, adding source and destination addresses.

12. The network access layer encapsulates the packet in a frame, addressing it for the local link.

13. The network access layer sends the frame as bits on the media.

14. Lower layers process and send the response to the requesting web client.

15. The response travels back to the source over multiple data links.

16. The requesting web client receives the response on the physical interface and sends the data up through the network access and Internet layers.

17. The requesting web client sends a TCP acknowledgment back to the web server.

18. The web page is displayed in the requesting device's browser.

Data Encapsulation Summary

Each layer of the TCP/IP model adds its own header information. As the data travels down through the layers, it is encapsulated with a new header. At the network access layer, a trailer is also added. This encapsulation process is described in five steps:

Step 1. Create and encapsulate the application data with any required application layer headers. For example, the HTTP OK message can be returned in an HTTP header, followed by part of the contents of a web page.

Step 2. Encapsulate the data supplied by the application layer inside a transport layer header. For end-user applications, a TCP or UDP header is typically used.

Step 3. Encapsulate the data supplied by the transport layer inside an Internet layer (IP) header. IP is the only protocol available in the TCP/IP network model at the Internet layer.

Step 4. Encapsulate the data supplied by the Internet layer inside a network access layer header and trailer. This is the only layer that uses both a header and a trailer.

Step 5. Transmit the bits. The physical layer encodes a signal onto the medium to transmit the frame.

The numbers in Figure 31-8 correspond to the five steps in the list, graphically showing the same encapsulation process.

Figure 31-8   Five Steps of Data Encapsulation

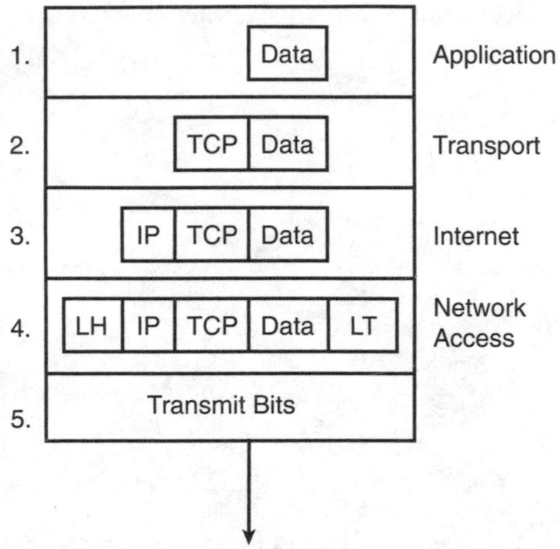

NOTE: The letters LH and LT stand for link header and link trailer, respectively, and refer to the data link layer header and trailer.

Devices

In today's wired networks, switches are almost exclusively used to connect end devices to a single LAN. Occasionally, you might see a hub connecting end devices, but hubs are really legacy devices. The following describes the difference between a hub and a switch:

- Hubs were typically chosen as an intermediary device within a very small LAN, in which bandwidth usage was not an issue or cost limitations were a factor. In today's networks, switches have replaced hubs.

- Switches replaced hubs as the local-area network (LAN) intermediary device because a switch can segment collision domains and provide enhanced security.

Switches

When choosing a switch, these are the main factors to consider:

- **Cost:** The cost is determined by the number and type of ports, network management capabilities, embedded security technologies, and optional advanced switching technologies.

- **Interface characteristics:** The number of ports must be sufficient both for now and for future expansion. Other characteristics include uplink speeds, a mixture of UTP and fiber, and modularity.

- **Hierarchical network layer:** Switches at the access layer have different requirements than switches at the distribution or core layers.

Access Layer Switches

Access layer switches facilitate the connection of end devices to the network. Features of access layer switches include the following:

- Port security
- VLANs
- Fast Ethernet/Gigabit Ethernet
- Power over Ethernet (PoE)
- Link aggregation
- Quality of service (QoS)

Distribution Layer Switches

Distribution layer switches receive the data from the access layer switches and forward it to the core layer switches. Features of distribution layer switches include the following:

- Layer 3 support
- High forwarding rate
- Gigabit Ethernet/10 Gigabit Ethernet
- Redundant components
- Security policies/access control lists
- Link aggregation
- QoS

Core Layer Switches

Core layer switches make up the backbone and are responsible for handling the majority of data on a switched LAN. Features of core layer switches include the following:

- Layer 3 support
- Very high forwarding rate
- Gigabit Ethernet/10 Gigabit Ethernet
- Redundant components
- Link aggregation
- QoS

Routers

Routers are the primary devices used to interconnect networks—LANs, WANs, and WLANs. When choosing a router, the main factors to consider are the following:

- **Expandability:** Provides flexibility to add new modules as needs change.

- **Media:** Determines the type of interfaces the router needs to support the various network connections.

- **Operating system features:** Determines the version of IOS loaded on the router. Different IOS versions support different feature sets. Features to consider include security, QoS, VoIP, routing complexity, and other services.

Figure 31-9 shows a Cisco 1941 router, which provides the following connections:

- **Console ports:** Two console ports for the initial configuration, using a regular RJ-45 port and a new USB Type-B (mini-B USB) connector

- **AUX port:** An RJ-45 port for remote management access

- **LAN interfaces:** Two Gigabit Ethernet interfaces for LAN access

- **Enhanced high-speed WAN interface card (eHWIC) slots:** Two slots that support different types of interface modules, including serial, digital subscriber line (DSL), switch port, and wireless

Figure 31-9 also shows two 4GB compact flash slots to provide increased storage space.

Figure 31-9   Backplane of the Cisco 1941 Router

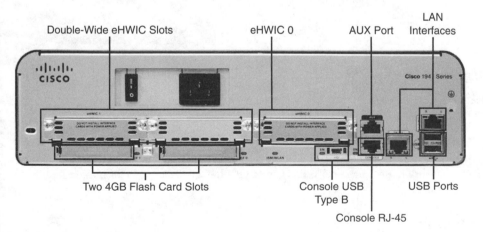

Specialty Devices

Although switches and routers make up the backbone of a network, many networks integrate various specialized network devices.

Firewalls

A firewall is a networking device, either hardware or software based, that controls access to the organization's network. This controlled access is designed to protect data and resources from an outside threat.

Organizations implement software firewalls through a network operating system (NOS) such as Linux/UNIX, Windows servers, and Mac OS X servers. The firewall is configured on the server to allow or block certain types of network traffic. Hardware firewalls are often dedicated network devices that can be implemented with little configuration.

Figure 31-10 shows a basic stateful firewall.

Figure 31-10   The Function of a Firewall

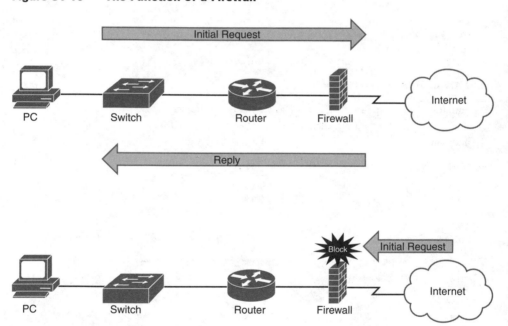

A stateful firewall allows traffic to originate from an inside, trusted network and go out to an untrusted network, such as the Internet. The firewall allows return traffic that comes back from the untrusted network to the trusted network. However, the firewall blocks traffic that originates from an untrusted network.

IDS and IPS

Both Intrusion Detection Systems (IDS) and Intrusion Prevention Systems (IPS) can recognize network attacks; they differ primarily in their network placement. An IDS device receives a copy of traffic to be analyzed. An IPS device is placed inline with the traffic, as Figure 31-11 shows.

Figure 31-11   IPS and IDS Comparison

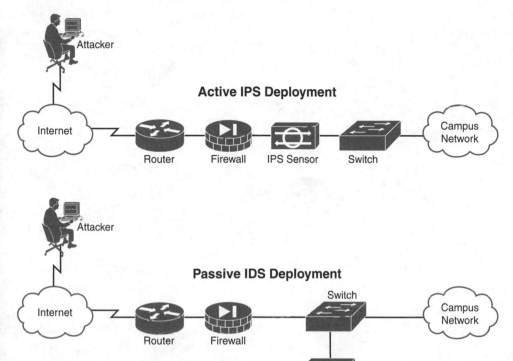

An IDS is a passive detection system. It can detect the presence of an attack, log the information, and send an alert.

An IPS has the same functionality as an IDS, but additionally, an IPS is an active device that continually scans the network, looking for inappropriate activity. It can shut down any potential threats. The IPS looks for any known signatures of common attacks and automatically tries to prevent those attacks.

Access Points and Wireless LAN Controllers

Wireless LANs (WLAN) are commonly a part of most networks. Users expect to be able to connect seamlessly as they move from location to location within a home, small business, or enterprise campus network. To enable this connectivity, network administrators manage a collection of wireless access points (AP) and wireless LAN controllers (WLC).

In small networks, APs are typically used when a router is already providing Layer 3 services, as in Figure 31-12.

Figure 31-12   Small Network with an AP

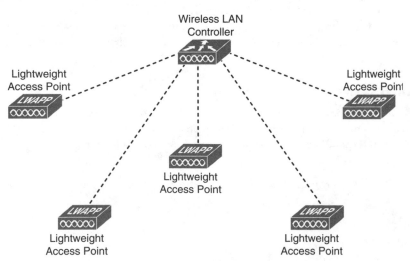

An AP has an Ethernet port that enables it to be connected to a switch port. In a home or small office network, an AP can simply be another wireless router with all the Layer 3 services turned off. You simply connect one of the AP's switch ports to the one of the switch ports on the wireless router.

APs are also used when the coverage area of an existing WLAN needs to be extended. In larger networks, a wireless LAN controller (WLC) is typically used to manage multiple APs, as in Figure 31-13.

Figure 31-13   Example of a Wireless LAN Controller Implementation

Wireless LAN
Controller

Lightweight
Access Point
LWAPP

Lightweight
Access Point
LWAPP

Lightweight
Access Point
LWAPP

Lightweight
Access Point
LWAPP

Lightweight
Access Point
LWAPP

WLCs can use the older Lightweight Access Point Protocol (LWAPP) or the more current Control and Provisioning of Wireless Access Points (CAPWAP). Using a WLC, VLAN pooling can be used to assign IP addresses to wireless clients from a pool of IP subnets and their associated VLANs.

Physical Layer

Before any network communications can occur, a wired or wireless physical connection must be established. The type of physical connection depends on the network setup. In larger networks, switches and APs are often two separate dedicated devices. In a very small business (three or four employees) or home network, wireless and wired connections are combined into one device and include a broadband method of connecting to the Internet. These wireless broadband routers offer a switching component with multiple ports and an AP, which allows wireless devices to connect as well. Figure 31-14 shows the back plane of a Cisco WRP500 Wireless Broadband Router.

Figure 31-14   Cisco WRP500 Wireless Broadband Router

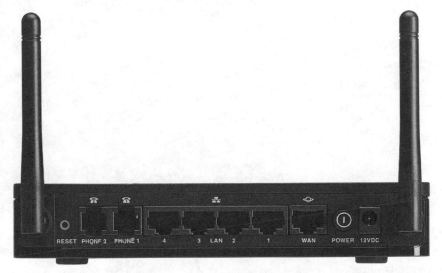

Network Media Forms and Standards

Three basic forms of network media exist:

- **Copper cable:** The signals are patterns of electrical pulses.

- **Fiber-optic cable:** The signals are patterns of light.

- **Wireless:** The signals are patterns of microwave transmissions.

Messages are encoded and then placed onto the media. Encoding is the process of converting data into patterns of electrical, light, or electromagnetic energy so that it can be carried on the media.

Table 31-6 summarizes the three most common networking media in use today.

Table 31-6   Networking Media

Media	Physical Components	Frame Encoding Technique	Signaling Methods
Copper cable	UTP Coaxial Connectors NICs Ports Interfaces	Manchester encoding Nonreturn to zero (NRZ) techniques 4B/5B codes used with Multi-Level Transition Level 3 (MLT-3) signaling 8B/10B PAM5	Changes in the electromagnetic field. Intensity of the electromagnetic field. Phase of the electromagnetic wave.
Fiber-optic cable	Single-mode fiber Multimode fiber Connectors NICs Interfaces Lasers and LEDs Photoreceptors	Pulses of light Wavelength multiplexing using different colors	A pulse equals 1. No pulse is 0.
Wireless	Access points NICs Radio Antennas	Direct Sequence Spread Spectrum (DSSS) Orthogonal frequency division multiplexing (OFDM)	Radio waves.

Each media type has its advantages and disadvantages. When choosing the media, consider each of the following:

- **Cable length:** Does the cable need to span a room or run from building to building?
- **Cost:** Does the budget allow for using a more expensive media type?
- **Bandwidth:** Does the technology used with the media provide adequate bandwidth?
- **Ease of installation:** Does the implementation team have the capability to install the cable, or is a vendor required?
- **Susceptible to EMI/RFI:** Will the local environment interfere with the signal?

Table 31-7 summarizes the media standards for LAN cabling.

Table 31-7   Media Standard, Cable Length, and Bandwidth

Ethernet Type	Bandwidth	Cable Type	Maximum Distance
10BASE-T	10 Mbps	Cat3/Cat5 UTP	100 m
100BASE-TX	100 Mbps	Cat5 UTP	100 m
100BASE-TX	200 Mbps	Cat5 UTP	100 m
100BASE-FX	100 Mbps	Multimode fiber	400 m
100BASE-FX	200 Mbps	Multimode fiber	2 km
1000BASE-T	1 Gbps	Cat5e UTP	100 m
1000BASE-TX	1 Gbps	Cat6 UTP	100 m
1000BASE-SX	1 Gbps	Multimode fiber	550 m
1000BASE-LX	1 Gbps	Single-mode fiber	2 km
10GBASE-T	10 Gbps	Cat6a/Cat7 UTP	100 m
10GBASE-SX4	10 Gbps	Multimode fiber	550 m
10GBASE-LX4	10 Gbps	Single-mode fiber	2 km

LAN Device Connection Guidelines

End devices are pieces of equipment that are either the original source or the final destination of a message. Intermediary devices connect end devices to the network, to assist in getting a message from the source end device to the destination end device.

Connecting devices in a LAN is usually done with unshielded twisted-pair (UTP) cabling. Although many newer devices have an automatic crossover feature that enables you to connect either a straight-through or a crossover cable, you still need to know the following basic rules:

Use straight-through cables for the following connections:

- Switch to router Ethernet port
- Computer to switch
- Computer to hub

Use crossover cables for the following connections:

- Switch to switch
- Switch to hub
- Hub to hub
- Router to router (Ethernet ports)
- Computer to computer
- Computer to router Ethernet port

LANs and WANs

A local-area network (LAN) is a network of computers and other components located relatively close together in a limited area. LANs can vary widely in size, from one computer connected to a router in a home office, to hundreds of computers in a corporate office. However, in general, a LAN spans a limited geographical area. The fundamental components of a LAN include the following:

- Computers

- Interconnections (NICs and the media)

- Networking devices (hubs, switches, and routers)

- Protocols (Ethernet, IP, ARP, DHCP, DNS, and so on)

A wide-area network (WAN) generally connects LANs that are geographically separated. A collection of LANs connected by one or more WANs is called an *internetwork*—thus, we have the Internet. The term *intranet* is often used to refer to a privately owned connection of LANs and WANs.

Depending on the type of service, connecting to the WAN normally works in one of four ways:

- RJ-11 connection to a dialup or DSL modem

- Cable coaxial connection to a cable modem

- 60-pin serial connection to a CSU/DSU

- RJ-45 T1 controller connection to a CSU/DSU

With the growing number of teleworkers, enterprises have an increasing need for secure, reliable, and cost-effective ways to connect people working in small offices or home offices (SOHO) or other remote locations to resources on corporate sites. Remote connection technologies to support teleworkers include the following:

- Traditional private WAN technologies, including Frame Relay, ATM, and leased lines

- IPsec virtual private networks (VPN)

- Remote secure VPN access through a broadband connection over the public Internet

Components needed for teleworker connectivity include the following:

- **Home office components:** Computer, broadband access (cable or DSL), and a VPN router or VPN client software installed on the computer

- **Corporate components:** VPN-capable routers, VPN concentrators, multifunction security appliances, authentication, and central management devices for resilient aggregation and termination of the VPN connections

Networking Icons

Before you can interpret networking diagrams or topologies, you must understand the symbols or icons used to represent different networking devices and media. The icons in Figure 31-15 are the most common networking symbols for CCNA studies.

Figure 31-15   Networking Icons

Desktop Computer	Laptop	Server
LAN Switch	Router	Multilayer Switch
IP Phone	Firewall	Hub
Wireless Router	Wireless Access Point	LAN Media
WAN Media	Wireless Media	

Physical and Logical Topologies

Network diagrams are usually referred to as *topologies*. A topology graphically displays the interconnection methods used between devices.

Physical topologies refer to the physical layout of devices and how they are cabled. Seven basic physical topologies exist (see Figure 31-16).

Figure 31-16   Physical Topologies

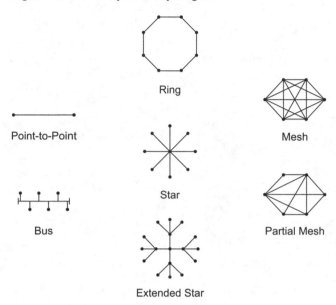

Logical topologies refer to the way that a signal travels from one point on the network to another and are largely determined by the access method—deterministic or nondeterministic. Ethernet is a nondeterministic access method. Logically, Ethernet operates as a bus topology. However, Ethernet networks are almost always physically designed as a star or extended star.

Other access methods use a deterministic access method. Token Ring and Fiber Distributed Data Interface (FDDI) both logically operate as a ring, passing data from one station to the next. Although these networks can be designed as a physical ring, like Ethernet, they are often designed as a star or extended star. Logically, however they operate like a ring.

 Activity: Determine the Device Type

Refer to the Digital Study Guide to complete this activity.

Hierarchical Campus Designs

Hierarchical campus design involves dividing the network into discrete layers. Each layer provides specific functions that define its role within the overall network. By separating the various functions that exist on a network, the network design becomes modular, which facilitates scalability and performance. The hierarchical design model is divided into three layers:

- **Access layer:** Provides local and remote user access
- **Distribution layer:** Controls the flow of data between the access and core layers
- **Core layer:** Acts as the high-speed redundant backbone

Figure 31-17 shows an example of the three-tiered hierarchical campus network design.

Figure 31-17   Three-Tiered Campus Design

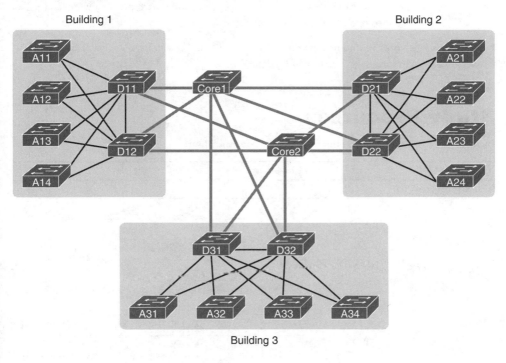

Building 3

For smaller networks, the core is often collapsed into the distribution layer for a two-tiered design, as in Figure 31-18.

Figure 31-18   Three-Tiered Campus Design

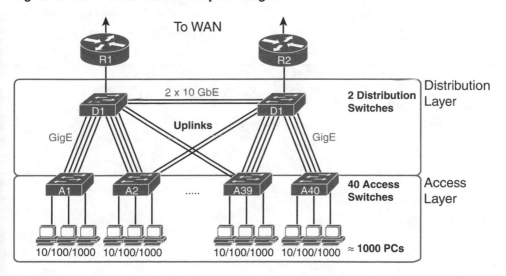

A two-tier design solves two major design needs:

- Provides a place to connect end-user devices (the access layer, with access switches)
- Connects the switches with a reasonable number of cables and switch ports by connecting all 40 access switches to two distribution switches

For very small networks and home networks, all three tiers can be seen in one device, such as the wireless broadband router shown earlier in Figure 31-14.

Study Resources

For today's exam topics, refer to the following resources for more study.

Resource	Location	Topic
Primary Resources		
Introduction to Networks	1	All
	3	All
	4	Media Access Control
ICND1 Official Cert Guide	1	All
	2	Building Physical Ethernet Networks with UTP
	5	TCP/IP Layer 4 Protocols: TCP and UDP
	10	Analyzing Campus LAN Topologies
		Analyzing LAN Physical Standard Choices
Supplemental Resources		
CCNA Video Series	1	Lesson 1: Network Reference Models and Protocols
		Lesson 2: Infrastructure Components
		Lesson 4: Network Architecture
		Lesson 5: Network Cabling

 Check Your Understanding

Refer to the Digital Study Guide to take a short quiz covering the content of this day.

Ethernet Switching

CCNA 200-125 Exam Topics

- Describe and verify switching concepts
- Interpret Ethernet frame format

Key Topics

Today we review the concepts behind Ethernet switching, including the history of switching development, how switching actually works, and the variety of switch features. We also review how to access Cisco devices, the basic IOS commands to navigate the command-line interface (CLI), and the details of Ethernet operation.

Evolution to Switching

Today's LANs almost exclusively use switches to interconnect end devices; however, this was not always the case. Initially, devices were connected to a physical bus, a long run of coaxial backbone cabling. With the introduction of 10BASE-T and UTP cabling, the hub gained popularity as a cheaper, easier way to connect devices. But even 10BASE-T with hubs had the following limitations:

- A frame sent from one device can collide with a frame sent by another device attached to that LAN segment. Devices were in the same collision domain sharing the bandwidth.

- Broadcasts sent by one device were heard and processed by all other devices on the LAN. Devices were in the same broadcast domain. Similar to hubs, switches forward broadcast frames out all ports except for the incoming port.

Ethernet bridges were soon developed to solve some of the inherent problems in a shared LAN. A bridge basically segmented a LAN into two collision domains, which reduced the number of collisions in a LAN segment. This increased the performance of the network by decreasing unnecessary traffic from another segment.

When switches arrived on the scene, these devices provided the same benefits of bridges, in addition to the following:

- A larger number of interfaces to break up the collision domain into more segments
- Hardware-based switching instead of using software to make the decision

In a LAN where all nodes are connected directly to the switch, the throughput of the network increases dramatically. With each computer connected to a separate port on the switch, each is in a separate collision domain and has its own dedicated segment. The three primary reasons for this increase follow:

- Dedicated bandwidth to each port

- Collision-free environment

- Full-duplex operation

Switching Logic

Ethernet switches selectively forward individual frames from a receiving port to the port where the destination node is connected. During this instant, the switch creates a full-bandwidth, logical, point-to-point connection between the two nodes.

Switches create this logical connection based on the source and destination Media Access Control (MAC) addresses in the Ethernet header. Specifically, the primary job of a LAN switch is to receive Ethernet frames and then make a decision to either forward the frame or ignore the frame. To accomplish this, the switch performs three actions:

1. Decides when to forward a frame or when to filter (not forward) a frame, based on the destination MAC address

2. Learns MAC addresses by examining the source MAC address of each frame the switch receives

3. Creates a (Layer 2) loop-free environment with other switches by using Spanning Tree Protocol (STP)

To make the decision to forward or filter, the switch uses a dynamically built MAC address table stored in RAM. By comparing the frame's destination MAC address with the fields in the table, the switch decides how to forward and/or filter the frame.

For example, in Figure 30-1, the switch receives a frame from Host A with the destination MAC address OC. The switch looks in its MAC table, finds an entry for the MAC address, and forwards the frame out port 6. The switch also filters the frame by not forwarding it out any other port, including the port on which the frame was received.

Figure 30-1   Switch Forwarding Based on MAC Address

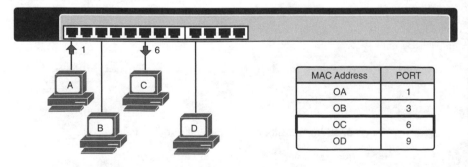

In addition to forwarding and filtering frames, the switch refreshes the timestamp for the source MAC address of the frame. In Figure 30-1, the MAC address for Host A, OA, is already in the MAC table, so the switch refreshes the entry. Entries that are not refreshed eventually are removed (after the default 300 seconds in Cisco IOS).

Continuing the example in Figure 30-1, assume that another device, Host E, is attached to port 10. Host B then sends a frame to the new Host E. The switch does not yet know where Host E is located, so it forwards the frame out all active ports except for the port on which the frame was received. The new Host E receives the frame. When it replies to Host B, the switch learns Host E's MAC address and port for the first time and stores it in the MAC address table. Subsequent frames destined for Host E then are sent out only port 10.

Finally, LAN switches must have a method for creating a loop-free path for frames to take within the LAN. Spanning Tree Protocol (STP) provides loop prevention in Ethernet networks where redundant physical links exist.

Collision and Broadcast Domains

A collision domain is the set of LAN interfaces whose frames could collide with each other. All shared media environments, such as those created by using hubs, are collision domains. When one host is attached to a switch port, the switch creates a dedicated connection, thereby eliminating the potential for a collision. Switches reduce collisions and improve bandwidth use on network segments because they provide dedicated bandwidth to each network segment.

Out of the box, however, a switch cannot provide relief from broadcast traffic. A collection of connected switches forms one large broadcast domain. If a frame with the destination address FFFF. FFFF.FFFF crosses a switch port, that switch must flood the frame out all other active ports. Each attached device must then process the broadcast frame at least up to the network layer. Routers and VLANs are used to segment broadcast domains. Day 28, "VLAN and Trunking Concepts and Configuration," reviews the use of VLANs to segment broadcast domains.

Frame Forwarding

Switches operate in several ways to forward frames. They can differ in forwarding methods, port speeds, memory buffering, and the OSI layers used to make the forwarding decision. The following sections discuss these concepts in greater detail.

Switch Forwarding Methods

Switches use one of the following forwarding methods to switch data between network ports:

- **Store-and-forward switching:** The switch stores received frames in its buffers, analyzes each frame for information about the destination, and evaluates the data integrity using the cyclic redundancy check (CRC) in the frame trailer. The entire frame is stored and the CRC is calculated before any of the frame is forwarded. If the CRC passes, the frame is forwarded to the destination.

- **Cut-through switching:** The switch buffers just enough of the frame to read the destination MAC address so that it can determine which port to forward the data. When the switch determines a match between the destination MAC address and an entry in the MAC address table, the frame is forwarded out the appropriate port(s). This happens as the rest of the initial frame is still being received. The switch does not perform any error checking on the frame.

- **Fragment-free:** The switch waits for the collision window (64 bytes) to pass before forwarding the frame. This means that each frame is checked into the data field to make sure that no fragmentation has occurred. Fragment-free mode provides better error checking than cut-through, with practically no increase in latency.

 Activity: Identify the Frame Forwarding Method

Refer to the Digital Study Guide to complete this activity.

Symmetric and Asymmetric Switching

Symmetric switching provides switched connections between ports with the same bandwidth, such as all 100-Mbps ports or all 1000-Mbps ports. An asymmetric LAN switch provides switched connections between ports of unlike bandwidth, such as a combination of 10-Mbps, 100-Mbps, and 1000-Mbps ports.

Memory Buffering

Switches store frames for a brief time in a memory buffer. Two methods of memory buffering exist:

- **Port-based memory:** Frames are stored in queues that are linked to specific incoming ports.

- **Shared memory:** Frames are deposited into a common memory buffer that all ports on the switch share.

Layer 2 and Layer 3 Switching

A Layer 2 LAN switch performs switching and filtering based only on MAC addresses. A Layer 2 switch is completely transparent to network protocols and user applications. A Layer 3 switch functions similarly to a Layer 2 switch. But instead of using only the Layer 2 MAC address information for forwarding decisions, a Layer 3 switch can also use IP address information. Layer 3 switches are also capable of performing Layer 3 routing functions, reducing the need for dedicated routers on a LAN. Because Layer 3 switches have specialized switching hardware, they can typically route data as quickly as they can switch data.

Ethernet Overview

802.3 is the IEEE standard for Ethernet, and both terms are commonly used interchangeably. The terms *Ethernet* and *802.3* both refer to a family of standards that together define the physical and data link layers of the definitive LAN technology. Figure 30-2 shows a comparison of Ethernet standards to the OSI model.

Figure 30-2   Ethernet Standards and the OSI Model

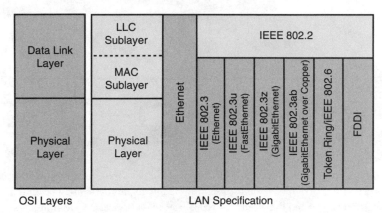

Ethernet separates the functions of the data link layer into two distinct sublayers:

- **Logical Link Control (LLC) sublayer:** Defined in the 802.2 standard
- **Media Access Control (MAC) sublayer:** Defined in the 802.3 standard

The LLC sublayer handles communication between the network layer and the MAC sublayer. In general, LLC provides a way to identify the protocol that is passed from the data link layer to the network layer. In this way, the fields of the MAC sublayer are not populated with protocol type information, as was the case in earlier Ethernet implementations.

The MAC sublayer has two primary responsibilities:

- **Data encapsulation:** Included here is frame assembly before transmission, frame parsing upon reception of a frame, data link layer MAC addressing, and error detection.
- **Media Access Control:** Because Ethernet is a shared media and all devices can transmit at any time, media access is controlled by a method called Carrier Sense Multiple Access with Collision Detection (CSMA/CD) when operating in half-duplex mode.

At the physical layer, Ethernet specifies and implements encoding and decoding schemes that enable frame bits to be carried as signals across both unshielded twisted-pair (UTP) copper cables and optical fiber cables. In early implementations, Ethernet used coaxial cabling.

Legacy Ethernet Technologies

Ethernet is best understood by first considering the two early Ethernet specifications, 10BASE5 and 10BASE2. With these two specifications, the network engineer installs a series of coaxial cables connecting each device on the Ethernet network, as in Figure 30-3.

Figure 30-3   Ethernet Physical and Logical Bus Topology

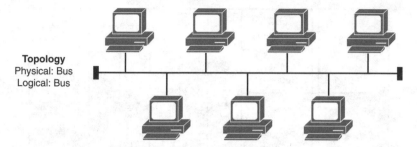

Topology
Physical: Bus
Logical: Bus

The series of cables creates an electrical circuit, called a *bus*, that is shared among all devices on the Ethernet. When a computer wants to send some bits to another computer on the bus, it sends an electrical signal and the electricity propagates to all devices on the Ethernet.

With the change of media to UTP and the introduction of the first hubs, Ethernet physical topologies migrated to a star, as shown in Figure 30-4.

Figure 30-4   Ethernet Physical Star and Logical Bus Topology

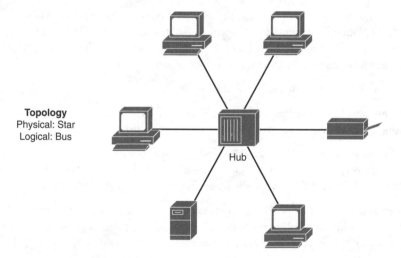

Topology
Physical: Star
Logical: Bus

Hub

Regardless of the change in the physical topology from a bus to a star, hubs logically operate similarly to a traditional bus topology and require the use of CSMA/CD.

CSMA/CD

Because Ethernet is a shared media in which every device has the right to send at any time, it also defines a specification to ensure that only one device sends traffic at a time. The CSMA/CD algorithm defines how the Ethernet logical bus is accessed.

CSMA/CD logic helps prevent collisions and also defines how to act when a collision does occur. The CSMA/CD algorithm works like this:

1. A device with a frame to send listens until the Ethernet is not busy.

2. When the Ethernet is not busy, the sender(s) begin(s) sending the frame.

3. The sender(s) listen(s) to make sure that no collision occurs.

4. If a collision occurs, the devices that were sending a frame each send a jamming signal to ensure that all stations recognize the collision.

5. When the jamming is complete, each sender randomizes a timer and waits that long before trying to resend the collided frame.

6. When each random timer expires, the process starts again from the beginning.

When CSMA/CD is in effect, a device's network interface card (NIC) operates in half-duplex mode, either sending or receiving frames. CSMA/CD is disabled when a NIC autodetects that it can operate in—or is manually configured to operate in—full-duplex mode. In full-duplex mode, a NIC can send and receive simultaneously.

Legacy Ethernet Summary

LAN hubs occasionally appear, but switches generally are used instead of hubs. Keep in mind the following key points about the history of Ethernet:

- The original Ethernet LANs created an electrical bus to which all devices connected.

- 10BASE2 and 10BASE5 repeaters extended the length of LANs by cleaning up the electrical signal and repeating it (a Layer 1 function), but without interpreting the meaning of the electrical signal.

- Hubs are repeaters that provide a centralized connection point for UTP cabling—but they still create a single electrical bus that the various devices share, just as with 10BASE5 and 10BASE2.

- Because collisions can occur in any of these cases, Ethernet defines the CSMA/CD algorithm, which tells devices how to both avoid collisions and take action when collisions do occur.

Current Ethernet Technologies

Refer to Figure 30-1 and notice the different 802.3 standards. Each new physical layer standard from the IEEE requires many differences at the physical layer. However, each of these physical layer standards uses the same 802.3 header, and each uses the upper LLC sublayer as well. Table 30-1 lists today's most commonly used IEEE Ethernet physical layer standards.

Table 30-1   Today's Most Common Types of Ethernet

Common Name	Speed	Alternative Name	Name of IEEE Standard	Cable Type, Maximum Length
Ethernet	10 Mbps	10BASE-T	802.3	Copper, 100 m
Fast Ethernet	100 Mbps	100BASE-TX	802.3u	Copper, 100 m
Gigabit Ethernet	1000 Mbps	1000BASE-LX	802.3z	Fiber, 550 m
Gigabit Ethernet	1000 Mbps	1000BASE-T	802.3ab	Copper, 100 m
10GigE (Gigabit Ethernet)	10 Gbps	10GBASE-T	802.3an	Copper, 100 m

UTP Cabling

The three most common Ethernet standards used today—10BASE-T (Ethernet), 100BASE-TX (Fast Ethernet, or FE), and 1000BASE-T (Gigabit Ethernet, or GE)—use UTP cabling. Some key differences exist, particularly with the number of wire pairs needed in each case and in the type (category) of cabling.

The UTP cabling in popular Ethernet standards includes either two or four pairs of wires. The cable ends typically use an RJ-45 connector. The RJ-45 connector has eight specific physical locations into which the eight wires in the cable can be inserted; these are called pin positions or, simply, pins.

The Telecommunications Industry Association (TIA) and the Electronics Industry Alliance (EIA) define standards for UTP cabling, with color coding for wires and standard pinouts on the cables. Figure 30-5 shows two TIA/EIA pinout standards, with the color coding and pair numbers listed.

Figure 30-5   TIA/EIA Standard Ethernet Cabling Pinouts

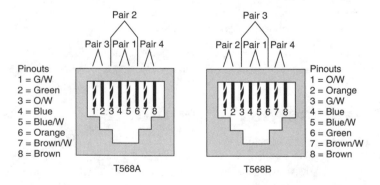

For the exam, you should be well prepared to choose which type of cable (straight-through or crossover) is needed in each part of the network. In short, devices on opposite ends of a cable that use the same pair of pins to transmit need a crossover cable. Devices that use an opposite pair of pins to transmit need a straight-through cable. Table 30-2 lists typical devices and the pin pairs they use, assuming that they use 10BASE-T and 100BASE-TX.

Table 30-2   10BASE-T and 100BASE-TX Pin Pairs Used

Devices That Transmit on 1,2 and Receive on 3,6	Devices That Transmit on 3,6 and Receive on 1,2
PC NICs	Hubs
Routers	Switches
Wireless access points (Ethernet interfaces)	—
Networked printers (printers that connect directly to the LAN)	—

1000BASE-T requires four wire pairs because Gigabit Ethernet transmits and receives on each of the four wire pairs simultaneously.

However, Gigabit Ethernet does have a concept of straight-through and crossover cables, with a minor difference in the crossover cables. The pinouts for a straight-through cable are the same—pin 1 to pin 1, pin 2 to pin 2, and so on.

A crossover cable has the 568A standard on one end and the 568B standard on the other end. This crosses the pairs at pins 1,2 and 3,6.

 Activity: Identify the 568A Pinouts

Refer to the Digital Study Guide to complete this activity.

 Activity: Identify the 568B Pinouts

Refer to the Digital Study Guide to complete this activity.

Benefits of Using Switches

A collision domain is a set of devices whose frames may collide. All devices on a 10BASE2, 10BASE5, or other network using a hub risk collisions between the frames that they send. Thus, devices on one of these types of Ethernet networks are in the same collision domain and use CSMA/CD to detect and resolve collisions.

LAN switches significantly reduce, or even eliminate, the number of collisions on a LAN. Unlike hubs, switches do not create a single shared bus. Instead, switches do the following:

- They interpret the bits in the received frame so that they can typically send the frame out the one required port instead of out all other ports.

- If a switch needs to forward multiple frames out the same port, the switch buffers the frames in memory, sending one at a time and thereby avoiding collisions.

In addition, switches with only one device cabled to each port of the switch allow the use of full-duplex operation. Full-duplex operation means that the NIC can send and receive concurrently, effectively doubling the bandwidth of a 100-Mbps link to 200 Mbps—100 Mbps for sending and 100 Mbps for receiving.

These seemingly simple switch features provide significant performance improvements, compared with using hubs. In particular, consider these points:

- If only one device is cabled to each port of a switch, no collisions can occur.

- Devices connected to one switch port do not share their bandwidth with devices connected to another switch port. Each has its own separate bandwidth, meaning that a switch with 100-Mbps ports has 100 Mbps of bandwidth per port.

Ethernet Addressing

The IEEE defines the format and assignment of LAN addresses. To ensure a unique MAC address, the first half of the address identifies the manufacturer of the card. This code is called the organizationally unique identifier (OUI). Each manufacturer assigns a MAC address with its own OUI as the first half of the address. The second half of the address is assigned by the manufacturer and is never used on another card or network interface with the same OUI. Figure 30-6 shows the structure of a unicast Ethernet address.

Figure 30-6   Structure of a Unicast Ethernet Address

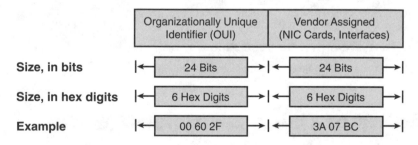

Ethernet also has group addresses, which identify more than one NIC or network interface. The IEEE defines two general categories of group addresses for Ethernet:

- **Broadcast addresses:** The broadcast address implies that all devices on the LAN should process the frame and has a value of FFFF.FFFF.FFFF.

- **Multicast addresses:** Multicast addresses allow a subset of devices on a LAN to communicate. When IP multicasts over an Ethernet, the multicast MAC addresses that IP uses follow this format: 0100.5exx.xxxx. The xx.xxxx portion is divided between IPv4 multicast (00:0000–7F. FFFF) and MPLS multicast (80:0000–8F:FFFF). Multiprotocol Label Switching (MPLS) is a CCNP topic.

Ethernet Framing

The physical layer helps you get a string of bits from one device to another. The framing of the bits allows the receiving device to interpret the bits. The term *framing* refers to the definition of the fields assumed to be in the data that is received. Framing defines the meaning of the bits transmitted and received over a network.

The framing used for Ethernet has changed a couple times over the years. Figure 30-7 shows each iteration of Ethernet, with the current version shown at the bottom.

Figure 30-7   Ethernet Frame Formats

DIX

Preamble	Destination	Source	Type	Data and Pad	FCS
8	6	6	2	46 – 1500	4

IEEE 802.3 (Original)

Preamble	SFD	Destination	Source	Length	Data and Pad	FCS
7	1	6	6	2	46 – 1500	4

IEEE 802.3 (Revised 1997)

	Preamble	SFD	Destination	Source	Length/ Type 2	Data and Pad	FCS
Bytes	7	1	6	6		46 – 1500	4

Table 30-3 further explains the fields in the last version shown in Figure 30-6.

Table 30-3   IEEE 802.3 Ethernet Field Descriptions

Field	Field Length in Bytes	Description
Preamble	7	Synchronization
Start Frame Delimiter (SFD)	1	Signifies that the next byte begins the Destination MAC field
Destination MAC Address	6	Identifies the intended recipient of this frame
Source MAC Address	6	Identifies the sender of this frame
Length	2	Defines the length of the data field of the frame (either length or type is present, but not both)
Type	2	Defines the type of protocol listed inside the frame (either length or type is present, but not both)
Data and Pad	46–1500	Holds data from a higher layer, typically a Layer 3 PDU (generic), and often an IP packet
Frame Check Sequence (FCS)	4	Provides a method for the receiving NIC to determine whether the frame experienced transmission errors

✔ **Activity: Order the Fields in a Frame**

Refer to the Digital Study Guide to complete this activity.

The Role of the Physical Layer

We have already discussed the most popular cabling used in LANs: UTP. To fully understand the operation of the network, you should know some additional basic concepts of the physical layer.

The OSI physical layer accepts a complete frame from the data link layer and encodes it as a series of signals that are transmitted onto the local media.

The delivery of frames across the local media requires the following physical layer elements:

- The physical media and associated connectors
- A representation of bits on the media
- Encoding of data and control information
- Transmitter and receiver circuitry on the network devices

Data is represented on three basic forms of network media:

- Copper cable
- Fiber
- Wireless (IEEE 802.11)

Bits are represented on the medium by changing one or more of the following characteristics of a signal:

- Amplitude
- Frequency
- Phase

The nature of the actual signals representing the bits on the media depends on the signaling method in use. Some methods use one attribute of a signal to represent a single 0 and use another attribute of a signal to represent a single 1. The actual signaling method and its detailed operation are not important to your CCNA exam preparation.

Study Resources

For today's exam topics, refer to the following resources for more study.

Resource	Location	Topic
Primary Resources		
Introduction to Networks	5	All
ICND1 Official Cert Guide	2	Sending Data in Ethernet Networks
	7	LAN Switching Concepts
	12	Predicting Where Switches Will Forward Frames
Supplemental Resources		
CCNA Video Series	1	Lesson 5: Network Cabling (EIA/TIA 568 Standards)
	2	Lesson 1: Fundamentals of Ethernet

Check Your Understanding

Refer to the Digital Study Guide to take a short quiz covering the content of this day.

Switch Configuration Basics

CCENT 100-101 ICND1 Exam Topics

- Configure and verify initial device configuration
- Troubleshoot interface and cable issues (collisions, errors, duplex, speed)

Key Topics

Today we review Cisco IOS basics and the commands necessary to perform a basic initial configuration of a switch. We also review verification techniques such as the **ping**, **traceroute**, and **show** commands.

Accessing and Navigating the Cisco IOS

By now, you are very familiar with connecting to Cisco devices and configuring them using the command-line interface (CLI). Here we quickly review methods for accessing and navigating the CLI.

Connecting to Cisco Devices

You can access a device directly or from a remote location. Figure 29-1 shows the many ways you can connect to Cisco devices.

The two ways to configure Cisco devices are as follows:

- **Console terminal:** Use an RJ-45–to–RJ-45 rollover cable and a computer with the terminal communications software (such as HyperTerminal or Tera Term) to establish a direct connection. Optionally, you can connect a mini-USB cable to the mini-USB console port, if available.

- **Remote terminal:** Use an external modem connected to the auxiliary port (routers only) to remotely configure the device.

After it is configured, you can access the device using three additional methods:

- Establish a terminal (vty) session using Telnet.

- Configure the device through the current connection (console or auxiliary), or download a previously written startup config file from a Trivial File Transfer Protocol (TFTP) server on the network.

- Download a configuration file using a network management software application such as CiscoWorks.

Figure 29-1 Sources for Cisco Device Configuration

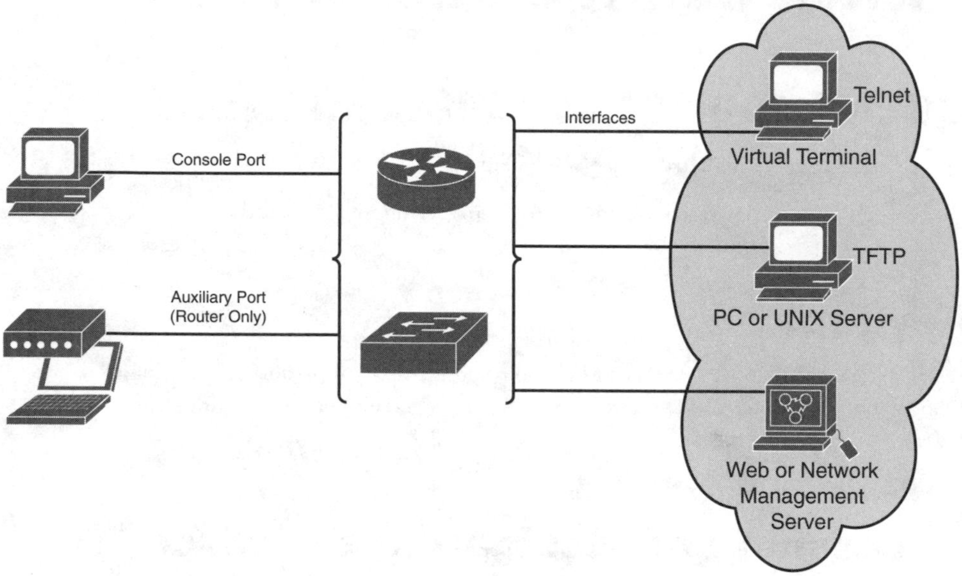

CLI EXEC Sessions

Cisco IOS separates the EXEC session into two basic access levels:

- **User EXEC mode:** Access to only a limited number of basic monitoring and troubleshooting commands, such as **show** and **ping**

- **Privileged EXEC mode:** Full access to all device commands, including configuration and management

Using the Help Facility

Cisco IOS has extensive command-line input help facilities, including context-sensitive help. The following summarizes the two types of help available:

- **Word help:** Enter a character sequence of an incomplete command immediately followed by a question mark (**sh?**) to get a list of available commands that start with the character sequence.

- **Command syntax help:** Enter the **?** command to get command syntax help to see all the available arguments to complete a command (**show ?**). Cisco IOS then displays a list of available arguments.

As part of the help facility, Cisco IOS displays console error messages when incorrect command syntax is entered. Table 29-1 shows sample error messages, what they mean, and how to get help.

Table 29-1   Console Error Messages

Example Error Message	Meaning	How to Get Help
switch# **cl** % Ambiguous command: "cl"	You did not enter enough characters for your device to recognize the command.	Reenter the command, followed by a question mark (?), without a space between the command and the question mark. The possible keywords that you can enter with the command display.
switch# **clock** % Incomplete command.	You did not enter all the keywords or values required by this command.	Reenter the command, followed by a question mark (?), with a space between the command and the question mark.
switch# **clock ste** ^ % Invalid input detected at '^' marker.	You entered the command incorrectly. The caret (^) marks the point of the error.	Enter a question mark (?) to display all the available commands or parameters.

CLI Navigation and Editing Shortcuts

Table 29-2 summarizes the shortcuts for navigating and editing commands in the CLI. Although not specifically tested on the CCNA exam, these shortcuts can save you time when using the simulator during the exam.

Table 29-2   Hot Keys and Shortcuts

Keyboard Command	What Happens
Navigation Key Sequences	
Up arrow or Ctrl-P	Displays the most recently used command. If you press the sequence again, the next most recent command appears, until the history buffer is exhausted. (The P stands for *previous*.)
Down arrow or Ctrl-N	Take you forward to the more recently entered commands, in case you have gone too far back into the history buffer. (The N stands for *next*.)
Left arrow or Ctrl-B	Moves the cursor backward in the currently displayed command without deleting characters. (The B stands for *back*.)
Right arrow or Ctrl-F	Moves the cursor forward in the currently displayed command without deleting characters. (The F stands for *forward*.)
Tab	Completes a partial command name entry.
Backspace	Moves the cursor backward in the currently displayed command, deleting characters.
Ctrl-A	Moves the cursor directly to the first character of the currently displayed command.
Ctrl-E	Moves the cursor directly to the end of the currently displayed command.
Ctrl-R	Redisplays the command line with all characters. This command is useful when messages clutter the screen.
Ctrl-D	Deletes a single character.
Esc-B	Moves back one word.
Esc-F	Moves forward one word.

Keyboard Command	What Happens
At the --More Prompt	
Enter key	Displays the next line.
Spacebar	Displays the next screen.
Any other alphanumeric key	Returns to the EXEC prompt.
Break Keys	
Ctrl-C	When in any configuration mode, ends the configuration mode and returns to privileged EXEC mode. When in setup mode, reverts back to the command prompt.
Ctrl-Z	When in any configuration mode, ends the configuration mode and returns to privileged EXEC mode. When in user or privileged EXEC mode, logs you out of the router.
Ctrl-Shift-6	Acts as an all-purpose break sequence. Use to abort DNS lookups, traceroutes, and pings.

Command History

By default, the Cisco IOS stores the last ten commands you entered in a history buffer. This gives you a quick way to move backward and forward in the history of commands, choose one, and then edit it before reissuing the command. To view or configure the command history buffer, use the commands in Table 29-3. Although this table shows the switch prompt, these commands are also appropriate for a router.

Table 29-3   Command History Buffer Commands

Command Syntax	Description
switch# **show history**	Displays the commands currently stored in the history buffer.
switch# **terminal history**	Enables terminal history. This command can be run from either user or privileged EXEC mode.
switch# **terminal history size 50**	Configures the terminal history size. The terminal history can maintain 0–256 command lines.
switch# **terminal no history size**	Resets the terminal history size to the default value of 20 command lines in Cisco IOS 15.
switch# **terminal no history**	Disables terminal history.

IOS Examination Commands

To verify and troubleshoot network operation, you use **show** commands. Figure 29-2 delineates the different **show** commands, as follows:

- Commands applicable to Cisco IOS (stored in RAM)
- Commands that apply to the backup configuration file stored in NVRAM
- Commands that apply to Flash or specific interfaces

Figure 29-2   Typical show Commands and the Information Provided

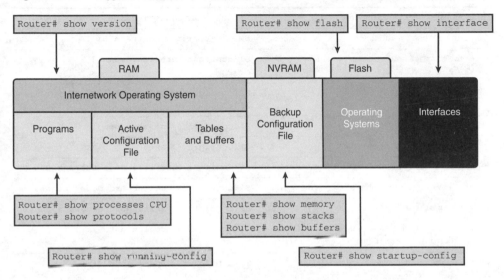

Subconfiguration Modes

To enter global configuration mode, enter the **configure terminal** command. From global configuration mode, Cisco IOS provides a multitude of subconfiguration modes. Table 29-4 summarizes the most common subconfiguration modes pertinent to the CCNA exam.

Table 29-4   Cisco Device Subconfiguration Modes

Prompt	Name of Mode	Examples of Commands Used to Reach This Mode
hostname(config)#	Global	configure terminal
hostname(config-line)#	Line	line console 0 line vty 0 15
hostname(config-if)#	Interface	interface fastethernet 0/0
hostname(config-router)#	Router	router rip router eigrp 100

 Activity: Identify the Cisco IOS Navigation Feature

Refer to the Digital Study Guide to complete this activity.

Basic Switch Configuration Commands

Table 29-5 reviews basic switch configuration commands.

Table 29-5   Basic Switch Configuration Commands

Command Description	Command Syntax
Enter global configuration mode.	Switch# **configure terminal**
Configure a name for the device.	Switch(config)# **hostname S1**
Enter the interface configuration mode for the VLAN 1 interface.	S1(config)# **interface vlan 1**
Configure the interface IP address.	S1(config-if)# **ip address 172.17.99.11 255.255.255.0**
Enable the interface.	S1(config-if)# **no shutdown**
Return to global configuration mode.	S1(config-if)# **exit**
Enter the interface to assign the VLAN.	S1(config)# **interface fastethernet 0/6**
Define the VLAN membership mode for the port.	S1(config-if)# **switchport mode access**
Assign the port to a VLAN.	S1(config-if)# **switchport access vlan 123**
Configure the interface duplex mode to enable AUTO duplex configuration.	S1(config-if)# **duplex auto**
Configure the interface speed and enable AUTO speed configuration.	S1(config-if)# **speed auto**
Enable auto-MDIX on the interface.	S1(config-if)# **mdix auto**
Return to global configuration mode.	S1(config-if)# **exit**
Configure the default gateway on the switch.	S1(config)# **ip default-gateway 172.17.50.1**
Configure the HTTP server for authentication using the **enable** password, which is the default method of HTTP server user authentication.	S1(config)# **ip http authentication enable**
Enable the HTTP server.	S1(config)# **ip http server**
Switch from global configuration mode to line configuration mode for console 0.	S1(config)# **line console 0**
Set **cisco** as the password for the console 0 line on the switch.	S1(config-line)# **password cisco**
Set the console line to require the password to be entered before access is granted.	S1(config-line)# **login**
Return to global configuration mode.	S1(config-if)# **exit**
Switch from global configuration mode to line configuration mode for vty terminals 0–15.	S1(config)# **line vty 0 15**
Set **cisco** as the password for the vty lines on the switch.	S1(config-line)# **password cisco**
Set the vty line to require the password to be entered before access is granted.	S1(config-line)# **login**

Command Description	Command Syntax
Return to global configuration mode.	`S1(config-line)# exit`
Configure **cisco** as the enable password to enter privileged EXEC mode.	`S1(config)# enable password cisco`
Configure **class** as the enable secret password to enter privileged EXEC mode. This password overrides **enable password**.	`S1(config)# enable secret class`
Encrypt all the system passwords that are stored in clear text.	`S1(config)# service password-encryption`
Configure a login banner. The # character delimits the beginning and end of the banner.	`S1 (config)# banner login #Authorized Personnel Only!#`
Configure a message of the day (MOTD) login banner. The # character delimits the beginning and end of the banner.	`S1(config)# banner motd #Device maintenance will be occurring on Friday!#`
Return to privileged EXEC mode.	`S1(config)# end`
Save the running configuration to the switch startup configuration.	`S1# copy running-config startup-config`

To configure multiple ports with the same command, use the **interface range** command. For example, to configure ports 6–10 as access ports belonging to VLAN 10, you enter the following:

```
Switch(config)# interface range FastEthernet 0/6 - 10
Switch(config-if-range)# switchport mode access
Switch(config-if-range)# switchport access vlan 10
```

 Packet Tracer Activity: Basic Switch Configuration

Refer to the Digital Study Guide to access the PKA file for this activity. You must have Packet Tracer software to run this activity. See the Introduction for details.

Half-Duplex, Full-Duplex, and Port Speed

Half-duplex communication is unidirectional data flow in which a device can either send or receive on an Ethernet LAN, but not both at the same time. Today's LAN networking devices and end device network interface cards (NIC) operate at full duplex as long as the device is connected to another device capable of full-duplex communication. Full-duplex communication increases the effective bandwidth by allowing both ends of a connection to transmit and receive data simultaneously; this is known as *bidirectional*. This microsegmented LAN is collision free. Gigabit Ethernet and 10-Gbps NICs require full-duplex connections to operate. Port speed is simply the bandwidth rating of the port. The most common speeds today are 100 Mbps, 1 Gbps, and 10 Gbps.

Although the default duplex and speed setting for Cisco Catalyst 2960 and 3560 switches is **auto**, you can manually configure the **speed** and **duplex** commands.

NOTE: Setting the duplex mode and speed of switch ports can cause issues if one end is mismatched or set to autonegotiation. In addition, all fiber-optic ports, such as 100BASE-FX ports, operate only at one preset speed and are always full duplex.

Automatic Medium-Dependent Interface Crossover (auto-MDIX)

In the past, switch-to-switch or switch-to-router connections required using different Ethernet cables (crossover or straight-through). Using the automatic medium-dependent interface crossover (auto-MDIX) feature on an interface eliminates this problem. When auto-MDIX is enabled, the interface automatically detects the required cable connection type (straight-through or crossover) and configures the connection appropriately.

The auto-MDIX feature is enabled by default on Catalyst 2960 and Catalyst 3560 switches. The Gigabit Ethernet standard requires auto-MDIX, so any 1000-Mbps port has this capability. When using auto-MDIX on an interface, the interface speed and duplex must be set to **auto** so that the feature operates correctly.

Verifying Network Connectivity

Using and interpreting the output of various testing tools is often the first step in isolating the cause of a network connectivity issue. The **ping** command can systematically test connectivity in the following manner:

- Can an end device ping itself?
- Can an end device ping its default gateway?
- Can an end device ping the destination?

By using the **ping** command in this ordered sequence, you can isolate problems faster. If local connectivity is not an issue—in other words, the end device can successfully ping its default gateway—using the traceroute utility can help isolate the point in the path from source to destination where the traffic stops.

As a first step in the testing sequence, verify the operation of the TCP/IP stack on the local host by pinging the loopback address, 127.0.0.1, as Example 29-1 demonstrates.

Example 29-1   Testing the TCP/IP Stack on a Windows PC

```
C:\> ping 127.0.0.1

Pinging 127.0.0.1 with 32 bytes of data:

Reply from 127.0.0.1: bytes=32 time<1ms TTL=64
Reply from 127.0.0.1: bytes=32 time<1ms TTL=64
Reply from 127.0.0.1: bytes=32 time<1ms TTL=64
Reply from 127.0.0.1: bytes=32 time<1ms TTL=64

Ping statistics for 127.0.0.1:
    Packets: Sent = 4, Received = 4, Lost = 0 (0% loss),
Approximate round trip times in milli-seconds:
    Minimum = 0ms, Maximum = 0ms, Average = 0ms
```

This test should succeed regardless of whether the host is connected to the network, so a failure indicates a software or hardware problem on the host itself. Either the network interface is not operating properly or support for the TCP/IP stack has been inadvertently removed from the operating system.

Next, verify connectivity to the default gateway. Determine the default gateway address using **ipconfig** and then attempt to ping it, as in Example 29-2.

Example 29-2   Testing Connectivity to the Default Gateway on a Windows PC

```
C:\> ipconfig


Windows IP Configuration


Ethernet adapter Local Area Connection:

        Connection-specific DNS Suffix  .  : cisco.com
        IP Address. . . . . . . . . . . : 192.168.1.25
        Subnet Mask . . . . . . . . . . : 255.255.255.0
        Default Gateway . . . . . . . . : 192.168.1.1

C:\> ping 192.160.1.1

Pinging 192.168.1.1 with 32 bytes of data:

Reply from 192.168.1.1: bytes=32 time=162ms TTL=255
Reply from 192.168.1.1: bytes=32 time=69ms TTL=255
Reply from 192.168.1.1: bytes=32 time=82ms TTL=255
Reply from 192.168.1.1: bytes=32 time=72ms TTL=255

Ping statistics for 192.168.1.1:
    Packets: Sent = 4, Received = 4, Lost = 0 (0% loss),
Approximate round trip times in milli-seconds:
    Minimum = 69ms, Maximum = 162ms, Average = 96ms
```

Failure here can indicate several problems, each of which must be checked in a systematic sequence. One possible order might be the following:

1. Is the cabling from the PC to the switch correct? Are link lights lit?
2. Is the configuration on the PC correct according to the logical map of the network?
3. Are the affected interfaces on the switch the cause of the problem? Is there a duplex, speed, or auto–MDIX mismatch? Are there VLAN misconfigurations?
4. Is the cabling from the switch to the router correct? Are link lights lit?
5. Is the configuration on the router interface correct according to the logical map of the network? Is the interface active?

Finally, verify connectivity to the destination by pinging it. Assume that you are trying to reach a server at 192.168.3.100. Example 29-3 shows a successful **ping** test to the destination.

Example 29-3   Testing Connectivity to the Destination on a Windows PC

```
PC> ping 192.168.3.100


Pinging 192.168.3.100 with 32 bytes of data:


Reply from 192.168.3.100: bytes=32 time=200ms TTL=126
Reply from 192.168.3.100: bytes=32 time=185ms TTL=126
Reply from 192.168.3.100: bytes=32 time=186ms TTL=126
Reply from 192.168.3.100: bytes=32 time=200ms TTL=126


Ping statistics for 192.168.3.100:
    Packets: Sent = 4, Received = 4, Lost = 0 (0% loss),
Approximate round trip times in milli-seconds:
    Minimum = 185ms, Maximum = 200ms, Average = 192ms
```

Failure here indicates a failure in the path beyond the default gateway interface because you already successfully tested connectivity to the default gateway. From a Windows PC, the best tool to use to find the break in the path is the **tracert** command (see Example 29-4).

NOTE: Both Mac OS X and Linux use the **traceroute** command.

Example 29-4   Tracing the Route from a Windows PC

```
C:\> tracert 192.168.3.100


Tracing route to 192.168.3.100 over a maximum of 30 hops:


  1    97 ms      75 ms      72 ms      192.168.1.1
  2   104 ms     119 ms     117 ms      192.168.2.2
  3    *          *          *          Request timed out.
  4    *          *          *          Request timed out.
  5    *          *          *          Request timed out.
  6   ^C
C:\>
```

NOTE: Failure at hops 3, 4, and 5 in Example 29-4 could indicate that these routers are configured to not send ICMP messages back to the source.

The last successful hop on the way to the destination was 192.168.2.2. If you have administrator rights to 192.168.2.2, you can continue your research by remotely accessing the command line on 192.168.2.2 and investigating why traffic will not go any further. Additionally, other devices between 192.168.2.2 and 192.168.3.100 could be the source of the problem. The point is, you want to use your **ping** and **tracert** tests, as well as your network documentation, to proceed in a logical sequence from source to destination.

Regardless of how simple or complex your network is, using **ping** and **tracert** from the source to the destination is a simple yet powerful way to systematically verify end-to-end connectivity, as well as locate breaks in a path from one source to one destination.

Troubleshoot Interface and Cable Issues

The physical layer is often the reason a network issue exists—power outage, disconnected cable, power-cycled devices, hardware failures, and so on. This section looks at some troubleshooting tools, in addition to the approach of actually walking over to the wiring closet or network device and "physically" checking layer 1.

Media Issues

Besides failing hardware, common physical layer issues occur with media. Consider a few examples:

- New equipment is installed that introduces electromagnetic interference (EMI) sources into the environment.

- Cable runs too close to powerful motors, such as an elevator.

- Poor cable management puts a strain on some RJ-45 connectors, causing one or more wires to break.

- New applications change traffic patterns.

- When new equipment is connected to a switch, the connection operates in half-duplex mode or a duplex mismatch occurs, which can lead to an excessive number of collisions.

Figure 29-3 shows an excellent troubleshooting flowchart that you can use in troubleshooting switch media issues.

Figure 29-3   Troubleshooting Switch Media Issues

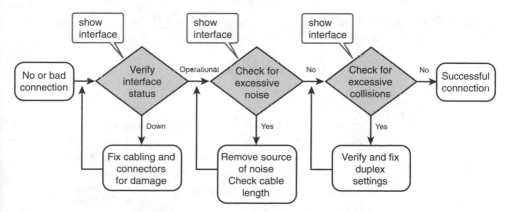

Next, take look at the output from the **show interface** and **show interface status** commands.

Interface Status and the Switch Configuration

Because today we are focusing on switch troubleshooting, we look at the **show** commands that help in troubleshooting the basic configuration.

Interface Status Codes

In general, interfaces are either "up" or "down." However, when an interface is "down" and you don't know why, the code in the **show interfaces** command provides more information to help you determine the reason. Table 29-6 lists the code combinations and some possible causes for the status indicated.

Table 29-6   LAN Switch Interface Status Codes

Line Status	Protocol Status	Interface Status	Typical Root Cause
Administratively Down	Down	disabled	The interface is configured with the **shutdown** command.
Down	Down	notconnect	No cable exists, the cable is bad, wrong cable pinouts are used, the two connected devices have mismatched speeds, or the device on the other end of the cable is powered off or the other interface is shut down.
Up	Down	notconnect	An interface up/down state is not expected on LAN switch interfaces. This indicates a Layer 2 problem on Layer 3 devices.
Down	Down (err-disabled)	err-disabled	Port security has disabled the interface. The network administrator must manually reenable the interface.
Up	Up	connect	The interface is working.

Duplex and Speed Mismatches

One of the more common problems is issues with speed and/or duplex mismatches. On switches and routers, the **speed** {**10** | **100** | **1000**} interface subcommand and the **duplex** {**half** | **full**} interface subcommand set these values. Note that configuring both speed and duplex on a switch interface disables the IEEE-standard autonegotiation process on that interface.

The **show interfaces status** and **show interfaces** commands list both the speed and duplex settings on an interface, as Example 29-5 shows.

Example 29-5   Commands to Verify Speed and Duplex Settings

```
S1# show interface status

Port      Name         Status        Vlan     Duplex   Speed Type
Fa0/1                  connected     trunk    full     100 10/100BaseTX
Fa0/2                  connected     1        half     100 10/100BaseTX
Fa0/3                  connected     1        a-full   a-100 10/100BaseTX
Fa0/4                  disabled      1        auto     auto 10/100BaseTX
Fa0/5                  disabled      1        auto     auto 10/100BaseTX
Fa0/6                  notconnect    1        auto     auto 10/100BaseTX
```

```
!Remaining output omitted
S1# show interface fa0/3
FastEthernet0/1 is up, line protocol is up (connected)
  Hardware is Fast Ethernet, address is 001b.5302.4e81 (bia 001b.5302.4e81)
  MTU 1500 bytes, BW 100000 Kbit, DLY 100 usec,
      reliability 255/255, txload 1/255, rxload 1/255
  Encapsulation ARPA, loopback not set
  Keepalive set (10 sec)
  Full-duplex, 100Mb/s, media type is 10/100BaseTX
  input flow-control is off, output flow-control is unsupported
  ARP type: ARPA, ARP Timeout 04:00:00
  Last input never, output 00:00:00, output hang never
  Last clearing of "show interface" counters never
  Input queue: 0/75/0/0 (size/max/drops/flushes); Total output drops: 0
  Queueing strategy: fifo
  Output queue: 0/40 (size/max)
  5 minute input rate 1000 bits/sec, 1 packets/sec
  5 minute output rate 0 bits/sec, 0 packets/sec
     2745 packets input, 330885 bytes, 0 no buffer
     Received 1386 broadcasts (0 multicast)
     0 runts, 0 giants, 0 throttles
     0 input errors, 0 CRC, 0 frame, 0 overrun, 0 ignored
     0 watchdog, 425 multicast, 0 pause input
     0 input packets with dribble condition detected
     56989 packets output, 4125809 bytes, 0 underruns
     0 output errors, 0 collisions, 1 interface resets
     0 babbles, 0 late collision, 0 deferred
     0 lost carrier, 0 no carrier, 0 PAUSE output
     0 output buffer failures, 0 output buffers swapped out
```

Notice that both commands show the duplex and speed settings of the interface. However, the **show interface status** command is preferred for troubleshooting duplex or speed mismatches because it shows exactly how the switch determined the duplex and speed of the interface. In the duplex column, **a-full** means the switch autonegotiated full duplex. The setting **full** or **half** means that the switch was configured at that duplex setting. Autonegotiation has been disabled. In the speed column, **a-100** means the switch autonegotiated 100 Mbps as the speed. The setting **10** or **100** means that the switch was configured at that speed setting.

Finding a duplex mismatch can be much more difficult than finding a speed mismatch because if the duplex settings do not match on the ends of an Ethernet segment, the switch interface will still be in a connect (up/up) state. In this case, the interface works, but the network might work poorly, with hosts experiencing poor performance and intermittent communication problems. To identify duplex mismatch problems, check the duplex setting on each end of the link and watch for incrementing collision and late collision counters, as highlighted in the output at the end of Example 29-5.

Common Layer 1 Problems On "Up" Interfaces

When a switch interface is "up," it does not necessarily mean that the interface is operating in an optimal state. For this reason, Cisco IOS tracks certain counters to help identify problems that can occur even though the interface is in a connect state. The output in Example 29-5 highlights these counters. Table 29-7 summarizes three general types of Layer 1 interface problems that can occur while an interface is in the "up," connected, state.

Table 29-7   Common LAN Layer 1 Problem Indicators

Type of Problem	Counter Values Indicating This Problem	Common Root Causes
Excessive noise	Many input errors, few collisions	Wrong cable category (Cat 5, 5E, 6), damaged cables, EMI
Collisions	More than roughly .1% of all frames are collisions	Duplex mismatch (seen on the half-duplex side), jabber, DoS attack
Late collisions	Increasing late collisions	Collision domain or single cable too long, duplex mismatch

Study Resources

For today's exam topics, refer to the following resources for more study.

Resource	Location	Topic
Primary Resources		
Introduction to Networks	2	IOS Bootcamp
	11	Network Troubleshooting
ICND1 Official Cert Guide	6	All
	8	All
	9	Configuring Switch Interfaces
	12	Analyzing Switch Interface Status and Statistics
	17	Enabling IPv4 Support on Cisco Router Interfaces
Supplemental Resources		
CCNA Portable Command Guide	4	All
	5	All
	6	All
CCNA Video Series	2	Lesson 2: Basic Cisco Catalyst Switch Configuration

Resource	Location	Topic
Supplemental Resources		
CCNA Network Simulator	ICND1	Chapter 6: Switch CLI Configuration Process I–II
		Chapter 6: Switch CLI Exec Mode
		Chapter 6: Configuring Local Usernames
		Chapter 6: Configuring Hostnames
		Chapter 6: Using the debug Command on a Router
		Chapter 8: Setting Switch Passwords
		Chapter 8: Terminal History I–II
		Chapter 8: Configuring Switch IP Settings
		Chapter 8: Switch IP Address
		Chapter 8: Switch IP Connectivity I
		Chapter 9: Switch Security
		Chapter 9: Interface Settings I–III
		Chapter 9: Interface Settings II
		Chapter 9: Interface Settings III
		Chapter 12: New Job I
		Chapter 12: Rebuild a Configuration
		Chapter 12: Router CLI Exec Mode I–II
		Chapter 12: Router CLI Exec Mode II
		Chapter 12: Router CLI Configuration Process
		Chapter 12: Setting Router Passwords
		Chapter 12: Interface Status V–VI

Check Your Understanding

Refer to the Digital Study Guide to take a short quiz covering the content of this day.

VLAN and Trunking Concepts and Configurations

CCENT 100-101 ICND1 Exam Topics

- Configure, verify, and troubleshoot VLANs (normal/extended range) spanning multiple switches

- Configure, verify, and troubleshoot interswitch connectivity

Key Points

Most large networks today implement virtual local-area networks (VLANs). Without VLANs, a switch considers every port to be in the same broadcast domain. With VLANs, switch ports can be grouped into different VLANs, essentially segmenting the broadcast domain. Today we review VLAN concepts, consider traffic types, discuss VLAN types, and review the concept of trunking, including Dynamic Trunking Protocol (DTP). Then we review the commands to configure and verify VLANs and trunking.

> **NOTE:** VLAN Trunking Protocol (VTP) is reviewed on Day 21, "VTP and Inter-VLAN Routing Configuration."

VLAN Concepts

Although a switch comes out of the box with only one VLAN, normally a switch is configured to have two or more VLANs. Doing so creates multiple broadcast domains by putting some interfaces into one VLAN and other interfaces into other VLANs.

Consider these reasons for using VLANs:

- Grouping users by department instead of by physical location

- Segmenting devices into smaller LANs to reduce processing overhead for all devices on the LAN

- Reducing the workload of STP by limiting a VLAN to a single access switch

- Enforcing better security by isolating sensitive data to separate VLANs

- Separating IP voice traffic from data traffic

- Assisting troubleshooting by reducing the size of the failure domain (the number of devices that can cause a failure or be affected by one)

Benefits of using VLANs include the following:

- **Security:** Sensitive data can be isolated to one VLAN, separating it from the rest of the network.

- **Cost reduction:** Cost savings result from less need for expensive network upgrades and more efficient use of existing bandwidth and uplinks.

- **Higher performance:** Dividing flat Layer 2 networks into multiple logical broadcast domains reduces unnecessary traffic on the network and boosts performance.

- **Broadcast storm mitigation:** VLAN segmentation prevents a broadcast storm from propagating throughout the entire network.

- **Ease of management and troubleshooting:** A hierarchical addressing scheme groups network addresses contiguously. Because a hierarchical IP addressing scheme makes problem components easier to locate, network management and troubleshooting are more efficient.

Traffic Types

The key to successful VLAN deployment is understanding the traffic patterns and the various traffic types in the organization. Table 28-1 lists the common types of network traffic to evaluate before placing devices and configuring VLANs.

Table 28-1   Traffic Types

Traffic Type	Description
Network management	Many types of network management traffic can be present on the network. To make network troubleshooting easier, some designers assign a separate VLAN to carry certain types of network management traffic.
IP telephony	Two types of IP telephony traffic exist: signaling information between end devices and the data packets of the voice conversation. Designers often configure the data to and from the IP phones on a separate VLAN designated for voice traffic so that they can apply quality-of-service measures to give high priority to voice traffic.
IP multicast	Multicast traffic can produce a large amount of data streaming across the network. Switches must be configured to keep this traffic from flooding to devices that have not requested it, and routers must be configured to ensure that multicast traffic is forwarded to the network areas where it is requested.
Normal data	Normal data traffic is typical application traffic that is related to file and print services, email, Internet browsing, database access, and other shared network applications.
Scavenger class	Scavenger class includes all traffic with protocols or patterns that exceed their normal data flows. Applications assigned to this class have little or no contribution to the organizational objectives of the enterprise and are typically entertainment-oriented.

Types of VLANs

Some VLAN types are defined by the type of traffic they support; others are defined by the specific functions they perform. The principal VLAN types and their descriptions follow:

- **Data VLAN:** Configured to carry only user-generated traffic, ensuring that voice and management traffic is separated from data traffic.

- **Default VLAN:** All the ports on a switch are members of the default VLAN when the switch is reset to factory defaults. The default VLAN for Cisco switches is VLAN 1. VLAN 1 has all the features of any VLAN, except that you cannot rename it and you cannot delete it. It is a security best practice to restrict VLAN 1 to serve as a conduit only for Layer 2 control traffic (for example, CDP), supporting no other traffic.

- **Black hole VLAN:** A security best practice is to define a black hole VLAN to be a dummy VLAN distinct from all other VLANs defined in the switched LAN. All unused switch ports are assigned to the black hole VLAN so that any unauthorized device connecting to an unused switch port is prevented from communicating beyond the switch to which it is connected.

- **Native VLAN:** This VLAN type serves as a common identifier on opposing ends of a trunk link. A security best practice is to define a native VLAN to be a dummy VLAN distinct from all other VLANs defined in the switched LAN. The native VLAN is not used for any traffic in the switched network unless legacy bridging devices happen to be present in the network or a multiaccess interconnection exists between switches joined by a hub.

- **Management VLAN:** The network administrator defines this VLAN as a means to access the management capabilities of a switch. By default, VLAN 1 is the management VLAN. It is a security best practice to define the management VLAN to be a VLAN distinct from all other VLANs defined in the switched LAN. You do this by configuring and activating a new VLAN interface.

- **Voice VLANs:** The voice VLAN feature enables switch ports to carry IP voice traffic from an IP phone. The network administrator configures a voice VLAN and assigns it to access ports. Then when an IP phone is connected to the switch port, the switch sends CDP messages that instruct the attached IP phone to send voice traffic tagged with the voice VLAN ID.

 Activity: Identify the Type of VLAN

Refer to the Digital Study Guide to complete this activity.

Voice VLAN Example

Figure 28-1 shows an example of using one port on a switch to connect a user's IP phone and PC. The switch port is configured to carry data traffic on VLAN 20 and voice traffic on VLAN 150. The Cisco IP Phone contains an integrated three-port 10/100 switch to provide the following dedicated connections:

- Port 1 connects to the switch or other VoIP device.

- Port 2 is an internal 10/100 interface that carries the IP Phone traffic.

- Port 3 (access port) connects to a PC or other device.

Figure 28-1   Cisco IP Phone Switching Voice and Data Traffic

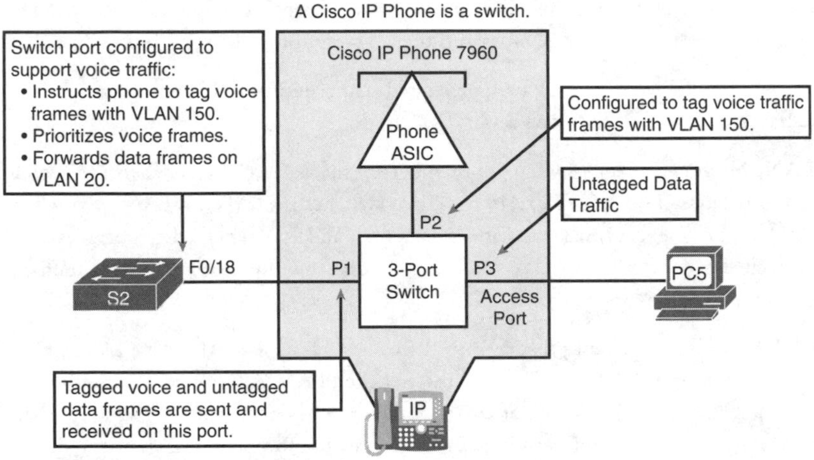

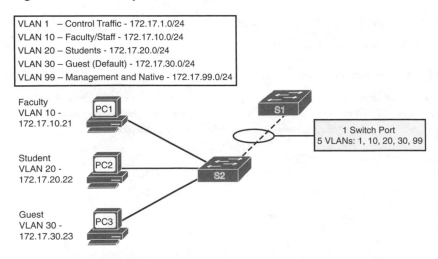

The traffic from the PC5 attached to the IP Phone passes through the IP Phone untagged. The link between S2 and the IP Phone acts as a modified trunk to carry both the tagged voice traffic and the untagged data traffic.

Trunking VLANs

A VLAN trunk is an Ethernet point-to-point link between an Ethernet switch interface and an Ethernet interface on another networking device, such as a router or a switch, carrying the traffic of multiple VLANs over the singular link. A VLAN trunk enables you to extend the VLANs across an entire network. A VLAN trunk does not belong to a specific VLAN; instead, it serves as a conduit for VLANs between switches. Figure 28-2 shows a small switched network with a trunk link between S1 and S2 carrying multiple VLAN traffic.

Figure 28-2   Example of a VLAN Trunk

When a frame is placed on a trunk link, information about the VLAN it belongs to must be added to the frame. This is accomplished by using IEEE 802.1Q frame tagging. When a switch receives a frame on a port configured in access mode and destined for a remote device through a trunk link, the switch takes apart the frame and inserts a VLAN tag, recalculates the frame check sequence (FCS), and sends the tagged frame out the trunk port. Figure 28-3 shows the 802.1Q tag inserted in an Ethernet frame.

Figure 28-3   Fields of the 802.1Q Tag Inside an Ethernet Frame

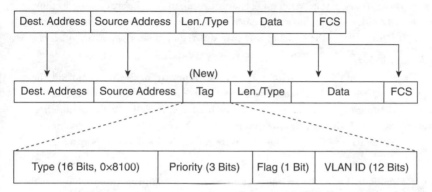

The VLAN tag field consists of a 16-bit Type field called the EtherType field and a Tag control information field. The EtherType field is set to the hexadecimal value of 0x8100. This value is called the tag protocol ID (TPID) value. With the EtherType field set to the TPID value, the switch receiving the frame knows to look for information in the Tag control information field. The Tag control information field contains the following:

- **3 bits of user priority:** Provides expedited transmission of Layer 2 frames, such as voice traffic

- **1 bit of Canonical Format Identifier (CFI):** Enables Token Ring frames to be easily carried across Ethernet links

- **12 bits of VLAN ID (VID):** Provides VLAN identification numbers

---

NOTE: Although 802.1Q is the recommended method for tagging frames, you should be aware of the Cisco proprietary legacy trunking protocol called Inter-Switch Link (ISL).

Dynamic Trunking Protocol

Dynamic Trunking Protocol (DTP) is a Cisco-proprietary protocol that negotiates both the status of trunk ports and the trunk encapsulation of trunk ports. DTP manages trunk negotiation only if the port on the other switch is configured in a trunk mode that supports DTP. A switch port on a Cisco Catalyst switch supports a number of trunking modes. The trunking mode defines how the port negotiates using DTP to set up a trunk link with its peer port. The following is a brief description of each trunking mode:

- If the switch is configured with the **switchport mode trunk** command, the switch port periodically sends DTP messages to the remote port, advertising that it is in an unconditional trunking state.

- If the switch is configured with the **switchport mode trunk dynamic auto** command, the local switch port advertises to the remote switch port that it is able to trunk but does not request to go to the trunking state. After a DTP negotiation, the local port ends up in the trunking state only if the remote port trunk mode has been configured so that the status is **on** or **desirable**. If both ports on the switches are set to **auto**, they do not negotiate to be in a trunking state. They negotiate to be in the access mode state.

- If the switch is configured with the **switchport mode dynamic desirable** command, the local switch port advertises to the remote switch port that it is able to trunk and asks the remote switch port to go to the trunking state. If the local port detects that the remote has been configured as **on, desirable,** or **auto** mode, the local port ends up in the trunking state. If the remote switch port is in the **nonegotiate** mode, the local switch port remains as a nontrunking port.

- If the switch is configured with the **switchport nonegotiate** command, the local port is then considered to be in an unconditional trunking state. Use this feature when you need to configure a trunk with a switch from another switch vendor.

Table 28-2 summarizes the results of DTP negotiations based on the different DTP configuration commands on a local and remote port.

Table 28-2 Trunk Negotiation Results Between a Local and a Remote Port

	Dynamic Auto	Dynamic Desirable	Trunk	Access
Dynamic Auto	Access	Trunk	Trunk	Access
Dynamic Desirable	Trunk	Trunk	Trunk	Access
Trunk	Trunk	Trunk	Trunk	Not recommended
Access	Access	Access	Not recommended	Access

VLAN Configuration and Verification

Refer to the topology in Figure 28-4 as we review the commands for configuring, verifying, and troubleshooting VLAN and trunking. The Packet Tracer activity later in the day uses this same topology.

Figure 28-4   Day 28 Sample Topology

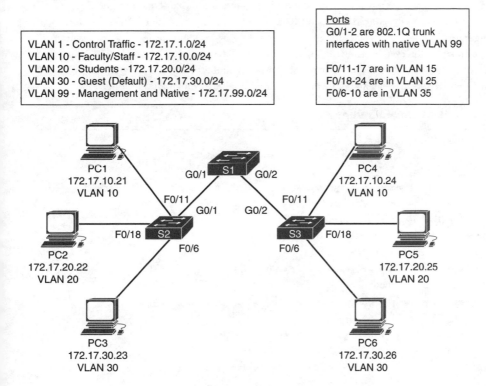

Ports
G0/1-2 are 802.1Q trunk
interfaces with native VLAN 99

F0/11-17 are in VLAN 15
F0/18-24 are in VLAN 25
F0/6-10 are in VLAN 35

VLAN 1 - Control Traffic - 172.17.1.0/24
VLAN 10 - Faculty/Staff - 172.17.10.0/24
VLAN 20 - Students - 172.17.20.0/24
VLAN 30 - Guest (Default) - 172.17.30.0/24
VLAN 99 - Management and Native - 172.17.99.0/24

The default configuration of a Cisco switch is to put all interfaces in VLAN 1. You can verify this with the **show vlan brief** command, as demonstrated for S2 in Example 28-1.

Example 28-1   Default VLAN Configuration

```
S2# show vlan brief

VLAN Name                             Status    Ports
---- -------------------------------- --------- -------------------------------
1    default                          active    Fa0/1, Fa0/2, Fa0/3, Fa0/4
                                                Fa0/5, Fa0/6, Fa0/7, Fa0/8
                                                Fa0/9, Fa0/10, Fa0/11, Fa0/12
                                                Fa0/13, Fa0/14, Fa0/15, Fa0/16
                                                Fa0/17, Fa0/18, Fa0/19, Fa0/20
                                                Fa0/21, Fa0/22, Fa0/23, Fa0/24
                                                Gig0/1, Gig0/2
1002 fddi-default                     active
1003 token-ring-default               active
1004 fddinet-default                  active
1005 trnet-default                    active
S2#
```

A VLAN is created in one of two ways: either in global configuration mode or directly under the interface. The advantage to configuring in global configuration mode is that you can then assign a name with the **name** *vlan-name* command. The advantage to configuring the VLAN in interface configuration mode is that you assign the VLAN to the interface and create the VLAN with just one command. However, to name the VLAN, you still have to go back to the global configuration method. Example 28-2 shows the creation of VLANs 10 and 20 using these two methods. VLAN 20 is then named, and the remaining VLANs are created in global configuration mode.

Example 28-2   Creating VLANs

```
S2# config t
Enter configuration commands, one per line.   End with CNTL/Z.
S2(config)# vlan 10
S2(config-vlan)# name Faculty/Staff
S2(config-vlan)# interface fa0/18
S2(config-if)# switchport access vlan 20
% Access VLAN does not exist. Creating vlan 20
S2(config-if)# vlan 20
S2(config-vlan)# name Students
S2(config-vlan)# vlan 30
S2(config-vlan)# name Guest(Default)
S2(config-vlan)# vlan 99
S2(config-vlan)# name Management&Native
S2(config-vlan)# end
%SYS-5-CONFIG_I: Configured from console by console
S2#
```

Notice in Example 28-3 that all the VLANs are created, but only VLAN 20 is assigned to an interface.

Example 28-3   Verifying VLAN Creation

```
S2# config t
Enter configuration commands, one per line.   End with CNTL/Z.
S2(config)# vlan 10
S2(config-vlan)# name Faculty/Staff
S2(config-vlan)# interface fa0/18
S2(config-if)# switchport access vlan 20
% Access VLAN does not exist. Creating vlan 20
S2(config-if)# vlan 20
S2(config-vlan)# name Students
S2(config-vlan)# vlan 30
S2(config-vlan)# name Guest(Default)
S2(config-vlan)# vlan 99
S2(config-vlan)# name Management&Native
S2(config-vlan)# end
%SYS-5-CONFIG_I: Configured from console by console
S2#
```

To assign the remaining interfaces to the VLANs specified in Figure 28-4, either you can configure one interface at a time or you can use the **range** command to configure all the interfaces that
belong to a VLAN with one command, as shown in Example 28-4.

Example 28-4   Assigning VLANs to Interfaces

```
S2# config t
Enter configuration commands, one per line.  End with CNTL/Z.
S2(config)# interface range fa 0/11 - 17
S2(config-if-range)# switchport access vlan 10
S2(config-if-range)# interface range fa 0/18 - 24
S2(config-if-range)# switchport access vlan 20
S2(config-if-range)# interface range fa 0/6 - 10
S2(config-if-range)# switchport access vlan 30
S2(config-if-range)# end
%SYS-5-CONFIG_I: Configured from console by console
S2#
```

The **show vlan brief** command in Example 28-5 verifies that all interfaces specified in Figure 28-4
have been assigned to the appropriate VLAN. Notice that unassigned interfaces still belong to the
default VLAN 1.

Example 28-5   Verifying VLAN Assignments to Interfaces

```
S2# show vlan brief

VLAN Name                             Status    Ports
---- -------------------------------- --------- ------------------------------
1    default                          active    Fa0/1, Fa0/2, Fa0/3, Fa0/4
                                                Fa0/5, Gig0/1, Gig0/2
10   Faculty/Staff                    active    Fa0/11, Fa0/12, Fa0/13, Fa0/14
                                                Fa0/15, Fa0/16, Fa0/17
20   Students                         active    Fa0/18, Fa0/19, Fa0/20, Fa0/21
                                                Fa0/22, Fa0/23, Fa0/24
30   Guest(Default)                   active    Fa0/6, Fa0/7, Fa0/8, Fa0/9
                                                Fa0/10
99   Management&Native                active
1002 fddi-default                     active
1003 token-ring-default               active
1004 fddinet-default                  active
1005 trnet-default                    active
S2#
```

You can also verify a specific interface's VLAN assignment with the **show interfaces** *type number*
switchport command, as shown for FastEthernet 0/11 in Example 28-6.

Example 28-6   Verifying an Interface's VLAN Assignment

```
S2# show interfaces fastethernet 0/11 switchport
Name: Fa0/11
Switchport: Enabled
Administrative Mode: dynamic auto
Operational Mode: static access
Administrative Trunking Encapsulation: dot1q
Operational Trunking Encapsulation: native
Negotiation of Trunking: On
Access Mode VLAN: 10 (Faculty/Staff)
Trunking Native Mode VLAN: 1 (default)
Voice VLAN: none
Administrative private-vlan host-association: none
Administrative private-vlan mapping: none
Administrative private-vlan trunk native VLAN: none
Administrative private-vlan trunk encapsulation: dot1q
Administrative private-vlan trunk normal VLANs: none
Administrative private-vlan trunk private VLANs: none
Operational private-vlan: none
Trunking VLANs Enabled: ALL
Pruning VLANs Enabled: 2-1001
Capture Mode Disabled
Capture VLANs Allowed: ALL
Protected: false
Appliance trust: none
S2#
```

For the sample topology shown in Figure 28-4, you would configure the VLANs on S1 and S3 as well, but only S3 needs VLANs assigned to interfaces.

Extended VLANs

VLANs are divided into a normal range or an extended range, as Table 28-3 describes.

Table 28-3   Comparing Normal and Extended VLANs

Type	Definition
Normal range VLANs	■ Normal range VLANs are used in small and medium-size business and enterprise networks.
	■ These VLANs are identified by VLAN IDs between 1 and 1005.
	■ IDs 1 and 1002 to 1005 are automatically created and cannot be removed.
	■ Configurations are stored within a VLAN database file called vlan.dat, which is stored in Flash memory.

Type	Definition
Extended range VLANs	■ Service providers and large organizations use extended range VLANs to extend their infrastructure to a greater number of customers.
	■ These VLANs are identified by a VLAN ID between 1006 and 4094.
	■ Extended range VLANs support fewer VLAN features than normal range VLANs.
	■ Configurations are saved in the running configuration file.

NOTE: A Cisco Catalyst 2960 switch can support up to 255 normal range and extended range VLANs. However, the number of VLANs configured affects the performance of the switch hardware.

By default, Cisco 2960 switches run VTP versions 1 and 2, which do not support extended VLANs. To configure an extended VLAN, you must first configure the switch in VTP transparent mode, as in Example 28-7.

Example 28-7   Configuring Extended VLANs on a Cisco 2960 Switch

```
Dist-A(config)# vlan 2500
Dist-A(config-vlan)# exit
% Failed to create VLANs 2500
Extended VLAN(s) not allowed in current VTP mode.
%Failed to commit extended VLAN(s) changes.
*Mar  1 01:08:32.825: %SW_VLAN-4-VLAN_CREATE_FAIL: Failed to create VLANs 2500:
extended VLAN(s) not allowed in current VTP mode
Dist-A(config)# vtp mode transparent
Setting device to VTP Transparent mode for VLANS.
Dist-A(config)# vlan 2500
Dist-A(config-vlan)# end
Dist-A# show vlan brief

VLAN Name                             Status    Ports
---- -------------------------------- --------- -------------------------------
1    default                          active    Fa0/1, Fa0/2, Fa0/3, Fa0/4
                                                Fa0/5, Fa0/6, Fa0/7, Fa0/8
                                                Fa0/9, Fa0/10, Fa0/11, Fa0/12
                                                Fa0/13, Fa0/14, Fa0/15, Fa0/16
                                                Fa0/17, Fa0/18, Fa0/19, Fa0/20
                                                Fa0/21, Fa0/22, Fa0/23, Fa0/24
                                                Gi0/1, Gi0/2
1002 fddi-default                     act/unsup
1003 token-ring-default               act/unsup
1004 fddinet-default                  act/unsup
1005 trnet-default                    act/unsup
2500 VLAN2500                         active
Dist-A#
```

Normal VLANs are saved in Flash memory in the vlan.dat file. You do not see normal VLAN configurations in the output of **show run**. However, extended VLAN configurations are saved in the running configuration and can be seen in **show run** (see Example 28-8).

Example 28-8   Viewing the Extended VLAN Configuration

```
Dist-A# show run
Building configuration...
<output omitted>
!
vtp mode transparent
!
<output omitted>
!
vlan 2500
!
<output omitted>
Dist-A#
```

NOTE: VTP version 3 supports extended VLANs, but the current exam topics cover only VTP versions 1 and 2.

Trunking Configuration and Verification

Following security best practices, we are configuring a different VLAN for the management and default VLAN. In a production network, you would want to use a different one for each: one for the management VLAN and one for the native VLAN. For expediency here, we are using VLAN 99 for both.

To begin, we first define a new management interface for VLAN 99, as in Example 28-9.

Example 28-9   Defining a New Management Interface

```
S1# config t
Enter configuration commands, one per line.   End with CNTL/Z.
S1(config)# interface vlan 99
%LINK-5-CHANGED: Interface Vlan99, changed state to up
S1(config-if)# ip address 172.17.99.31 255.255.255.0
S1(config-if)# end
%SYS-5-CONFIG_I: Configured from console by console
S1#
```

Repeat the configuration on S2 and S3. The IP address is used to test connectivity to the switch, as well as the IP address the network administrator uses for remote access (Telnet, SSH, SDM, HTTP, and so on).

Depending on the switch model and Cisco IOS version, DTP might have already established trunking between two switches that are directly connected. For example, the default trunk configuration for 2950 switches is **dynamic desirable**. Therefore, a 2950 will initiate trunk negotiations. For our purposes, assume that the switches are all 2960s. The 2960 default trunk configuration is **dynamic auto**, in which the interface will not initiate trunk negotiations.

In Example 28-10, the first five interfaces on S1 are configured for trunking. Also notice that the native VLAN is changed to VLAN 99.

Example 28-10   Trunk Configuration and Native VLAN Assignment

```
S1# config t
Enter configuration commands, one per line.  End with CNTL/Z.
S1(config)# interface range g0/1 - 2
S1(config-if-range)# switchport mode trunk
S1(config-if-range)# switchport trunk native vlan 99
S1(config-if-range)# end
%SYS-5-CONFIG_I: Configured from console by console
S1#
%CDP-4-NATIVE_VLAN_MISMATCH: Native VLAN mismatch discovered on FastEthernet0/1
   (99), with S2 FastEthernet0/1 (1).
%CDP-4-NATIVE_VLAN_MISMATCH: Native VLAN mismatch discovered on FastEthernet0/3
   (99), with S3 FastEthernet0/3 (1).
```

If you wait for the next round of CDP messages, you should get the error message shown in Example 28-10. Although the trunk is working between S1 and S2 and between S1 and S3, the switches do not agree on the native VLAN. Repeat the trunking commands on S2 and S3 to correct the native VLAN mismatch.

NOTE: The encapsulation type—dot1q or isl—might need to be configured, depending on the switch model. If so, the syntax for configuring the encapsulation type is as follows:

```
Switch(config-if)# switchport trunk encapsulation { dot1q | isl | negotiate }
```

The 2960 Series supports only 802.1Q, so this command is not available.

To verify that trunking is operational, use the commands in Example 28-11.

Example 28-11   Verifying Trunk Configuration

```
S1# show interfaces trunk
Port          Mode          Encapsulation  Status        Native vlan
Gig0/1        on            802.1q         trunking      99
Gig0/2        on            802.1q         trunking      99


Port          Vlans allowed on trunk
Gig0/1        1-1005
Gig0/2        1-1005
```

```
Port          Vlans allowed and active in management domain
Gig0/1        1,10,20,30,99
Gig0/2        1,10,20,30,99


Port          Vlans in spanning tree forwarding state and not pruned
Gig0/1        1,10,20,30,99
Gig0/2        1,10,20,30,99

S1# show interface g0/1 switchport
Name: Gig0/1
Switchport: Enabled
Administrative Mode: trunk
Operational Mode: trunk
Administrative Trunking Encapsulation: dot1q
Operational Trunking Encapsulation: dot1q
Negotiation of Trunking: On
Access Mode VLAN: 1 (default)
Trunking Native Mode VLAN: 99 (Management&Native)
Voice VLAN: none
Administrative private-vlan host-association: none
Administrative private-vlan mapping: none
Administrative private-vlan trunk native VLAN: none
Administrative private-vlan trunk encapsulation: dot1q
Administrative private-vlan trunk normal VLANs: none
Administrative private-vlan trunk private VLANs: none
Operational private-vlan: none
Trunking VLANs Enabled: ALL
Pruning VLANs Enabled: 2-1001
Capture Mode Disabled
Capture VLANs Allowed: ALL
Protected: false
Appliance trust: none
S1#
```

Remember, hosts on the same VLAN must be configured with an IP address and subnet mask on the same subnet. The ultimate test of your configuration, then, is to verify that end devices on the same VLAN can now ping each other. If not, use the verification commands to systematically track down the problem with your configuration.

Packet Tracer Activity: VLAN and Trunking Configuration

Refer to the Digital Study Guide to access the PKA file for this activity. You must have Packet Tracer software to run this activity. See the Introduction for details.

VLAN Troubleshooting

If connectivity issues arise between VLANs and you have already resolved potential IP addressing issues, you can use the flowchart in Figure 28-5 to methodically track down any issues related to VLAN configuration errors.

Figure 28-5   VLAN Troubleshooting Flow Chart

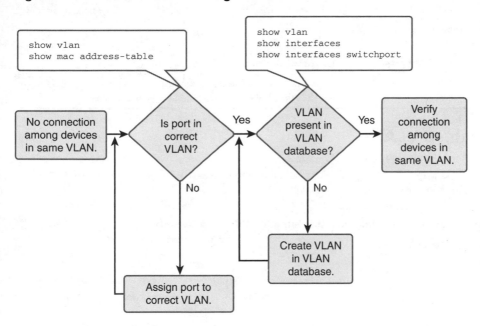

The flowchart in Figure 28-5 works in this way:

Step 1.   Use the **show vlan** command to check whether the port belongs to the expected VLAN. If the port is assigned to the wrong VLAN, use the **switchport access vlan** command to correct the VLAN membership. Use the **show mac address-table** command to check which addresses were learned on a particular port of the switch and see the VLAN to which that port is assigned.

Step 2.   If the VLAN to which the port is assigned is deleted, the port becomes inactive. Use the **show vlan** or **show interfaces switchport** commands to discover issues with deleted VLANs. If the port is inactive, it is not functional until the missing VLAN is created using the **vlan** *vlan_id* command.

Table 28-4 summarizes these commands, which can be particularly helpful in troubleshooting VLAN issues.

Table 28-4   VLAN Troubleshooting Commands

EXEC Command	Description
show vlan show vlan brief	Lists each VLAN and all interfaces assigned to that VLAN (but does not include operational trunks)
show vlan id *num*	Lists both access and trunk ports in the VLAN
show interfaces switchport show interfaces *type number* switchport	Identifies the interface's access VLAN and voice VLAN, the configured and operational mode (access or trunk), and the state of the port (up or down)
show mac address-table	Lists MAC table entries, including the associated VLAN
show interface status	Summarizes the status listing for all interfaces (connected, notconnect, err-disabled), the VLAN, duplex, speed, and type of port

Disabled VLANs

VLANs can be manually disabled. You can verify that VLANs are active with the **show vlan** command. As Example 28-12 shows, VLANs can be in one of two states: either *active* or *act/lshut*. The second of these states means that the VLAN is shut down.

Example 28-12   Enabling and Disabling VLANs on a Switch

```
S1# show vlan brief
VLAN Name                             Status    Ports
---- -------------------------------- --------- -------------------------------
1    default                          active    Fa0/1, Fa0/2, Fa0/3, Fa0/4
                                                 Fa0/5, Fa0/6, Fa0/7, Fa0/8
                                                 Fa0/9, Fa0/10, Fa0/11, Fa0/12
                                                 Fa0/14, Fa0/15, Fa0/16, Fa0/17
                                                 Fa0/18, Fa0/19, Fa0/20, Fa0/21
                                                 Fa0/22, Fa0/23, Fa0/24, Gi0/1
10   VLAN0010                         act/lshut Fa0/13
20   VLAN0020                         active
30   VLAN0030                         act/lshut
40   VLAN0040                         active
S1# configure terminal
Enter configuration commands, one per line. End with CNTL/Z.
S1(config)# no shutdown vlan 10
S1(config)# vlan 30
S1(config-vlan)# no shutdown
S1(config-vlan)#
```

The highlighted commands in Example 28-12 show the two configuration methods you can use to enable a shutdown VLAN.

Trunking Troubleshooting

To summarize issues with VLANs and trunking, the four potential issues are as follows:

Step 1. Identify all access interfaces and their assigned access VLANs, and reassign them into the correct VLANs, as needed.

Step 2. Determine whether the VLANs exist and are active on each switch. If not, configure and activate the VLANs to resolve problems, as needed.

Step 3. Check the allowed VLAN lists on the switches on both ends of the trunk and ensure that the lists of allowed VLANs are the same.

Step 4. Ensure that, for any links that should use trunking, one switch does not think it is trunking, while the other switch does not think it is trunking.

The previous section reviewed Steps 1 and 2. Next, we review Steps 3 and 4.

Check Both Ends of a Trunk

For the CCNA, you should be ready to notice a couple oddities that happen with some unfortunate configuration choices on trunks.

It is possible to configure a different allowed VLAN list on the opposite ends of a VLAN trunk. As Figure 28-6 shows, when the VLAN lists do not match, the trunk cannot pass traffic for that VLAN.

Figure 28-6   Mismatched VLAN-Allowed Lists on a Trunk

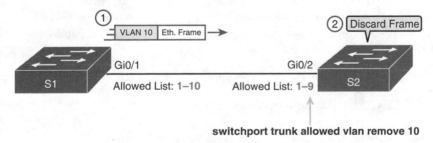

You can isolate this problem only by comparing the allowed lists on both ends of the trunk. Example 28-11 displays the output of the **show interfaces trunk** command on S2.

To compare the allowed VLANs on each switch, you need to look at the second of three lists of VLANs listed by the **show interfaces trunk** command. See the output in Example 28-13.

Example 28-13   Verifying the Allowed VLANs on S2

```
S2# show interfaces trunk
Port          Mode          Encapsulation  Status        Native vlan
Gi0/2         desirable     802.1q         trunking      1


Port          Vlans allowed on trunk
Gi0/2         1-4094


Port          Vlans allowed and active in management domain
Gi0/2         1-9


Port          Vlans in spanning tree forwarding state and not pruned
Gi0/2         1-9
```

To add VLAN 10 to S2's trunk, enter the following commands:

```
S2(config)# interface g0/2
S2(config-if)# switchport trunk allowed vlan add 10
```

The keyword **add** provides the capability to add one or more VLANs to the trunk without having to specify again all the existing VLANs that are already allowed.

Check Trunking Operational States

Trunks can also be misconfigured. In some cases, both switches conclude that their interfaces do not trunk. In other cases, one switch believes that its interface is correctly trunking, while the other switch does not.

The most common incorrect configuration—which results in both switches not trunking—is a configuration that uses the **switchport mode dynamic auto** command on both switches on the link. The keyword **auto** does not mean that trunking happens automatically. Instead, both switches passively wait on the other device on the link to begin negotiations.

With this particular incorrect configuration, the **show interfaces switchport** command on both switches confirms both the administrative state (auto) and the fact that both switches operate as static access ports. Example 28-14 highlights those parts of the output for S2.

Example 28-14   Verifying the Trunking State for a Specific Interface

```
SW2# show interfaces gigabit0/2 switchport
Name: Gi0/2
Switchport: Enabled
Administrative Mode: dynamic auto
Operational Mode: static access
Administrative Trunking Encapsulation: dot1q
Operational Trunking Encapsulation: native
! lines omitted for brevity
```

Always check the trunk's operational state on both sides of the trunk. The best commands to check trunking-related facts are **show interfaces trunk** and **show interfaces switchport**.

Study Resources

For today's exam topics, refer to the following resources for more study.

Resource	Location	Topic
Primary Resources		
Routing and Switching Essentials	6	VLAN Segmentation
Scaling Networks	2	VTP, Extended VLANs, and DTP
ICND1 Official Cert Guide	11	All
	12	Analyzing VLANs and VLAN Trunks
Supplemental Resources		
CCNA Portable Command Guide	7	All
	8	All
CCNA Video Series	2	Lesson 3: Virtual LANs (VLANs)
		Lesson 4: Trunking
		Lesson 6: Troubleshooting Switch Operation
		Checking a Port's VLAN Membership
		Checking a Trunk's Status
CCNA Network Simulator	ICND1	Chapter 11: Configuring VLANs
		Chapter 11: VLAN Trunking I–II
		Chapter 11: VLANs I–III
		Chapter 11: VLAN Configuration I–V
		Chapter 11: Trunking Configuration I–IV

Check Your Understanding

Refer to the Digital Study Guide to take a short quiz covering the content of this day.

IPv4 Addressing

CCENT 100-101 ICND1 Exam Topics

- Compare and contrast IPv4 address types
- Describe the need for private IPv4 addressing
- Configure, verify, and troubleshoot IPv4 addressing and subnetting

Key Topics

Today we focus on reviewing the structure of an IPv4 address, the classes, and private and public IPv4 addresses. Then we turn our focus to IPv4 subnetting.

By now, you should be able to subnet quickly. For example, you should be able to quickly answer a question such as the following:

If you are given a /16 network, what subnet mask would you use to maximize the total number of subnets while still providing enough addresses for the largest subnet with 500 hosts?

The answer is 255.255.254.0, or /23. This gives you 128 subnets with 510 usable hosts per subnet. You should be able to quickly calculate this information.

The CCNA exam promises to contain many subnetting and subnetting-related questions. Therefore, we devote some time to this necessary skill and also look at designing addressing schemes using variable-length subnet masking (VLSM).

IPv4 Addressing

Although IPv6 is rapidly permeating the networks of the world, most networks still have a large IPv4 implementation. Especially on private networks, migration away from IPv4 will take years to complete. Clearly, IPv4 and your skill in its use are still in demand.

Header Format

Figure 27-1 shows the layout of the IPv4 header.

Figure 27-1   IPv4 Header Format

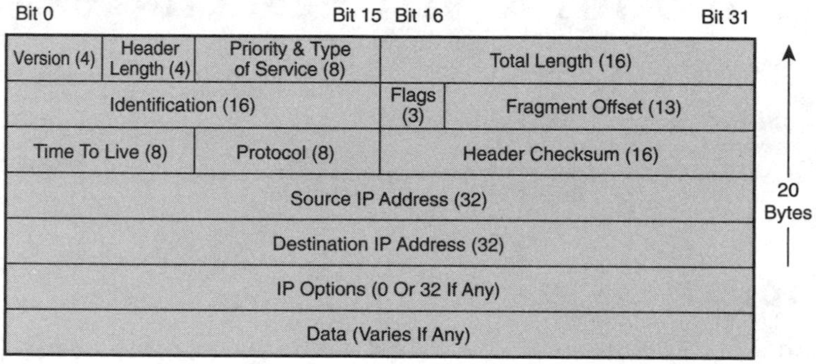

Note that each IP packet carries this header, which includes a source IP address and destination IP address.

An IP address consists of two parts:

- The high-order, or leftmost, bits specify the network address component (network ID) of the address.

- The low-order, or rightmost, bits specify the host address component (host ID) of the address.

Classes of Addresses

From the beginning, IPv4 was designed with class structure: Classes A, B, C, D, and E. Class D is used for multicasting addresses and Class E is reserved for experimentation. Classes A, B, and C are assigned to network hosts. To provide a hierarchical structure, these classes are divided into network and host portions, as Figure 27-2 shows. The high-order bits specify the network ID, and the low-order bits specify the host ID.

Figure 27-2   Network/Host Boundary for Each Class of IPv4 Address

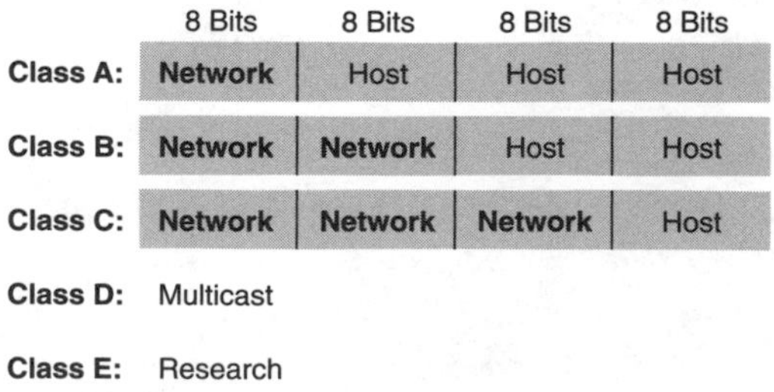

In a classful addressing scheme, devices that operate at Layer 3 can determine the address class of an IP address from the format of the first few bits in the first octet. Initially, this was important so that a networking device could apply the default subnet mask for the address and determine the host address. Table 27-1 summarizes how addresses are divided into classes, the default subnet mask, the number of networks per class, and the number of hosts per classful network address.

Table 27-1   IPv4 Address Classes

Address Class	First Octet Range (Decimal)	First Octet Bits (Highlighted Bits Do Not Change)	Network (N) and Host (H) Portions of Addresses	Default Subnet Mask (Decimal and Binary)	Number of Possible Networks and Hosts per Network
A	1–127	00000000–01111111	N.H.H.H	255.0.0.0 11111111.00000000.00000000.00000000	2^7 or 128 networks $2^{24}-2$ or 16,777,214 hosts per network
B	128–191	10000000–10111111	N.N.H.H	255.255.0.0 11111111.11111111.00000000.00000000	2^{14} or 16,384 networks $2^{16}-2$ or 65,534 hosts per network
C	192–223	11000000–11011111	N.N.N.H	255.255.255.0 11111111.11111111.11111111.00000000	2^{21} or 2,097,152 networks 2^8-2 or 254 hosts per network
D	224–239	11100000–11101111	Not used for host addressing		
E	240–255	11110000–11111111	Not used for host addressing		

In the last column, the −2 for hosts per network is to account for the reserved network and broadcast addresses for each network. These two addresses cannot be assigned to hosts.

NOTE: We do not review the process of converting between binary and decimal. At this point in your studies, you should be comfortable moving between the two numbering systems. If not, take some time to practice this necessary skill. You can search the Internet for binary conversion tricks, tips, and games to help you practice. The Cisco Learning Network has a fun game you can play here: https://learningnetwork.cisco.com/docs/DOC-1803.

Purpose of the Subnet Mask

Subnet masks are always a series of 1 bits followed by a series of 0 bits. The boundary where the series changes from 1s to 0s is the boundary between the network and the host. This is how a device that operates at Layer 3 determines the network address for a packet, by finding the bit boundary where the series of 1 bits ends and the series of 0 bits begins. The bit boundary for default subnet masks breaks on the octet boundary. Determining the network address for an IP address that uses a default mask is easy.

For example, a router receives a packet destined for 192.168.1.51. By ANDing the IP address and the subnet mask, the router determines the network address for the packet. By the ANDing rules, a 1 AND a 1 equals 1. All other possibilities equal 0. Table 27-2 shows the results of the ANDing operation. Notice that the host bits in the last octet are ignored.

Table 27-2   ANDing an IP Address and Subnet Mask to Find the Network Address

Destination Address	192.168.1.51	11000000.10101000.00000001.00110011
Subnet Mask	255.255.255.0	11111111.11111111.11111111.00000000
Network Address	192.168.1.0	11000000.10101000.00000001.00000000

The bit boundary can now occur in just about any place in the 32 bits. Table 27-3 summarizes the values for the last nonzero octet in a subnet mask.

Table 27-3   Subnet Mask Binary Values

Mask (Decimal)	Mask (Binary)	Network Bits	Host Bits
0	00000000	0	8
128	10000000	1	7
192	11000000	2	6
224	11100000	3	5
240	11110000	4	4
248	11111000	5	3
252	11111100	6	2
254	11111110	7	1
255	11111111	8	0

Private and Public IP Addressing

RFC 1918, "Address Allocation for Private Internets," eased the demand for IP addresses by reserving the following addresses for use in private internetworks:

- **Class A:** 10.0.0.0/8 (10.0.0.0–10.255.255.255)

- **Class B:** 172.16.0.0/12 (172.16.0.0–172.31.255.255)

- **Class C:** 192.168.0.0/16 (192.168.0.0–192.168.255.255)

If you are addressing a nonpublic intranet, these private addresses are normally used instead of globally unique public addresses. This provides flexibility in your addressing design. Any organization can take full advantage of an entire Class A address (10.0.0.0/8). Forwarding traffic to the public Internet requires translation to a public address using Network Address Translation (NAT). But by overloading an Internet-routable address with many private addresses, a company needs only a handful of public addresses. Day 9 reviews NAT operation and configuration in greater detail.

Activity: Identify Private and Public Addresses

Refer to the Digital Study Guide to complete this activity.

Subnetting in Four Steps

Everyone has a preferred method of subnetting. Each teacher uses a slightly different strategy to help students master this crucial skill and each of the suggested study resources has a slightly different way of approaching this subject.

The method I prefer consists of four steps:

Step 1.   Determine how many bits to borrow, based on the host requirements.

Step 2.   Determine the new subnet mask.

Step 3.   Determine the subnet multiplier.

Step 4.   List the subnets, including subnetwork address, host range, and broadcast address.

The best way to demonstrate this method is to use an example. Assume that you are given the network address 192.168.1.0 with the default subnet mask 255.255.255.0. The network address and subnet mask can be written as 192.168.1.0/24. The /24 represents the subnet mask in a shorter notation and means that the first 24 bits are network bits.

Now further assume that you need 30 hosts per network and want to create as many subnets for the given address space as possible. With these network requirements, you can now subnet the address space.

Determine How Many Bits to Borrow

To determine the number of bits you can borrow, you first must know how many host bits you have to start with. Because the first 24 bits are network bits in this example, the remaining 8 bits are host bits.

Because our requirement specifies 30 host addresses per subnet, we need to first determine the minimum number of host bits to leave. The remaining bits can be borrowed:

Host Bits = Bits Borrowed + Bits Left

To provide enough address space for 30 hosts, we need to leave 5 bits. Use the following formula:

$2^{BL} - 2$ = number of host addresses

The exponent BL is bits left in the host portion.

Remember, the −2 is to account for the network and broadcast addresses that cannot be assigned to hosts.

In this example, leaving 5 bits in the host portion provides the right number of host addresses:

$2^5 - 2 = 30$

Because we have 3 bits remaining in the original host portion, we borrow all these bits to satisfy the requirement to "create as many subnets as possible." To determine how many subnets we can create, use the following formula:

2^{BB} = number of subnets

The exponent BB is bits borrowed from the host portion.

In this example, borrowing 3 bits from the host portion creates eight subnets: $2^3 = 8$.

As Table 27-4 shows, the 3 bits are borrowed from the leftmost bits in the host portion. The highlighted bits in the table show all possible combinations of manipulating the 8 bits borrowed to create the subnets.

Table 27-4   Binary and Decimal Value of the Subnetted Octet

Subnet Number	Last Octet Binary Value	Last Octet Decimal Value
0	00000000	.0
1	00100000	.32
2	01000000	.64
3	01100000	.96
4	10000000	.128
5	10100000	.160
6	11000000	.192
7	11100000	.224

Determine the New Subnet Mask

Notice in Table 27-4 that the network bits now include the 3 borrowed host bits in the last octet. Add these 3 bits to the 24 bits in the original subnet mask, and you have a new subnet mask, /27. In decimal format, you turn on the 128, 64, and 32 bits in the last octet, for a value of 224. The new subnet mask is thus 255.255.255.224.

Determine the Subnet Multiplier

Notice in Table 27-4 that the last octet decimal value increments by 32 with each subnet number. The number 32 is the subnet multiplier. You can quickly find the subnet multiplier using one of two methods:

- **Method 1:** Subtract the last nonzero octet of the subnet mask from 256. In this example, the last nonzero octet is 224. The subnet multiplier is therefore 256 − 224 = 32.

- **Method 2:** The decimal value of the last bit borrowed is the subnet multiplier. In this example, we borrowed the 128 bit, the 64 bit, and the 32 bit. The 32 bit is the last bit we borrowed and is, therefore, the subnet multiplier.

By using the subnet multiplier, you no longer have to convert binary subnet bits to decimal.

List the Subnets, Host Ranges, and Broadcast Addresses

Listing the subnets, host ranges, and broadcast addresses helps you see the flow of addresses within one address space. Table 27-5 documents our subnet addressing scheme for the 192.168.1.0/24 address space.

Table 27-5   Subnet Addressing Scheme for 192.168.1.0/24: 30 Hosts Per Subnet

Subnet Number	Subnet Address	Host Range	Broadcast Address
0	192.168.1.0	192.168.1.1–192.168.1.30	192.168.1.31
1	192.168.1.32	192.168.1.33–192.168.1.62	192.168.1.63
2	192.168.1.64	192.168.1.65–192.168.1.94	192.168.1.95
3	192.168.1.96	192.168.1.97–192.168.1.126	192.168.1.127
4	192.168.1.128	192.168.1.129–192.168.1.158	192.168.1.159
5	192.168.1.160	192.168.1.161–192.168.1.190	192.168.1.191
6	192.168.1.192	192.168.1.193–192.168.1.222	192.168.1.223
7	192.168.1.224	192.168.1.225–192.168.1.254	192.168.1.255

Following are three examples using the four subnetting steps. For brevity, Step 4 lists only the first three subnets.

Subnetting Example 1

Subnet the address space 172.16.0.0/16 to provide at least 80 host addresses per subnet while creating as many subnets as possible.

1. There are 16 host bits. Leave 7 bits for host addresses ($2^7 - 2 = 126$ host addresses per subnet). Borrow the first 9 host bits to create as many subnets as possible ($2^9 = 512$ subnets).

2. The original subnet mask is /16, or 255.255.0.0. Turn on the next 9 bits starting in the second octet, for a new subnet mask of /25 or 255.255.255.128.

3. The subnet multiplier is 128, which can be found as 256 − 128 = 128, or because the 128 bit is the last bit borrowed.

4. Table 27-6 lists the first three subnets, host ranges, and broadcast addresses.

Table 27-6   Subnet Addressing Scheme for Example 1

Subnet Number	Subnet Address	Host Range	Broadcast Address
0	172.16.0.0	172.16.0.1–172.16.0.126	172.16.0.127
1	172.16.0.128	172.16.0.129–172.16.0.254	172.16.0.255
2	172.16.1.0	172.16.1.1–172.16.1.126	172.16.1.127

Subnetting Example 2

Subnet the address space 172.16.0.0/16 to provide at least 80 subnet addresses.

1. There are 16 host bits. Borrow the first 7 host bits to create at least 80 subnets ($2^7 - 2 = 126$ subnets). That leaves 9 bits for host addresses, or $2^9 - 2 = 510$ host addresses per subnet.

2. The original subnet mask is /16, or 255.255.0.0. Turn on the next 7 bits starting in the second octet, for a new subnet mask of /23, or 255.255.254.0.

3. The subnet multiplier is 2, which can be found as 256 − 254 = 2, or because the 2 bit is the last bit borrowed.

4. Table 27-7 lists the first three subnets, host ranges, and broadcast addresses.

Table 27-7   Subnet Addressing Scheme for Example 2

Subnet Number	Subnet Address	Host Range	Broadcast Address
0	172.16.0.0	172.16.0.1–172.16.1.254	172.16.1.255
1	172.16.2.0	172.16.2.1–172.16.3.254	172.16.3.255
2	172.16.4.0	172.16.4.1–172.16.5.254	172.16.5.255

Subnetting Example 3

Subnet the address space 172.16.10.0/23 to provide at least 60 host addresses per subnet while creating as many subnets as possible.

1. There are 9 host bits. Leave 6 bits for host addresses ($2^6 - 2 = 62$ host addresses per subnet). Borrow the first 3 host bits to create as many subnets as possible ($2^3 = 8$ subnets).

2. The original subnet mask is /23, or 255.255.254.0. Turn on the next 3 bits starting with the last bit in the second octet, for a new subnet mask of /26, or 255.255.255.192.

3. The subnet multiplier is 64, which can be found as 256 − 192 = 64, or because the 64 bit is the last bit borrowed.

4. Table 27-8 lists the first three subnets, host ranges, and broadcast addresses.

Table 27-8   Subnet Addressing Scheme for Example 3

Subnet Number	Subnet Address	Host Range	Broadcast Address
0	172.16.10.0	172.16.10.1–172.16.10.62	172.16.10.63
1	172.16.10.64	172.16.10.65–172.16.10.126	172.16.10.127
2	172.16.10.128	172.16.10.129–172.16.10.190	172.16.10.191

PacketTracer Activity: Basic Subnetting Scenario

Refer to the Digital Study Guide to access the PKA file for this activity. You must have
Packet Tracer software to run this activity. See the Introduction for details.

VLSM

You probably noticed that the starting address space in Subnetting Example 3 is not an entire classful address. In fact, it is subnet 5 from Subnetting Example 2. In Subnetting Example 3, therefore,
we "subnetted a subnet." That is what VLSM is in a nutshell—subnetting a subnet.

With VLSM, you can customize your subnets to fit your network. Subnetting works the same way.
You just have to do it more than once to complete your addressing scheme. To avoid overlapping
address spaces, start with your largest host requirement, create a subnet for it, and then continue
with the next-largest host requirement.

Consider a small example. Given the address space 172.30.4.0/22 and the network requirements in
Figure 27-3, apply an addressing scheme that conserves the most addresses for future growth.

Figure 27-3   VLSM Example Topology

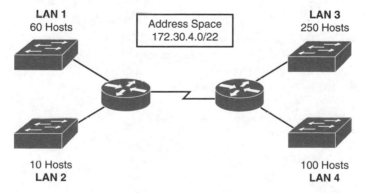

We need five subnets: four LAN subnets and one WAN subnet. Starting with the largest host
requirement on LAN 3, begin subnetting the address space.

To satisfy the 250-host requirement, we leave 8 host bits ($2^8 - 2 = 254$ hosts per subnet). Because
we have 10 host bits total, we borrow 2 bits to create the first round of subnets ($2^2 = 4$ subnets).
The starting subnet mask is /22, or 255.255.252.0. We turn on the next 2 bits in the subnet mask to
get /24, or 255.255.255.0. The multiplier is 1. The four subnets are as follows:

- **Subnet 0:** 172.30.4.0/24

- **Subnet 1:** 172.30.5.0/24

- **Subnet 2:** 172.30.6.0/24

- **Subnet 3:** 172.30.7.0/24

Assigning Subnet 0 to LAN 3, we are left with three /24 subnets. Continuing on to the next-largest host requirement on LAN 4, we take Subnet 1, 172.30.5.0/24, and subnet it further.

To satisfy the 100-host requirement, we leave 7 bits ($2^7 - 2 = 128$ hosts per subnet). Because we have 8 host bits total, we can borrow only 1 bit to create the subnets ($2^1 = 2$ subnets). The starting subnet mask is /24, or 255.255.255.0. We turn on the next bit in the subnet mask to get /25, or 255.255.255.128. The multiplier is 128. The two subnets are as follows:

- **Subnet 0:** 172.30.5.0/25

- **Subnet 1:** 172.30.5.128/25

Assigning Subnet 0 to LAN 4, we are left with one /25 subnet and two /24 subnets. Continuing on to the next-largest host requirement on LAN 1, we take Subnet 1, 172.30.5.128/25, and subnet it further.

To satisfy the 60-host requirement, we leave 6 bits ($2^6 - 2 = 62$ hosts per subnet). Because we have 7 host bits total, we borrow 1 bit to create the subnets ($2^1 = 2$ subnets). The starting subnet mask is /25, or 255.255.255.128. We turn on the next bit in the subnet mask to get /26, or 255.255.255.192. The multiplier is 64. The two subnets are as follows:

- **Subnet 0:** 172.30.5.128/26

- **Subnet 1:** 172.30.5.192/26

Assigning Subnet 0 to LAN 1, we are left with one /26 subnet and two /24 subnets. Finishing our LAN subnetting with LAN 2, we take Subnet 1, 172.30.5.192/26, and subnet it further.

To satisfy the ten-host requirement, we leave 4 bits ($2^4 - 2 = 14$ hosts per subnet). Because we have 6 host bits total, we borrow 2 bits to create the subnets ($2^2 = 4$ subnets). The starting subnet mask is /26, or 255.255.255.192. We turn on the next 2 bits in the subnet mask to get /28, or 255.255.255.240. The multiplier is 16. The four subnets are as follows:

- **Subnet 0:** 172.30.5.192/28

- **Subnet 1:** 172.30.5.208/28

- **Subnet 2:** 172.30.5.224/28

- **Subnet 3:** 172.30.5.240/28

Assigning Subnet 0 to LAN 2, we are left with three /28 subnets and two /24 subnets. To finalize our addressing scheme, we need to create a subnet for the WAN link, which needs only two host addresses. We take Subnet 1, 172.30.5.208/28, and subnet it further.

To satisfy the two-host requirement, we leave 2 bits ($2^2 - 2 = 2$ hosts per subnet). Because we have 4 host bits total, we borrow 2 bits to create the subnets ($2^2 = 4$ subnets). The starting subnet mask is /28, or 255.255.255.240. We turn on the next 2 bits in the subnet mask to get /30, or 255.255.255.252. The multiplier is 4. The four subnets are as follows:

- **Subnet 0:** 172.30.5.208/30
- **Subnet 1:** 172.30.5.212/30
- **Subnet 2:** 172.30.5.216/30
- **Subnet 3:** 172.30.5.220/30

We assign Subnet 0 to the WAN link. We are left with three /30 subnets, two /28 subnets, and two /24 subnets.

 Packet Tracer Activity: VLSM Subnetting Scenario

Refer to the Digital Study Guide to access the PKA file for this activity. You must have Packet Tracer software to run this activity. See the Introduction for details.

Study Resources

For today's exam topics, refer to the following resources for more study.

Resource	Location	Topic
Primary Resources		
Introduction to Networks	7	IPv4 Network Addresses
		Connectivity Verification
	8	All
ICND1 Official Cert Guide	13	All
	14	All
	15	All
	16	All
	20	Verifying Host IPv4 Settings
		IPv4 Address Types
Supplemental Resources		
CCNA Portable Command Guide	1	All
	2	All
CCNA Video Series	1	Lesson 7: IPv4 Addressing
CCNA Network Simulator		Subnet ID Calculation I–XI
		IP Address Rejection I–XI

 Check Your Understanding

Refer to the Digital Study Guide to take a short quiz covering the content of this day.

Day 26

IPv6 Addressing

CCNA 200-125 Exam Topics

- Compare and contrast IPv6 address types
- Identify the appropriate IPv6 addressing scheme to satisfy addressing requirements in a LAN/WAN environment
- Configure, verify, and troubleshoot IPv6 addressing
- Configure and verify IPv6 Stateless Address Auto Configuration

Key Topics

In the early 1990s, the Internet Engineering Task Force (IETF) grew concerned about the exhaustion of the IPv4 network addresses and began to look for a replacement for this protocol. This activity led to the development of what is now known as IPv6. Today's review focuses on the IPv6 protocol and IPv6 address types. We also review the various ways to implement IPv6 addressing, including subnetting, autoconfiguring hosts, and running IPv6 and IPv4 in a dual-stack configuration.

> **NOTE:** If you have not yet purchased a copy of Rick Graziani's *IPv6 Fundamentals* to add to your library of study tools, now is the time to do so. His book is my definitive source for everything IPv6.

Overview and Benefits of IPv6

Scaling networks today requires a limitless supply of IP addresses and improved mobility that private addressing and NAT alone cannot meet. IPv6 satisfies the increasingly complex requirements of hierarchical addressing that IPv4 does not provide. The main benefits and features of IPv6 include the following:

- **Extended address space:** A 128-bit address space represents about 340 trillion trillion trillion addresses.
- **Stateless address autoconfiguration:** IPv6 provides host devices with a method for generating their own routable IPv6 addresses. IPv6 also supports stateful configuration using DHCPv6.
- **Eliminates the need for NAT/PAT:** NAT/PAT was conceived as part of the solution to IPv4 address depletion. With IPv6, address depletion is no longer an issue. NAT64, however, does play an important role in providing backward compatibility with IPv4.

- **Simpler header:** A simpler header offers several advantages over IPv4:

  - Better routing efficiency for performance and forwarding-rate scalability

  - No broadcasts and, thus, no potential threat of broadcast storms

  - No requirement for processing checksums

  - Simpler and more efficient extension header mechanisms

- **Mobility and security:** Mobility and security help ensure compliance with mobile IP and IPsec standards:

  - IPv4 does not automatically enable mobile devices to move without breaks in established network connections.

  - In IPv6, mobility is built in, which means that any IPv6 node can use mobility when necessary.

  - IPsec is enabled on every IPv6 node and is available for use, making the IPv6 Internet more secure.

- **Transition strategies:** You can incorporate existing IPv4 capabilities with the added features of IPv6 in several ways:

  - You can implement a dual-stack method, with both IPv4 and IPv6 configured on the interface of a network device.

  - You can use tunneling, which will become more prominent as the adoption of IPv6 grows.

The IPv6 Protocol

Table 26-1 compares the binary and alphanumeric representations of IPv4 and IPv6 addresses.

Table 26-1   IPv4 and IPv6 Address Comparison

	IPv4 (4 Octets)	IPv6 (16 Octets)
Binary representation	11000000.101010 00.00001010. 01100101	10100101.00100100.01110010.11010011.00101100.1000 0000.11011101.00000010.00000000.00101001.11101100. 01111010.00000000.00101011.11101010.01110011
Alphanumeric representation	192.168.10.101	A524:72D3:2C80:DD02:0029:EC7A:002B:EA73
Total IP addresses	4,294,967,296 or 2^{32}	3.4 * 10^{38} or 2^{128}

Figure 26-1 compares the IPv4 header with the main IPv6 header. Notice that the IPv6 header is represented in 64-bit words instead of the 32-bit words used by IPv4.

Figure 26-1   IPv6 Header Format

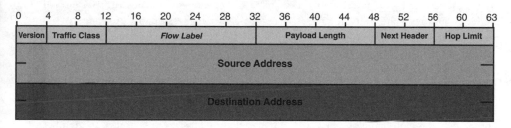

NOTE: Refer to RFC 2460 and the "Study Resources" section for the full specification of IPv6.

IPv6 Address Types

IPv4 has three address types: unicast, multicast, and broadcast. IPv6 does not use broadcasts. Instead, IPv6 uses unicast, multicast, and anycast. Figure 26-2 illustrates these three types of IPv6 addresses.

Figure 26-2   IPv6 Address Types

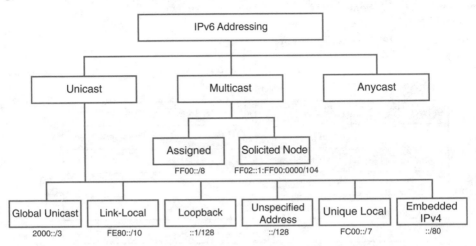

Unicast

The first classification of IPv6 address types shown in Figure 26-2 is the unicast address. A unicast address uniquely identifies an interface on an IPv6 device. A packet sent to a unicast address is received by the interface that is assigned to that address. Similar to IPv4, source IPv6 addresses must be a unicast address. Because unicast addressing—as opposed to multicast and anycast addressing—is the major focus for a CCNA candidate, we spend some time reviewing the Unicast branch in Figure 26-2.

Global Unicast Address

IPv6 has an address format that enables aggregation upward, eventually to the ISP. An IPv6 global unicast address is globally unique. Similar to a public IPv4 address, it can be routed in the Internet without modification. An IPv6 global unicast address consists of a 48-bit global routing prefix, a 16-bit subnet ID, and a 64-bit interface ID. Use Rick Graziani's method of breaking down the IPv6 address with the 3-1-4 Rule (also known as the *pi rule* for 3.14), shown in Figure 26-3.

Figure 26-3   Graziani's 3-1-4 Rule for Remembering the Global Unicast Address Structure

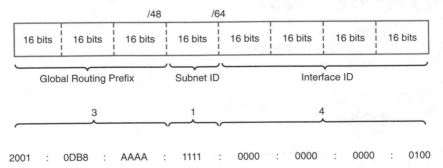

Each number refers to the number of hextets, or 16-bit segments, of that portion of the address:

- **3:** Three hextets for the global routing prefix

- **1:** One hextet for the subnet ID

- **4:** Four hextets for the interface ID

Global unicast addresses that are currently assigned by the Internet Assigned Numbers Authority (IANA) use the range of addresses that start with binary value 001 (2000::/3). This range represents one-eighth of the total IPv6 address space and is the largest block of assigned addresses. Figure 26-4 shows how the IPv6 address space is divided into an eight-piece pie based on the value of the first 3 bits.

Figure 26-4   Allocation of IPv6 Address Space

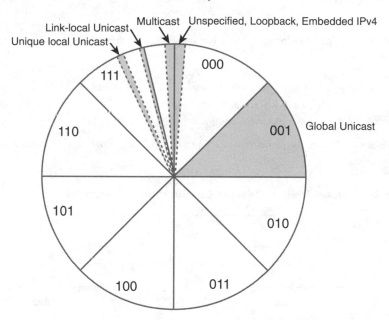

Using the 2000::/3 pie piece, the IANA assigns /23 or shorter address blocks to the five Regional Internet Registries (RIR). From there, ISPs are assigned /32 or shorter address blocks. ISPs then assign sites—their customers—a /48 or shorter address block. Figure 26-5 shows the breakdown of global routing prefixes.

Figure 26-5   Classification of Global Routing Prefix Sizes

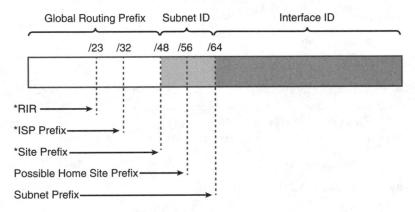

*This is a minimum allocation. The prefix-length may be less if it can be justified.

In IPv6, an interface can be configured with multiple global unicast addresses, which can be on the same or different subnets. In addition, an interface does not have to be configured with a global unicast address, but it must at least have a link-local address.

A global unicast address can be further classified into the various configuration options available, as Figure 26-6 shows.

Figure 26-6   Global Unicast Address Configuration Options

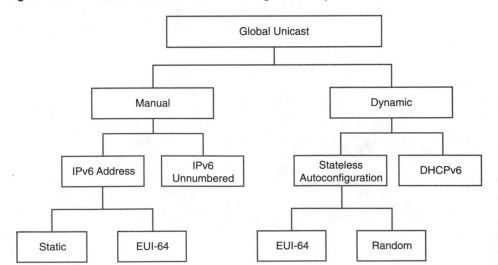

We review EUI-64 and stateless address autoconfiguration in more detail later in this day. We review the rest of the configuration options in Figure 26-6 in more detail in the upcoming days. For now, Table 26-2 summarizes them as follows.

Table 26-2   Summary of Global Unicast Configuration Options

Global Unicast Configuration Option		Description
Manual	Static	Similar to IPv4, the IPv6 address and prefix are statically configured on the interface.
	EUI-64	The prefix is configured manually. The EUI-64 process uses the MAC address to generate the 64-bit interface ID.
	IPv6 Unnumbered	Similar to IPv4, an interface can be configured to use the IPv6 address of another interface on the same device.
Dynamic	Stateless address autoconfiguration	SLAAC determines the prefix and prefix length from neighbor discovery router advertisement messages and then creates the interface ID using the EUI-64 method.
	DHCPv6	Similar to IPv4, a device can receive some or all of its addressing from a DHCPv6 server.

Link-Local Address

As Figure 26-2 shows, link-local addresses are a type of unicast address. Link-local addresses are confined to a single link. They need to be unique only to that link because packets with a link-local source or destination address are not routable off the link.

Link-local addresses are configured in one of three ways:

- Dynamically, using EUI-64
- Random-generated interface ID
- Statically, entering the link-local address manually

Link-local addresses provide a unique benefit in IPv6. A device can create its link-local address completely on its own. Link-local unicast addresses are in the range of FE80::/10 to FEBF::/10, as Table 26-3 shows.

Table 26-3   Range of Link-Local Unicast Addresses

Link-Local Unicast Address	Range of First Hextet	Range of First Hextet in Binary
FE80::/10	FE80	1111 1110 10 00 0000
	FEBF	1111 1110 10 11 1111

Figure 26-7 shows the format of a link-local unicast address.

Figure 26-7   Link-Local Unicast Address

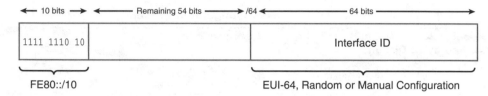

Loopback Address

The loopback address for IPv6 is an all-0s address except for the last bit, which is set to a 1. As in IPv4, an end device uses the IPv6 loopback address to send an IPv6 packet to itself to test the TCP/IP stack. The loopback address cannot be assigned to an interface and is not routable outside the device.

Unspecified Address

The unspecified unicast address is the all-0s address, represented as ::. It cannot be assigned to an interface but is reserved for communications when the sending device does not have a valid IPv6 address yet. For example, a device uses :: as the source address when using the duplicate address detection (DAD) process. The DAD process ensures a unique link-local address. Before a device can begin using its newly created link-local address, it sends out an all-nodes multicast to all devices on the link with its new address as the destination. If the device receives a response, it knows that link-local address is in use and, therefore, needs to create another link-local address.

Unique Local Address

Unique local addresses (ULA) are defined by RFC 4193, "Unique Local IPv6 Unicast Addresses." Figure 26-8 shows the format for ULAs.

Figure 26-8   Unique Local Address

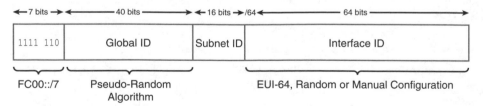

These are private addresses. However, unlike in IPv4, IPv6 ULAs are globally unique. This is possible because of the relatively large amount of address space in the Global ID portion shown in Figure 26-8: 40 bits, or more than 1 trillion unique global IDs. As long as a site uses the Pseudo-Random Global ID Algorithm, it will have a very high probability of generating a unique global ID.

Unique local addresses have the following characteristics:

- Possess a globally unique prefix or at least have a very high probability of being unique

- Allow sites to be combined or privately interconnected without address conflicts or addressing renumbering

- Remain independent of any Internet service provider and can be used within a site without having Internet connectivity

- If accidentally leaked outside a site by either routing or the Domain Name System (DNS), don't cause a conflict with any other addresses

- Can be used just like a global unicast address

IPv4 Embedded Address

IPv4 and IPv6 packets are not compatible. Features such as NAT-PT (now deprecated) and NAT64 are required to translate between the two address families. IPv4-mapped IPv6 addresses are used by transition mechanisms on hosts and routers to create IPv4 tunnels that deliver IPv6 packets over IPv4 networks.

NOTE: NAT64 is beyond the scope of the CCNA exam topics.

To create an IPv4-mapped IPv6 address, the IPv4 address is embedded within the low-order 32 bits of IPv6. Basically, IPv6 just puts an IPv4 address at the end, adds 16 all-1 bits, and pads the rest of the address. The address does not have to be globally unique. Figure 26-9 illustrates this IPv4-mapped IPv6 address structure.

Figure 26-9   IPv4-Mapped IPv6 Address

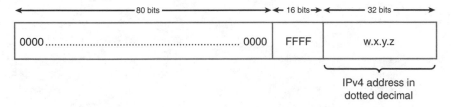

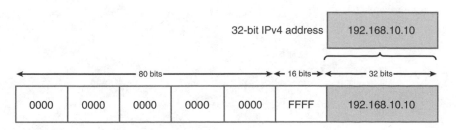

IPv6 compressed format ::FFFF.192.168.10.10

Multicast

The second major classification of IPv6 address types in Figure 26-2 is multicast. Multicast is a technique used for a device to send a single packet to multiple destinations simultaneously. An IPv6 multicast address defines a group of devices known as a multicast group and is equivalent to IPv4 224.0.0.0/4. IPv6 multicast addresses have the prefix FF00::/8.

Two types of IPv6 multicast addresses are used:

- Assigned multicast

- Solicited node multicast

Assigned Multicast

Assigned multicast addresses are used in context with specific protocols.

Two common IPv6 assigned multicast groups include the following:

- **FF02::1 All-nodes multicast group:** This is a multicast group that all IPv6-enabled devices join. Similar to a broadcast in IPv4, all IPv6 interfaces on the link process packets sent to this address. For example, a router sending an ICMPv6 Router Advertisement (RA) uses the all-nodes FF02::1 address. IPv6-enabled devices can then use the RA information to learn the link's address information such as prefix, prefix length, and the default gateway.

- **FF02::2 All-routers multicast group:** This is a multicast group that all IPv6 routers join. A router becomes a member of this group when it is enabled as an IPv6 router with the **ipv6 unicast-routing** global configuration command. A packet sent to this group is received and processed by all IPv6 routers on the link or network. For example, IPv6-enabled devices send ICMPv6 Router Solicitation (RS) messages to the all-routers multicast address requesting an RA message.

Solicited-Node Multicast

In addition to every unicast address assigned to an interface, a device has a special multicast address known as a solicited-node multicast address (see Figure 26-2). These multicast addresses are automatically created using a special mapping of the device's unicast address with the solicited-node multicast prefix FF02:0:0:0:0:1:FF00::/104.

As Figure 26-10 shows, solicited-node multicast addresses are used for two essential IPv6 mechanisms, both part of Neighbor Discovery Protocol (NDP):

Figure 26-10   Uses of Solicited-Node Multicasts

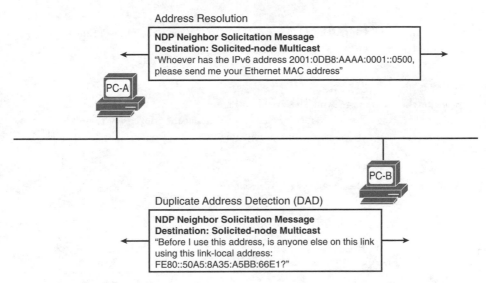

Address Resolution

NDP Neighbor Solicitation Message
Destination: Solicited-node Multicast
"Whoever has the IPv6 address 2001:0DB8:AAAA:0001::0500,
please send me your Ethernet MAC address"

PC-A

PC-B

Duplicate Address Detection (DAD)

NDP Neighbor Solicitation Message
Destination: Solicited-node Multicast
"Before I use this address, is anyone else on this link
using this link-local address:
FE80::50A5:8A35:A5BB:66E1?"

- **Address resolution:** In this mechanism, which is equivalent to ARP in IPv4, an IPv6 device sends an NS message to a solicited-node multicast address to learn the link layer address of a device on the same link. The device recognizes the IPv6 address of the destination on that link but needs to know its data-link address.

- **Duplicate address detection (DAD):** As reviewed earlier, DAD allows a device to verify that its unicast address is unique on the link. An NS message is sent to the device's own solicited-node multicast address to determine whether anyone else has this same address.

As Figure 26-11 shows, the solicited-node multicast address consists of two parts:

Figure 26-11   Solicited-Node Multicast Address Structure

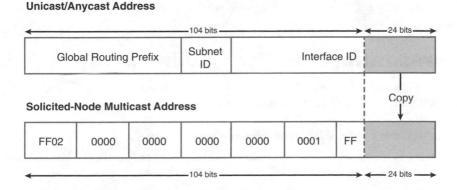

Unicast/Anycast Address

|←————————————— 104 bits —————————————→|←— 24 bits —→|

| Global Routing Prefix | Subnet ID | Interface ID | |

Copy

Solicited-Node Multicast Address

| FF02 | 0000 | 0000 | 0000 | 0000 | 0001 | FF | |

|←————————————— 104 bits —————————————→|←— 24 bits —→|

FF02:0:0:0:0:1:FF00::/104

- **FF02:0:0:0:0:FF00::/104 multicast prefix:** This is the first 104 bits of the all solicited-node multicast address.

- **Least significant 24 bits:** These bits are copied from the far-right 24 bits of the global unicast or link-local unicast address of the device.

Anycast

The last major classification of IPv6 address types in Figure 26-2 is the anycast address. It is an address that can be assigned to more than one device or interface. A packet sent to an anycast address is routed to the "nearest" device that is configured with the anycast address, as Figure 26-12 shows.

Figure 26-12   Example of Anycast Addressing

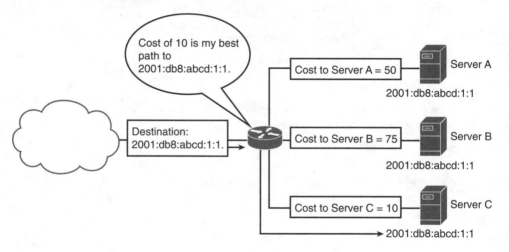

 Activity: Identify the Type of IPv6 Address

Refer to the Digital Study Guide to complete this activity.

Representing the IPv6 Address

The IPv6 address can look rather intimidating to someone who is used to IPv4 addressing. However, the IPv6 address can be easier to read and is much simpler to subnet than IPv4.

Conventions for Writing IPv6 Addresses

IPv6 conventions use 32 hexadecimal numbers, organized into eight hextets of four hex digits separated by a colon, to represent a 128-bit IPv6 address. For example:

2340:1111:AAAA:0001:1234:5678:9ABC

To make things a little easier, two rules allow you to shorten what must be configured for an IPv6 address:

- **Rule 1:** Omit the leading 0s in any given hextet.

- **Rule 2:** Omit the all-0s hextets. Represent one or more consecutive hextets of all hex 0s with a double colon (::), but only for one such occurrence in a given address.

For example, consider the following address. The highlighted hex digits represent the portion of the address that can be abbreviated.

FE00:0000:0000:0001:0000:0000:0000:0056

This address has two locations in which one or more hextets have four hex 0s, so two main options work for abbreviating this address, using the :: abbreviation in one of the locations. The following two options show the two briefest valid abbreviations:

- FE00::1:0:0:0:56

- FE00:0:0:1::56

In the first example, the second and third hextets preceding 0001 were replaced with ::. In the second example, the fifth, sixth, and seventh hextets were replaced with ::. In particular, note that the :: abbreviation, meaning "one or more hextets of all 0s," cannot be used twice because that would be ambiguous. Therefore, the abbreviation FE00::1::56 would not be valid.

Conventions for Writing IPv6 Prefixes

IPv6 prefixes represent a range or block of consecutive IPv6 addresses. The number that represents the range of addresses, called a *prefix*, is usually seen in IP routing tables, just as you see IP subnet numbers in IPv4 routing tables.

As with IPv4, when writing or typing a prefix in IPv6, the bits past the end of the prefix length are all binary 0s. The following IPv6 address is an example of an address assigned to a host:

2000:1234:5678:9ABC:1234:5678:9ABC:1111/64

The prefix in which this address resides is as follows:

2000:1234:5678:9ABC:**0000:0000:0000:0000**/64

When abbreviated, this is

2000:1234:5678:9ABC::/64

If the prefix length does not fall on a hextet boundary (is not a multiple of 16), the prefix value should list all the values in the last hextet. For example, assume that the prefix length in the previous example is /56. By convention, the rest of the fourth hextet is written, after being set to binary 0s, as follows:

2000:1234:5678:9A**00**::/56

The following list summarizes some key points about how to write IPv6 prefixes:

- The prefix has the same value as the IP addresses in the group for the first number of bits, as defined by the prefix length.

- Any bits after the prefix length number of bits are binary 0s.

- The prefix can be abbreviated with the same rules as IPv6 addresses.

- If the prefix length is not on a hextet boundary, write down the value for the entire hextet.

Table 26-4 shows several sample prefixes, their formats, and a brief explanation.

Table 26-4   Example IPv6 Prefixes and Their Meanings

Prefix	Explanation	Incorrect Alternative
2000::/3	All addresses whose first 3 bits are equal to the first 3 bits of hex number 2000 (bits are 001)	2000/3 (omits ::) 2::/3 (omits the rest of the first hextet)
2340:1140::/26	All addresses whose first 26 bits match the listed hex number	2340:114::/26 (omits the last digit in the second hextet)
2340:1111::/32	All addresses whose first 32 bits match the listed hex number	2340:1111/32 (omits ::)

 Activity: Compress IPv6 Address Representations

Refer to the Digital Study Guide to complete this activity.

IPv6 Subnetting

In many ways, subnetting IPv6 addresses is much simpler than subnetting IPv4 addresses. A typical site is assigned an IPv6 address space with a /48 prefix length. Because the least significant bits are used for the interface ID, that leaves 16 bits for the subnet ID and a /64 subnet prefix length, as Figure 26-13 shows.

Figure 26-13   /64 Subnet Prefix

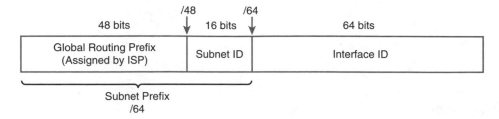

For our subnetting examples, we use 2001:0DB8:000A::/48, or simply 2001:DB8:A::/48, which includes subnets 2001:DB8:A::/64 through 2001:DB8:A:FFFF::/64. That's 2^{16}, or 65,536 subnets, each with 2^{64}, or 18 quintillion, interface addresses.

Subnetting the Subnet ID

To subnet in a small to medium-size business, simply increment the least significant bits of the subnet ID (as in Example 26-1) and assign /64 subnets to your networks.

Example 26-1   Subnetting the Subnet ID

```
2001:DB8:A:0001::/64
2001:DB8:A:0002::/64
2001:DB8:A:0003::/64
2001:DB8:A:0004::/64
2001:DB8:A:0005::/64
```

Of course, if you are administering a larger implementation, you can use the four hexadecimal digits of the subnet ID to design a quick and simple four-level hierarchy. Most large enterprise networks have plenty of room to design a logical address scheme that aggregates addresses for an optimal routing configuration. If not, applying for and receiving another /48 address is not difficult.

Subnetting into the Interface ID

If you extend your subnetting into the interface ID portion of the address, it is a best practice to subnet on the nibble boundary. A nibble is 4 bits or one hexadecimal digit. For example, let's borrow the first 4 bits from the interface ID portion of the network address 2001:DB8:A:1::/64. That means the network 2001:DB8:A:1::/64 would now have 2^4, or 16, subnets from 2001:DB8:A:1:0000::/68 to 2001:DB8:A:1:F000::/68. Listing the subnets is easy, as Example 26-2 shows.

Example 26-2   Subnetting into the Interface ID

```
2001:DB8:A:1:0000::/68
2001:DB8:A:1:1000::/68
2001:DB8:A:1:2000::/68
2001:DB8:A:1:3000::/68
        thru
2001:DB8:A:1:F000::/68
```

EUI-64 Concept

Day 24, "Basic Router Configuration," reviews static IPv6 addressing, including how to configure the router to use EUI-64 addressing (EUI stands for Extended Unique Identifier). Today we are reviewing the concept behind the EUI-64 configuration.

Recall from Figure 26-13 that the second half of the IPv6 address is called the interface ID. The value of the interface ID portion of a global unicast address can be set to any value, as long as no other host in the same subnet attempts to use the same value. However, the size of the interface ID was chosen to allow easy autoconfiguration of IP addresses by plugging the MAC address of a network card into the interface ID field in an IPv6 address.

MAC addresses are 6 bytes (48 bits) in length. To complete the 64-bit interface ID, IPv6 fills in 2 more bytes by separating the MAC address into two 3-byte halves. It then inserts hex FFFE between the halves and sets the seventh bit in the first byte to binary 1 to form the interface ID field. Figure 26-14 shows this format, called the EUI-64 format.

For example, the following two lines list a host's MAC address and corresponding EUI-64 format interface ID, assuming the use of an address configuration option that uses the EUI-64 format:

- **MAC address:** 0034:5678:9ABC

- **EUI-64 interface ID:** 0234:56FF:FE78:9ABC

Figure 26-14   IPv6 Address Format with Interface ID and EUI-64

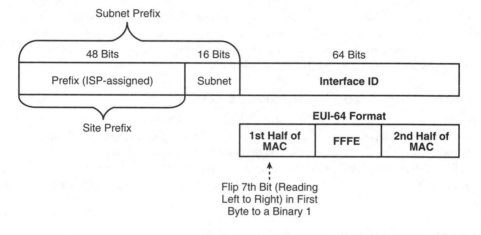

NOTE: To change the seventh bit (reading left to right) in the example, convert hex 00 to binary 00000000, change the seventh bit to 1 (00000010), and then convert back to hex, for hex 02 as the first two digits.

Stateless Address Autoconfiguration

IPv6 supports two methods of dynamic configuration of IPv6 addresses:

- **Stateless Address Autoconfiguration (SLAAC):** A host dynamically learns the /64 prefix through the IPv6 Neighbor Discovery Protocol (NDP) and then calculates the rest of its address by using an EUI-64 method.

- **DHCPv6:** This works the same conceptually as DHCP in IPv4. We review DHCPv6 on Day 7, "DHCP and DNS."

By using the EUI-64 process and the Neighbor Discovery Protocol (NDP), SLAAC allows a device to determine its entire global unicast address without any manual configuration or a

DHCPv6 server. Figure 26-15 illustrates the SLAAC process between a host and a router config-ured with the **ipv6 unicast-routing** command, which means that it will send and receive NDP messages.

Figure 26-15   Neighbor Discovery and the SLAAC Process

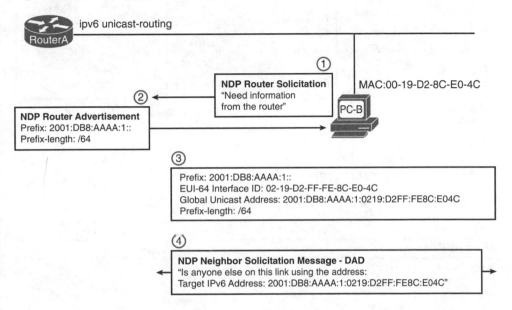

Migration to IPv6

Two major transition strategies are currently used to migrate to IPv6:

- **Dual-stacking:** In this integration method, a node has implementation and connectivity to both an IPv4 and IPv6 network. This is the recommended option and involves running IPv4 and IPv6 at the same time.

- **Tunneling:** Tunneling is a method for transporting IPv6 packets over IPv4-only networks by encapsulating the IPv6 packet inside IPv4. Several tunneling techniques are available.

Because of the simplicity of running dual-stack, it will most likely be the preferred strategy as IPv4-only networks begin to disappear. But it will probably still be decades before we see enterprise networks running exclusively IPv6. Figure 26-16 illustrates one way Wendell Odom thinks about the transition to IPv6: "But who knows how long it will take?"

Remember this advice: "Dual-stack where you can; tunnel where you must." These two methods are the most common techniques to transition from IPv4 to IPv6. Dual-stacking is easy enough. Just configure all your devices to use both IPv4 and IPv6 addressing. Tunneling, however, is more complex and beyond the scope of the CCNA exam topics.

Figure 26-16   Transition to IPv6 Using Dual-Stack

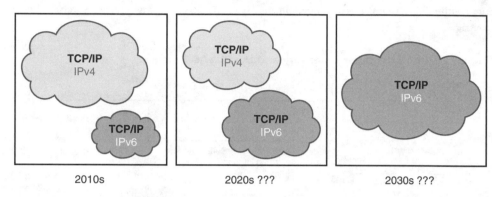

Study Resources
===============

For today's exam topics, refer to the following resources for more study.

Resource	Location	Topic
Primary Resources		
Introduction to Networks	7	IPv6 Network Addresses
	8	Design Considerations for IPv6
ICND1 Official Cert Guide	28	All
	29	All
	30	All
	31	All
Supplemental Resources		
CCNA Video Series	1	Lesson 8: IPv6 Addressing
CCNA Network Simulator	ICND1	Chapter 30: IPv6 Subnet ID Calculation I–X
		Chapter 30: IPv6 Route Selection I–X
		Chapter 30: IPv6 Configuration I–II
		Chapter 30: IPv6 Address Configuration I–IX
		Chapter 30: IPv6 EUI-64 Calculation Drills I–X
		Chapter 30: IPv6 Addressing Troubleshooting

? **Check Your Understanding**

Refer to the Digital Study Guide to take a short quiz covering the content of this day.

Basic Routing Concepts

CCNA 200-125 Exam Topics

- Describe the routing concepts
- Compare and contrast static routing and dynamic routing
- Compare and contrast distance vector and link state routing protocols
- Compare and contrast interior and exterior routing protocols

Key Topics

Today we review basic routing concepts, including exactly how a packet is processed by intermediary devices (routers) on its way from source to destination. We then review the basic routing methods, including connected, static, and dynamic routes. We conclude the day's review with a deep dive into the operation of dynamic routing protocols.

Packet Forwarding

Packet forwarding by routers is accomplished through path determination and switching functions. The path determination function is the process of how the router determines which path to use when forwarding a packet. To determine the best path, the router searches its routing table for a network address that matches the packet's destination IP address.

This search results in one of three path determinations:

- **Directly connected network:** If the destination IP address of the packet belongs to a device on a network that is directly connected to one of the router's interfaces, that packet is forwarded directly to that device. This means that the destination IP address of the packet is a host address on the same network as this router's interface.

- **Remote network**: If the destination IP address of the packet belongs to a remote network, the packet is forwarded to another router. Remote networks can be reached only by forwarding packets to another router.

- **No route determined:** If the destination IP address of the packet does not belong to a connected or remote network and the router does not have a default route, the packet is discarded. The router sends an Internet Control Message Protocol (ICMP) Unreachable message to the source IP address of the packet.

In the first two results, the router completes the process by switching the packet out the correct interface. It does this by reencapsulating the IP packet into the appropriate Layer 2 data-link frame format for the exit interface. The type of interface determines the type of Layer 2 encapsulation. For example, if the exit interface is Fast Ethernet, the packet is encapsulated in an Ethernet frame. If the exit interface is a serial interface configured for PPP, the IP packet is encapsulated in a PPP frame.

Path Determination and Switching Function Example

Let's review the process of path determination and switching functions that routers perform as a packet travels from source to destination. This scenario uses the topology in Figure 25-1.

Figure 25-1   Packet Forwarding Sample Topology

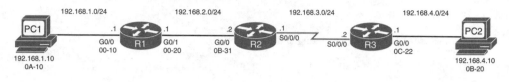

NOTE: For brevity, Figure 25-1 shows only the last two octets of the MAC address.

---

1. PC1 has a packet to send to PC2.

   Using the AND operation on the destination's IP address and PC1's subnet mask, PC1 has determined that the IP source and IP destination addresses are on different networks. Therefore, PC1 checks its Address Resolution Protocol (ARP) table for the IP address of the default gateway and its associated MAC address. It then encapsulates the packet in an Ethernet header and forwards it to R1.

2. Router R1 receives the Ethernet frame.

   Router R1 examines the destination MAC address, which matches the MAC address of the receiving interface, G0/0. R1 will therefore copy the frame into its buffer to be processed.

   R1 decapsulates the Ethernet frame and reads the destination IP address. Because it does not match any of R1's directly connected networks, the router consults its routing table to route this packet.

   R1 searches the routing table for a network address and subnet mask that include this packet's destination IP address as a host address on that network. It selects the entry with the longest match (longest prefix). R1 encapsulates the packet in the appropriate frame format for the exit interface and switches the frame to the interface (G0/1 in this example). The interface then forwards it to the next hop.

3. Packet arrives at Router R2.

   R2 performs the same functions as R1, but this time, the exit interface is a serial interface— not Ethernet. Therefore, R2 encapsulates the packet in the appropriate frame format for the serial interface and sends it to R3. For this example, assume that the interface is using High-Level Data Link Control (HDLC), which uses the data-link address 0x8F. Remember, serial interfaces do not use MAC addresses.

4. Packet arrives at R3.

   R3 decapsulates the data-link HDLC frame. The search of the routing table results in a network that is one of R3's directly connected networks. Because the exit interface is a directly connected Ethernet network, R3 needs to resolve the destination IP address of the packet with a destination MAC address.

   R3 searches for the packet's destination IP address of 192.168.4.10 in its ARP cache. If the entry is not in the ARP cache, R3 sends an ARP request out its G0/0 interface.

PC2 sends back an ARP reply with its MAC address. R3 updates its ARP cache with an entry for 192.168.4.10 and the MAC address returned in the ARP reply.

The IP packet is encapsulated into a new data-link Ethernet frame and sent out R3's G0/0 interface.

5. The Ethernet frame with the encapsulated IP packet arrives at PC2.

PC2 examines the destination MAC address, which matches the MAC address of the receiving interface—that is, its own Ethernet NIC. PC2 will therefore copy the rest of the frame. PC2 sees that the Ethernet Type field is 0x800, which means that the Ethernet frame contains an IP packet in the data portion of the frame. PC2 decapsulates the Ethernet frame and passes the IP packet to its operating system's IP process.

Routing Methods

A router can learn routes from three basic sources:

- **Directly connected routes:** Automatically entered in the routing table when an interface is activated with an IP address

- **Static routes**: Manually configured by the network administrator and entered in the routing table if the exit interface for the static route is active

- **Dynamic routes:** Learned by the routers through sharing routes with other routers that use the same routing protocol

In many cases, the complexity of the network topology, the number of networks, and the need for the network to automatically adjust to changes require the use of a dynamic routing protocol. Dynamic routing certainly has several advantages over static routing; however, networks still use static routing. In fact, networks typically use a combination of both static and dynamic routing.

Table 25-1 compares dynamic and static routing features. From this comparison, you can list the advantages of each routing method. The advantages of one method are the disadvantages of the other.

Table 25-1   Dynamic Versus Static Routing

Feature	Dynamic Routing	Static Routing
Configuration complexity	Generally stays independent of the network size	Increases with network size
Required administrator knowledge	Requires advanced knowledge	Requires no extra knowledge
Topology changes	Automatically adapts to topology changes	Requires administrator intervention
Scaling	Suitable for simple and complex topologies	Suitable for simple topologies
Security	Less secure	More secure
Resource usage	Uses CPU, memory, and link bandwidth	Requires no extra resources
Predictability	Uses a route that depends on the current topology	Always uses the same route to the destination

Activity: Compare Dynamic and Static Routing

Refer to the Digital Study Guide to complete this activity.

Classifying Dynamic Routing Protocols

Figure 25-2 shows a timeline of IP routing protocols, along with a chart to help you memorize the various ways to classify routing protocols.

Figure 25-2 Routing Protocols' Evolution and Classification

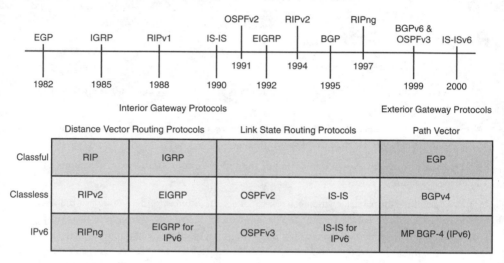

CCENT exam topics include configuration of single-area Open Shortest Path First version 2 (OSPFv2) and single-area OSPFv3. CCNA exam topics include configuration of Enhanced Interior Gateway Routing Protocol (EIGRP) for IPv4, EIGRP for IPv6, multiarea OSPFv2, and multiarea OPSFv3.

Routing protocols are classified into different groups according to their characteristics:

- IGP or EGP

- Distance vector or link state

- Classful or classless

IGP and EGP

An autonomous system (AS) is a collection of routers under a common administration that presents a common, clearly defined routing policy to the Internet. Typical examples are a large company's internal network and an ISP's network. Most company networks are not autonomous systems; they are a network within their own ISP's autonomous system. Because the Internet is based on the autonomous system concept, two types of routing protocols are required:

- **Interior gateway protocols (IGP):** Used for intra-AS routing—that is, routing inside an AS

- **Exterior gateway protocols (EGP):** Used for inter-AS routing—that is, routing between autonomous systems

Distance Vector Routing Protocols

Distance vector means that routes are advertised as vectors of distance and direction. Distance is defined in terms of a metric such as hop count, and direction is the next-hop router or exit interface. Distance vector protocols typically use the Bellman-Ford algorithm for the best-path route determination.

Some distance vector protocols periodically send complete routing tables to all connected neighbors. In large networks, these routing updates can become enormous, causing significant traffic on the links.

Although the Bellman-Ford algorithm eventually accumulates enough knowledge to maintain a database of reachable networks, the algorithm does not allow a router to know the exact topology of an internetwork. The router knows only the routing information received from its neighbors.

Distance vector protocols use routers as signposts along the path to the final destination. The only information a router knows about a remote network is the distance or metric to reach that network and which path or interface to use to get there. Distance vector routing protocols do not have an actual map of the network topology.

Distance vector protocols work best in these situations:

- The network is simple and flat and does not require a hierarchical design.

- The administrators do not have enough knowledge to configure and troubleshoot link-state protocols.

- Specific types of networks, such as hub-and-spoke networks, are being implemented.

- Worst-case convergence times in a network are not a concern.

Link-State Routing Protocols

In contrast to distance vector routing protocol operation, a router configured with a link-state routing protocol can create a complete view, or topology, of the network by gathering information from all the other routers. Think of a link-state routing protocol as having a complete map of the network topology. The signposts along the way from source to destination are not necessary because all link-state routers are using an identical map of the network. A link-state router uses the link-state information to create a topology map and to select the best path to all destination networks in the topology.

With some distance vector routing protocols, routers send periodic updates of their routing information to their neighbors. Link-state routing protocols do not use periodic updates. After the network has converged, a link-state update is sent only when the topology changes.

Link-state protocols work best in these situations:

- The network design is hierarchical, usually occurring in large networks.

- The administrators have a good knowledge of the implemented link-state routing protocol.

- Fast convergence of the network is crucial.

Classful Routing Protocols

Classful routing protocols do not send subnet mask information in routing updates. The first routing protocols, such as Routing Information Protocol (RIP), were classful. This was at a time when network addresses were allocated based on classes: Class A, B, or C. A routing protocol did not need to include the subnet mask in the routing update because the network mask could be determined based on the first octet of the network address.

Classful routing protocols can still be used in some of today's networks, but because they do not include the subnet mask, they cannot be used in all situations. Classful routing protocols cannot be used when a network is subnetted using more than one subnet mask. In other words, classful routing protocols do not support variable-length subnet masking (VLSM).

Other limitations are a factor with classful routing protocols, including their inability to support discontiguous networks and supernets. Classful routing protocols include Routing Information Protocol version 1 (RIPv1) and Interior Gateway Routing Protocol (IGRP). CCNA exam topics do not include either RIPv1 or IGRP.

Classless Routing Protocols

Classless routing protocols include the subnet mask with the network address in routing updates. Today's networks are no longer allocated based on classes, and the subnet mask cannot be determined by the value of the first octet. Classless routing protocols are required in most networks today because of their support for VLSM and discontiguous networks and supernets. Classless routing protocols are Routing Information Protocol version 2 (RIPv2), Enhanced IGRP (EIGRP), Open Shortest Path First (OSPF), Intermediate System–to–Intermediate System (IS-IS), and Border Gateway Protocol (BGP).

Dynamic Routing Metrics

In some cases, a routing protocol learns of more than one route to the same destination from the same routing source. To select the best path, the routing protocol must be capable of evaluating and differentiating among the available paths. A *metric* is used for this purpose. Two different routing protocols might choose different paths to the same destination because they use different metrics. Metrics used in IP routing protocols include the following:

- **RIP—Hop count:** Best path is chosen by the route with the lowest hop count.

- **IGRP and EIGRP—Bandwidth, delay, reliability, and load:** Best path is chosen by the route with the smallest composite metric value calculated from these multiple parameters. By default, only bandwidth and delay are used.

- **IS-IS and OSPF—Cost:** Best path is chosen by the route with the lowest cost. The Cisco implementation of OSPF uses bandwidth to determine the cost.

The metric associated with a certain route can be best viewed using the **show ip route** command. The metric value is the second value in the brackets for a routing table entry. In Example 25-1, R2 has a route to the 192.168.8.0/24 network that is two hops away.

Example 25-1   Routing Table for R2

```
R2# show ip route

<output omitted>

Gateway of last resort is not set

R     192.168.1.0/24 [120/1] via 192.168.2.1, 00:00:20, Serial0/0/0
      192.168.2.0/24 is variably subnetted, 2 subnets, 2 masks
C        192.168.2.0/24 is directly connected, Serial0/0/0
L        192.168.2.2/32 is directly connected, Serial0/0/0
      192.168.3.0/24 is variably subnetted, 2 subnets, 2 masks
C        192.168.3.0/24 is directly connected, GigabitEthernet0/0
L        192.168.3.1/32 is directly connected, GigabitEthernet0/0
      192.168.4.0/24 is variably subnetted, 2 subnets, 2 masks
C        192.168.4.0/24 is directly connected, Serial0/0/1
L        192.168.4.2/32 is directly connected, Serial0/0/1
R     192.168.5.0/24 [120/1] via 192.168.4.1, 00:00:25, Serial0/0/1
R     192.168.6.0/24 [120/1] via 192.168.2.1, 00:00:20, Serial0/0/0
                     [120/1] via 192.168.4.1, 00:00:25, Serial0/0/1
R     192.168.7.0/24 [120/1] via 192.168.4.1, 00:00:25, Serial0/0/1
R     192.168.8.0/24 [120/2] via 192.168.4.1, 00:00:25, Serial0/0/1
```

Notice in the output that one network, 192.168.6.0/24, has two routes. RIP will load-balance
between these equal-cost routes. All the other routing protocols are capable of automatically load
balancing traffic for up to four equal-cost routes, by default. EIGRP is also capable of load balancing
across unequal-cost paths.

Administrative Distance

Sometimes a router learns a route to a remote network from more than one routing source.
For example, a static route might have been configured for the same network/subnet mask that
was learned dynamically by a dynamic routing protocol, such as RIP. The router must choose
which route to install.

Although less common, more than one dynamic routing protocol can be deployed in the same
network. In some situations, it might be necessary to route the same network address using
multiple routing protocols, such as RIP and OSPF. Because different routing protocols use different
metrics—RIP uses hop count and OSPF uses bandwidth—it is not possible to compare metrics to
determine the best path.

Administrative distance (AD) defines the preference of a routing source. Each routing source—
including specific routing protocols, static routes, and even directly connected networks—is
prioritized in order of most preferable to least preferable using an AD value. Cisco routers use
the AD feature to select the best path when they learn about the same destination network from
two or more different routing sources.

The AD value is an integer value from 0 to 255. The lower the value, the more preferred the route source. An administrative distance of 0 is the most preferred. Only a directly connected network has an AD of 0, which cannot be changed. An AD of 255 means the router will not believe the source of that route, and it will not be installed in the routing table.

In the routing table in Example 25-1, the AD value is the first value listed in the brackets. You can see that the AD value for RIP routes is 120. You can also verify the AD value with the **show ip protocols** command, as Example 25-2 demonstrates.

Example 25-2   Verifying the AD Value with the show ip protocols Command

```
R2# show ip protocols

Routing Protocol is "rip"
  Outgoing update filter list for all interfaces is not set
  Incoming update filter list for all interfaces is not set
  Sending updates every 30 seconds, next due in 21 seconds
  Invalid after 180 seconds, hold down 180, flushed after 240
  Redistributing: rip
  Default version control: send version 1, receive any version
    Interface              Send  Recv  Triggered RIP  Key-chain
    GigabitEthernet0/0      1     1 2
    Serial0/0/0             1     1 2
    Serial0/0/1             1     1 2
  Automatic network summarization is in effect
  Maximum path: 4
  Routing for Networks:
    192.168.2.0
    192.168.3.0
    192.168.4.0
  Routing Information Sources:
    Gateway         Distance       Last Update
    192.168.2.1        120         00:00:01
    192.168.4.1        120         00:00:01
  Distance: (default is 120)

R2#
```

Table 25-2 shows a chart of the different administrative distance values for various routing protocols.

Table 25-2   Default Administrative Distances

Route Source	AD
Connected	0
Static	1
EIGRP summary route	5

Route Source	AD
External BGP	20
Internal EIGRP	90
IGRP	100
OSPF	110
IS-IS	115
RIP	120
External EIGRP	170
Internal BGP	200

IGP Comparison Summary

Table 25-3 compares several features of the currently most popular IGPs: RIPv2, OSPF, and EIGRP.

Table 25-3   Comparing Features of IGPs: RIPv2, OSPF, and EIGRP

Features	RIPv2	OSPF	EIGRP
Metric	Hop count	Bandwidth	Function of bandwidth, delay
Sends periodic updates	Yes (30 seconds)	No	No
Full or partial routing updates	Full	Partial	Partial
Where updates are sent	(224.0.0.9)	(224.0.0.5, 224.0.0.6)	(224.0.0.10)
Route considered unreachable	16 hops	Depends on MaxAge of LSA, which is never incremented past 3,600 seconds	A delay of all 1s
Supports unequal-cost load balancing	No	No	Yes

 Activity: Compare Dynamic Routing Protocol Features

Refer to the Digital Study Guide to complete this activity.

Routing Loop Prevention

Without preventive measures, distance vector routing protocols can cause severe routing loops in the network. A routing loop is a condition in which a packet is continuously transmitted within a series of routers without ever reaching its intended destination network. A routing loop can occur when two or more routers have inaccurate routing information to a destination network.

Several mechanisms are available to eliminate routing loops, primarily with distance vector routing protocols. These mechanisms include the following:

- **A maximum metric to prevent count to infinity**: To eventually stop the incrementing of a metric during a routing loop, infinity is defined by setting a maximum metric value. For example, RIP defines infinity as 16 hops, an unreachable metric. When the routers "count to infinity," they mark the route as unreachable.

- **Hold-down timers**: Routers are instructed to hold any changes that might affect routes for a specified period of time. If a route is identified as down or possibly down, any other information for that route containing the same status, or worse, is ignored for a predetermined amount of time (the hold-down period) so that the network has time to converge.

- **Split horizon**: A routing loop is prevented by not allowing advertisements to be sent back through the interface where they originated. The split horizon rule stops a router from incrementing a metric and then sending the route back to its source.

- **Route poisoning or poison reverse**: The route is marked as unreachable in a routing update that is sent to other routers. *Unreachable* is interpreted as a metric that is set to the maximum.

- **Triggered updates**: A routing table update is sent immediately in response to a routing change. Triggered updates do not wait for update timers to expire. The detecting router immediately sends an update message to adjacent routers.

- **TTL field in the IP header**: The Time To Live (TTL) field avoids a situation in which an undeliverable packet circulates endlessly on the network. With TTL, the source device of the packet sets the 8-bit field with a value. This TTL value is decreased by 1 by every router in the path until the packet reaches its destination. If the TTL value reaches 0 before the packet arrives at its destination, the packet is discarded and the router sends an ICMP error message back to the source of the IP packet.

Link-State Routing Protocol Features

Just as distance vector protocols send routing updates to their neighbors, link-state protocols send link-state updates to neighboring routers, which then forward that information to their neighbors, and so on. Also similar to distance vector protocols, at the end of the process, routers that use link-state protocols add the best routes to their routing tables, based on metrics. However, beyond this level of explanation, these two types of routing protocol algorithms have little in common.

Building the LSDB

Link-state routers flood detailed information about the internetwork to all the other routers so that every router has the same information about the internetwork. Routers use this link-state database (LSDB) to calculate the current best routes to each subnet.

OSPF, the most popular link-state IP routing protocol, advertises information in routing update messages of various types. The updates contain information called link-state advertisements (LSA).

Figure 25-3 shows the general idea of the flooding process. R8 is creating and flooding its router LSA. Note that Figure 25-3 shows only a subset of the information in R8's router LSA.

Figure 25-3   Flooding LSAs Using a Link-State Routing Protocol

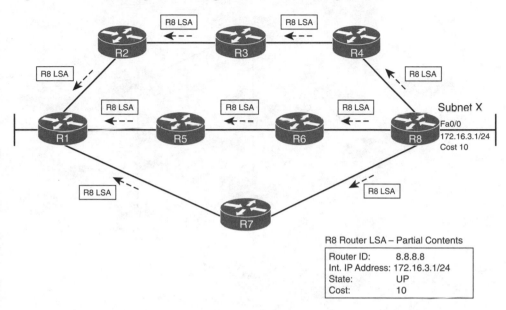

R8 Router LSA – Partial Contents

Router ID: 8.8.8.8
Int. IP Address: 172.16.3.1/24
State: UP
Cost: 10

Figure 25-3 shows the rather basic flooding process. R8 is sending the original LSA for itself, and the other routers are flooding the LSA by forwarding it until every router has a copy.

After the LSA has been flooded, even if the LSAs do not change, link-state protocols require periodic reflooding of the LSAs by default every 30 minutes. However, if an LSA changes, the router immediately floods the changed LSA. For example, if Router R8's LAN interface failed, R8 would need to reflood the R8 LSA, stating that the interface is now down.

Calculating the Dijkstra Algorithm

The flooding process alone does not cause a router to learn what routes to add to the IP routing table. Link-state protocols must then find and add routes to the IP routing table using the Dijkstra Shortest Path First (SPF) algorithm.

The SPF algorithm is run on the LSDB to create the SPF tree. The LSDB holds all the information about all the possible routers and links. Each router must view itself as the starting point, and each subnet as the destination, and use the SPF algorithm to build its own SPF tree to pick the best route to each subnet.

Figure 25-4 shows a graphical view of route possibilities from the results of the SPF algorithm run by router R1 when trying to find the best route to reach subnet 172.16.3.0/24 (based on Figure 25-3).

Figure 25-4   SPF Tree to Find R1's Route to 172.16.3.0/24

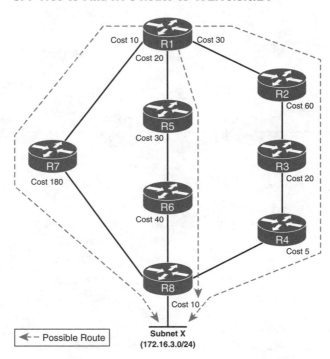

To pick the best route, a router's SPF algorithm adds the cost associated with each link between itself and the destination subnet, over each possible route. Figure 25-4 shows the costs associated with each route beside the links. The dashed lines show the three routes R1 finds between itself and subnet X (172.16.3.0/24).

Table 25-4 lists the three routes shown in Figure 25-2, with their cumulative costs. You can see that R1's best route to 172.16.3.0/24 starts by going through R5.

Table 25-4   Comparing R1's Three Alternatives for the Route to 172.16.3.0/24

Route	Location in Figure 25-2	Cumulative Cost
R1–R7–R8	Left	10 + 180 + 10 = 200
R1–R5–R6–R8	Middle	20 + 30 + 40 + 10 = 100
R1–R2–R3–R4–R8	Right	30 + 60 + 20 + 5 + 10 = 125

As a result of the SPF algorithm's analysis of the LSDB, R1 adds a route to subnet 172.16.3.0/24 to its routing table, with the next-hop router of R5.

Convergence with Link-State Protocols

Remember, when an LSA changes, link-state protocols react swiftly, converging the network and using the currently best routes as quickly as possible. For example, imagine that the link between

R5 and R6 fails in the internetwork of Figures 25-3 and 25-4. R1 then uses the following process to switch to a different route:

1. R5 and R6 flood LSAs, stating that their interfaces are now in a down state.

2. All routers run the SPF algorithm again to see if any routes have changed.

3. All routers replace routes, as needed, based on the results of SPF. For example, R1 changes its route for subnet X (172.16.3.0/24) to use R2 as the next-hop router.

These steps allow the link-state routing protocol to converge quickly—much more quickly than distance vector routing protocols.

Study Resources

For today's exam topics, refer to the following resources for more study.

Resource	Location	Topic
Primary Resources		
Routing and Switching Essentials	1	Router Operation
	3	Dynamic Routing Protocols
ICND1 Official Cert Guide	4	IPv4 Routing
	18	IP Routing
	19	RIP and Routing Protocol Concepts
ICND2 Official Cert Guide	7	Comparing Dynamic Routing Protocol Features
	9	EIGRP and Distance Vector Routing Protocols
Supplemental Resources		
CCNA Video Series	3	Lesson 3: Routing Fundamentals Administrative Distance Split Horizon Metric Next Hop Address Passive Interfaces
		Lesson 5: Routing Information Protocol (RIP) RIP Overview
		Lesson 6: Open Shortest Path First (OSPF) Introduction to Dijkstra's Algorithm Dijkstra's Algorithm Calculation OSPF Overview

Check Your Understanding

Refer to the Digital Study Guide to take a short quiz covering the content of this day.

Basic Router Configuration

CCNA 200-125 Exam Topics

- Configure, verify, and troubleshoot IPv4 addressing and subnetting
- Configure, verify, and troubleshoot IPv6 addressing

Key Topic

Today we review basic router configuration. First, we focus on configuring and verifying initial settings, including IPv4 addressing. Then we review IPv6 addressing and network connectivity verification. Most of this should be very familiar at this point in your studies because these skills are fundamental to all other router configuration tasks.

Basic Router Configuration with IPv4

Figure 24-1 shows the topology and IPv4 addressing scheme that we use to review basic router configuration and verification tasks.

Figure 24-1   IPv4 Example Topology

Device	Interface	IP Address	Subnet Mask	Default Gateway
R1	G0/0	192.168.1.1	255.255.255.0	N/A
R1	S0/0/0	192.168.2.1	255.255.255.0	N/A
R2	G0/0	192.168.3.1	255.255.255.0	N/A
R2	S0/0/0	192.168.2.2	255.255.255.0	N/A
PC1	N/A	192.168.1.10	255.255.255.0	192.168.1.1
PC2	N/A	192.168.3.10	255.255.255.0	192.168.3.1

When configuring a router, certain basic tasks are performed:

- Naming the router
- Setting passwords
- Configuring interfaces
- Configuring a banner
- Saving changes on a router
- Verifying basic configuration and router operations

Command Syntax

Table 24-1 shows the basic router configuration command syntax used to configure R1 in the following example.

Table 24-1   Basic Router Configuration Command Syntax

Configuration Task	Commands
Naming the router	Router(config)# **hostname** *name*
Setting passwords	Router(config)# **enable secret** *password*
	Router(config)# **line console** *0*
	Router(config-line)# **password** *password*
	Router(config-line)# **login**
	Router(config)# **line vty 0 15**
	Router(config-line)# **transport input ssh**
	Router(config-line)# **login local**
	Router(config)# **username** *name* **password** *password*
Configuring a message-of-the-day banner	Router(config)# **banner** *motd* # *message* #
Configuring an interface	Router(config)# **interface** *type* *number*
	Router(config-if)# **ip address** *address* *mask*
	Router(config-if)# **description** *description*
	Router(config-if)# **no shutdown**
Saving changes on a router	Router# **copy running-config startup-config**
Examining the output of **show** commands	Router# **show running-config**
	Router# **show ip route**
	Router# **show ip interface brief**
	Router# **show interfaces**

Configuration Example

Let's walk through a basic configuration for R1. First, enter privileged EXEC mode and then global configuration mode:

```
Router> enable
Router# config t
```

Next, name the router and enter the encrypted password for entering privileged EXEC mode. This command overrides the older **enable password** *password* command, so we are not entering that one:

```
Router(config)# hostname R1
R1(config)# enable secret class
```

Next, configure the console password and require that it be entered with the login password:

```
R1(config)# line console 0
R1(config-line)# password cisco
R1(config-line)# login
```

Configuring SSH and disabling Telnet are security best practices, so configure the vty lines to use only SSH.

NOTE: SSH configuration is not shown here; assume that it is already configured. To review SSH configuration, refer to Day 12, "LAN Security."

```
R1(config)# line vty 0 15
R1(config-line)# transport input ssh
R1(config-line)# login local
R1(config-line)# exit
R1(config)# username admin password cisco
```

Encrypt all the clear-text passwords in the running configuration using the **service-password encryption** command:

```
R1(config)# service password encryption
```

Configure the message-of-the-day (MOTD) banner. A delimiting character such as a # is used at both the beginning and the end of the message. At a minimum, a banner should warn against unauthorized access. A good security policy prohibits configuring a banner that welcomes an unauthorized user:

```
R1(config)# banner motd #
Enter TEXT message.   End with the character '#'.
******************************************
WARNING!! Unauthorized Access Prohibited!!
******************************************
#
```

Now configure the individual router interfaces with IP addresses and other information. First, enter interface configuration mode by specifying the interface type and number. Next, configure the IP address and subnet mask:

```
R1(config)# interface Serial0/0/0
R1(config-if)# ip address 192.168.2.1 255.255.255.0
```

It is good practice to configure a description on each interface to help document the network information:

```
R1(config-if)# description Ciruit#VBN32696-123 (help desk:1-800-555-1234)
```

Activate the interface:

```
R1(config-if)# no shutdown
```

Assuming that the other side of the link is activated on R2, the serial interface is now up. Finish R1 by configuring the GigabitEthernet 0/0 interface:

```
R1(config-if)# interface GigabitEthernet0/0
R1(config-if)# ip address 192.168.1.1 255.255.255.0
R1(config-if)# description R1 LAN
R1(config-if)# no shutdown
```

Assume that R2 is fully configured and can route back to the 192.168.1.0/24 LAN attached to R1. We need to add a static route to R1 to ensure connectivity to R2's LAN. Static routing is reviewed in more detail on Day 25, "Basic Routing Concepts." For now, enter the following command to configure a directly attached static route to R2's LAN:

```
R1(config)# ip route 192.168.3.0 255.255.255.0 Serial 0/0/0
```

To save the configuration, enter the **copy running-config startup-config** command or the **copy run start** command.

Verification Example

You can use the **show running-config** command to verify the full current configuration on the router. However, a few other basic commands can help you not only verify your configuration, but also begin troubleshooting any potential problems.

First, make sure that the networks for your interfaces are now in the routing table by using the **show ip route** command (see Example 24-1).

Example 24-1 The show ip route Command

```
R1# show ip route
Codes: L - local, C - connected, S - static, R - RIP, M - mobile, B - BGP
       D - EIGRP, EX - EIGRP external, O - OSPF, IA - OSPF inter area
       N1 - OSPF NSSA external type 1, N2 - OSPF NSSA external type 2
       E1 - OSPF external type 1, E2 - OSPF external type 2
       i - IS-IS, su - IS-IS summary, L1 - IS-IS level-1, L2 - IS-IS level-2
       ia - IS-IS inter area, * - candidate default, U - per-user static route
       o - ODR, P - periodic downloaded static route, H - NHRP, l - LISP
       + - replicated route, % - next hop override

Gateway of last resort is not set

      192.168.1.0/24 is variably subnetted, 2 subnets, 2 masks
C        192.168.1.0/24 is directly connected, GigabitEthernet0/0
L        192.168.1.1/32 is directly connected, GigabitEthernet0/0
      192.168.2.0/24 is variably subnetted, 2 subnets, 2 masks
C        192.168.2.0/24 is directly connected, Serial0/0/0
L        192.168.2.1/32 is directly connected, Serial0/0/0
S     192.168.3.0/24 is directly connected, Serial0/0/0
R1#
```

If a network is missing, check your interface status with the **show ip interface brief** command (see Example 24-2).

Example 24-2   The show ip interface brief Command

```
R1# show ip interface brief
Interface                    IP-Address    OK? Method  Status                     Protocol
Embedded-Service-Engine0/0   unassigned    YES unset   administratively down down down
GigabitEthernet0/0           192.168.1.1   YES manual  up                         up
GigabitEthernet0/1           unassigned    YES unset   administratively down down
Serial0/0/0                  192.168.2.1   YES manual  up                         up
Serial0/0/1                  unassigned    YES unset   administratively down down
R1#
```

The output from the **show ip interface brief** command provides you with three important pieces of information:

- IP address

- Line status (column 5)

- Protocol status (column 6)

The IP address should be correct, and the status codes should be up and up. Table 24-2 summarizes the two status codes and their meanings.

Table 24-2   Interface Status Codes

Name	Location	General Meaning
Line status	First status code	Refers to the Layer 1 status—for example, is the cable installed, is it the right/wrong cable, is the device on the other end powered on?
Protocol status	Second status code	Refers generally to the Layer 2 status. It is always down if the line status is down. If the line status is up, a protocol status of down is usually caused by mismatched data link layer configuration.

Four combinations of settings are possible for the status codes when troubleshooting a network. Table 24-3 lists the four combinations, along with an explanation of the typical reasons why an interface is in that state.

Table 24-3   Combinations of Interface Status Codes

Line and Protocol Status	Typical Reasons
Administratively down, down	The interface has a **shutdown** command configured on it.
down, down	The interface has a **no shutdown** command configured, but the physical layer has a problem. For example, no cable has been attached to the interface (or with Ethernet), the switch interface on the other end of the cable is shut down, or the switch is powered off.

Line and Protocol Status	Typical Reasons
up, down	This almost always refers to data link layer problems, most often configuration problems. For example, serial links have this combination when one router was configured to use PPP and the other defaults to use HDLC. However, a clocking or hardware issue can also be to blame.
up, up	All is well and the interface is functioning.

If necessary, use the more verbose **show interface** command if you need to track down a problem with an interface, to get the output for every physical and virtual interface. You can also specify one interface. Example 24-3 shows the output for GigabitEthernet 0/0.

Example 24-3   The show interface gigabitethernet 0/0 Command

```
R1# show interface gigabitethernet 0/0
GigabitEthernet0/0 is up, line protocol is up
  Hardware is CN Gigabit Ethernet, address is 30f7.0da3.0da0 (bia 30f7.0da3.0da0)
  Description: R1 LAN
  Internet address is 192.168.1.1/24
  MTU 1500 bytes, BW 100000 Kbit/sec, DLY 100 usec,
     reliability 255/255, txload 1/255, rxload 1/255
  Encapsulation ARPA, loopback not set
  Keepalive set (10 sec)
  Full Duplex, 100Mbps, media type is RJ45
  output flow-control is unsupported, input flow-control is unsupported
  ARP type: ARPA, ARP Timeout 04:00:00
  Last input 00:00:00, output 00:00:01, output hang never
  Last clearing of "show interface" counters never
  Input queue: 0/75/0/0 (size/max/drops/flushes); Total output drops: 0
  Queueing strategy: fifo
  Output queue: 0/40 (size/max)
  5 minute input rate 0 bits/sec, 0 packets/sec
  5 minute output rate 0 bits/sec, 0 packets/sec
     387 packets input, 59897 bytes, 0 no buffer
     Received 252 broadcasts (0 IP multicasts)
     0 runts, 0 giants, 0 throttles
     0 input errors, 0 CRC, 0 frame, 0 overrun, 0 ignored
     0 watchdog, 86 multicast, 0 pause input
     281 packets output, 35537 bytes, 0 underruns
     0 output errors, 0 collisions, 1 interface resets
     56 unknown protocol drops
     0 babbles, 0 late collision, 0 deferred
     0 lost carrier, 0 no carrier, 0 pause output
     0 output buffer failures, 0 output buffers swapped out
R1#
```

This command has a lot of output. However, sometimes this is the only way to find a problem.

Table 24-4 parses and explains each important part of the **show interface** output.

Table 24-4   show interface Output Explanation

Output	Description
GigabitEthernet...is {up | down | administratively down}	Whether the interface hardware is currently active or down, or whether an administrator has taken it down.
line protocol is {up | down}	Whether the software processes that handle the line protocol consider the interface usable (that is, whether keepalives are successful). If the interface misses three consecutive keepalives, the line protocol is marked as down.
Hardware	Hardware type (for example, MCI Ethernet, serial communications interface [SCI], cBus Ethernet) and address.
Description	Text string description configured for the interface (max 240 characters).
Internet address	IP address followed by the prefix length (subnet mask).
MTU	Maximum transmission unit (MTU) of the interface.
BW	Bandwidth of the interface, in kilobits per second. The bandwidth parameter is used to compute routing protocol metrics and other calculations.
DLY	Delay of the interface, in microseconds.
rely	Reliability of the interface as a fraction of 255 (255/255 is 100 percent reliability), calculated as an exponential average over 5 minutes.
load	Load on the interface as a fraction of 255 (255/255 is completely saturated), calculated as an exponential average over 5 minutes.
Encapsulation	Encapsulation method assigned to an interface.
Loopback	Whether loopback is set. Can indicate a problem with the carrier.
Keepalive	Whether keepalives are set.
ARP type	Type of Address Resolution Protocol (ARP) assigned.
Last input	Number of hours, minutes, and seconds since the last packet was successfully received by an interface. Useful for knowing when a dead interface failed.
output	Number of hours, minutes, and seconds since the last packet was successfully transmitted by an interface. Useful for knowing when a dead interface failed.
output hang	Number of hours, minutes, and seconds (or never) since the interface was last reset because of a transmission that took too long. When the number of hours in any of the previous fields exceeds 24 hours, the number of days and hours is printed. If that field overflows, asterisks are printed.
Last clearing	Time at which the counters that measure cumulative statistics shown in this report (such as number of bytes transmitted and received) were last reset to 0. Note that variables that might affect routing (for example, load and reliability) are not cleared when the counters are cleared. Asterisks indicate elapsed time too large to be displayed. Reset the counters with the **clear interface** command.

Output	Description
Output queue, input queue, drops queue	Number of packets in output and input queues. Each number is followed by a slash (/), the maximum size of the queue, and the number of packets dropped because of a full queue.
Five minute input rate, Five minute output rate	Average number of bits and packets transmitted per second in the last 5 minutes. If the interface is not in promiscuous mode, it senses network traffic that it sends and receives (instead of all network traffic). The 5-minute input and output rates should be used only as an approximation of traffic per second during a given 5-minute period. These rates are exponentially weighted averages with a time constant of 5 minutes. A period of four time constants must pass before the average will be within 2 percent of the instantaneous rate of a uniform stream of traffic over that period.
packets input	Total number of error-free packets the system received.
bytes input	Total number of bytes, including data and MAC encapsulation, in the error-free packets received by the system.
no buffers	Number of received packets discarded because the main system had no buffer space. Compare with ignored count. Broadcast storms on Ethernet are often responsible for no input buffer events.
Received...broadcasts	Total number of broadcast or multicast packets received by the interface. The number of broadcasts should be kept as low as practicable. An approximate threshold is less than 20 percent of the total number of input packets.
runts	Number of Ethernet frames that are discarded because they are smaller than the minimum Ethernet frame size. Any Ethernet frame that is less than 64 bytes is considered a runt. Runts are usually caused by collisions. If more than one runt per million bytes is received, it should be investigated.
giants	Number of Ethernet frames that are discarded because they exceed the maximum Ethernet frame size. Any Ethernet frame that is larger than 1518 bytes is considered a giant.
input error	Runts, giants, no buffer, cyclic redundancy check (CRC), frame, overrun, and ignored counts. Other input-related errors can also increase the input error count, and some datagrams can have more than one error. Therefore, this sum might not balance with the sum of enumerated input error counts.
CRC	CRC generated by the originating LAN station or far-end device not matching the checksum calculated from the data received. On a LAN, this usually indicates noise or transmission problems on the LAN interface or the LAN bus itself. A high number of CRCs is usually the result of collisions or a station transmitting bad data.

Output	Description
frame	Number of packets received as incorrectly having a CRC error and a noninteger number of octets. On a LAN, this is usually the result of collisions or a malfunctioning Ethernet device.
overrun	Number of times the receiver hardware could not hand-receive data to a hardware buffer because the input rate exceeded the capability of the receiver to handle the data.
ignored	Number of received packets ignored by the interface because the interface hardware ran low on internal buffers. These buffers are different from the system buffers mentioned in the buffer description. Broadcast storms and bursts of noise can cause the ignored count to increase.
input packets with dribble condition detected	Dribble bit error indicates that a frame is slightly too long. This frame error counter is incremented just for informational purposes; the router accepts the frame.
packets output	Total number of messages transmitted by the system.
bytes	Total number of bytes, including data and MAC encapsulation, transmitted by the system.
underruns	Number of times that the transmitter has been running faster than the router can handle. This might never be reported on some interfaces.
output errors	Sum of all errors that prevented the final transmission of datagrams out of the interface being examined. Note that this might not balance with the sum of the enumerated output errors because some datagrams might have more than one error and others might have errors that do not fall into any of the specifically tabulated categories.
collisions	Number of messages retransmitted because of an Ethernet collision. This is usually the result of an overextended LAN (too-long Ethernet or transceiver cable, more than two repeaters between stations, or too many cascaded multiport transceivers). A packet that collides is counted only once in output packets.
interface resets	Number of times an interface has been completely reset. This can happen if packets queued for transmission were not sent within several seconds. On a serial line, this can be caused by a malfunctioning modem that is not supplying the transmit clock signal, or it can be caused by a cable problem. If the system notices that the carrier detect line of a serial interface is up but the line protocol is down, it periodically resets the interface in an effort to restart it. Interface resets can also occur when an interface is looped back or shut down.

 Activity: Order the Steps for IPv4 Router Configuration

Refer to the Digital Study Guide to complete this activity.

Basic Router Configuration with IPv6

In this section, we use the topology in Figure 24-2 to review the basic commands for enabling IPv6 on a router.

Figure 24-2   IPv6 Example Topology

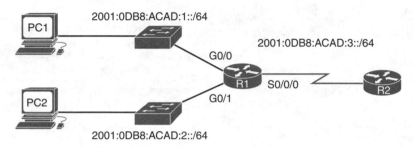

Command Syntax

First, you must enable IPv6 routing using the following command in global configuration mode:

```
R1(config)# ipv6 unicast-routing
```

Among other actions, this command configures the router to begin listening for and responding to Neighbor Discovery (ND) messages on all active IPv6 interfaces.

To configure an IPv6 address on a router's interface, you have one of several options:

- Configure the interface to use the EUI-64 method of addressing:

  ```
  Router(config)# ipv6 address ipv6-prefix/prefix-length eui-64
  ```

- Configure the full global unicast address. To manually configure a full IPv6 address, use the following command syntax:

  ```
  Router(config)# ipv6 address ipv6-address/prefix-length
  ```

- Configure the interface as unnumbered (see Day 26, "IPv6 Addressing").

- Configure the interface as a DHCPv6 client (see Day 7, "DHCP and DNS").

NOTE: To manually configure an interface's link-local address, use the following command syntax:

```
Router(config)# ipv6 address ipv6-address/prefix-length link-local
```

Configuration Example

The preferred method often is to manually configure the full IPv6 address because you can control the number of hexadecimal digits you must type when testing connectivity or troubleshooting a problem. You can see this by comparing the EUI-64 method to a full configuration. In Example 24-4, the interfaces on R1 are all configured using the EUI-64 method.

Example 24-4   Configuring Interfaces Using the EUI-64 Method

```
R1(config)# interface g0/0
R1(config-if)# ipv6 address 2001:db8:acad:1::/64 eui-64
R1(config-if)# interface g0/1
R1(config-if)# ipv6 address 2001:db8:acad:2::/64 eui-64
R1(config-if)# interface s0/0/0
R1(config-if)# ipv6 address 2001:db8:acad:3::/64 eui-64
R1(config-if)# do show ipv6 interface brief
GigabitEthernet0/0          [up/up]
    FE80::2D0:97FF:FE20:A101
    2001:DB8:ACAD:1:2D0:97FF:FE20:A101
GigabitEthernet0/1          [up/up]
    FE80::2D0:97FF:FE20:A102
    2001:DB8:ACAD:2:2D0:97FF:FE20:A102
Serial0/0/0                 [down/down]
    FE80::20C:CFFF:FE77:A401
    2001:DB8:ACAD:3:20C:CFFF:FE77:A401
<output omitted>
```

Notice the number of hexadecimal digits in the IPv6 addresses highlighted in the output from the **show ipv6 interface brief** command. Imagine having to ping the GigabitEthernet 0/0 address 2001:DB8:ACAD:1:2D0:97FF:FE20:A101.

Furthermore, notice that the link-local addresses are also rather complex. To reduce the complexity of the router's configuration, verification, and troubleshooting, it is a good practice to manually configure the link-local address as well as the IPv6 global unicast address. In Example 24-5, R1 is reconfigured with simpler IPv6 addresses and with FE80::1 as the link-local address on all interfaces. Remember, the link-local address needs to be unique only on that interface's link.

Example 24-5   Full IPv6 Address and Link-Local Address Configuration

```
R1(config-if)# interface g0/0
R1(config-if)# no ipv6 address 2001:db8:acad:1::/64 eui-64
R1(config-if)# ipv6 address 2001:db8:acad:1::1/64
R1(config-if)# ipv6 address fe80::1 link-local
R1(config-if)# interface g0/1
R1(config-if)# no ipv6 address 2001:db8:acad:2::/64 eui-64
R1(config-if)# ipv6 address 2001:db8:acad:2::1/64
R1(config-if)# ipv6 address fe80::1 link-local
R1(config-if)# interface s0/0/0
R1(config-if)# no ipv6 address 2001:db8:acad:3::/64 eui-64
R1(config-if)# ipv6 address 2001:db8:acad:3::1/64
R1(config-if)# ipv6 address fe80::1 link-local
R1(config-if)# do show ipv6 interface brief
```

```
GigabitEthernet0/0           [up/up]
    FE80::1
    2001:DB8:ACAD:1::1
GigabitEthernet0/1           [up/up]
    FE80::1
    2001:DB8:ACAD:2::1
Serial0/0/0                  [down/down]
    FE80::1
    2001:DB8:ACAD:3::1
<output omitted>
```

NOTE: If you do not remove the previous IPv6 address configuration, each interface will have two IPv6 global unicast addresses. This is different than in IPv4, where simply configuring another IPv4 address with the **ip address** command overwrites any previous configuration. However, only one link-local address can exist per interface.

Compare the highlighted output from the **show ipv6 interface brief** command in Example 24-5 with the output in Example 24-4. You can see that simplifying the IPv6 addressing implementation can make your verification and troubleshooting job much easier.

To verify the full configuration of an interface, use the **show ipv6 interface** command. Example 24-6 shows the output for R1's GigabitEthernet 0/0 interface.

Example 24-6 The show ipv6 interface gigabitethernet 0/0 Command

```
R1# show ipv6 interface gigabitethernet 0/0
GigabitEthernet0/0 is up, line protocol is up
  IPv6 is enabled, link-local address is FE80::1
  No Virtual link-local address(es):
  Global unicast address(es):
    2001:DB8:ACAD:1::1, subnet is 2001:DB8:ACAD:1::/64
  Joined group address(es):
    FF02::1
    FF02::1:FF00:1
  MTU is 1500 bytes
  ICMP error messages limited to one every 100 milliseconds
  ICMP redirects are enabled
  ICMP unreachables are sent
  ND DAD is enabled, number of DAD attempts: 1
  ND reachable time is 30000 milliseconds
  ND advertised reachable time is 0 milliseconds
  ND advertised retransmit interval is 0 milliseconds
  ND router advertisements are sent every 200 seconds
  ND router advertisements live for 1800 seconds
  ND advertised default router preference is Medium
  Hosts use stateless autoconfig for addresses.
```

Focus on the highlighted output. IPv6 is enabled on this interface with a nice, short link–local address. The global unicast address and its subnet are listed, as is the address of multicast groups that this interface automatically joined. Do you remember what the FF02::1 and FF02::1:FF00:1 addresses are used for? If not, revisit Day 26.

That's all the IPv6 configurations for today. As we continue to review the exam topics in the upcoming days, we will incorporate IPv6 topics.

 Activity: Order the Steps for IPv6 Router Configuration

Refer to the Digital Study Guide to complete this activity.

Verifying IPv4 and IPv6 Network Connectivity

As reviewed on Day 29, "Switch Configuration Basics," ping and traceroute are helpful tools for verifying network connectivity. Example 24-7 demonstrates successful ping output on the router.

Example 24-7   Successful ping Output on a Router

```
R1# ping 192.168.3.10

Type escape sequence to abort.
Sending 5, 100-byte ICMP Echos to 192.168.3.10, timeout is 2 seconds:
!!!!!
Success rate is 100 percent (5/5), round-trip min/avg/max = 1/2/4 ms
!Pinging an IPv6 destination
R1# ping 2001:db8:acad:1:290:dff:fee5:8095

Type escape sequence to abort.
Sending 5, 100-byte ICMP Echos to 2001:DB8:ACAD:1:290:CFF.FEE5:8095, timeout is
2   seconds:
!!!!!
Success rate is 100 percent (5/5), round-trip min/avg/max = 0/9/46 ms

R1#
```

Unsuccessful ping output shows periods (.) instead of exclamation points (!), as Example 24-8 demonstrates. The output would be the same in IPv6.

Example 24-8   Unsuccessful ping Output on a Router

```
R1# ping 192.168.3.2

Type escape sequence to abort.
Sending 5, 100-byte ICMP Echos to 192.168.3.2, timeout is 2 seconds:
.....
Success rate is 0 percent (0/5)
R1#
```

Example 24-9 shows output from a successful **traceroute** command.

Example 24-9   Successful traceroute Output on a Router

```
R1# traceroute 192.168.3.10
Type escape sequence to abort.
Tracing the route to 192.168.3.10

  1    192.168.2.2     71 msec    70 msec    72 msec
  2    192.168.3.10    111 msec  133 msec   115 msec
R1#
!Tracing to an IPv6 destination.
R2# traceroute 2001:db8:acad:1:290:cff:fee5:8095
Type escape sequence to abort.
Tracing the route to 2001:DB8:ACAD:1:290:CFF:FEE5:8095

  1    2001:DB8:ACAD:3::11 msec     1 msec     1 msec
  2    2001:DB8:ACAD:1:290:CFF:FEE5:80951 msec    1 msec    0 msec
R2#
```

Unsuccessful traces show the last successful hop and the asterisks for each attempt until the user cancels. To cancel the **traceroute** command on a router, use the key combination **Ctrl–Shift–6** and then press the **x** key. Example 24-10 shows unsuccessful **traceroute** output. The output would be the same with IPv6.

Example 24-10   Unsuccessful traceroute Output on a Router

```
R1# traceroute 192.168.3.2
Type escape sequence to abort.
Tracing the route to 192.168.3.2

  1    192.168.2.2     71 msec    70 msec    72 msec
  2    *      *      *
  3    *      *      *
  4    *      *      *
  5    *
R1#
```

Using Telnet or SSH to remotely access another device also tests connectivity. More important, these remote access methods test whether a device has been correctly configured so that you can access it for management purposes. This can be important when a device is truly remote (for example, across town or in another city). Day 12 reviews SSH configuration and verification in greater detail.

During the basic configuration tasks earlier, we entered the commands to properly configure the vty lines for SSH remote access. If you are accessing a device configured with SSH from a PC, you use the SSH setting in your terminal client. However, you can use the **ssh** command on a router or switch to access another device configured with SSH. Example 24-11 shows how to use SSH to remotely access R2 from R1.

Example 24-11   Remote Access Using SSH

```
R1# ssh?
  -c     Select encryption algorithm
  -l     Log in using this user name
  -m     Select HMAC algorithm
  -o     Specify options
  -p     Connect to this port
  -v     Specify SSH Protocol Version
  -vrf   Specify vrf name
  WORD   IP address or hostname of a remote system

R1# ssh -l?
  WORD   Login name

R1# ssh -l admin?
  -c     Select encryption algorithm
  -m     Select HMAC algorithm
  -o     Specify options
  -p     Connect to this port
  -v     Specify SSH Protocol Version
  -vrf   Specify vrf name
  WORD   IP address or hostname of a remote system

R1# ssh -l admin 192.168.2.2
Password:

*******************************************
WARNING!! Unauthorized Access Prohibited!!
*******************************************

R2>
```

NOTE: During your CCNA studies and lab practice, you most likely used a Telnet configuration to remotely access your lab equipment. Although Telnet is easier to use than SSH, remember that SSH is considered best practice. Therefore, during the CCNA exam, be ready to use SSH to remotely access devices on simulation questions because Telnet might not be configured or allowed.

 Packet Tracer Activity: Dual-Stack Router Address Configuration

Refer to the Digital Study Guide to access the PKA file for this activity. You must have Packet Tracer software to run this activity. See the Introduction for details.

Basic IP Addressing Troubleshooting

If you are sure you manually configured the correct IP address and subnet mask (IPv4) or network prefix (IPv6), then basic IP addressing issues are usually the result of a misconfigured default gateway or duplicate addresses.

Default Gateway

A misconfigured default gateway is one of the most common problems in either a static or dynamically assigned IP addressing scheme. For a device to communicate across multiple networks, it must be configured with an IP address, a subnet mask or network prefix, and a default gateway.

The default gateway is used when the host wants to send a packet to a device on another network. The default gateway address is generally the router interface address attached to the local network to which the host is connected.

To resolve a default gateway that was manually configured incorrectly, consult the topology and addressing documentation to verify what the device's default gateway should be—normally, a router attached to the same LAN.

NOTE: A misconfigured DHCP server can also cause a default gateway issue. Some DHCP server configurations, such as the Easy IP IOS feature, might require the administrator to manually configure the default gateway address. If this is configured incorrectly, no devices will have access beyond the LAN. DHCP is reviewed on Day 7.

Duplicate IP Addresses

Under some circumstances, duplicate IP address conflicts can occur between a statically configured network device and a PC obtaining automatic IP addressing information from the DHCP server. To resolve such an IP addressing conflict, you can do one of the following:

- Convert the network device with the static IP address to a DHCP client

- On the DHCP server, exclude the static IP address of the end device from the DHCP pool of addresses

The first solution is a quick fix that you can do in the field. However, the device more than likely needs a static configuration. The second solution might be the better long-term choice. However, it requires that you have administrative privileges to configure the DHCP server.

You might also encounter IP addressing conflicts when manually configuring IP on an end device in a network that uses only static IP addresses. In this case, you must determine which IP addresses are available on the particular IP subnet and configure accordingly. This case illustrates why it is so important for a network administrator to maintain detailed documentation, including IP address assignments and topologies, for end devices.

Study Resources

For today's exam topics, refer to the following resources for more study.

Resource	Location	Topic
Primary Resources		
Routing and Switching Essentials	1	Router Initial Configuration
ICND1 Official Cert Guide	17	Enabling IPv4 Support on Cisco Router Interfaces
	30	Implementing Unicast IPv6 Addresses on Routers
Supplemental Resources		
CCNA Portable Command Guide	11	All
CCNA Video Series	3	Lesson 2: Basic Router Configuration and Verification
CCNA Network Simulator	ICND1	Chapter 17: New Job I
		Chapter 17: Rebuild a Configuration
		Chapter 17: Router CLI Exec Mode I–II
		Chapter 17: Router CLI Configuration Process
		Chapter 17: Setting Router Passwords
		Chapter 30: IPv6 Configuration I–II
		Chapter 30: IPv6 Address Configuration I–IX
		Chapter 30: IPv6 EUI-64 Calculation Drills I–X
		Chapter 30: IPv6 Addressing Troubleshooting

 Check Your Understanding

Refer to the Digital Study Guide to take a short quiz covering the content of this day.

Static and Default Route Configuration

CCNA 200-125 Exam Topics

- Configure, verify, and troubleshoot IPv4 and IPv6 static routing.

Key Topics

Today we focus on static and default routing for IPv4 and IPv6. Static routes are a common part of an enterprise's routing policy. Static routes can be used to force traffic to use a specific path or to establish a default route out of the enterprise. The network administrator hard-codes static routes into the routing table. Thus, a network administrator must monitor and maintain static routes to ensure connectivity.

Static and Default Routing Overview

When a router configured with a dynamic routing protocol can learn routes from other routers without additional input from the network administrator, why would you use static routing? Situations vary and other reasons might be unique to a particular implementation, but, in general, you use static routing in these cases:

- Use static routes:
  - In a small network that requires only simple routing
  - In a hub-and-spoke network topology
  - When you want to create a quick ad hoc route
  - As a backup when the primary route fails
- Do not use static routes:
  - In a large network
  - When the network is expected to scale

Static routes are commonly used when you are routing from a larger network to a stub network (a network that is accessed by a single link). Static routes can also be useful for specifying a default route or gateway of last resort. For example, in Figure 23-1, R2 is attached to a stub network.

Figure 23-1   Example of a Stub Network

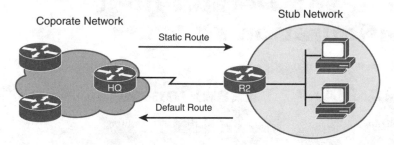

In Figure 23-1, no other route out of the stub network exists except to send packets to HQ. Therefore, it makes sense to configure R2 with a default route pointing out the interface attached to HQ. Similarly, HQ has only one way to route packets destined for the stub network attached to R2. Therefore, it makes sense to configure HQ with a static route pointing out the interface attached to R2. Yes, you could configure both routers with a dynamic routing protocol, but that can introduce a level of complexity that might not be necessary in a stub network situation.

IPv4 Static Route Configuration

To configure a static route, use the **ip route** command with the following relevant syntax:

```
Router(config)# ip route network-address subnet-mask {ip-address | exit-interface}
[administrative-distance]
```

The explanation for each parameter follows:

- *network-address:* The destination network address of the remote network to be added to the routing table.

- *subnet-mask:* The subnet mask of the remote network to be added to the routing table. The subnet mask can be modified to summarize a group of networks.

One or both of the following parameters are used:

- *ip-address*: Commonly referred to as the next-hop router's IP address

- *exit-interface*: Outgoing interface used in forwarding packets to the destination network

Also shown is the *administrative-distance* optional parameter. This is used when configuring a floating static route, as you see later in today's review.

Figure 23-2 shows the topology we use today in reviewing IPv4 static and default routing.

Figure 23-2   IPv4 Static and Default Routing Topology

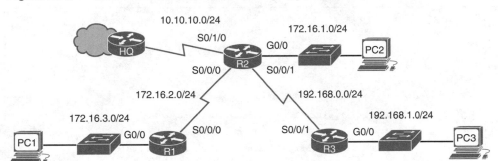

Table 23-1 shows the IPv4 addressing scheme we use with the topology in Figure 23-2.

Table 23-1   IPv4 Addressing Scheme

Device	Interface	IP Address	Subnet Mask	Default Gateway
HQ	S0/0/0	10.10.10.1	255.255.255.0	—
R1	G0/0	172.16.3.1	255.255.255.0	—
	S0/0/0	172.16.2.2	255.255.255.0	—
R2	G0/0	172.16.1.1	255.255.255.0	—
	S0/0/0	172.16.2.1	255.255.255.0	—
	S0/0/1	192.168.0.1	255.255.255.0	—
	S0/1/0	10.10.10.2	255.255.255.0	—
R3	G0/0	192.168.1.1	255.255.255.0	—
	S0/0/1	192.168.0.2	255.255.255.0	—
PC1	NIC	172.16.3.10	255.255.255.0	172.16.3.1
PC2	NIC	172.16.1.10	255.255.255.0	172.16.1.1
PC3	NIC	192.168.2.10	255.255.255.0	192.168.2.1

Assume that R1 is configured and knows about its own directly connected networks. Example 23-1 shows the routing table for R1 before any static routing is configured.

Example 23-1   R1 Routing Table Before Static Routes Are Configured

```
R1# show ip route
<output omitted>


Gateway of last resort is not set


      172.16.0.0/16 is variably subnetted, 4 subnets, 2 masks
C        172.16.2.0/24 is directly connected, Serial0/0/0
L        172.16.2.2/32 is directly connected, Serial0/0/0
C        172.16.3.0/24 is directly connected, GigabitEthernet0/0
L        172.16.3.1/32 is directly connected, GigabitEthernet0/0
R1#
```

R1 does not know about these remote networks:

- 172.16.1.0/24: The LAN on R2

- 192.168.0.0/24: The serial network between R2 and R3

- 192.168.1.0/24: The LAN on R3

- 10.10.10.0/24: The serial network between R2 and HQ

- 0.0.0.0/0: All other networks accessible through HQ

IPv4 Static Routes Using the Next-Hop Parameter

Using the next-hop parameter, R1 can be configured with three static routes—one for each network R1 does not yet know about. Example 23-2 shows the command syntax.

Example 23-2   Static Route Configuration with Next-Hop Parameter

```
R1(config)# ip route 172.16.1.0 255.255.255.0 172.16.2.1
R1(config)# ip route 192.168.0.0 255.255.255.0 172.16.2.1
R1(config)# ip route 192.168.1.0 255.255.255.0 172.16.2.1
R1(config)# ip route 10.10.10.0 255.255.255.0 172.16.2.1
```

The interface that routes to the next hop must be up and up before the static routes can be entered in the routing table. Example 23-3 verifies that the static routes are now in the routing table.

Example 23-3   R1 Routing Table After Static Routes Are Configured

```
R1# show ip route
<output omitted>


Gateway of last resort is not set


      10.0.0.0/24 is subnetted, 1 subnets
S        10.10.10.0/24 [1/0] via 172.16.2.1
```

```
|      172.16.0.0/16 is variably subnetted, 5 subnets, 2 masks
| S        172.16.1.0/24 [1/0] via 172.16.2.1
| C        172.16.2.0/24 is directly connected, Serial0/0/0
| L        172.16.2.2/32 is directly connected, Serial0/0/0
| C        172.16.3.0/24 is directly connected, GigabitEthernet0/0
| L        172.16.3.1/32 is directly connected, GigabitEthernet0/0
| S     192.168.0.0/24 [1/0] via 172.16.2.1
| S     192.168.1.0/24 [1/0] via 172.16.2.1
| R1#
```

When using the next-hop parameter, the router must have a route in the table to the network that the next-hop address belongs to. Highlighted in Example 23-3, we see that R1 does indeed have a route to the 172.16.2.0/24 network, which includes the next-hop address 172.16.2.1. However, configuring a next-hop address requires the router to perform a recursive lookup to find the exit interface before it can send the packet out the Serial 0/0/0 interface.

IPv4 Static Routes Using the Exit Interface Parameter

To avoid a recursive lookup and have a router immediately send packets to the exit interface, configure the static route using the exit-interface parameter instead of the next-hop (*ip-address*) parameter.

For example, on R2, we can configure static routes to the R1 and R3 LANs by specifying the exit interface:

```
R2(config)# ip route 172.16.3.0 255.255.255.0 serial 0/0/0
R2(config)# ip route 192.168.1.0 255.255.255.0 serial 0/0/1
```

Any previous static routes to this network using a next-hop IP address should be removed. R2 now has two static routes in its routing table (see Example 23-4) that it can use immediately to route to the 172.16.3.0/24 and 192.168.1.0/24 networks without having to do a recursive route lookup.

Example 23-4   R2 Routing Table After Static Route Is Configured

```
R2# show ip route
<output omitted>

Gateway of last resort is not set

     10.0.0.0/8 is variably subnetted, 2 subnets, 2 masks
C        10.10.10.0/24 is directly connected, Serial0/1/0
L        10.10.10.2/32 is directly connected, Serial0/1/0
     172.16.0.0/16 is variably subnetted, 5 subnets, 2 masks
C        172.16.1.0/24 is directly connected, GigabitEthernet0/0
L        172.16.1.1/32 is directly connected, GigabitEthernet0/0
C        172.16.2.0/24 is directly connected, Serial0/0/0
L        172.16.2.1/32 is directly connected, Serial0/0/0
```

```
S          172.16.3.0/24 is directly connected, Serial0/0/0
       192.168.0.0/24 is variably subnetted, 2 subnets, 2 masks
C          192.168.0.0/24 is directly connected, Serial0/0/1
L          192.168.0.1/32 is directly connected, Serial0/0/1
S      192.168.1.0/24 is directly connected, Serial0/0/1
R2#
```

NOTE: Although the highlighted output in Example 23-4 shows that the routes are directly connected, technically, that is not true. However, as far as R2 is concerned, the exit interface is the way to get to the destination, much like truly directly connected routes. Another benefit to using the exit interface configuration instead of the next-hop address configuration is that the static route does not depend upon the IP address stability of the next hop. Most of the time, using the exit interface configuration is the best practice, so we use the exit interface configuration for all static and default routes as we continue with the reviews.

IPv4 Default Route Configuration

A default route is a special kind of static route used to represent all routes with zero or no bits matching. In other words, when no routes have a more specific match in the routing table, the default route is a match.

The destination IP address of a packet can match multiple routes in the routing table. For example, consider having the following two static routes in the routing table:

```
       172.16.0.0/24 is subnetted, 3 subnets
S          172.16.1.0 is directly connected, Serial0/0/0
S          172.16.0.0/16 is directly connected, Serial0/0/1
```

A packet destined for 172.16.1.10, the packet's destination IP address, matches both routes. However, the 172.16.1.0 route is the more specific route because the destination matches the first 24 bits, whereas the destination matches only the first 16 bits of the 172.16.0.0 route. Therefore, the router uses the route with the most specific match.

A default route is a route that matches all packets. Commonly called a quad-zero route, a default route uses 0.0.0.0 (thus the term *quad-zero*) for both the network-address and the subnet-mask parameter, as in this syntax:

```
Router(config)# ip route 0.0.0.0 0.0.0.0 {ip-address | exit-interface}
```

Referring to the topology in Figure 23-2, assume that HQ has a connection to the Internet. From the perspective of R2, all default traffic can be sent to HQ for routing outside the domain known to R2.

The following command configures R2 with a default route pointing to HQ:

```
R2(config)# ip route 0.0.0.0 0.0.0.0 serial 0/1/0
```

R2 now has a gateway of last resort listed in the routing table—a candidate default route indicated by the asterisk (*) next to the S code (see Example 23-5).

Example 23-5 R2 Routing Table After Default Route Is Configured

```
R2# show ip route
<some codes omitted>
        * - candidate default, U - per-user static route, o - ODR
        P - periodic downloaded static route

Gateway of last resort is 0.0.0.0 to network 0.0.0.0

     10.0.0.0/8 is variably subnetted, 2 subnets, 2 masks
C        10.10.10.0/24 is directly connected, Serial0/1/0
L        10.10.10.2/32 is directly connected, Serial0/1/0
     172.16.0.0/16 is variably subnetted, 5 subnets, 2 masks
C        172.16.1.0/24 is directly connected, GigabitEthernet0/0
L        172.16.1.1/32 is directly connected, GigabitEthernet0/0
C        172.16.2.0/24 is directly connected, Serial0/0/0
L        172.16.2.1/32 is directly connected, Serial0/0/0
S        172.16.3.0/24 is directly connected, Serial0/0/0
     192.168.0.0/24 is variably subnetted, 2 subnets, 2 masks
C        192.168.0.0/24 is directly connected, Serial0/0/1
L        192.168.0.1/32 is directly connected, Serial0/0/1
S     192.168.1.0/24 is directly connected, Serial0/0/1
S*    0.0.0.0/0 is directly connected, Serial0/1/0
R2#
```

From R1 and R3's perspective, R2 is the default route. The following commands configure R1 and R3 with a default route pointing to R2:

```
R1(config)# ip route 0.0.0.0 0.0.0.0 serial 0/0/0
!
R3(config)# ip route 0.0.0.0 0.0.0.0 serial 0/0/1
```

Again, we can verify that the default route is now in the routing table for R1 (see Example 23-6).

Example 23-6 R1 and R3 Routing Tables After Default Route Is Configured

```
!R1!!!!!!!!!!!!!
R1# show ip route
<some codes omitted>
        * - candidate default, U - per-user static route, o - ODR
        P - periodic downloaded static route

Gateway of last resort is 0.0.0.0 to network 0.0.0.0

     172.16.0.0/16 is variably subnetted, 4 subnets, 2 masks
C        172.16.2.0/24 is directly connected, Serial0/0/0
L        172.16.2.2/32 is directly connected, Serial0/0/0
```

```
C          172.16.3.0/24 is directly connected, GigabitEthernet0/0
L          172.16.3.1/32 is directly connected, GigabitEthernet0/0
S*   0.0.0.0/0 is directly connected, Serial0/0/0
R1#
!
!R3!!!!!!!!!!!!!
R3# show ip route
<some codes omitted>
          * - candidate default, U - per-user static route, o - ODR
          P - periodic downloaded static route

Gateway of last resort is 0.0.0.0 to network 0.0.0.0

     192.168.0.0/24 is variably subnetted, 2 subnets, 2 masks
C          192.168.0.0/24 is directly connected, Serial0/0/1
L          192.168.0.2/32 is directly connected, Serial0/0/1
     192.168.1.0/24 is variably subnetted, 2 subnets, 2 masks
C          192.168.1.0/24 is directly connected, GigabitEthernet0/0
L          192.168.1.1/32 is directly connected, GigabitEthernet0/0
S*   0.0.0.0/0 is directly connected, Serial0/0/1
R3#
```

After evaluating the complete routing tables for R1, R2, and R3 shown in Examples 23-5 and 23-6, you can see that R1 and R3 need only one route out—a default route. R2 acts as a hub router to the R1 and R3 spokes. Therefore, it needs two static routes pointing to the R1 and R3 LANs. R2 also has a route out to HQ for any destinations it does not know about. But what about HQ? Currently, HQ does not have routes back to any of the networks accessible through R2. Any traffic from PC1, PC2, and PC3 is thus currently confined to the R1, R2, and R3 networks. None of these PCs can ping the HQ interface address 10.10.10.1. In the traceroute output in Example 23-7, failure occurs after R2 responds. This is because HQ receives the ICMP requests from PC1 but does not have a route back to the 172.16.3.0/24 network. Therefore, HQ drops the packets.

Example 23-7   A traceroute from PC1 to HQ Fails

```
C:\> tracert 10.10.10.1

Tracing route to 10.10.10.1 over a maximum of 30 hops:

  1    0 ms       0 ms      1 ms       172.16.3.1
  2    0 ms       0 ms      1 ms       172.16.2.1
  3    *          *         *          Request timed out.
  4    ^C
C:\>
```

Let's configure HQ with static routes to complete the static route configuration for the topology in Figure 23-2.

IPv4 Summary Static Route Configuration

Before configuring five separate static routes for each of the networks in Figure 23-2, notice that the 172.16 networks can be summarized into one route and that the 192.168 networks can be summarized into one route. Example 23-8 shows the five routes in binary, with the bits in common highlighted.

Example 23-8   Summary Route Calculation for HQ Static Routes

```
Summary calculation for the 172.16 networks:
10101100.00010000.00000001.00000000
10101100.00010000.00000010.00000000
10101100.00010000.00000011.00000000
Summary calculation for the 192.168 networks:
11000000.10101000.00000000.00000000
11000000.10101000.00000001.00000000
```

The summary route for the 172.16 networks is 172.16.0.0/22 because the three network addresses have 22 bits in common. Although this summary static route is not part of the current addressing scheme, it also includes the route 172.16.0.0/24. The summary route for the 192.168 networks is 192.168.0.0/23 because the two network addresses have 23 bits in common.

You can now configure HQ with two summary static routes instead of five individual static routes:

```
HQ(config)# ip route 172.16.0.0 255.255.252.0 serial 0/0/0
HQ(config)# ip route 192.168.0.0 255.255.254.0 Serial0/0/0
```

Now PC1 can successfully trace a route to the HQ interface, as Example 23-9 shows.

Example 23-9   A traceroute from PC1 to HQ Succeeds

```
C:\> tracert 10.10.10.1

Tracing route to 10.10.10.1 over a maximum of 30 hops:

  1    1 ms       0 ms       0 ms       172.16.3.1
  2    0 ms       1 ms       2 ms       172.16.2.1
  3    1 ms       2 ms       1 ms       10.10.10.1

Trace complete.

C:\>
```

The trace is successful because HQ now has a route back to PC1's network, as in Example 23-10.

Example 23-10   HQ Routing Table with IPv4 Summary Static Routes

```
HQ# show ip route
<output omitted>


Gateway of last resort is not set


      10.0.0.0/8 is variably subnetted, 2 subnets, 2 masks
C        10.10.10.0/24 is directly connected, Serial0/0/0
L        10.10.10.1/32 is directly connected, Serial0/0/0
      172.16.0.0/22 is subnetted, 1 subnets
S        172.16.0.0/22 is directly connected, Serial0/0/0
S        192.168.0.0/23 is directly connected, Serial0/0/
HQ#
```

IPv6 Static Routing

Static routing with IPv6 is similar to IPv4. We use the same topology but change the addressing to IPv6 (see Figure 23-3).

Figure 23-3   Static and Default Routing IPv6 Topology

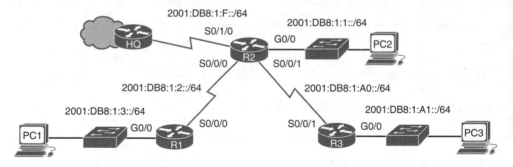

Table 23-2 shows the IPv6 addressing scheme we use with the topology in Figure 23-3.

Table 23-2   IPv6 Addressing Scheme

Device	Interface	IPv6 Address/Prefix	Default Gateway
HQ	S0/0/0	2001:DB8:1:F::1/64	—
	Link-local	FE80::F	
R1	G0/0	2001:DB8:1:3::1/64	—
	S0/0/0	2001:DB8:1:2::2/64	—
		FE80::1	

Device	Interface	IPv6 Address/Prefix	Default Gateway
R2	G0/0	2001:DB8:1:1::1/64	—
	S0/0/0	2001:DB8:1:2::1/64	—
	S0/0/1	2001:DB8:1:A0::1/64	—
	S0/1/0	2001:DB8:1:F::2/64	—
	Link-local	FE80::2	—
R3	G0/0	2001:DB8:1:A1::1/64	—
	S0/0/1	2001:DB8:1:A0::2/64	—
	Link-local	FE80::3	—
PC1	NIC	2001:DB8:1:3:209:7CFF:FE9A:1A87/64	FE80::1
PC2	NIC	2001:DB8:1:1:204:9AFF:FEE3:C943/64	FE80::2
PC3	NIC	2001:DB8:1:A1:201:C9FF:FEE5:D3A/64	FE80::3

NOTE: The IPv6 addressing for the PCs is set to autoconfiguration. Pinging from PC to PC would not really be much fun. However, the IPv6 addresses are not manually set so that you can practice your knowledge of how EUI-64 works. Can you figure out the MAC address for each PC? If not, review Day 26, "IPv6 Addressing." (Hint: FFFE and flip the bit.) If you are following along using a simulator, you might want to consider manually configuring the PCs with easier IPv6 addresses—2001:DB8:1:3::A/64 on PC1, for example. This will greatly improve your pinging experience.

IPv6 Static Route Configuration

The command syntax for IPv6 static routing is similar to the syntax for IPv4:

```
Router(config)# ipv6 route ipv6-prefix/prefix-length {ipv6-address | exit
  interface} [administrative-distance]
```

Therefore, the following commands configure R2 with static routes to the R1 and R3 LANs:

```
R2(config)# ipv6 route 2001:DB8:1:3::/64 Serial0/0/0
R2(config)# ipv6 route 2001:DB8:1:A1::/64 Serial0/0/1
```

As highlighted in the output from the **show ipv6 route** command in Example 23-11, R2 now has routes in the routing table to the R1 and R3 LANs.

Example 23-11   R2 IPv6 Routing Table After Static Routes Are Configured

```
R2# show ipv6 route
IPv6 Routing Table - 11 entries
<code output omitted>
C    2001:DB8:1:1::/64 [0/0]
     via ::, GigabitEthernet0/0
L    2001:DB8:1:1::1/128 [0/0]
     via ::, GigabitEthernet0/0
```

```
C   2001:DB8:1:2::/64 [0/0]
      via ::, Serial0/0/0
L   2001:DB8:1:2::1/128 [0/0]
      via ::, Serial0/0/0
S   2001:DB8:1:3::/64 [1/0]
      via ::, Serial0/0/0
C   2001:DB8:1:F::/64 [0/0]
      via ::, Serial0/1/0
L   2001:DB8:1:F::2/128 [0/0]
      via ::, Serial0/1/0
C   2001:DB8:1:A0::/64 [0/0]
      via ::, Serial0/0/1
L   2001:DB8:1:A0::1/128 [0/0]
      via ::, Serial0/0/1
S   2001:DB8:1:A1::/64 [1/0]
      via ::, Serial0/0/1
L   FF00::/8 [0/0]
      via ::, Null0
```

IPv6 Default Route Configuration

The following is the command syntax for an IPv6 default route:

```
Router(config)# ipv6 route ::/0 {ipv6-address | exit-interface}
```

Just as with the quad-zero in IPv4, the double colon (::) means all 0s or any address, and the /0 means any prefix length.

Continuing with the example in Figure 23-3, we can configure R1, R2, and R3 with the following default routes:

```
R1(config)# ipv6 route ::/0 serial 0/0/0
R2(config)# ipv6 route ::/0 serial 0/1/0
R3(config)# ipv6 route ::/0 serial 0/0/1
```

The highlights in Example 23-12 show the default routes for R1, R2, and R3.

Example 23-12   Default Routes in the Routing Tables for R1, R2, and R3

```
!R1!!!!!!!!!!!!
R1# show ipv6 route
IPv6 Routing Table - 6 entries
<code output omitted>
S   ::/0 [1/0]
      via ::, Serial0/0/0
<output for connected and local routes omitted>

!R2!!!!!!!!!!!!
```

```
R2# show ipv6 route
IPv6 Routing Table - 12 entries
<code output omitted>
S    ::/0 [1/0]
     via ::, Serial0/1/0
S    2001:DB8:1:3::/64 [1/0]
     via ::, Serial0/0/0
S    2001:DB8:1:A1::/64 [1/0]
     via ::, Serial0/0/1
<output for connected and local routes omitted>


!R3!!!!!!!!!!!!
R3# show ipv6 route
IPv6 Routing Table - 6 entries
<code output omitted>
S    ::/0 [1/0]
     via ::, Serial0/0/1
<output for connected and local routes omitted>
```

IPv6 Summary Static Route Configuration

Similar to the IPv4 static routing scenario, HQ can be configured with two summary static routes to the R1, R2, and R3 LANs. Example 23-13 shows the first four hextets (64 bits) of the five routes in binary, with the bits in common highlighted.

Example 23-13   Summary Route Calculation for HQ Static Routes

```
Summary calculation for the first four hextets of 2001:DB8:1:1::/64,
2001:DB8:1:2::/64, and 2001:DB8:1:3::/64 networks:
0010000000000001:0000110110111000:0000000000000001:0000000000000001::
0010000000000001:0000110110111000:0000000000000001:0000000000000010::
0010000000000001:0000110110111000:0000000000000001:0000000000000011::
Summary calculation for the first four hextets of 2001:DB8:1:A0::/64 and
  2001:DB8:1:A1::/64 networks:
0010000000000001:0000110110111000:0000000000000001:0000000010100000::
0010000000000001:0000110110111000:0000000000000001:0000000010100001::
```

Therefore, the first summary route is 2001:DB8:1::/62 because the three network addresses have 62 bits in common. Although this summary static route is not part of the current addressing scheme, it also includes the network 2001:DB8:1::/64. The second summary route is 2001:DB8:1:A0::/63 because the two network addresses have 63 bits in common.

You can now configure HQ with the following two summary static routes:

```
HQ(config)# ipv6 route 2001:DB8:1::/62 Serial0/0/0
HQ(config)# ipv6 route 2001:DB8:1:A0::/63 Serial0/0/0
```

Now HQ has two summary routes, as you can see in the highlighted entries in Example 23-14.

Example 23-14 HQ Routing Table with IPv6 Summary Static Routes

```
HQ# show ipv6 route
IPv6 Routing Table - 5 entries
<output omitted>
S    2001:DB8:1::/62 [1/0]
     via ::, Serial0/0/0
C    2001:DB8:1:F::/64 [0/0]
     via ::, Serial0/0/0
L    2001:DB8:1:F::1/128 [0/0]
     via ::, Serial0/0/0
S    2001:DB8:1:A0::/63 [1/0]
     via ::, Serial0/0/0
L    FF00::/8 [0/0]
     via ::, Null0
HQ#
```

 Packet Tracer Activity: Dual-Stack Static and Default Routing Configuration

Refer to the Digital Study Guide to access the PKA file for this activity. You must have Packet Tracer software to run this activity. See the Introduction for details.

Study Resources

For today's exam topics, refer to the following resources for more study.

Resource	Location	Topic
Primary Resources		
Routing and Switching Essentials	2	All
ICND1 Official Cert Guide	18	All
	32	Static IPv6 Routes
Supplemental Resources		
CCNA Portable Command Guide	12	All
CCNA Video Series	3	Lesson 3: Routing Fundamentals
		Configuring Static Routes for IPv4
		Configuring Static Routes for IPv6

Resource	Location	Topic
Supplemental Resources		
CCNA Network Simulator	ICND1	Chapter 18: Static Routing I–II
		Chapter 18: Configuring Default Routes
		Chapter 18: Configuring Router IP Settings
		Chapter 18: Configuring IP Addresses I–IV
		Chapter 18: IP Addressing I–III
		Chapter 18: Connected Routes
		Chapter 18: Static Routes I–IV
		Chapter 18: Default Route I–II

Check Your Understanding

Refer to the Digital Study Guide to take a short quiz covering the content of this day.

RIPv2 Implementation

CCNA 200-125 Exam Topics

- Configure, verify, and troubleshoot RIPv2 for IPv4 (excluding authentication, filtering, manual summarization, redistribution)
- Interpret the components of a routing table
- Describe how a routing table is populated by different routing information sources

Key Topic

Routing protocols specify a method for dynamically sending and receiving routing updates between routers. The simplest routing protocol to configure and understand is Routing Information Protocol (RIP). RIP is rarely used in networks today, but its simplicity makes RIP valuable to networking students who want to understand the basic operation of routing protocols. In fact, RIP is the only routing protocol the CCENT/ICND1 exam covers. RIP was chosen for this exam because a routing protocol was needed to address the other exam topics related to interpreting and describing the routing table. OSPF and EIGRP are more complex in operation than RIP, so they are reserved for the CCNA/ICND2 exam.

Today we review RIP operation, configuration, verification, and troubleshooting. We also use RIP to review how a routing table is built and examine the components of a routing table.

RIP Concepts

Because RIPv2 is an enhancement of RIPv1, you should be able to compare and contrast the two versions' concepts and configurations. First, let's look briefly at RIPv1.

RIPv1 Message Format

RIPv1 is a classful distance vector routing protocol for IPv4. It uses hop count as its only metric for path selection; a hop count greater than 15 is considered unreachable. RIPv1 routing messages are encapsulated in a UDP segment using port number 520 and are broadcast every 30 seconds. Figure 22-1 shows the RIPv1 message encapsulation from the data link layer up to and including the RIPv1 message.

Figure 22-1   RIPv1 Message Encapsulation

Data Link Frame Header	IP Packet Header	UDP Segment Header	RIP Message (512 Bytes: Up to 25 Routes)

Data Link Frame

MAC Source Address = Address of Sending Interface
MAC Destination Address = Broadcast: FF-FF-FF-FF-FF-FF

IP Packet

IP Source Address = Address of Sending Interface
IP Destination Address = Broadcast: 255.255.255.255
Protocol Field = 17 for UDP

UDP Segment

Source Port = 520
Destination Port = 520

RIP Message

Command: Request (1); Response (2)
Version = 1
Address Family ID = 2 for IP
Routes: Network IP Address
Metric: Hop Count

RIPv1 Operation

Notice in the RIP message that RIP uses two message types specified in the Command field. Command 1 is a Request message and Command 2 is a Response message.

Each RIP-configured interface sends out a Request message upon startup, requesting that all RIP neighbors send their complete routing tables. RIP-enabled neighbors send back a Response message. When the requesting router receives the responses, it evaluates each route entry. If a route entry is new, the receiving router installs the route in the routing table. If the route is already in the table, the existing entry is replaced if the new entry has a better hop count. The startup router then sends a triggered update out all RIP-enabled interfaces containing its own routing table so that RIP neighbors can learn any new routes.

RIPv1 does not send subnet mask information in the update. Therefore, a router either uses the subnet mask configured on a local interface or applies the default subnet mask based on the address class. Because of this limitation, RIPv1 networks cannot be discontiguous, nor can they implement VLSM or supernetting.

RIP has a default administrative distance of 120. When compared to other interior gateway protocols, RIP is the least-preferred routing protocol.

RIPv1 Configuration

Figure 22-2 and Table 22-1 show the RIPv1 topology for the first scenario and the addressing scheme we use to review RIPv1 configuration and verification.

Figure 22-2   RIPv1 Topology: Scenario A

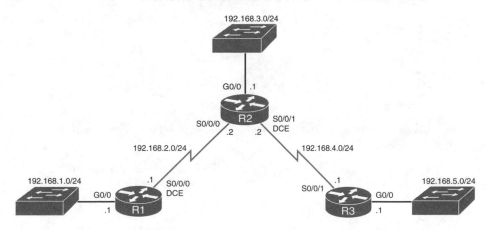

Table 22-1   Scenario A Addressing Scheme

Device	Interface	IP Address	Subnet Mask
R1	G0/0	192.168.1.1	255.255.255.0
	S0/0/0	192.168.2.1	255.255.255.0
R2	G0/0	192.168.3.1	255.255.255.0
	S0/0/0	192.168.2.2	255.255.255.0
	S0/0/1	192.168.4.2	255.255.255.0
R3	G0/0	192.168.5.1	255.255.255.0
	S0/0/1	192.168.4.1	255.255.255.0

Figure 22-2 shows six separate classful networks, so each network must be configured individually. Assuming that the interfaces on R1, R2, and R3 are configured and active, Example 22-1 shows the RIPv1 configuration for the routers.

Example 22-1   RIPv1 Standard Configuration: Scenario A

```
R1(config)# router rip
R1(config-router)# network 192.168.1.0
R1(config-router)# network 192.168.2.0

R2(config)# router rip
R2(config-router)# network 192.168.2.0
R2(config-router)# network 192.168.3.0
R2(config-router)# network 192.168.4.0

R3(config)# router rip
R3(config-router)# network 192.168.4.0
R3(config-router)# network 192.168.5.0
```

RIPv1 Verification and Troubleshooting

The following verification commands, used in order, quickly verify whether routing is operational as intended.

- **show ip route**
- **show ip protocols**
- **debug ip rip**

If routing is not functioning correctly, these commands will help you track down the problem in the most efficient manner.

To verify that routing is operational, start with the **show ip route** command. For the topology in Figure 22-2, all routes should be in the routing table for each router. Example 22-2 shows the routing table for R2.

Example 22-2   R2 Routing Table with RIP Routes Installed

```
R2# show ip route
Codes: L - local, C - connected, S - static, R - RIP, M - mobile, B - BGP
<some codes omitted>


Gateway of last resort is not set

R      192.168.1.0/24 [120/1] via 192.168.2.1, 00:00:19, Serial0/0/0
       192.168.2.0/24 is variably subnetted, 2 subnets, 2 masks
C         192.168.2.0/24 is directly connected, Serial0/0/0
L         192.168.2.2/32 is directly connected, Serial0/0/0
       192.168.3.0/24 is variably subnetted, 2 subnets, 2 masks
C         192.168.3.0/24 is directly connected, GigabitEthernet0/0
L         192.168.3.1/32 is directly connected, GigabitEthernet0/0
       192.168.4.0/24 is variably subnetted, 2 subnets, 2 masks
C         192.168.4.0/24 is directly connected, Serial0/0/1
L         192.168.4.2/32 is directly connected, Serial0/0/1
R      192.168.5.0/24 [120/1] via 192.168.4.1, 00:00:13, Serial0/0/1
R2#
```

To better understand the output from the **show ip route** command, let's focus on one RIP route learned by R2 and interpret the output shown in the routing table:

```
R 192.168.5.0/24 [120/1] via 192.168.4.1, 00:00:23, Serial0/0/1
```

Table 22-2 lists and describes each part of the output.

Table 22-2   Interpreting a RIP Route

Output	Description
R	Identifies the source of the route as RIP.
192.168.5.0	Indicates the address of the remote network.

Output	Description
/24	Indicates the subnet mask used for this network.
[120/1]	Shows the administrative distance (120) and the metric (1 hop).
via 192.168.4.1,	Specifies the address of the next-hop router (R2) to send traffic to for the remote network.
00:00:23,	Specifies the amount of time since the route was updated (here, 23 seconds). Another update is due in 7 seconds.
Serial0/0/1	Specifies the local interface through which the remote network can be reached.

If the routing table is missing one or more expected routes, use the **show ip protocols** command on the local router first to make sure RIP is configured and operating correctly. This command displays the routing protocol that is currently configured on the router. You can check the output to verify most RIP parameters to confirm the following:

- RIP routing is configured.

- The correct interfaces are sending and receiving RIP updates.

- The router is advertising the correct networks.

- RIP neighbors are sending updates.

Figure 22-3 shows the output from the **show ip protocols** command, with numbers by each portion of the output. The descriptions that follow the figure correspond to the numbers in the figure.

Figure 22-3   Interpreting show ip protocols Output

```
R2# show ip protocols
*** IP Routing is NSF aware ***

①—Routing Protocol is "rip"
②  { Outgoing update filter list for all interfaces is not set
     { Incoming update filter list for all interfaces is not set
③  { Sending updates every 30 seconds, next due in 23 seconds
     { Invalid after 180 seconds, hold down 180, flushed after 240
②——Redistributing: rip
     ⌠ Default version control: send version 1, receive any version
     │   Interface            Send  Recv  Triggered RIP  Key-chain
④  { GigabitEthernet0/0      1     1 2
     │   Serial0/0/0          1     1 2
     ⌡   Serial0/0/1          1     1 2
⑤  { Automatic network summarization is in effect
     { Maximum path: 4
     ⌠ Routing for Networks:
⑥  {   192.168.2.0
     │   192.168.3.0
     ⌡   192.168.4.0
     ⌠ Routing Information Sources:
     │   Gateway           Distance       Last Update
⑦  {   192.168.2.1            120         00:00:08
     │   192.168.4.1            120         00:00:05
     ⌡ Distance: (default is 120)
```

1. The first line of output verifies that RIP routing is configured and running on R2.

2. The filtering and redistribution information shown here is a CCNP-level topic.

3. These timers show when the next round of updates will be sent out from this router—23 seconds from now, in the example.

4. This block of output contains information about which RIP version is currently configured and which interfaces are participating in RIP updates. Notice that the router is sending version 1 updates but will receive both version 1 and version 2.

5. This part of the output shows that R2 is currently summarizing at the classful network boundary and, by default, will use up to four equal-cost routes to load-balance traffic.

6. The classful networks configured with the network command are listed next. If R2 has an active interface for the configured network, R2 will include the network in its RIP updates.

7. Here the RIP neighbors are listed as Routing Information Sources. Gateway is the next-hop IP address of the neighbor that is sending updates to R2. Distance is the AD that R2 uses for updates sent by this neighbor.

Most RIP configuration errors involve an incorrect network statement configuration, a missing network statement configuration, or the configuration of discontiguous subnets in a classful environment. As shown in Figure 22-4, **debug ip rip** helps in finding issues with RIP updates.

Figure 22-4   Interpreting debug ip rip Output

```
R2# debug ip rip
RIP protocol debugging is on
①  RIP: received v1 update from 192.168.2.1 on Serial0/0/0
        192.168.1.0 in 1 hops
②  RIP: received v1 update from 192.168.4.1 on Serial0/0/1
        192.168.5.0 in 1 hops
    RIP: sending v1 update to 255.255.255.255 via GigabitEthernet0/0
    (192.168.3.1)
    RIP: build update entries
③      network 192.168.1.0 metric 2
        network 192.168.2.0 metric 1
        network 192.168.4.0 metric 1
        network 192.168.5.0 metric 2
    RIP: sending v1 update to 255.255.255.255 via Serial0/0/1
    (192.168.4.2)
④  RIP: build update entries
        network 192.168.1.0 metric 2
        network 192.168.2.0 metric 1
        network 192.168.3.0 metric 1
    RIP: sending v1 update to 255.255.255.255 via Serial0/0/0
    (192.168.2.2)
⑤  RIP: build update entries
        network 192.168.3.0 metric 1
        network 192.168.4.0 metric 1
        network 192.168.5.0 metric 2
⑥  R2# undebug all
    All possible debugging has been turned off
```

This command displays RIP routing updates as they are sent and received, which gives you the opportunity to track down potential sources of a routing problem. The following list corresponds to the numbers in Figure 22-4.

1. You see an update coming in from R1 on interface Serial 0/0/0. Notice that R1 sends only one route to the 192.168.1.0 network. No other routes are sent because doing so would violate the split horizon rule. R1 is not allowed to advertise networks back to R2 that R2 previously sent to R1.

2. The next update that is received comes from R3. Again, because of the split horizon rule, R3 sends only one route: the 192.168.5.0 network.

3. R2 sends out its own updates. First, R2 does not have any passive interfaces configured. Therefore, R2 builds an update to send out the GigabitEthernet 0/0 interface even though there are no routers to receive the update. The update includes the entire routing table except for network 192.168.3.0, which is attached to GigabitEthernet 0/0.

4. Next, R2 builds an update to send to R3. Three routes are included. R2 does not advertise the network R2 and R3 share, nor does it advertise the 192.168.5.0 network because of split horizon.

5. Finally, R2 builds an update to send to R1. Three routes are included. R2 does not advertise the network that R2 and R1 share, nor does it advertise the 192.168.1.0 network because of split horizon.

6. To stop monitoring RIP updates on R2, enter the **no debug ip rip** command or **undebug all**, as in Figure 22-4.

Passive Interfaces

In the topology in Figure 22-2, notice that there is no reason to send updates out the GigabitEthernet interfaces on any of the routers. Therefore, you should configure these as passive interfaces for two reasons:

- To enhance security by preventing someone attached to one of the LANs from intercepting, inspecting, and possibly modifying the RIP updates

- To improve the efficiency of the routers' processing

Use the **passive-interface** command to stop sending RIP updates out the GigabitEthernet interfaces, as in Example 22-3 for R2. The **show ip protocols** command is then used to verify the passive interface configuration.

Example 22-3   Disabling Updates with the passive-interface Command

```
R2(config)# router rip
R2(config-router)# passive-interface GigabitEthernet 0/0
R2(config-router)# do show ip protocols
*** IP Routing is NSF aware ***
Routing Protocol is "rip"
  Outgoing update filter list for all interfaces is not set
  Incoming update filter list for all interfaces is not set
  Sending updates every 30 seconds, next due in 19 seconds
  Invalid after 180 seconds, hold down 180, flushed after 240
  Redistributing: rip
  Default version control: send version 1, receive any version
    Interface              Send  Recv  Triggered RIP  Key-chain
    Serial0/0/0              1     1 2
    Serial0/0/1              1     1 2
    Interface              Send  Recv  Triggered RIP  Key-chain
  Automatic network summarization is in effect
  Maximum path: 4
  Routing for Networks:
    192.168.2.0
    192.168.3.0
    192.168.4.0
  Passive Interface(s):
    GigabitEthernet0/0
  Routing Information Sources:
    Gateway         Distance      Last Update
    192.168.2.1         120       00:00:13
    192.168.4.1         120       00:00:05
  Distance: (default is 120)
```

Notice that the GigabitEthernet interface is no longer listed under **Interface**, but instead is listed under a new section called Passive Interface(s). Also notice that the network 192.168.3.0 is still listed under Routing for Networks, which means that this network is still included as a route entry in RIP updates that are sent to R1 and R3. All routing protocols support the **passive-interface** command.

Automatic Summarization

RIP automatically summarizes at the classful network boundary. Figure 22-5 and Table 22-3 show the RIPv1 topology for Scenario B and the addressing scheme we use for the rest of this RIPv1 review.

Figure 22-5   RIPv1 Topology: Scenario B

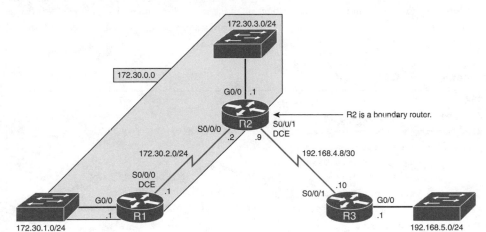

Table 22-3   RIPv1 Scenario B Addressing Scheme

Device	Interface	IP Address	Subnet Mask
R1	G0/0	172.30.1.1	255.255.255.0
	S0/0/0	172.30.2.1	255.255.255.0
R2	G0/0	172.30.3.1	255.255.255.0
	S0/0/0	172.30.2.2	255.255.255.0
	S0/0/1	192.168.4.9	255.255.255.252
R3	G0/0	192.168.5.1	255.255.255.0
	S0/0/1	192.168.4.10	255.255.255.252

Assuming that all interfaces are configured and activated, Example 22-4 shows the RIP
configuration for R1, R2, and R3.

Example 22-4   RIPv1 Standard Configuration: Scenario B

```
R1(config)# router rip
R1(config-router)# network 172.30.0.0

R2(config)# router rip
R2(config-router)# network 172.30.0.0
R2(config-router)# network 192.168.4.0

R3(config)# router rip
R3(config-router)# network 192.168.4.0
R3(config-router)# network 192.168.5.0
```

Notice that, in the RIP configuration for all routers, the classful network address was entered instead
of each subnet. If we had entered the subnets instead, Cisco IOS would have summarized them to

the classful network address. This is because a RIP router either uses the subnet mask configured on a local interface or applies the default subnet mask based on the address class. Therefore, RIPv1 cannot support discontiguous subnets, supernets, or VLSM addressing schemes. Example 22-5 shows what R2 sends in its updates to R1 and R3.

Example 22-5   R2 RIPv1 Updates

```
R2# debug ip rip
RIP protocol debugging is on
RIP: sending v1 update to 255.255.255.255 via Serial0/0/0 (172.30.2.2)
RIP: build update entries
        subnet 172.30.3.0 metric 1
        network 192.168.4.0 metric 1
        network 192.168.5.0 metric 2
RIP: sending v1 update to 255.255.255.255 via Serial0/0/1 (192.168.4.9)
RIP: build update entries
        network 172.30.0.0 metric 1
```

When R2 sends updates to R1, it sends the 172.30.3.0 network because the Serial 0/0/0 interface is using a /24 mask for the 172.30.2.0 network. However, it summarizes the 192.168.4.8 subnet to 192.168.4.0 before sending the update to R1 because R1 applies the default classful mask to the routing update. R2 is a boundary router for the 192.168.4.0 network. For its update to R3, R2 summarizes subnets 172.30.1.0, 172.30.2.0, and 172.30.3.0 to the classful network 172.30.0.0 because R2 is the boundary router for the 172.30.0.0 network and assumes R3 does not have any other way to get to the 172.30.0.0 network.

Default Routing and RIPv1

Using the same addressing scheme from Table 22-3, let's modify the topology as shown in Figure 22-6 so that R2 and R3 are using static and default routing.

Figure 22-6   RIPv1 Topology: Scenario B (Modified)

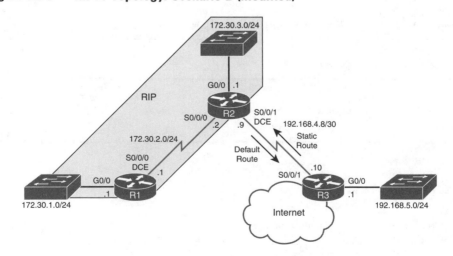

Example 22-6 shows the configuration changes made to R2 and R3. R3 is providing service to the Internet, so R2 will use a default route to send all traffic for unknown destinations to R3. R3 will use a summary route to send all traffic to the 172.30.0.0 subnets.

Example 22-6   Configuration Changes to R2 and R3

```
R2(config)# router rip
R2(config-router)# no network 192.168.4.0
R2(config-router)# exit
R2(config)# ip route 0.0.0.0 0.0.0.0 serial 0/0/1
```

```
R3(config)# no router rip
R3(config)# ip route 172.30.0.0 255.255.252.0 serial 0/0/1
```

We could configure R1 with a default route pointing to R2. A better and more scalable solution, however, is to use the **default-information originate** command to have R2 propagate its default route to R1 in its RIP routing updates.

```
R2(config)# router rip
R2(config-router)# default-information originate
```

As Example 22-7 shows, R1 now has a RIP route tagged with the asterisk (*) code, indicating that this route is a default gateway.

Example 22-7   Verifying Default Route Propagation

```
R1# show ip route
<output omitted>
Gateway of last resort is 172.30.2.2 to network 0.0.0.0

R*      0.0.0.0/0 [120/1] via 172.30.2.2, 00:00:00, Serial0/0/0
        172.30.0.0/16 is variably subnetted, 5 subnets, 2 masks
C          172.30.1.0/24 is directly connected, GigabitEthernet0/0
L          172.30.1.1/32 is directly connected, GigabitEthernet0/0
C          172.30.2.0/24 is directly connected, Serial0/0/0
L          172.30.2.1/32 is directly connected, Serial0/0/0
R          172.30.3.0/24 [120/1] via 172.30.2.2, 00:00:00, Serial0/0/0
R1#
```

RIPv2 Configuration

As in Version 1, RIPv2 is encapsulated in a UDP segment using port 520 and can carry up to 25 routes. Figure 22-7 shows the RIPv1 and RIPv2 message formats.

Figure 22-7   RIPv1 and RIPv2 Message Formats

RIPv1

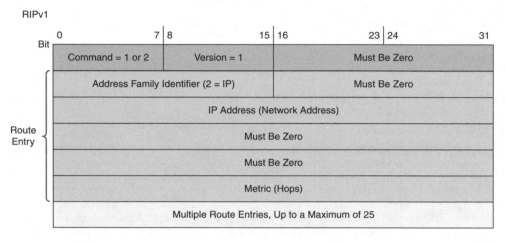

RIPv2

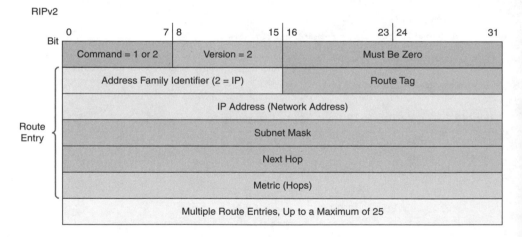

For review purposes, the most important extension RIPv2 provides is the addition of the subnet mask field, which allows a 32-bit mask to be included in the RIP route entry. As a result, the receiving router no longer depends on the subnet mask of the inbound interface or the classful mask when determining the subnet mask for a route. This means that RIPv1's three main limitations—lack of discontiguous network designs, supernetting, and VLSM support—are no longer an issue.

By default, the RIP process on Cisco routers sends RIPv1 messages but can receive both RIPv1 and RIPv2. You can see this in the **show ip protocols** output shown previously in Example 22-3. To enable the sending of RIPv2 messages in our topology, enter the command **version 2** in router configuration mode, as in Example 22-8.

Example 22-8   Configuring RIPv2

```
R2(config)# router rip
R2(config-router)# version 2
R2(config-router)# do show ip protocols
*** IP Routing is NSF aware ***

Routing Protocol is "rip"
  Outgoing update filter list for all interfaces is not set
  Incoming update filter list for all interfaces is not set
  Sending updates every 30 seconds, next due in 24 seconds
  Invalid after 180 seconds, hold down 180, flushed after 240
  Redistributing: rip
  Default version control: send version 2, receive version 2
    Interface              Send  Recv  Triggered RIP  Key-chain
    GigabitEthernet0/0      2     2
    Serial0/0/0             2     2
  Automatic network summarization is in effect
<output omitted>
```

With this configuration, R2 will now send and receive only RIPv2 messages. That means we must con-figure R1 with the **version 2** command as well because R2 will ignore the RIPv1 messages sent by R1.

 Packet Tracer Activity: RIPv2 Configuration

Refer to the Digital Study Guide to access the PKA file for this activity. You must have Packet Tracer software to run this activity. See the Introduction for details.

Disabling Autosummarization

Notice this line in the **show ip protocols** output from Example 22-8:

```
Automatic network summarization is in effect
```

By default, RIPv2 automatically summarizes networks to the classful boundary just as in RIPv1. To support discontiguous subnets and VLSM, you must first disable automatic summarization with the **no auto-summary** command on all RIPv2 routers to ensure that individual subnets are sent in routing updates—not the classful network address.

RIPv2 Verification and Troubleshooting

You can verify and troubleshoot RIPv2 in several ways. You can use many of the same commands for RIPv2 to verify and troubleshoot other routing protocols. Beginning with the basics is always best:

- Make sure all the links (interfaces) are up and operational.

- Check the cabling.

- Make sure you have the correct IP address and subnet mask on each interface.

- Remove any configuration commands that are no longer necessary or have been replaced by other commands.

Commands to use are the same as for RIPv1, as well as your standard use of **show ip interface brief**, **show run**, and **ping**. But also consider the following RIPv2 specific issues:

- **Version:** A good place to begin troubleshooting a network that is running RIP is to verify that the version 2 command is configured on all routers. RIPv1 does not support discontiguous subnets, VLSM, or CIDR supernet routes.

- **Network statements:** Another source of problems might be incorrectly configured or missing network statements configured with the network command. Remember, the network command does two things:

  - It enables the routing protocol to send and receive updates on any local interfaces that belong to that network.

  - It includes the configured network in its routing updates to its neighboring routers.

  A missing or incorrect network statement results in missed routing updates, as well as routing updates not being sent or received on an interface.

- **Automatic summarization:** If specific subnets must be sent instead of just summarized routes, make sure automatic summarization has been disabled with the **no auto-summary** command.

 Packet Tracer Activity: RIPv2 Troubleshooting

Refer to the Digital Study Guide to access the PKA file for this activity. You must have Packet Tracer software to run this activity. See the Introduction for details.

Study Resources

For today's exam topics, refer to the following resources for more study.

Resource	Location	Topic
Primary Resources		
Routing and Switching Essentials	3	RIPv2
ICND1 Official Cert Guide	19	All
Supplemental Resources		
CCNA Video Series	3	Lesson 5: Routing Information Protocol (RIP)
CCNA Network Simulator	ICND1	Chapter 19: RIP-2 Configuration I–II
		Chapter 19: RIP Configuration I–VI
		Chapter 19: RIP Verification I–II
		Chapter 19: IP Route Selection I–X
		Chapter 19: IP VLSM Route Selection I–VII

 Check Your Understanding

Refer to the Digital Study Guide to take a short quiz covering the content of this day.

VTP and Inter-VLAN Routing Configuration

CCNA 200-125 Exam Topics

- Configure, verify, and troubleshoot interswitch connectivity.

- Configure, verify, and troubleshoot inter-VLAN routing

Key Topics

Today we review two topics: VLAN Trunking Protocol (VTP) and inter-VLAN routing. Manually configuring VLANs across all switches in an enterprise network can become unmanageable. Therefore, Cisco developed VTP to help network administrators in large networks implement VLAN configurations. Because Layer 2 switches cannot perform the routing function, it is necessary to implement a Layer 3 device to route between VLANs.

VTP Concepts

VTP is a Layer 2 messaging protocol that maintains VLAN configuration consistency by managing the additions, deletions, and name changes of VLANs across networks.

VLAN trunking protocol (VTP) allows a network administrator to manage VLANs on a switch configured as a VTP server. The VTP server distributes and synchronizes VLAN information over trunk links to VTP-enabled switches throughout the switched network. This minimizes the problems caused by incorrect configurations and configuration inconsistencies.

> **NOTE:** The CCNA exam covers VTP version 1 and version 2. Extended-range VLANs (IDs greater than 1005) are not supported by VTP version 1 or version 2. VTP version 3 adds support for extended VLANs.

Table 21-1 describes the VTP components.

Table 21-1   VTP Components

VTP Component	Definitions
VTP domain	A VTP domain consists of one or more interconnected switches.
	All switches in a domain share VLAN configuration details using VTP advertisements.
	Switches in different VTP domains do not exchange VTP messages.
	A router or Layer 3 switch defines the boundary of each domain.

VTP Component	Definitions
VTP advertisements	Each switch in the VTP domain sends periodic global configuration advertisements from each trunk port to a reserved multicast address.
	Neighboring switches receive these advertisements and update their VTP and VLAN configurations as necessary.
VTP modes	A switch can be configured in one of three VTP modes: server, client, or transparent.
VTP password	Switches in the VTP domain can also be configured with a password.

Table 21-2 describes the VTP modes.

Table 21-2   VTP Modes

VTP Mode	Definition
VTP server	VTP servers advertise the VTP domain VLAN information to other VTP-enabled switches in the same VTP domain.
	VTP servers store the VLAN information for the entire domain in NVRAM.
	The VTP server is where VLANs can be created, deleted, or renamed for the domain.
VTP client	VTP clients function the same way as VTP servers, but you cannot create, change, or delete VLANs on a VTP client.
	A VTP client stores the VLAN information for the entire domain only while the switch is on.
	Reloading a VTP client causes it to lose all VLAN information until a VTP server updates the client.
	You must configure VTP client mode on a switch.
VTP transparent	Transparent switches do not participate in VTP except to forward VTP advertisements to VTP clients and VTP servers.
	VLANs that are created, renamed, or deleted on transparent switches are local to that switch only.
	To create an extended VLAN, a switch must be configured as a VTP transparent switch when using VTP versions 1 or 2.

Table 21-3 compares the difference in the functions of the three modes.

Table 21-3   VTP Mode Function

Function	Server	Client	Transparent
Sends VTP messages only out ISL or 802.1Q trunks	Yes	Yes	Yes
Allows CLI configuration of VLANs	Yes	No	Yes
Can use normal-range VLANs (1–1005)	Yes	Yes	Yes
Can use extended-range VLANs (1006–4095)	No	No	Yes
Synchronizes its own config database when receiving VTP messages with a higher revision number	Yes	Yes	No

Function	Server	Client	Transparent
Creates and sends periodic VTP updates every 5 minutes	Yes	Yes	No
Does not process received VTP updates, but does forward received VTP updates out other trunks	No	No	Yes

VTP Configuration and Verification

This section uses the sample topology in Figure 21-1.

Figure 21-1   VTP Topology

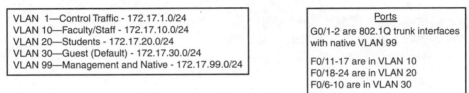

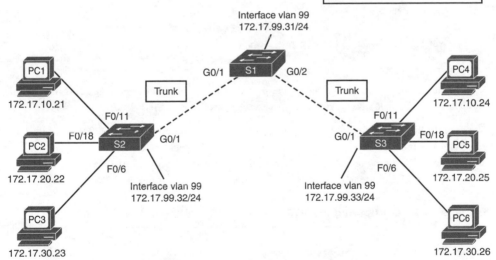

After choosing which switch will be the server and which switches will be clients, use the following steps to configure VTP:

Step 1.   Configure the VTP mode using the **vtp mode {server | client}** global configuration command.

Step 2.   (Optional, but recommended) On both clients and servers, configure the same case-sensitive password using the **vtp password** *password-value* global configuration command.

Step 3.   Configure the VTP (case-sensitive) domain name using the **vtp domain** *domain-name* global configuration command.

Step 4.   (Optional) Configure VTP pruning on the VTP servers using the **vtp pruning** global configuration command.

Step 5. (Optional) Enable VTP version 2 with the **vtp version 2** global configuration command.

Step 6. Bring up trunks between the switches.

Before configuring VTP, look at the default VTP state of S1. To do so, use the command **show vtp status**, as in Example 21-1.

Example 21-1 Default VTP Configuration on S1

```
S1# show vtp status
VTP Version                     : 2
Configuration Revision          : 0
Maximum VLANs supported locally : 255
Number of existing VLANs        : 5
VTP Operating Mode              : Server
VTP Domain Name                 :
VTP Pruning Mode                : Disabled
VTP V2 Mode                     : Disabled
VTP Traps Generation            : Disabled
MD5 digest                      : 0x7D 0x5A 0xA6 0x0E 0x9A 0x72 0xA0 0x3A
Configuration last modified by 0.0.0.0 at 0-0-00 00:00:00
Local updater ID is 0.0.0.0 (no valid interface found)
```

Notice that the configuration revision number is 0 and that the number of existing VLANs is 5—the five default VLANs that always exist on the switch. Also notice that S1 is already a VTP server.

The commands in Example 21-2 configure S1 as the server using **cisco** as the VTP password and **CCNA** as the VTP domain name. Because S2 and S3 share all the same VLANs, we are not configuring VTP pruning (enabled globally with the command **vtp pruning**). We also leave VTP in the default version 1 mode (enabled globally with the command **vtp version 2**).

Example 21-2 Configuring the VTP Server

```
S1# config t
Enter configuration commands, one per line. End with CNTL/Z.
S1(config)# vtp mode server
Device mode already VTP SERVER.
S1(config)# vtp password cisco
Setting device VLAN database password to cisco
S1(config)# vtp domain CCNA
Changing VTP domain name from NULL to CCNA
S1(config)# end
%SYS-5-CONFIG_I: Configured from console by console
S1#
```

We configured the VTP password before the VTP domain name for a specific reason. As soon as the VTP domain name is configured, S1 begins sending out VTP messages on all trunk links that are active.

If switches on the other end of the trunk are using the default VTP configuration (server mode, null as the domain name, and no password), they start using the domain name sent in the VTP messages. This can cause VLAN database corruption if the receiving switch has a higher configuration revision number than the configured server. The receiving switch is also a VTP server and sends out its VLAN database to the configured VTP server. By configuring the password first, we avoid the potential for this to happen. After the switches on the other end of the trunks are configured as clients, their configuration revision number is reset to 0. Then when the domain name and password are configured, the VTP server will request VTP updates.

We explicitly configured S1 as a VTP server instead of assuming it is in the default VTP server mode. The VTP password is not shown in the running-config or the startup-config. You can verify the VTP password with the **show vtp password** command.

Example 21-3 shows the commands to configure S2 as a client with the same password and domain name as S1. Repeat the same commands on S3.

Example 21-3   Configure the VTP Clients

```
S2# config t
Enter configuration commands, one per line. End with CNTL/Z.
S2(config)# vtp mode client
Setting device to VTP CLIENT mode.
S2(config)# vtp password cisco
Setting device VLAN database password to cisco
S2(config)# vtp domain CCNA
Changing VTP domain name from NULL to CCNA
S2(config)# end
%SYS-5-CONFIG_I: Configured from console by console
S2#
```

Again, verify the configuration with the **show vtp status** and **show vtp password** commands.

At this point, configure the VLANs on the VTP server, S1. You will not be able to create VLANs on S2 or S3. If you try, you will get the following console message:

```
S3(config)# vlan 10
VTP VLAN configuration not allowed when device is in CLIENT mode.
S3(config)#
```

Remember, however, that on the client switches, you will still be able to assign switch ports to specific VLANs.

After configuring the VLANs on S1, notice that the configuration revision number is incremented for each modification to the VLAN database. If you made no errors in your configuration, the configuration revision number should be 8, as in Example 21-4—one increment for each time you added one of the four VLANs and one increment for each time you named one of the VLANs. The server now has a total of nine VLANs: five default VLANs and four configured VLANs.

Example 21-4   Verifying the VTP Status and VLANs on the VTP Server

```
S1# show vtp status
VTP Version                    : 2
Configuration Revision         : 8
Maximum VLANs supported locally : 255
Number of existing VLANs       : 9
VTP Operating Mode             : Server
VTP Domain Name                : CCNA
VTP Pruning Mode               : Disabled
VTP V2 Mode                    : Disabled
VTP Traps Generation           : Disabled
MD5 digest                     : 0x69 0xB6 0x9B 0x54 0x91 0xF6 0xD9 0x39
Configuration last modified by 0.0.0.0 at 3-1-93 00:00:46
Local updater ID is 172.17.99.31 on interface Vl99 (lowest numbered VLAN
   interface found)
S1# show vlan brief


VLAN Name                            Status    Ports
---- -------------------------------- --------- -------------------------------
1    default                         active    Fa0/1, Fa0/2, Fa0/3, Fa0/4
                                                Fa0/5, Fa0/6, Fa0/7, Fa0/8
                                                Fa0/9, Fa0/10, Fa0/11, Fa0/12
                                                Fa0/13, Fa0/14, Fa0/15, Fa0/16
                                                Fa0/17, Fa0/18, Fa0/19, Fa0/20
                                                Fa0/21, Fa0/22, Fa0/23, Fa0/24
10   Faculty/Staff                   active
20   Students                        active
30   Guest(Default)                  active
99   Management&Native               active
1002 fddi-default                    active
1003 token-ring-default              active
1004 fddinet-default                 active
1005 trnet-default                   active
S1#
```

S2 and S3 have not received the VLANs yet because the trunks are not active between the switches and S1. In this case, configure the appropriate S1 interfaces to trunk and assign VLAN 99 as the native VLAN. In some cases, DTP autonegotiates the trunk links on S2 and S3. Now both client switches should have received VTP advertisements for S1. As Example 21-5 shows, both S2 and S3 have synchronized VLAN databases.

Example 21-5   Verifying S2 and S3 VTP Status

```
S2# show vtp status
VTP Version                    : 2
Configuration Revision         : 8
Maximum VLANs supported locally : 255
Number of existing VLANs       : 9
VTP Operating Mode             : Client
VTP Domain Name                : CCNA
VTP Pruning Mode               : Disabled
VTP V2 Mode                    : Disabled
VTP Traps Generation           : Disabled
MD5 digest                     : 0x0E 0xBA 0xA9 0x60 0xA2 0xB7 0x1B 0xA7
Configuration last modified by 0.0.0.0 at 3-1-93 00:00:46
S2#
```

```
S3# show vtp status
VTP Version                    : 2
Configuration Revision         : 8
Maximum VLANs supported locally : 255
Number of existing VLANs       : 9
VTP Operating Mode             : Client
VTP Domain Name                : CCNA
VTP Pruning Mode               : Disabled
VTP V2 Mode                    : Disabled
VTP Traps Generation           : Disabled
MD5 digest                     : 0x0E 0xBA 0xA9 0x60 0xA2 0xB7 0x1B 0xA7
Configuration last modified by 0.0.0.0 at 3-1-93 00:00:46
S3#
```

Inter-VLAN Routing Concepts

Inter-VLAN communications cannot occur without a Layer 3 device. Three options are available when implementing inter-VLAN routing:

- Traditional or legacy inter-VLAN routing
- Router on a stick
- Multilayer switch

Let's briefly review the concept of each method.

Legacy Inter-VLAN Routing

Legacy inter-VLAN routing requires multiple physical interfaces on both the router and the switch. When using a router to facilitate inter-VLAN routing, the router interfaces can be connected to separate VLANs. Devices on those VLANs send traffic through the router to reach other VLANs.

For example, in Figure 21-2, each S2 interface connected to R1 is assigned to a VLAN. The router is already configured with the appropriate IP addressing on each of its interfaces, so no additional configuration is required. However, you can see that if you used a separate interface for each VLAN on a router, you would quickly run out of interfaces.

Figure 21-2   Legacy Inter-VLAN Routing

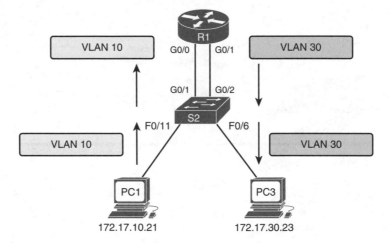

Router on a Stick

Today router software permits configuring one router interface as multiple trunks using subinterfaces. In Figure 21-3, the physical GigabitEthernet 0/0 interface is logically subdivided into two logical interfaces. The one switch trunk is configured to trunk both VLAN 10 and VLAN 30, and each subinterface on the router is assigned a separate VLAN. The router performs inter-VLAN routing by accepting VLAN-tagged traffic on the trunk interface coming from the adjacent switch. The router then forwards the routed traffic, VLAN-tagged for the destination VLAN, out the same physical interface as it used to receive the traffic.

Figure 21-3   Router on a Stick

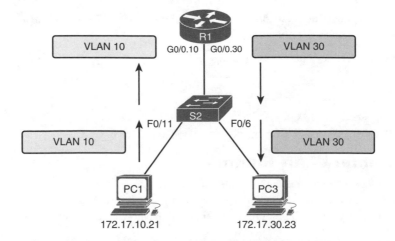

Multilayer Switch

Router on a stick works fine in a small business with one or two routers. But the most scalable solution in enterprise networks today is to use a multilayer switch to replace both the router and the switch, as in Figure 21-4. A multilayer switch performs both functions: switching traffic within the same VLAN and routing traffic between VLANs.

Figure 21-4   Multilayer Switch

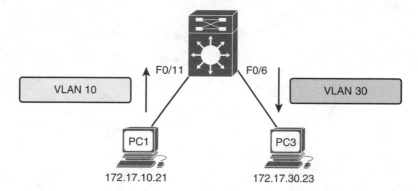

Multilayer switching is more scalable than any other inter-VLAN routing implementation, for these reasons:

- Routers have a limited number of available interfaces to connect to networks.

- Limited amounts of traffic can be accommodated on the physical link at one time.

With a multilayer switch, packets are forwarded down a single trunk line to obtain new VLAN-tagging information. A multilayer switch does not completely replace the functionality of a router but can be thought of as a Layer 2 device that is upgraded to have some routing capabilities.

Router on a Stick Configuration and Verification

When configuring inter-VLAN routing using the router on a stick model, the physical interface of the router must be connected to a trunk link on the adjacent switch. On the router, subinterfaces are created for each unique VLAN on the network. Each subinterface is assigned an IP address specific to its subnet/VLAN and is also configured to tag frames for that VLAN. This way, the router can keep the traffic from each subinterface separated as it traverses the trunk link back to the switch.

Configuring inter-VLAN routing is pretty straightforward. Refer to the sample topology in Figure 21-5 to review the commands.

Figure 21-5   Topology for Inter-VLAN Routing

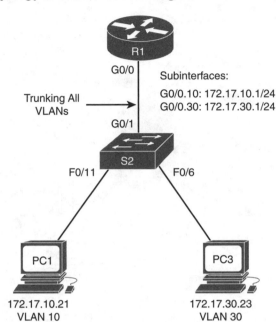

This router on a stick topology is configured using the following steps on the router:

Step 1.   Activate the physical interface that is trunking with the switch using the **no shutdown** command.

Step 2.   Enter subinterface configuration mode for the first VLAN that needs routing. One convention is to use the VLAN number as the subinterface number. For example, the **interface g0/1.10** command enters subinterface configuration mode for VLAN 10.

Step 3.   Configure the trunking encapsulation type using the subinterface configuration command **encapsulation {dot1q | isl}** *vlan-number* [**native**]. Set the encapsulation to **dot1q**.

   •   Inter-switch link (ISL) encapsulation, a Cisco proprietary trunking method, existed before the IEEE 802.1Q standard, which is now the recommended best practice. However, older switches that are still in use might support only ISL. In those cases, you substitute the **dot1q** keyword for **isl**.

   •   On some routers, the optional keyword **native** must be configured for the native VLAN before the router will route native VLAN traffic. The following examples do not use native VLAN routing; refer to your Study Resources for more on this topic.

Step 4.   Configure the IP address and subnet mask.

Step 5.   Repeat Steps 2–4 for each additional VLAN that needs routing.

Assuming that the switch is already configured with VLANs and trunking, Example 21-6 shows the commands to configure R1 to provide routing between VLAN 10 and VLAN 30.

Example 21-6   Configuring R1 to Route Between VLANs

```
R1(config)# interface g0/0
R1(config-if)# no shutdown
R1(config-if)# interface g0/1.10
R1(config-subif)# encapsulation dot1q 10
R1(config-subif)# ip address 172.17.10.1 255.255.255.0
R1(config-subif)# interface g0/1.30
R1(config-subif)# encapsulation dot1q 30
R1(config-subif)# ip address 172.17.30.1 255.255.255.0
```

To verify the configuration, use the **show vlans**, **show ip route**, and **show ip interface brief** commands to make sure that the new networks are in the routing table and that the subinterfaces are up and up, as in Example 21-7.

Example 21-7   Verifying the Inter-VLAN Routing Configuration

```
R1# show vlans
<output omitted>
Virtual LAN ID:  10 (IEEE 802.1Q Encapsulation)
   vLAN Trunk Interface:   GigabitEthernet0/0.10
   Protocols Configured:   Address:        Received:       Transmitted:
          IP              172.17.10.1            0               0
<output omitted>
Virtual LAN ID:  30 (IEEE 802.1Q Encapsulation)
   vLAN Trunk Interface:   GigabitEthernet0/0.30
   Protocols Configured:   Address:        Received:       Transmitted:
          IP              172.17.30.1            0               0
<output omitted>
R1# show ip route
<output omitted>


Gateway of last resort is not set


     172.17.0.0/16 is variably subnetted, 4 subnets, 2 masks
C        172.17.10.0/24 is directly connected, GigabitEthernet0/0.10
L        172.17.10.1/32 is directly connected, GigabitEthernet0/0.10
C        172.17.30.0/24 is directly connected, GigabitEthernet0/0.30
L        172.17.30.1/32 is directly connected, GigabitEthernet0/0.30
R1# show ip interface brief
Interface               IP-Address      OK? Method Status               Protocol
GigabitEthernet0/0      unassigned      YES unset  up                   up
GigabitEthernet0/0.10   172.17.10.1     YES manual up                   up
GigabitEthernet0/0.30   172.17.30.1     YES manual up                   up
```

```
GigabitEthernet0/1      unassigned      YES unset   administratively down down
Serial0/0/0             unassigned      YES manual  administratively down down
Serial0/0/1             unassigned      YES manual  administratively down down
Vlan1                   unassigned      YES manual  administratively down down
R1#
```

Assuming that the switch and PCs are configured correctly, the two PCs should now be able to ping each other. R1 will route the traffic between VLAN 10 and VLAN 30.

Multilayer Switch Inter-VLAN Routing Configuration and Verification

Most enterprise networks use multilayer switches to achieve high-packet processing rates using hardware-based switching. All Catalyst multilayer switches support the following types of Layer 3 interfaces:

- **Switch virtual interface (SVI):** Virtual VLAN interface used for inter-VLAN routing
- **Routed port:** Similar to a physical interface on a Cisco IOS router

All Layer 3 Cisco Catalyst switches support routing protocols (3500, 4500, and 6500 series). Catalyst 2960 Series switches running Cisco IOS Release 12.2(55) or later support static routing.

Creating Additional SVIs

The SVI for the default VLAN (VLAN1) already exists to permit remote switch administration. For a topology such as the one in Figure 21-6, additional SVIs must be explicitly created.

Figure 21-6   Switched Virtual Interfaces

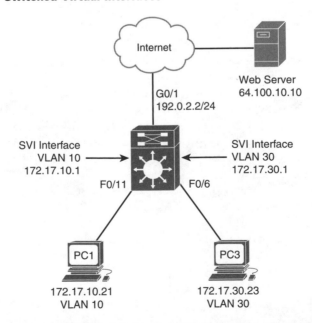

Create an SVI using the **interface vlan** *vlan-id* command. The *vlan-id* used corresponds to the VLAN tag associated with data frames coming from that VLAN. For example, when creating an SVI as a gateway for VLAN 10, use the **interface VLAN 10** command. Assign an IP address and enable the new SVI with the **no shutdown** command.

In addition, the switch must be configured to do Layer 3 routing with the **ip routing** global configuration command.

The following are some advantages of SVIs (the only disadvantage is that multilayer switches are more expensive):

- They are much faster than routers on a stick because everything is hardware switched and routed.

- No external links are needed from the switch to the router for routing.

- They are not limited to one link. Layer 2 EtherChannels can be used between the switches to get more bandwidth.

- Latency is much lower because it does not need to leave the switch.

Example 21-8 shows the configuration for the Layer 3 switch in Figure 21-6.

Example 21-8   Configuring a Switch to Use SVIs for Routing

```
MLS(config)# ip routing
MLS(config)# vlan 10
MLS(config)# vlan 30
MLS(config)# interface vlan 10
MLS(config-if)# ip address 172.17.10.1 255.255.255.0
MLS(config-if)# interface vlan 30
MLS(config-if)# ip address 172.30.10.1 255.255.255.0
MLS(config-if)# interface f0/11
MLS(config-if)# switchport mode access
MLS(config-if)# switchport access vlan 10
MLS(config-if)# interface f0/6
MLS(config-if)# switchport mode access
MLS(config-if)# switchport access vlan 30
MLS(config-if)# end
MLS# show ip route
<Code output omitted>

Gateway of last resort is not set

      172.17.0.0/24 is subnetted, 2 subnets
C        172.17.10.0 is directly connected, Vlan10
C        172.17.30.0 is directly connected, Vlan30
MLS#
```

Because the command **ip routing** is configured, MLS has a routing table. PC1 and PC3 can now ping each other.

Configuring a Layer 3 Routed Port

In Figure 21-6, notice that the GigabitEthernet 0/1 interface has an IP address assigned to it. To configure this interface as a routed port, turn off switching with the **no switchport** interface configuration command. Then configure the IP address as normal. The **ip routing** command was enabled in the previous step. However, the Layer 3 switch still needs a default route to send traffic to the Internet. Example 21-9 shows the commands to configure the routed port and default route.

Example 21-9   Configuring a Switch with a Routed Port

```
MLS(config)# interface g0/1
MLS(config-if)# no switchport
MLS(config-if)# ip address 192.0.2.2 255.255.255.0
!The no shutdown command is not required because switch interfaces are already
  activated.
MLS(config-if)# exit
MLS(config)# ip route 0.0.0.0 0.0.0.0 g0/1
MLS(config)# exit
MLS# show ip route
<Code output omitted>


Gateway of last resort is 0.0.0.0 to network 0.0.0.0


     172.17.0.0/24 is subnetted, 2 subnets
C        172.17.10.0 is directly connected, Vlan10
C        172.17.30.0 is directly connected, Vlan30
C    192.0.2.0/24 is directly connected, GigabitEthernet0/1
S*   0.0.0.0/0 is directly connected, GigabitEthernet0/1
MLS#
```

The **show ip route** command verifies that the Layer 3 switch has a route to the Internet. PC1 and PC3 can now access the web server.

 PacketTracer Activity: Router and Layer 3 Switch Inter-VLAN Routing Configuration

Refer to the Digital Study Guide to access the PKA file for this activity. You must have Packet Tracer software to run this activity. See the Introduction for details.

Study Resources

For today's exam topics, refer to the following resources for more study.

Resource	Location	Topic
Primary Resources		
Routing and Switching Essentials v6	6	Inter-VLAN Routing Using Routers
Scaling Networks v6	2	All

Resource	Location	Topic
Primary Resources		
ICND1 Official Cert Guide	18	Routing Between Subnets on VLANs
ICND2 Official Cert Guide	5	All
	19	All
Supplemental Resources		
CCNA Portable Command Guide	8	All
CCNA Video Series	2	VLAN Trunking Protocol (VTP)
CCNA Network Simulator	ICND1, 18	Router-on-a-Stick Configuration I
		Router-on-a-Stick Configuration II
		Router-on-a-Stick Verification I
		Router-on-a-Stick Verification II
	ICND2, 5	VTP I
		VTP Transparent Mode
	ICND2, 19	Router-on-a-Stick to MLS I
		Router-on-a-Stick to MLS II

 Check Your Understanding

Refer to the Digital Study Guide to take a short quiz covering the content of this day.

OSPF Operation

CCNA 200-125 Exam Topics

- Configure, verify, and troubleshoot single area and multiarea OSPFv2 for IPv4

- Configure, verify, and troubleshoot single area and multiarea OSPFv3 for IPv6

Key Topics

Today we review the basic operation of OSPF. OSPFv2 is used for IPv4 routing and OSPFv3 is used for IPv6 routing. Although the two versions share the same basic operation principles, we also review how they differ.

Single-Area OSPF Operation

The Internet Engineering Task Force (IETF) chose OSPF over Intermediate System–to–Intermediate System (IS-IS) as its recommended interior gateway protocol (IGP). In 1998, the OSPFv2 specification was updated in RFC 2328 and is the current RFC for OSPF. RFC 2328, "OSPF Version 2," is on the IETF website at http://www.ietf.org/rfc/rfc2328. Cisco IOS Software chooses OSPF routes over RIP routes because OSPF has an administrative distance of 110 versus RIP's AD of 120.

OSPF Message Format

The data portion of an OSPF message is encapsulated in a packet. This data field can include one of five OSPF packet types. Figure 20-1 shows an encapsulated OSPF message in an Ethernet frame.

The OSPF packet header is included with every OSPF packet, regardless of its type. The OSPF packet header and packet type-specific data are then encapsulated in an IP packet. In the IP packet header, the protocol field is set to 89 to indicate OSPF, and the destination address is typically set to one of two multicast addresses: 224.0.0.5 or 224.0.0.6. If the OSPF packet is encapsulated in an Ethernet frame, the destination MAC address is also a multicast address: 01-00-5E-00-00-05 or 01-00-5E-00-00-06.

Figure 20-1   Encapsulated OSPF Message

Data Link Frame Header	IP Packet Header	OSPF Packet Header	OSPF Packet Type-Specific Data

Data Link Frame (Ethernet Fields Shown Here)

MAC Source Address = Address of Sending Interface
MAC Destination Address = Multicast: 01-00-5E-00-00-05 or 01-00-5E-00-00-06

IP Packet

IP Source Address = Address of Sending Interface
IP Destination Address = Multicast: 224.0.0.5 or 224.0.0.6
Protocol Field = 89 for OSPF

OSPF Packet Header

Type Code for OSPF Packet Type
Router ID and Area ID

OSPF Packet Types

0x01 Hello
0x02 Database Description
0x03 Link State Request
0x04 Link State Update
0x05 Link State Acknowledgment

OSPF Packet Types

These five OSPF packet types each serve a specific purpose in the routing process:

- **Hello:** Hello packets establish and maintain adjacency with other OSPF routers.

- **DBD:** The database description (DBD) packet contains an abbreviated list of the sending router's link-state database. Receiving routers use it to check against the local link-state database.

- **LSR:** Receiving routers can request more information about any entry in the DBD by sending a link-state request (LSR).

- **LSU:** Link-state update (LSU) packets reply to LSRs and announce new information. LSUs contain 11 types of link-state advertisements (LSA).

- **LSAck:** When an LSU is received, the router sends a link-state acknowledgment (LSAck) to confirm receipt of the LSU.

 Activity: Identify the OSPF Packet Type

Refer to the Digital Study Guide to complete this activity.

Neighbor Establishment

OSPF neighbors exchange hello packets to establish adjacency. Figure 20-2 shows the OSPF header and hello packet.

Figure 20-2   OSPF Packet Header and Hello Packet

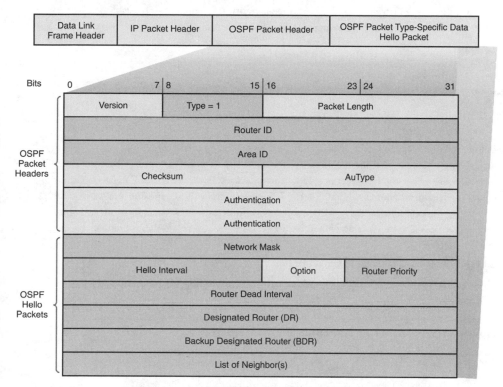

Important fields shown in the figure include the following:

- **Type**: OSPF packet type: Hello (Type 1), DBD (Type 2), LS Request (Type 3), LS Update (Type 4), LS ACK (Type 5)

- **Router ID**: ID of the originating router

- **Area ID**: Area from which the packet originated

- **Network Mask**: Subnet mask associated with the sending interface

- **Hello Interval**: Number of seconds between the sending router's hellos

- **Router Priority**: Used in DR/BDR election

- **Designated Router (DR)**: Router ID of the DR, if any

- **Backup Designated Router (BDR)**: Router ID of the BDR, if any

- **List of Neighbors**: The OSPF Router ID of the neighboring router(s)

Hello packets are used to do the following:

- Discover OSPF neighbors and establish neighbor adjacencies

- Advertise parameters on which two routers must agree to become neighbors

- Elect the DR and BDR on multiaccess networks such as Ethernet and Frame Relay

Receiving an OSPF hello packet on an interface confirms for a router that another OSPF router exists on this link. OSPF then establishes adjacency with the neighbor. To establish adjacency, two OSPF routers must have the following matching interface values:

- Hello Interval

- Dead Interval

- Network Type

- Area ID

Before both routers can establish adjacency, both interfaces must be part of the same network, including the same subnet mask. Full adjacency will happen after both routers have exchanged any necessary LSUs and have identical link-state databases. By default, OSPF hello packets are sent to the multicast address 224.0.0.5 (*ALLSPFRouters*) every 10 seconds on multiaccess and point-to-point segments, and every 30 seconds on nonbroadcast multiaccess (NBMA) segments (Frame Relay, X.25, ATM). The default dead interval is four times the hello interval.

Link-State Advertisements

LSUs are the packets used for OSPF routing updates. An LSU packet can contain 11 types of LSAs, as Figure 20-3 shows.

Figure 20-3   LSUs Contain LSAs

Type	Packet Name	Description
1	Hello	Discovers neighbors and builds adjacencies between them.
2	DBD	Checks for database synchronization between routers.
3	LSR	Requests specific link-state records from router to router.
4	LSU	Sends specifically requested link-state records.
5	LSAck	Acknowledges the other packet types.

The acronyms LSA and LSU are often used interchangeably.

An LSU contains one or more LSAs.

LSAs contain route information for destination networks.

LSA specifics are discussed in CCNP.

LSA Type	Description
1	Router LSAs
2	Network LSAs
3 or 4	Summary LSAs
5	Autonomous System External LSAs
6	Multicast OSPF LSAs
7	Defined for Not-So-Stubby Areas
8	External Attributes LSA for Border Gateway Protocol (BGP)
9, 10, 11	Opaque LSAs

OSPF DR and BDR

Multiaccess networks create two challenges for OSPF regarding the flooding of LSAs:

- Creation of multiple adjacencies, with one adjacency for every pair of routers

- Extensive flooding of LSAs

The solution to managing the number of adjacencies and the flooding of LSAs on a multiaccess network is the designated router (DR). To reduce the amount of OSPF traffic on multiaccess networks, OSPF elects a DR and a backup DR (BDR). The DR is responsible for updating all other OSPF routers when a change occurs in the multiaccess network. The BDR monitors the DR and takes over as DR if the current DR fails. All other routers become DROTHERs. A DROTHER is a router that is neither the DR nor the BDR.

OSPF Algorithm

Each OSPF router maintains a link-state database containing the LSAs received from all other routers. When a router has received all the LSAs and built its local link-state database, OSPF uses Dijkstra's shortest path first (SPF) algorithm to create an SPF tree. This algorithm accumulates costs along each path, from source to destination. The SPF tree is then used to populate the IP routing table with the best paths to each network.

For example, in Figure 20-4, each path is labeled with an arbitrary value for cost. The cost of the shortest path for R2 to send packets to the LAN attached to R3 is 27 (20 + 5 + 2 = 27). Notice that this cost is not 27 for all routers to reach the LAN attached to R3. Each router determines its own cost to each destination in the topology. In other words, each router uses the SPF algorithm to calculate the cost of each path to a network and determines the best path to that network from its own perspective.

Table 20-1 lists the shortest path to each LAN for R1, along with the cost.

Table 20-1   SPF Tree for R1

Destination	Shortest Path	Cost
R2 LAN	R1 to R2	22
R3 LAN	R1 to R3	7
R4 LAN	R1 to R3 to R4	17
R5 LAN	R1 to R3 to R4 to R5	27

You should be able to create a similar table for each of the other routers in Figure 20-4.

Figure 20-4   Dijkstra's Shortest Path First Algorithm

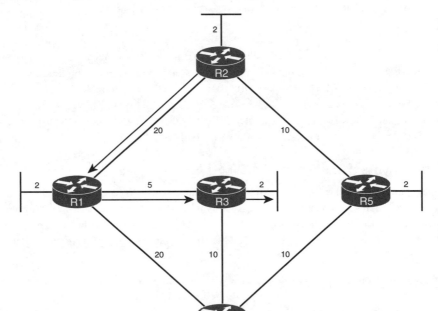

Shortest Path for Host on R2 LAN to Reach Host on R3 LAN:
R2 to R1 (20) + R1 to R3 (5) + R3 to LAN (2) = 27

Link-State Routing Process

The following list summarizes the link-state routing process OSPF uses. All OSPF routers complete the following generic link-state routing process to reach a state of convergence:

1. Each router learns about its own links and its own directly connected networks. This is done by detecting that an interface is in the up state, including a Layer 3 address.

2. Each router is responsible for establishing adjacency with its neighbors on directly connected networks by exchanging hello packets.

3. Each router builds a link-state packet (LSP) containing the state of each directly connected link. This is done by recording all the pertinent information about each neighbor, including neighbor ID, link type, and bandwidth.

4. Each router floods the LSP to all neighbors, who then store all LSPs received in a database. Neighbors then flood the LSPs to their neighbors until all routers in the area have received the LSPs. Each router stores a copy of each LSP received from its neighbors in a local database.

5. Each router uses the database to construct a complete map of the topology and computes the best path to each destination network. The SPF algorithm is used to construct the map of the topology and determine the best path to each network. All routers have a common map or tree of the topology, but each router independently determines the best path to each network within that topology.

OSPFv2 Versus OSPFv3

In 1999, OSPFv3 for IPv6 was published in RFC 2740. In 2008, OSPFv3 was updated in RFC 5340 as OSPF for IPv6. However, it is still referred to as OSPFv3.

OSPFv3 has the same functionality as OSPFv2 but uses IPv6 as the network layer transport, communicating with OSPFv3 peers and advertising IPv6 routes. OSPFv3 also uses the SPF algorithm as the computation engine to determine the best paths throughout the routing domain.

As with all IPv6 routing protocols, OSPFv3 has separate processes from its IPv4 counterpart. OSPFv2 and OSPFv3 each have separate adjacency tables, OSPF topology tables, and IP routing tables.

Similarities Between OSPFv2 and OSPFv3

OSPFv3 operates much like OSPFv2. Table 20-2 summarizes the operational features that OSPFv2 and OSPFv3 share.

Table 20-2   OSPFv2 and OSPFv3 Similarities

Feature	OSPFv2 and OSPFv3
Link state	Yes
Routing algorithm	SPF
Metric	Cost
Areas	Support the same two-level hierarchy
Packet types	Use the same hello, DBD, LSR, LSU, and LSAck packets
Neighbor discovery	Transition through the same states using hello packets
LSDB synchronization	Exchange contents of their LSDB between two neighbors
DR and BDR	Use the same function and election process
Router ID	Use a 32-bit Router ID and the same process in determining the 32-bit Router ID

Differences Between OSPFv2 and OSPFv3

Table 20-3 lists the major differences between OSPFv2 and OSPFv3.

Table 20-3   OSPFv2 and OSPFv3 Differences

Feature	OSPFv2	OSPFv3
Advertising	IPv4 networks	IPv6 prefixes
Source address	IPv4 source address	IPv6 link-local address
Destination address	Choice of: Neighbor IPv4 unicast address 224.0.0.5, all–OSPF-routers multicast address 224.0.0.6, DR/BDR multicast address	Choice of: Neighbor IPv6 link-local address FF02::5, all–OSPFv3-routers multicast address FF02::6, DR/BDR multicast address
Advertising networks	Configured using the **network** router configuration command	Configured using the **ipv6 ospf area** interface configuration command
IP unicast routing	IPv4 unicast routing enabled by default	Requires configuration of the **ipv6 unicast-routing** global configuration command
Authentication	Plain text and MD5	IPsec

 Activity: Compare OSPFv2 and OSPFv3

Refer to the Digital Study Guide to complete this activity.

Multiarea OSPF Operation

Single-area OSPF works fine in smaller networks in which the number of links is manageable. However, consider an OSPF single-area network with 900 routers and several thousand subnets. In this situation, the single-area design causes the following problems:

- **Large routing tables:** By default, OSPF does not summarize routing updates.

- **Large link-state database (LSDB):** In a single area, each router must maintain a database of all active links in the routing domain, regardless of whether that router is currently using a particular link.

- **Frequent SPF calculations:** In a large network, changes to the LSDB can cause routers to spend many CPU cycles recalculating the SPF algorithm and updating the routing table.

To address these issues, OSPF supports hierarchical design through the uses of multiple OSPF areas. Multiarea OSPF is useful in larger network deployments to reduce processing and memory overhead. This breaks the one large LSDB into several smaller LSDBs by using multiple OSPF areas.

Multiarea OSPF Design

Multiarea OSPF design follows a couple basic rules:

- Put all interfaces connected to the same subnet inside the same area.

- An area should be contiguous.

- Some routers might be internal to an area, with all interfaces assigned to that single area.

- Some routers might be Area Border Routers (ABR) because some interfaces connect to the backbone area and some connect to nonbackbone areas.

- All nonbackbone areas must connect to the backbone area (area 0) by having at least one ABR connected to both the backbone area and the nonbackbone area.

Figure 20-5 shows a simple multiarea OSPF design with two areas (Area 1 and Area 2) connected to a backbone, Area 0.

Figure 20-5   Sample Multiarea OSPF Design

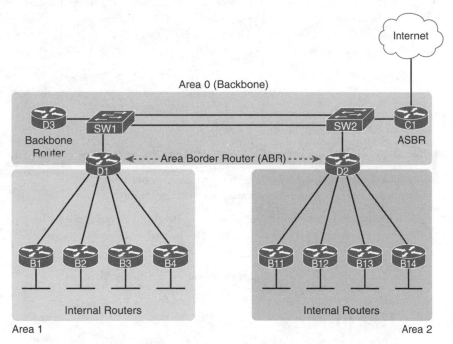

The figure also shows a few important multiarea OSPF design terms. Table 20-4 summarizes the meaning of these terms.

Table 20-4   Multiarea OSPF Design Terminology

Term	Description
Area Border Router (ABR)	An OSPF router with interfaces connected to the backbone area and to at least one other area.
Backbone router	A router connected to the backbone area (includes ABRs).
Internal router	A router in one area (not the backbone area).
Autonomous System Boundary Router (ASBR)	A router that has at least one interface connected to an external network. An external network is a network that is not part of the routing domain, such as EIGRP, BGP, or one with static routing to the Internet, as Figure 20-5 shows.

Term	Description
Area	A set of routers and links that shares the same detailed LSDB information, but not with routers in other areas, for better efficiency.
Backbone area	A special OSPF area to which all other areas must connect, such as Area 0.
Intra-area route	A route to a subnet inside the same area as the router.
Interarea route	A route to a subnet in an area the router is not a part of.

Multiarea OSPF Improves Performance

In multiarea OSPF, all areas must connect to the backbone area. Routing still occurs between the areas. ABRs send interarea routes between areas. However, the CPU intensive routing operation of recalculating the SPF algorithm is done only for routes within an area. A change in one area does not cause an SPF algorithm recalculation in other areas.

In Figure 20-5, assume that a link fails in Area 1. Only the routers in Area 1 exchange LSAs. D1, the ABR for Area 1, will send one update to Area 0 after Area 1 has converged on the new information.

The following list summarizes how multiarea OSPF improves OSPF performance:

- The smaller per-area LSDB requires less memory.

- Routers require fewer CPU cycles to process the smaller per-area LSDB with the SPF algorithm, reducing CPU overhead and improving convergence time.

- Changes in the network (for example, links failing and recovering) require SPF calculations only on routers connected to the area where the link changed state, reducing the number of routers that must rerun SPF.

- Less information must be advertised between areas, reducing the bandwidth required to send LSAs.

Study Resources

For today's exam topics, refer to the following resources for more study.

Resource	Location	Topic
Primary Resources		
Scaling Networks v6	8	OSPF Characteristics
		Single-Area OSPFv2 (OSPF Router ID)
		Single-Area OSPFv3 (OSPFv2 vs. OSPFv3)
	9	Multiarea OSPF Operation
ICND2 Official Cert Guide	7	OSPF Concepts and Operation
		OSPF Area Design

Resource	Location	Topic
Supplemental Resources		
CCNA Portable Command Guide	15	OSPFv2 versus OSPFv3
		Multiarea OSPF Router Types
CCNA Video Series	3	OSPF Overview
		OSPF Neighbor Formation
		OSPF Areas

Check Your Understanding

Refer to the Digital Study Guide to take a short quiz covering the content of this day.

Single-Area OSPF Implementation

CCNA 200-125 Exam Topics

- Configure, verify, and troubleshoot single area and multiarea OSPFv2 for IPv4
- Configure, verify, and troubleshoot single area and multiarea OSPFv3 for IPv6

Key Topics

Today we review the basic implementation of OSPFv2 and OSPFv3 for single-area network designs. We review the commands to configure and verify the implementation. Tomorrow we review the basic implementation of multiarea OSPF.

Single-Area OSPFv2 Configuration

To review the single-area OSPFv2 configuration commands, we use the topology in Figure 19-1 and the addressing scheme in Table 19-1.

Table 19-1   Addressing Scheme for OSPFv2

Device	Interface	IP Address	Subnet Mask
R1	G0/0	172.16.1.1	255.255.255.0
	S0/0/0	172.16.3.1	255.255.255.252
	S0/0/1	192.168.10.5	255.255.255.252
R2	G0/0	172.16.2.1	255.255.255.0
	S0/0/0	172.16.3.2	255.255.255.252
	S0/0/1	192.168.10.9	255.255.255.252
R3	G0/0	192.168.1.1	255.255.255.0
	S0/0/0	192.168.10.6	255.255.255.252
	S0/0/1	192.168.10.10	255.255.255.252

Figure 19-1   OSPFv2 Configuration Topology

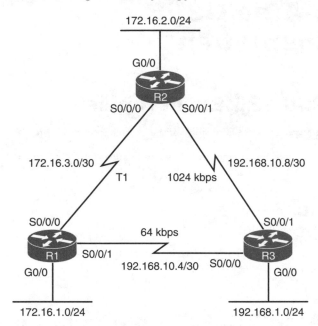

The router ospf Command

OSPF is enabled with the **router ospf** *process-id* global configuration command:

```
R1(config)# router ospf process-id
```

The *process-id* is a number between 1 and 65,535 and is chosen by the network administrator. The process ID is locally significant. It does not have to match other OSPF routers to establish adjacencies with those neighbors. This differs from Enhanced Interior Gateway Routing Protocol (EIGRP). The EIGRP process ID and autonomous system number must match before two EIGRP neighbors will become adjacent.

For our review, we enable OSPF on all three routers using the same process ID of 10.

Router ID

The router ID plays an important role in OSPF by uniquely identifying each router in the OSPF routing domain. Cisco routers derive the router ID based on three criteria in the following order:

1. The router uses the IP address configured with the OSPF **router-id** command.

2. If the router ID is not configured, the router chooses the highest IP address of any of its loopback interfaces.

3. If no loopback interfaces are configured, the router chooses the highest active IP address of any of its physical interfaces.

The router ID can be viewed with several commands, including **show ip ospf interfaces, show ip protocols**, and **show ip ospf.**

Because the network administrator can control the OSPF **router-id** command and because loop-back interfaces clutter the routing table, it is a best practice to configure the **router-id** command. The **router-id** command accepts an IPv4 address as its only argument. Example 19-1 shows the router ID configurations for the routers in our topology.

Example 19-1   Router ID Configurations

```
R1(config-router)# router-id 1.1.1.1
```

```
R2(config-router)# router-id 2.2.2.2
```

```
R3(config-router)# router-id 3.3.3.3
```

The router ID is selected when OSPF is configured with its first OSPF **network** command, so the **router-id** command should already be configured. However, you can force OSPF to release its current ID and use the configured router ID by clearing the OSPF routing process:

```
Router# clear ip ospf process
```

The network Command

The **network** command is used in router configuration mode:

```
Router(config-router)# network network-address wildcard-mask area area-id
```

The OSPF **network** command uses a combination of *network-address* and *wildcard-mask*. The network address, along with the wildcard mask, specifies the interface or range of interfaces that will be enabled for OSPF using this **network** command.

The wildcard mask is customarily configured as the inverse of a subnet mask. For example, R1's Serial 0/0/0 interface is on the 172.16.3.0/30 network. The subnet mask for this interface is /30 or 255.255.255.252. The inverse of the subnet mask results in the wildcard mask 0.0.0.3.

The **area** *area-id* refers to the OSPF area. An OSPF area is a group of routers that share link-state information. All OSPF routers in the same area must have the same link-state information in their link-state databases. Therefore, all the routers within the same OSPF area must be configured with the same area ID on all routers. By convention, the area ID is 0.

As an alternative, OSPFv2 can be enabled using the **network** *intf-ip-address* **0.0.0.0 area** *area-id* router configuration mode command.

Example 19-2 shows the **network** commands for all three routers, enabling OSPF on all interfaces. For R1, the alternative interface IP address and quad zero wildcard mask is configured.

Example 19-2   Configuring OSPF Networks

```
R1(config)# router ospf 10
R1(config-router)# network 172.16.1.1 0.0.0.0 area 0
R1(config-router)# network 172.16.3.1 0.0.0.0 area 0
R1(config-router)# network 192.168.10.5 0.0.0.0 area 0
```

```
R2(config)# router ospf 10
R2(config-router)# network 172.16.2.0 0.0.0.255 area 0
R2(config-router)# network 172.16.3.0 0.0.0.3 area 0
R2(config-router)# network 192.168.10.8 0.0.0.3 area 0
```

```
R3(config)# router ospf 10
R3(config-router)# network 192.168.1.0 0.0.0.255 area 0
R3(config-router)# network 192.168.10.4 0.0.0.3 area 0
R3(config-router)# network 192.168.10.8 0.0.0.3 area 0
```

Passive Interfaces

By default, OSPF messages are forwarded out all OSPF-enabled interfaces. However, these messages really need to be sent out only interfaces that connect to other OSPF-enabled routers. Sending out unneeded messages on a LAN affects the network in three ways:

- **Inefficient use of bandwidth:** Available bandwidth is consumed transporting unnecessary messages.

- **Inefficient use of resources:** All devices on the LAN must process the message.

- **Increased security risk:** OSPF messages can be intercepted and routing updates can be modified, corrupting the routing table.

Use the **passive-interface** command to prevent OSPF updates from being sent out unnecessary interfaces. For our topology in Figure 19-1, each router's GigabitEthernet 0/0 interface should be set to passive with the following command:

```
Router(config)# passive-interface gigabitethernet 0/0
```

As an alternative, all interfaces can be made passive using the **passive-interface default** command. Then interfaces that should not be passive can be reenabled using the **no passive-interface** *interface* command.

Modifying the OSPF Metric

Cisco IOS Software uses the cumulative bandwidths of the outgoing interfaces from the router to the destination network as the cost value. At each router, the cost for an interface is calculated using the following formula:

Cisco IOS Cost for OSPF = 10^8/bandwidth in bps

In this calculation, the value 10^8 is known as the *reference bandwidth*. Table 19-2 shows the default OSPF costs using the default reference bandwidth for several types of interfaces.

Table 19-2   Cisco Default OSPF Cost Values

Interface Type	10^8/bps = Cost	Cost
10 Gigabit Ethernet (10 Gbps)	10^8/10,000,000,000 bps = 1	1
Gigabit Ethernet (1 Gbps)	10^8/1,000,000,000 bps = 1	1
Fast Ethernet (100 Mbps)	10^8/100,000,000 bps = 1	1
Ethernet (10 Mbps)	10^8/10,000,000 bps = 10	10
T1 (1.544 Mbps)	10^8/1,544,000 bps = 64	64
128 kbps	10^8/128,000 bps = 781	781
64 kbps	10^8/64,000 bps = 1562	1562

In Table 19-2, 10GigE, Gigabit Ethernet, and Fast Ethernet all have the same cost. That is because the OSPF cost value must be an integer. This was not an issue before the introduction of gigabit and higher data rates.

However, today's networks are certainly running at gigabit speeds. Therefore, as a matter of policy, you should change the reference bandwidth to accommodate networks with links faster than 100,000,000 bps (100 Mbps). Use the following command to change the reference bandwidth:

```
Router(config-router)# auto-cost reference-bandwidth Mbps
```

Because the value entered is in megabits per second, changing the reference bandwidth to 10000 ensures that all OSPF routers are ready to accurately calculate the cost for 10GigE networks. When used, this command should be entered on all routers so that the OSPF routing metric remains consistent. In fact, the Cisco IOS replies with the follow syslog message when you configure the **auto-cost reference-bandwidth** command:

```
% OSPF: Reference bandwidth is changed.
        Please ensure reference bandwidth is consistent across all routers.
```

For our topology in Figure 19-1, we enter the commands shown in Example 19-3.

Example 19-3   Changing the OSPF Reference Bandwidth

```
R1(config-router)# auto-cost reference-bandwidth 10000

R2(config-router)# auto-cost reference-bandwidth 10000

R3(config-router)# auto-cost reference-bandwidth 10000
```

Table 19-3 shows the modified cost values with the new reference bandwidth of 10,000,000,000 bps, or 10^{10}.

Table 19-3   OSPF Cost Values with Modified Reference Bandwidth = 10000

Interface Type	10^{10}/bps = Cost	Cost
10 Gigabit Ethernet (10 Gbps)	10^{10}/10,000,000,000 bps = 1	1
Gigabit Ethernet (1 Gbps)	10^{10}/1,000,000,000 bps = 1	10
Fast Ethernet (100 Mbps)	10^{10}/100,000,000 bps = 1	100
Ethernet (10 Mbps)	10^{10}/10,000,000 bps = 10	1000
T1 (1.544 Mbps)	10^{10}/1,544,000 bps = 64	6477
128 kbps	10^{10}/128,000 bps = 781	78125
64 kbps	10^{10}/64,000 bps = 1562	156250 (see the Note)

NOTE: Although the cost for a 64 kbps speed calculates to 156250, the maximum OSPF cost for a Cisco router interface is 65535.

But we are not done: We still have one more adjustment to make to ensure that OSPF is using accurate costs. On Cisco routers, the default bandwidth on most serial interfaces is set to T1 speed, or 1.544 Mbps. But in our topology in Figure 19-1, we have the following actual speeds:

- The link between R1 and R2 is running at 1544 kbps (default value).

- The link between R2 and R3 is running at 1024 kbps.

- The link between R1 and R3 is running at 64 kbps.

You can modify the OSPF metric in two ways:

- Use the **bandwidth** command to modify the bandwidth value the Cisco IOS Software uses in calculating the OSPF cost metric.

- Use the **ip ospf cost** command, which enables you to directly specify the cost of an interface.

An advantage of configuring a cost over setting the interface bandwidth is that the router does not have to calculate the metric when the cost is manually configured. Also, the **ip ospf cost** command is useful in multivendor environments, where non-Cisco routers can use a metric other than bandwidth to calculate the OSPF costs.

Table 19-4 shows the two alternatives that can be used in modifying the costs of the serial links in the topology in Figure 19-1. The right side of the figure shows the **ip ospf cost** command equivalents of the **bandwidth** commands on the left.

Table 19-4   Comparing the bandwidth and ip ospf cost Commands

Adjusting the Interface Bandwidth	=	Manually Setting the OSPF Cost
R1(config)# **interface S0/0/1** R1(config-if)# **bandwidth 64**	=	R1(config)# **interface S0/0/1** R1(config-if)# **ip ospf cost 65535**
R2(config)# **interface S0/0/1** R2(config-if)# **bandwidth 1024**	=	R2(config)# **interface S0/0/1** R2(config-if)# **ip ospf cost 9765**

Adjusting the Interface Bandwidth	=	Manually Setting the OSPF Cost
R3(config)# **interface S0/0/0**	=	R3(config)# **interface S0/0/0**
R3(config-if)# **bandwidth 64**		R3(config-if)# **ip ospf cost 65535**
R3(config)# **interface S0/0/1**	=	R3(config)# **interface S0/0/1**
R3(config-if)# **bandwidth 1024**		R3(config-if)# **ip ospf cost 9765**

NOTE: The 64 kbps interface is set to the maximum cost of 65535.

Verifying OSPFv2

To verify any routing configuration, you will most likely depend on the **show ip interface brief**, **show ip route**, and **show ip protocols** commands. All the expected interfaces should be up and up and should be configured with the correct IP address. The routing table should have all the expected routes. The protocol status should show routing for all expected networks, as well as show all expected routing sources. Example 19-4 shows R1's output from these three basic commands.

Example 19-4 R1 Basic Routing Verification Commands

```
R1# show ip route
<output omitted>

Gateway of last resort is not set

      172.16.0.0/16 is variably subnetted, 5 subnets, 3 masks
C        172.16.1.0/24 is directly connected, GigabitEthernet0/0
L        172.16.1.1/32 is directly connected, GigabitEthernet0/0
O        172.16.2.0/24 [110/6576] via 172.16.3.2, 00:04:57, Serial0/0/0
C        172.16.3.0/30 is directly connected, Serial0/0/0
L        172.16.3.1/32 is directly connected, Serial0/0/0
O     192.168.1.0/24 [110/16341] via 172.16.3.2, 00:00:41, Serial0/0/0
      192.168.10.0/24 is variably subnetted, 3 subnets, 2 masks
C        192.168.10.4/30 is directly connected, Serial0/0/1
L        192.168.10.5/32 is directly connected, Serial0/0/1
O        192.168.10.8/30 [110/16241] via 172.16.3.2, 00:00:41, Serial0/0/0
R1# show ip interface brief
Interface                     IP-Address      OK? Method Status                Protocol
Embedded-Service-Engine0/0    unassigned      YES unset  administratively down  down
GigabitEthernet0/0            172.16.1.1      YES manual up                     up
GigabitEthernet0/1            unassigned      YES unset  administratively down  down
Serial0/0/0                   172.16.3.1      YES manual up                     up
Serial0/0/1                   192.168.10.5    YES manual up                     up
```

```
R1# show ip protocols
*** IP Routing is NSF aware ***


Routing Protocol is "ospf 10"
  Outgoing update filter list for all interfaces is not set
  Incoming update filter list for all interfaces is not set
  Router ID 1.1.1.1
  Number of areas in this router is 1. 1 normal 0 stub 0 nssa
  Maximum path: 4
  Routing for Networks:
    172.16.1.0 0.0.0.255 area 0
    172.16.3.0 0.0.0.3 area 0
    192.168.10.4 0.0.0.3 area 0
  Passive Interface(s):
    GigabitEthernet0/0
  Routing Information Sources:
    Gateway         Distance      Last Update
    3.3.3.3         110           00:09:00
    2.2.2.2         110           00:09:00
  Distance: (default is 110)
```

You can verify that expected neighbors have established adjacency with the **show ip ospf neighbor** command. Example 19-5 shows the neighbor tables for all three routers.

Example 19-5   Verifying Neighbor Adjacency

```
R1# show ip ospf neighbor


Neighbor ID     Pri   State        Dead Time    Address         Interface
3.3.3.3          0    FULL/   -    00:00:37     192.168.10.6    Serial0/0/1
2.2.2.2          0    FULL/   -    00:00:37     172.16.3.2      Serial0/0/0


R2# show ip ospf neighbor


Neighbor ID     Pri   State        Dead Time    Address         Interface
3.3.3.3          0    FULL/   -    00:00:38     192.168.10.10   Serial0/0/1
1.1.1.1          0    FULL/   -    00:00:37     172.16.3.1      Serial0/0/0


R3# show ip ospf neighbor


Neighbor ID     Pri   State        Dead Time    Address         Interface
2.2.2.2          0    FULL/   -    00:00:37     192.168.10.9    Serial0/0/1
1.1.1.1          0    FULL/   -    00:00:30     192.168.10.5    Serial0/0/0
```

For each neighbor, this command displays the following output:

- **Neighbor ID:** The router ID of the neighboring router.

- **Pri:** The OSPF priority of the interface. These all show 0 because point-to-point links do not elect a DR or BDR.

- **State:** The OSPF state of the interface. FULL state means that the router's interface is fully adjacent with its neighbor and they have identical OSPF link-state databases.

- **Dead Time:** The amount of time remaining that the router will wait to receive an OSPF hello packet from the neighbor before declaring the neighbor down. This value is reset when the interface receives a hello packet.

- **Address:** The IP address of the neighbor's interface to which this router is directly connected.

- **Interface:** The interface on which this router has formed adjacency with the neighbor.

The **show ip ospf** command in Example 19-6 for R1 can also be used to examine the OSPF process ID and router ID. In addition, this command displays the OSPF area information and the last time that the SPF algorithm was calculated.

Example 19-6   The show ip ospf Command

```
R1# show ip ospf
Routing Process "ospf 10" with ID 1.1.1.1
 Start time: 00:29:52.316, Time elapsed: 00:45:15.760
 Supports only single TOS(TOS0) routes
 Supports opaque LSA
 Supports Link-local Signaling (LLS)
 Supports area transit capability
 Supports NSSA (compatible with RFC 3101)
 Event-log enabled, Maximum number of events: 1000, Mode: cyclic
 Router is not originating router-LSAs with maximum metric
 Initial SPF schedule delay 5000 msecs
 Minimum hold time between two consecutive SPFs 10000 msecs
 Maximum wait time between two consecutive SPFs 10000 msecs
 Incremental-SPF disabled
 Minimum LSA interval 5 secs
 Minimum LSA arrival 1000 msecs
 LSA group pacing timer 240 secs
 Interface flood pacing timer 33 msecs
 Retransmission pacing timer 66 msecs
 Number of external LSA 0. Checksum Sum 0x000000
 Number of opaque AS LSA 0. Checksum Sum 0x000000
 Number of DCbitless external and opaque AS LSA 0
 Number of DoNotAge external and opaque AS LSA 0
 Number of areas in this router is 1. 1 normal 0 stub 0 nssa
 Number of areas transit capable is 0
```

```
External flood list length 0
IETF NSF helper support enabled
Cisco NSF helper support enabled
Reference bandwidth unit is 10000 mbps
    Area BACKBONE(0)
        Number of interfaces in this area is 3
        Area has no authentication
        SPF algorithm last executed 00:18:32.788 ago
        SPF algorithm executed 7 times
        Area ranges are
        Number of LSA 3. Checksum Sum 0x01BB59
        Number of opaque link LSA 0. Checksum Sum 0x000000
        Number of DCbitless LSA 0
        Number of indication LSA 0
        Number of DoNotAge LSA 0
        Flood list length 0
```

The quickest way to verify OSPF interface settings is to use the **show ip ospf interface brief**
command. As shown in the output for R1 in Example 19-7, this command provides a detailed list
for every OSPF-enabled interface. The command is also useful for quickly viewing the cost of each
interface and determining whether the network statements were correctly configured.

Example 19-7   The show ip ospf interface brief Command

```
R1# show ip ospf interface brief
Interface     PID   Area         IP Address/Mask       Cost   State Nbrs F/C
Se0/0/1       10    0            192.168.10.5/30       65535  P2P   1/1
Se0/0/0       10    0            172.16.3.1/30         6476   P2P   1/1
Gi0/0         10    0            172.16.1.1/24         100    DR    0/0
```

Single-Area OSPFv3 Configuration

OSPFv3 configuration requires the same basic steps as OSPFv2: pick and configure a process ID,
enable the process on each interface, and assign the correct OSPF area to each interface. However,
the way in which these steps are implemented is quite different.

Figure 19-2 shows the topology we use to review the OSPFv3 configuration steps.

Figure 19-2   OSPFv3 Configuration Topology

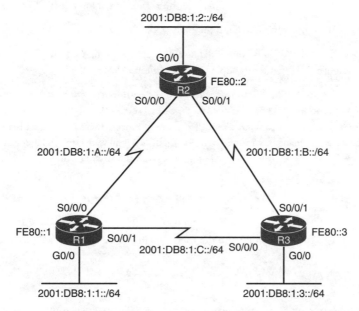

To ease our configuration and verification steps, we use the simplified IPv6 addressing scheme in Table 19-5.

Table 19-5   Addressing Scheme for OSPFv3

Device	Interface	IPv6 Address/Prefix
R1	G0/0	2001:DB8:1:1::1/64
	S0/0/0	2001:DB8:1:A::1/64
	S0/0/1	2001:DB8:1:C::1/64
	Link-local	FE80::1
R2	G0/0	2001:DB8:1:2::1/64
	S0/0/0	2001:DB8:1:A::2/64
	S0/0/1	2001:DB8:1:B::1/64
	Link-local	FE80::2
R3	G0/0	2001:DB8:1:3::1/64
	S0/0/0	2001:DB8:1:C::2/64
	S0/0/1	2001:DB8:1:B::2/64
	Link-local	FE80::3

The Router ID in OSPFv3

As with OSPFv2, OSPFv3 chooses the router ID in the following order:

1. If the **router-id** command is configured, use the manually configured IPv4 router ID.

2. If the router ID is not configured, use the highest configured loopback interface IPv4 address.

3. If no loopback IPv4 address is configured, use the highest configured interface IPv4 address. The interface can be in either the up/up state or the up/down state.

Also as with OSPFv2, you configure the router ID with the **router-id** command in router configuration mode. However, notice that both OSPFv2 and OSPFv3 use an IPv4 address for the router ID. This means that before a router can start an OSPFv3 routing process, there must be an IPv4 address configured—either an interface or a router ID. If not, the router will return the following syslog message when you attempt to enable the OSPFv3 routing process with the **ipv6 router ospf** command:

```
R1(config)# ipv6 router ospf 10
*Jun  3 13:06:06.579: %OSPFv3-4-NORTRID: Process OSPFv3-10-IPv6 could not pick a
   s router-id, please configure manually
```

The next step on R1, then, is to configure the router ID. It can be any IPv4 address. For simplicity, we use 1.1.1.1:

```
R1(config-rtr)# router-id 1.1.1.1
```

To make sure that costs are accurately calculated for the 10GigE interfaces when they become available, we change the reference bandwidth to 10,000,000,000 bps, or 10000 Mbps, with the **auto-cost reference-bandwidth** command:

```
R1(config-rtr)# auto-cost reference-bandwidth 10000
% OSPFv3-10-IPv6:  Reference bandwidth is changed.
        Please ensure reference bandwidth is consistent across all routers.
```

A syslog message reminds us to do this on every router.

As in OSPFv2, we can stop sending updates out the GigabitEthernet 0/0 interface with the **passive-interface** command:

```
R1(config-rtr)# passive-interface g0/0
```

That's it for router configuration commands. Next, we simply enable OSPFv3 on each of the active interfaces, as in Example 19-8.

Example 19-8   Enable OSPFv3 on Interfaces

```
R1(config-rtr)# exit
R1(config)# interface GigabitEthernet 0/0
R1(config-if)# ipv6 ospf 10 area 0
R1(config-if)# interface Serial0/0/0
R1(config-if)# ipv6 ospf 10 area 0
R1(config-if)# interface Serial0/0/1
R1(config-if)# ipv6 ospf 10 area 0
```

Configure R2 and R3 with similar commands (we can use 2.2.2.2 and 3.3.3.3 for R2 and R3, respectively), and OSPFv3 is fully operational.

Verifying OSPFv3

In Table 19-6, notice that every OSPFv2 command shown is also available for OSPFv3—just substitute **ipv6** for **ip**.

Table 19-6   OSPFv2 and Matching OSPFv3 show Commands

To Display Details About...	OSPFv2	OSPFv3
OSPF process	show ip ospf	show ipv6 ospf
All sources of routing information	show ip protocols	show ipv6 protocols
Details about OSPF-enabled interfaces	show ip ospf interface	show ipv6 ospf interface
Concise info about OSPF-enabled interfaces	show ip ospf interface brief	show ipv6 ospf interface brief
List of neighbors	show ip ospf neighbor	show ipv6 ospf neighbor
Summary of LSDB	show ip ospf database	show ipv6 ospf database
OSPF-learned routes	show ip route ospf	show ipv6 route ospf

Examples 19-9–19-15 show the output from R1 for the OSPFv3 verification commands in Table 19-6. The **bandwidth** command configured during single-area OSPF configuration is still in effect, as reflected in the output for OSPF cost values.

Example 19-9   Verify the OSPF Process

```
R1# show ipv6 ospf
 Routing Process "ospfv3 10" with ID 1.1.1.1
 Supports NSSA (compatible with RFC 3101)
 Event-log enabled, Maximum number of events: 1000, Mode: cyclic
 Router is not originating router-LSAs with maximum metric
 Initial SPF schedule delay 5000 msecs
 Minimum hold time between two consecutive SPFs 10000 msecs
 Maximum wait time between two consecutive SPFs 10000 msecs
 Minimum LSA interval 5 secs
 Minimum LSA arrival 1000 msecs
 LSA group pacing timer 240 secs
 Interface flood pacing timer 33 msecs
 Retransmission pacing timer 66 msecs
Retransmission limit dc 24 non-dc 24
 Number of external LSA 0. Checksum Sum 0x000000
 Number of areas in this router is 1. 1 normal 0 stub 0 nssa
 Graceful restart helper support enabled
Reference bandwidth unit is 1000 mbp
RFC1583 compatibility enabled
    Area BACKBONE(0)
```

```
              Number of interfaces in this area is 3
              SPF algorithm executed 4 times
              Number of LSA 11. Checksum Sum 0x05AD44
              Number of DCbitless LSA 0
              Number of indication LSA 0
              Number of DoNotAge LSA 0
              Flood list length 0
R1#
```

Example 19-10   Verify Sources of Routing Information

```
R1# show ipv6 protocols
IPv6 Routing Protocol is "connected"
IPv6 Routing Protocol is "application"
IPv6 Routing Protocol is "ospf 10"
  Router ID 1.1.1.1
  Number of areas: 1 normal, 0 stub, 0 nssa
  Interfaces (Area 0):
    Serial0/0/1
    Serial0/0/0
    GigabitEthernet0/0
  Redistribution:
    None
IPv6 Routing Protocol is "ND"
R1#
```

Example 19-11   Verify Details of an OSPF-Enabled Interface

```
R1# show ipv6 ospf interface serial 0/0/0
Serial0/0/0 is up, line protocol is up
  Link Local Address FE80::1, Interface ID 6
  Area 0, Process ID 10, Instance ID 0, Router ID 1.1.1.1
  Network Type POINT_TO_POINT, Cost: 6476
  Transmit Delay is 1 sec, State POINT_TO_POINT
  Timer intervals configured, Hello 10, Dead 40, Wait 40, Retransmit 5
    Hello due in 00:00:07
  Graceful restart helper support enabled
  Index 1/2/2, flood queue length 0
  Next 0x0(0)/0x0(0)/0x0(0)
  Last flood scan length is 3, maximum is 3
  Last flood scan time is 0 msec, maximum is 0 msec
  Neighbor Count is 1, Adjacent neighbor count is 1
    Adjacent with neighbor 2.2.2.2
  Suppress hello for 0 neighbor(s)
R1#
```

Example 19-12   Verify OSPF Interface Status

```
R1# show ipv6 ospf interface brief
Interface    PID   Area           Intf ID    Cost   State Nbrs F/C
Se0/0/1      10    0              7          65535  P2P   1/1
Se0/0/0      10    0              6          6476   P2P   1/1
Gi0/0        10    0              3          100    DR    0/0
R1#
```

Example 19-13   Verify OSPF Neighbor Table

```
R1# show ipv6 ospf neighbor

            OSPFv3 Router with ID (1.1.1.1) (Process ID 10)


Neighbor ID     Pri   State         Dead Time    Interface ID   Interface
3.3.3.3         0     FULL/  -      00:00:31     6              Serial0/0/1
2.2.2.2         0     FULL/  -      00:00:38     6              Serial0/0/0
R1#
```

Example 19-14   Verify the OSPF Link-State Database

```
R1# show ipv6 ospf database

            OSPFv3 Router with ID (1.1.1.1) (Process ID 10)

              Router Link States (Area 0)

ADV Router       Age        Seq#        Fragment ID  Link count  Bits
1.1.1.1          1042       0x80000004  0            2           None
2.2.2.2          1264       0x80000002  0            2           None
3.3.3.3          1260       0x80000002  0            2           None

              Link (Type-8) Link States (Area 0)

ADV Router       Age        Seq#        Link ID     Interface
1.1.1.1          1042       0x80000002  7           Se0/0/1
3.3.3.3          1265       0x80000001  6           Se0/0/1
1.1.1.1          1042       0x80000002  6           Se0/0/0
2.2.2.2          1313       0x80000001  6           Se0/0/0
1.1.1.1          1042       0x80000002  3           Gi0/0

              Intra Area Prefix Link States (Area 0)

ADV Router       Age        Seq#        Link ID     Ref-lstype  Ref-LSID
1.1.1.1          1042       0x80000003  0           0x2001      0
2.2.2.2          1308       0x80000002  0           0x2001      0
3.3.3.3          1260       0x80000002  0           0x2001      0
R1#
```

Example 19-15   Verify OSPF Routes in the Routing Table

```
R1# show ipv6 route ospf
IPv6 Routing Table - default - 10 entries
<output omitted>
O   2001:DB8:1:2::/64 [110/6576]
      via FE80::2, Serial0/0/0
O   2001:DB8:1:3::/64 [110/16341]
      via FE80::2, Serial0/0/0
O   2001:DB8:1:B::/64 [110/16241]
      via FE80::2, Serial0/0/0
R1#
```

 Packet Tracer Activity: Dual-Stack Single-Area OSPF Configuration

Refer to the Digital Study Guide to access the PKA file for this activity. You must have Packet Tracer software to run this activity. See the Introduction for details.

Study Resources

For today's exam topics, refer to the following resources for more study.

Resource	Location	Topic
Primary Resources		
Scaling Networks v6	8	Single-Area OSPFv2
		Single-Area OSPFv3
ICND2 Official Cert Guide	8	Implementing Single-Area OSPFv2
	23	OSPFv3 Configuration
		OSPFv3 Verification and Troubleshooting
Supplemental Resources		
CCNA Portable Command Guide	15	Configuring OSPF
		Using Wildcard Masks with OSPF Areas
		Loopback Interfaces
		Router ID
		Passive Interfaces
		Modifying Cost Metrics
		OSPF auto-cost reference-bandwidth
		Enabling OSPF for IPv6 on an Interface
		Verifying OSPFv2 and OSPFv3 Configurations
		Configuration Example: Single-Area OSPF

Resource	Location	Topic
Supplemental Resources		
CCNA Video Series	3	Lesson 6: OSPFv2 Configuration
		Lesson 6: OSPFv2 Verification
		Lesson 6: OSPF Cost Calculation
		Lesson 6: OSPF Cost Configuration
		Lesson 6: OSPF Passive Interfaces
		Lesson 6: OSPFv3 Configuration
		Lesson 6: OSPFv3 Verification
CCNA Network Simulator	ICND2	Chapter 8: OSPF Configuration I–III
		Chapter 8: OSPF Serial Configuration I–VI
		Chapter 8: OSPF Router ID I–II
		Chapter 8: OSPF Neighbors I–V
		Chapter 8: OSPF Interface Configuration I–II
		Chapter 23: OSPF for IPv6 Serial Configuration I–VI
		Chapter 23: OSPF for IPv6 Router ID I–II
		Chapter 23: OSPF for IPv6 Neighbors I–VI

Check Your Understanding

Refer to the Digital Study Guide to take a short quiz covering the content of this day.

Multiarea OSPF Implementation

CCNA 200-125 Exam Topics

- Configure, verify, and troubleshoot single area and multiarea OSPFv2 for IPv4
- Configure, verify, and troubleshoot single area and multiarea OSPFv3 for IPv6

Key Topics

Today we review the basic implementation of OSPFv2 and OSPFv3 for multiarea network designs, including reviewing the commands to configure and verify the implementation. Tomorrow we review how to modify and troubleshoot OSPF implementations.

Multiarea OSPFv2 Implementation

For multiarea OSPF implementation, we change up the OSPF topology from yesterday's review, adding areas, adding more LANs, and changing the addressing scheme. The topology in Figure 18-1 helps to review the commands to configure multiarea OSPFv2.

Figure 18-1   Multiarea OSPFv2 Topology

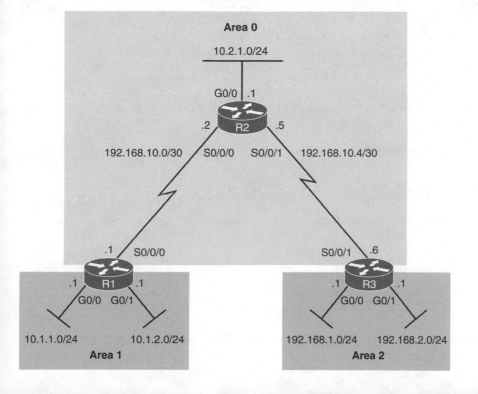

Table 18-1 shows the addressing scheme for the topology in Figure 18-1.

Table 18-1   Addressing Scheme for Multiarea OSPFv2

Device	Interface	IP Address	Subnet Mask
R1	G0/0	10.1.1.1	255.255.255.0
	G0/1	10.1.2.1	255.255.255.0
	S0/0/0	192.168.10.1	255.255.255.252
R2	G0/0	10.2.1.1	255.255.255.0
	S0/0/0	192.168.10.2	255.255.255.252
	S0/0/1	192.168.10.5	255.255.255.252
R3	G0/0	192.168.1.1	255.255.255.0
	G0/1	192.168.2.1	255.255.255.0
	S0/0/1	192.168.10.6	255.255.255.252

No special commands work to implement multiarea OSPF. A router simply becomes an ABR when you configure two or more **network** statements in different areas. In the configuration in Example 18-1, multiarea OSPF is implemented and R1 becomes an ABR between area 0 and area 1.

Example 18-1   Configuring Multiarea OSPFv2 on R1

```
R1(config)# router ospf 10
R1(config-router)# router-id 1.1.1.1
R1(config-router)# network 10.1.1.1 0.0.0.0 area 1
R1(config-router)# network 10.1.2.1 0.0.0.0 area 1
R1(config-router)# network 192.168.10.0 0.0.0.0 area 0
R1(config-router)# end
```

The same verification commands used to verify single-area OSPFv2 works to verify the multiarea OSPF topology in the figure:

- **show ip ospf neighbor**
- **show ip ospf**
- **show ip ospf interface**

These commands verify specific multiarea OSPFv2 information:

- **show ip protocols**
- **show ip ospf interface brief**
- **show ip route ospf**
- **show ip ospf database**

Use the **show ip protocols** command to verify the OSPFv2 status. Example 18-2 verifies that R1 is participating in two areas.

Example 18-2   Verifying Multiarea OSPFv2 Status on R1

```
R1# show ip protocols
*** IP Routing is NSF aware ***

Routing Protocol is "ospf 10"
  Outgoing update filter list for all interfaces is not set
  Incoming update filter list for all interfaces is not set
  Router ID 1.1.1.1
  Number of areas in this router is 2. 2 normal 0 stub 0 nssa
  Maximum path: 4
  Routing for Networks:
    10.1.1.0 0.0.0.255 area 1
    10.1.2.0 0.0.0.255 area 1
    192.168.10.0 0.0.0.3 area 0
  Routing Information Sources:
    Gateway         Distance      Last Update
    1.1.1.1              110      00:00:21
    2.2.2.2              110      00:29:54
    3.3.3.3              110      00:29:54
  Distance: (default is 110)

R1#
```

The **show ip ospf interface brief** command displays that area each interface belongs to, as Example 18-3 shows.

Example 18-3   Verifying OSPFv2-Enable Interfaces on R1

```
R1# show ip ospf interface brief
Interface    PID   Area     IP Address/Mask     Cost  State Nbrs F/C
Se0/0/0      10    0        192.168.10.1/30     64    P2P   1/1
Gi0/1        10    1        10.1.2.1/24         1     DR    0/0
Gi0/0        10    1        10.1.1.1/24         1     DR    0/0
R1#
```

The **show ip route ospf** command verifies that R1 is receiving interarea routes from R2. Routes listed with the code **o IA** in Example 18-4 are from R3 in area 2.

Example 18-4   Verifying Multiarea OSPFv2 Routes on R1

```
R1# show ip route ospf | begin Gateway
Gateway of last resort is not set

      10.0.0.0/8 is variably subnetted, 5 subnets, 2 masks
O        10.2.1.0 [110/65] via 192.168.10.2, 00:37:34, Serial0/0/0
O IA 192.168.1.0 [110/129] via 192.168.10.2, 00:36:56, Serial0/0/0
O IA 192.168.2.0 [110/129] via 192.168.10.2, 00:36:56, Serial0/0/0
      192.168.10.0/24 is variably subnetted, 3 subnets, 2 masks
O        192.168.10.4 [110/128] via 192.168.10.2, 00:37:16, Serial0/0/0
R1#
```

Use the **show ip ospf database** command to verify the contents of the OSPFv2 LSDB, as in Example 18-5.

Example 18-5   Verifying the OSPFv2 LSDB on R1

```
R1# show ip ospf database


            OSPF Router with ID (1.1.1.1) (Process ID 10)


            Router Link States (Area 0)


Link ID          ADV Router       Age         Seq#        Checksum Link count
1.1.1.1          1.1.1.1          230         0x80000002 0x00FFAD 2
2.2.2.2          2.2.2.2          216         0x80000003 0x001E95 5
3.3.3.3          3.3.3.3          215         0x80000002 0x00F6FD 2


            Summary Net Link States (Area 0)


Link ID          ADV Router       Age         Seq#        Checksum
10.1.1.0         1.1.1.1          230         0x80000001 0x00DB50
10.1.2.0         1.1.1.1          230         0x80000001 0x00D05A
192.168.1.0      3.3.3.3          205         0x80000001 0x007C49
192.168.2.0      3.3.3.3          205         0x80000001 0x007153


            Router Link States (Area 1)


Link ID          ADV Router       Age         Seq#        Checksum Link count
1.1.1.1          1.1.1.1          230         0x80000004 0x00817A 2


            Summary Net Link States (Area 1)


Link ID          ADV Router       Age         Seq#        Checksum
10.2.1.0         1.1.1.1          220         0x80000001 0x005298
192.168.1.0      1.1.1.1          203         0x80000001 0x00D8A4
192.168.2.0      1.1.1.1          203         0x80000001 0x00CDAE
192.168.10.0     1.1.1.1          220         0x80000001 0x00BBCC
192.168.10.4     1.1.1.1          210         0x80000001 0x003143
R1#
```

Multiarea OSPFv3 Implementation

The topology in Figure 18-2 helps as we review the commands to configure multiarea OSPFv3.

Figure 18-2   Multiarea OSPFv3 Topology

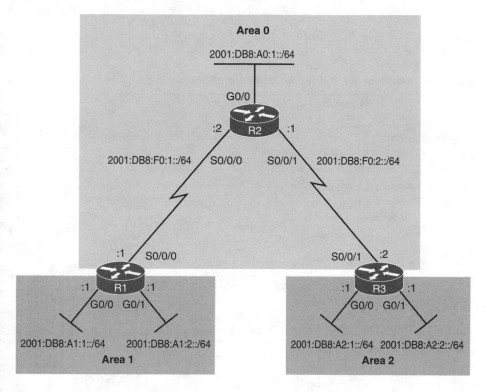

Table 18-2 shows the addressing scheme for the topology in Figure 18-2.

Table 18-2   Addressing Scheme for Multiarea OSPFv2

Device	Interface	IPv6 Address/Prefix
R1	G0/0	2001:DB8:A1:1::1/64
	G0/1	2001:DB8:A1:2::1/64
	S0/0/0	2001:DB8:F0:1::1/64
	Link Local	FE80::1
R2	G0/0	2001:DB8:A0:1::1/64
	S0/0/0	2001:DB8:F0:1::2/64
	S0/0/1	2001:DB8:F0:2::1/64
	Link Local	FE80::2
R3	G0/0	2001:DB8:A2:1::1/64
	G0/1	2001:DB8:A2:2::1/64
	S0/0/1	2001:DB8:F0:2::2/64
	Link Local	FE80::3

As in OSPFv2, implementing the multiarea OSPFv3 topology in Figure 18-2 is simple. No special commands are required. A router simply becomes an ABR when it has two interfaces in different areas.

In Example 18-6, R1 is assigned the router ID 1.1.1.1. Then OSPF is enabled for area 1 on the two LAN interfaces and area 0 on the serial interface.

Example 18-6   Configuring Multiarea OSPFv3 on R1

```
R1(config)# ipv6 router ospf 10
R1(config-rtr)# router-id 1.1.1.1
R1(config-rtr)# exit
R1(config)# interface GigabitEthernet 0/0
R1(config-if)# ipv6 ospf 10 area 1
R1(config-if)# interface GigabitEthernet 0/1
R1(config-if)# ipv6 ospf 10 area 1
R1(config-if)# interface Serial 0/0/0
R1(config-if)# ipv6 ospf 10 area 0
R1(config-if)# end
R1#
```

As in OSPFv2, OSPFv3 provides similar OSPFv3 verification commands, with **ip** replaced with **ipv6**:

- **show ipv6 protocols**
- **show ipv6 ospf interface brief**
- **show ipv6 route ospf**
- **show ipv6 ospf database**

In Example 18-7, the command output from **show ipv6 protocols** displays the OSPFv3 settings on R1. Notice that the command confirms that R1 is attached to two areas.

Example 18-7   Verifying Multiarea OSPFv3 Status on R1

```
R1# show ipv6 protocols
IPv6 Routing Protocol is "connected"
IPv6 Routing Protocol is "application"
IPv6 Routing Protocol is "ospf 10"
  Router ID 1.1.1.1
  Area border router
  Number of areas: 2 normal, 0 stub, 0 nssa
  Interfaces (Area 0):
    Serial0/0/0
  Interfaces (Area 1):
    GigabitEthernet0/1
    GigabitEthernet0/0
  Redistribution:
    None
IPv6 Routing Protocol is "ND"
R1#
```

In Example 18-8, the **show ipv6 ospf interface brief** command verifies the area to which each interface belongs.

Example 18-8   Verifying Multiarea OSPFv3-Enabled Interfaces on R1

```
R1# show ipv6 ospf interface brief
Interface    PID   Area          Intf ID    Cost   State Nbrs F/C
Se0/0/0      10    0             6          64     P2P   1/1
Gi0/1        10    1             4          1      DR    0/0
Gi0/0        10    1             3          1      DR    0/0
R1#
```

The **show ipv6 route ospf** command in Example 18-9 verifies that R1 has received interarea routes from R2 and can now route to the R3 LANs.

Example 18-9   Verifying Multiarea OSPFv3 Routes on R1

```
R1# show ipv6 route ospf
IPv6 Routing Table - default - 11 entries
Codes: C - Connected, L - Local, S - Static, U - Per-user Static route
       B - BGP, R - RIP, H - NHRP, I1 - ISIS L1
       I2 - ISIS L2, IA - ISIS interarea, IS - ISIS summary, D - EIGRP
       EX - EIGRP external, ND - ND Default, NDp - ND Prefix, DCE - Destination
       NDr - Redirect, O - OSPF Intra, OI - OSPF Inter, OE1 - OSPF ext 1
       OE2 - OSPF ext 2, ON1 - OSPF NSSA ext 1, ON2 - OSPF NSSA ext 2
       a - Application
O    2001:DB8:A0:1::/64 [110/65]
     via FE80::2, Serial0/0/0
OI   2001:DB8:A2:1::/64 [110/846]
     via FE80::2, Serial0/0/0
OI   2001:DB8:A2:2::/64 [110/846]
     via FE80::2, Serial0/0/0
O    2001:DB8:F0:2::/64 [110/845]
     via FE80::2, Serial0/0/0
R1#
```

Use the **show ipv6 ospf database** command to verify the contents of the OSPFv3 LSDB, as in Example 18-10.

Example 18-10   Verifying the Multiarea OSPFv3 LSDB on R1

```
R1# show ipv6 ospf database

            OSPFv3 Router with ID (1.1.1.1) (Process ID 10)

            Router Link States (Area 0)
```

ADV Router	Age	Seq#	Fragment ID	Link count	Bits
1.1.1.1	1604	0x80000003	0	1	B
2.2.2.2	1588	0x80000003	0	2	None
3.3.3.3	1585	0x80000002	0	1	B

Inter Area Prefix Link States (Area 0)

ADV Router	Age	Seq#	Prefix
1.1.1.1	22	0x80000002	2001:DB8:A1:1::/64
1.1.1.1	22	0x80000002	2001:DB8:A1:2::/64
3.3.3.3	1580	0x80000001	2001:DB8:A2:1::/64
3.3.3.3	1580	0x80000001	2001:DB8:A2:2::/64

Link (Type-8) Link States (Area 0)

ADV Router	Age	Seq#	Link ID	Interface
1.1.1.1	22	0x80000003	6	Se0/0/0
2.2.2.2	1601	0x80000002	6	Se0/0/0

Intra Area Prefix Link States (Area 0)

ADV Router	Age	Seq#	Link ID	Ref-lstype	Ref-LSID
1.1.1.1	22	0x80000002	0	0x2001	0
2.2.2.2	1600	0x80000002	0	0x2001	0
3.3.3.3	1585	0x80000001	0	0x2001	0

Router Link States (Area 1)

ADV Router	Age	Seq#	Fragment ID	Link count	Bits
1.1.1.1	22	0x80000003	0	0	B

Inter Area Prefix Link States (Area 1)

ADV Router	Age	Seq#	Prefix
1.1.1.1	22	0x80000002	2001:DB8:F0:1::/64
1.1.1.1	1600	0x80000001	2001:DB8:A0:1::/64
1.1.1.1	1590	0x80000001	2001:DB8:F0:2::/64
1.1.1.1	1578	0x80000001	2001:DB8:A2:1::/64
1.1.1.1	1578	0x80000001	2001:DB8:A2:2::/64

Link (Type-8) Link States (Area 1)

ADV Router	Age	Seq#	Link ID	Interface
1.1.1.1	22	0x80000003	4	Gi0/1
1.1.1.1	22	0x80000003	3	Gi0/0

```
            Intra Area Prefix Link States (Area 1)

ADV Router        Age         Seq#         Link ID    Ref-lstype  Ref-LSID
 1.1.1.1          22          0x80000002   0          0x2001      0
R1#
```

Packet Tracer Activity: Dual-Stack Multiarea OSPF Configuration

Refer to the Digital Study Guide to access the PKA file for this activity. You must have Packet Tracer software to run this activity. See the Introduction for details.

Study Resources

For today's exam topics, refer to the following resources for more study.

Resource	Location	Topic
Primary Resources		
Scaling Networks v6	9	All
ICND2 Official Cert Guide	8	Implementing Multiarea OSPFv2
Supplemental Resources		
CCNA Portable Command Guide	15	Configuring Multiarea OSPF
		Configuration Example: Multiarea OSPF
CCNA Video Series	3	Lesson 6: OSPFv2 Configuration
		Lesson 6: OSPFv2 Verification
		Lesson 6: OSPFv3 Configuration
		Lesson 6: OSPFv3 Verification
CCNA Network Simulator	ICND2	Chapter 8: OSPF Configuration I–III
		Chapter 8: OSPF Serial Configuration I–VI
		Chapter 8: OSPF Router ID I–II
		Chapter 8: OSPF Neighbors I–V
		Chapter 8: OSPF Interface Configuration I–II
		Chapter 23: OSPF for IPv6 Serial Configuration I–VI
		Chapter 23: OSPF for IPv6 Router ID I–II
		Chapter 23: OSPF for IPv6 Neighbors I–VI

Check Your Understanding

Refer to the Digital Study Guide to take a short quiz covering the content of this day.

Fine-Tuning and Troubleshooting OSPF

CCNA 200-125 Exam Topics

- Configure, verify, and troubleshoot single area and multiarea OSPFv2 for IPv4
- Configure, verify, and troubleshoot single area and multiarea OSPFv3 for IPv6

Key Topics

Today's review focuses on fine-tuning and troubleshooting both OSPFv2 and OSPFv3. Fine-tuning OSPF involves modifying timers, conducting DR/BDR elections, and propagating a default route. We also turn our focus to troubleshooting the OSPF process.

OSPFv2 Configuration Example

To fine-tune OSPFv2, we use the topology in Figure 17-1 and the addressing scheme in Table 17-1.

Figure 17-1   OSPFv2 Configuration Topology

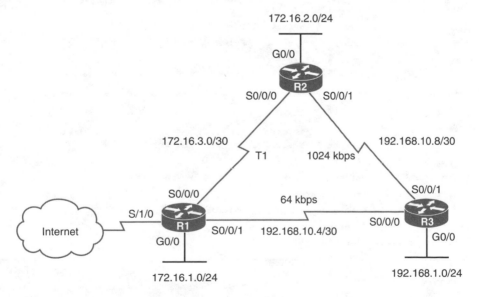

Table 17-1   Addressing Scheme for OSPFv2

Device	Interface	IP Address	Subnet Mask
R1	G0/0	172.16.1.1	255.255.255.0
	S0/0/0	172.16.3.1	255.255.255.252
	S0/0/1	192.168.10.5	255.255.255.252
	S0/1/0	209.165.200.226	255.255.255.224
R2	G0/0	172.16.2.1	255.255.255.0
	S0/0/0	172.16.3.2	255.255.255.252
	S0/0/1	192.168.10.9	255.255.255.252
R3	G0/0	192.168.1.1	255.255.255.0
	S0/0/0	192.168.10.6	255.255.255.252
	S0/0/1	192.168.10.10	255.255.255.252

Example 17-1 shows the network commands for all three routers, enabling OSPFv2 on all interfaces.

Example 17-1   Configuring OSPF Networks

```
R1(config)# router ospf 10
R1(config-router)# router-id 1.1.1.1
R1(config-router)# network 172.16.1.0 0.0.0.255 area 0
R1(config-router)# network 172.16.3.0 0.0.0.3 area 0
R1(config-router)# network 192.168.10.4 0.0.0.3 area 0
R1(config-router)# passive-interface g0/0
R1(config-router)# auto-cost reference-bandwidth 10000
R1(config-router)# interface S0/0/1
R1(config-if)# bandwidth 64

R2(config)# router ospf 10
R2(config-router)# router-id 2.2.2.2
R2(config-router)# network 172.16.2.0 0.0.0.255 area 0
R2(config-router)# network 172.16.3.0 0.0.0.3 area 0
R2(config-router)# network 192.168.10.8 0.0.0.3 area 0
R2(config-router)# passive-interface g0/0
R2(config-router)# auto-cost reference-bandwidth 10000
R2(config-router)# interface S0/0/1
R2(config-if)# bandwidth 1024

R3(config)# router ospf 10
R3(config-router)# router-id 3.3.3.3
R3(config-router)# network 192.168.1.0 0.0.0.255 area 0
R3(config-router)# network 192.168.10.4 0.0.0.3 area 0
```

```
R3(config-router)# network 192.168.10.8 0.0.0.3 area 0
R3(config-router)# passive-interface g0/0
R3(config-router)# auto-cost reference-bandwidth 10000
R3(config-router)# interface S0/0/0
R3(config-if)# bandwidth 64
R3(config-if)# interface S0/0/1
R3(config-if)# bandwidth 1024
```

Modifying OSPFv2

This section reviews the concepts and commands to redistribute a default route, tune OSPF interfaces, and manipulate the designated router/backup designated router (DR/BDR) election process.

Redistributing a Default Route

In Figure 17-1, R1 has a link to the Internet that makes R1 an Autonomous System Boundary Router (ASBR). We therefore configure a default route to the Internet and redistribute the default static route to R2 and R3 with the **default-information originate** command, as in Example 17-2.

Example 17-2   ASBR Static Default Route Configuration

```
R1(config)# ip route 0.0.0.0 0.0.0.0 Serial 0/1/0
R1(config)# router ospf 10
R1(config-router)# default-information originate
```

Both R2 and R3 should now have default routes identified with the **O*E2** code, as in Example 17-3.

Example 17-3   R2 and R3 OSPF Routes with Default Route

```
R2# show ip route ospf
      172.16.0.0/16 is variably subnetted, 5 subnets, 3 masks
O        172.16.1.0 [110/6477] via 172.16.3.1, 00:02:45, Serial0/0/0
O     192.168.1.0 [110/6486] via 192.168.10.10, 00:00:55, Serial0/0/1
      192.168.10.0/24 is variably subnetted, 3 subnets, 2 masks
O        192.168.10.4 [110/12952] via 192.168.10.10, 00:00:55, Serial0/0/1
O*E2 0.0.0.0/0 [110/1] via 172.16.3.1, 00:00:09, Serial0/0/0


R3# show ip route ospf
      172.16.0.0/16 is variably subnetted, 3 subnets, 2 masks
O        172.16.1.0 [110/6477] via 192.168.10.5, 00:26:01, Serial0/0/0
O        172.16.2.0 [110/6486] via 192.168.10.9, 00:26:01, Serial0/0/1
O        172.16.3.0 [110/6540] via 192.168.10.5, 00:26:01, Serial0/0/0
O*E2 0.0.0.0/0 [110/1] via 192.168.10.9, 00:01:19, Serial0/0/1
```

Modifying Hello and Dead Intervals

The default hello interval on multiaccess and point-to-point networks is 10 seconds. Nonbroadcast multiaccess (NBMA) networks default to a 30-second hello interval. The default dead interval is four times the hello interval.

It might be desirable to change the OSPF timers so that routers detect network failures in less time. Doing this increases traffic, but sometimes a need for quick convergence outweighs the extra traffic.

You can modify OSPF hello and dead intervals manually by using the following interface commands:

```
Router(config-if)# ip ospf hello-interval seconds
Router(config-if)# ip ospf dead-interval seconds
```

Although the dead interval defaults to four times the hello interval and does not have to be explicitly configured, it is a good practice to document the new dead interval in the configuration. Example 17-4 shows the hello interval and dead interval modified to 5 seconds and 20 seconds, respectively, on the Serial 0/0/0 interface for R1.

Example 17-4   Modifying Hello and Dead Intervals on R1

```
R1(config)# interface serial 0/0/0
R1(config-if)# ip ospf hello-interval 5
R1(config-if)# ip ospf dead-interval 20
R1(config-if)# end
```

Remember, unlike Enhanced Interior Gateway Routing Protocol (EIGRP), OSPF hello and dead intervals must be equivalent between neighbors. Therefore, R2 should be configured with the same intervals.

OSPF Network Types

OSPF defines five network types:

- **Point-to-point:** Two routers interconnected over a common link. No other routers are on the link. This is often the configuration in WAN links.

- **Broadcast multiaccess:** Multiple routers interconnected over an Ethernet network.

- **NBMA:** Multiple routers interconnected in a network that does not allow broadcasts, such as Frame Relay.

- **Point-to-multipoint:** Multiple routers interconnected in a hub-and-spoke topology over an NBMA network. Often used to connect branch sites (spokes) to a central site (hub).

- **Virtual links:** Special OSPF network used to interconnect distant OSPF areas to the backbone area.

Multiaccess networks create two challenges for OSPF regarding the flooding of LSAs:

- **Creation of multiple adjacencies:** Ethernet networks can potentially interconnect many OSPF routers over a common link. Using the formula $n(n − 1) / 2$, where n equals the number of routers, 5 routers would require 10 separate neighbor adjacencies; 10 routers would require 45.

- **Extensive flooding of LSAs:** Link-state routers flood their link-state packets when OSPF is initialized or when the topology changes. This flooding can become excessive without a mechanism to reduce the number of adjacencies.

DR/BDR Election

The solution to managing the number of adjacencies and the flooding of LSAs on a multiaccess network is the designated router (DR). To reduce the amount of OSPF traffic on multiaccess networks, OSPF elects a DR and backup DR (BDR). The DR is responsible for updating all other OSPF routers when a change occurs in the multiaccess network. The BDR monitors the DR and takes over as DR if the current DR fails.

The following criteria are used to elect the DR and BDR:

1. The DR is the router with the highest OSPF interface priority.

2. The BDR is the router with the second-highest OSPF interface priority.

3. If OSPF interface priorities are equal, the highest router ID breaks the tie.

When the DR is elected, it remains the DR until one of the following conditions occurs:

- The DR fails.

- The OSPF process on the DR fails.

- The multiaccess interface on the DR fails.

If the DR fails, the BDR assumes the role of DR, and an election is held to choose a new BDR. If a new router enters the network after the DR and BDR have been elected, it will not become the DR or the BDR even if it has a higher OSPF interface priority or router ID than the current DR or BDR. The new router can be elected the BDR if the current DR or BDR fails. If the current DR fails, the BDR becomes the DR, and the new router can be elected the new BDR.

Without additional configuration, you can control the routers that win the DR and BDR elections by doing either of the following:

- Boot the DR first, followed by the BDR, and then boot all other routers.

- Shut down the interface on all routers, followed by a **no shutdown** on the DR, then the BDR, and then all other routers.

The recommended way to control DR/BDR elections, however, is to change the interface priority.

Controlling the DR/BDR Election

Because the DR becomes the focal point for the collection and distribution of LSAs in a multiaccess network, this router must have sufficient CPU and memory capacity to handle the responsibility. Instead of relying on the router ID to decide which routers are elected the DR and BDR, it is better to control the election of these routers with the **ip ospf priority** interface command:

```
Router(config-if)# ip ospf priority {0 - 255}
```

The priority value defaults to 1 for all router interfaces, which means the router ID determines the DR and BDR. If you change the default value from 1 to a higher value, however, the router with

the highest priority becomes the DR and the router with the next highest priority becomes the
BDR. A value of 0 makes the router ineligible to become a DR or BDR.

All the routers in Figure 17-2 booted at the same time with a complete OSPF configuration. In
such a situation, R3 is elected the DR, and R2 is elected the BDR based on the highest router IDs,
as you can see in the output for the neighbor table on R1 in Example 17-5.

Figure 17-2   Multiaccess Topology

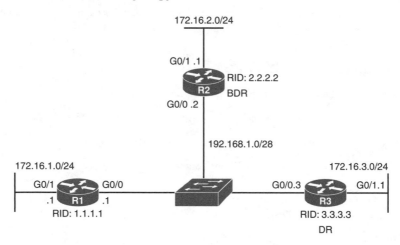

Example 17-5   Verifying the DR and BDR

```
R1# show ip ospf neighbor
Neighbor ID      Pri  State        Dead Time   Address       Interface
2.2.2.2            1  FULL/BDR     00:00:32    192.168.1.2   GigabitEthernet0/0
3.3.3.3            1  FULL/DR      00:00:38    192.168.1.3   GigabitEthernet0/0
R1#
```

Assume that R1 is the better candidate to be DR and that R2 should be BDR. Example 17-6
shows a way to control the DR/BDR election in the topology in Figure 17-2.

Example 17-6   Modifying the OSPF Interface Priority

```
R1(config)# interface gigabitethernet 0/0
R1(config-if)# ip ospf priority 200

R2(config)# interface gigabitethernet 0/0
R2(config-if)# ip ospf priority 100
```

Notice that we changed both routers. Although R2 was the BDR without doing anything, it would
lose this role to R3 if we had not configured R2's priority to be higher than the default.

Before R1 can become DR, the OSPF process needs to restart. This can be done by shutting down
the interfaces or simply entering the **clear ip ospf process** command in privileged EXEC mode,
as in Example 17-7. The neighbor table on R3 shows that R1 is now the DR and R2 is the BDR.

Example 17-7   Restarting the OSPF Process and Verifying New DR and BDR

```
R1# clear ip ospf process
Reset ALL OSPF processes? [no]: y
R1#
```

```
R2# clear ip ospf process
Reset ALL OSPF processes? [no]: y
R2#
```

```
R3# clear ip ospf process
Reset ALL OSPF processes? [no]: y
R2#
R3# show ip ospf neighbor

Neighbor ID     Pri   State       Dead Time   Address       Interface
2.2.2.2         100   FULL/BDR    00:00:38    192.168.1.2   GigabitEthernet0/0
1.1.1.1         200   FULL/DR     00:00:30    192.168.1.1   GigabitEthernet0/0
R3#
```

OSPFv3 Configuration Example

To fine-tune OSPFv3, we use the topology in Figure 17-3 and the addressing scheme in Table 17-2.

Figure 17-3   OSPFv3 Configuration Topology

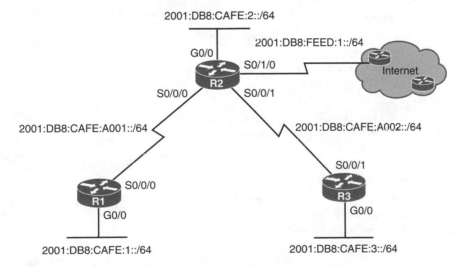

Table 17-2   Addressing Scheme for OSPFv3

Device	Interface	IPv6 Address/Prefix
R1	G0/0	2001:DB8:CAFE:1::1/64
	S0/0/0	2001:DB8:CAFE:A001::2/64
	Link-local	FE80::1
	Router ID	1.1.1.1
R2	G0/0	2001:DB8:CAFE:2::1/64
	S0/0/0	2001:DB8:CAFE:A001::1/64
	S0/0/1	2001:DB8:CAFE:A002::1/64
	S0/1/0	2001:DB8:FEED:1::2/64
	Link-local	FE80::2
	Router ID	2.2.2.2
R3	G0/0	2001:DB8:CAFE:3::1/64
	S0/0/1	2001:DB8:CAFE:A002::2/64
	Link-local	FE80::3
	Router ID	3.3.3.3

Example 17-8 shows the configuration commands for R2 to enable IPv6 and OSPFv3 on all interfaces. The commands are the same for R1 and R3.

Example 17-8   Enabling IPv6 and OSPFv3 on R2

```
R2(config)# ipv6 unicast-routing
R2(config)# ipv6 router ospf 10
R2(config-rtr)# router-id 2.2.2.2
R2(config-rtr)# auto-cost reference-bandwidth 1000
R2(config-rtr)# interface g0/0
R2(config-if)# ipv6 add 2001:db8:cafe:2::1/64
R2(config-if)# ipv6 add fe80::1 l
R2(config-if)# ipv6 ospf 10 area 0
R2(config-if)# interface s0/0/0
R2(config-if)# ipv6 add 2001:db8:cafe:a001::1/64
R2(config-if)# ipv6 add fe80::2 link-local
R2(config-if)# ipv6 ospf 10 area 0
R2(config-if)# interface s0/0/1
R2(config-if)# ipv6 add 2001:db8:cafe:a002::1/64
R2(config-if)# ipv6 add fe80::2 link-local
R2(config-if)# ipv6 ospf 10 area 0
R2(config-if)# interface s0/1/0
R2(config-if)# ipv6 add 2001:db8:feed:1::2/64
R2(config-if)# ipv6 add fe80::2 link-local
```

```
R2(config-if)# end
R2# show ipv6 ospf neighbor


Neighbor ID     Pri   State         Dead Time   Interface ID   Interface
3.3.3.3           0   FULL/  -       00:00:38    4              Serial0/0/1
1.1.1.1           0   FULL/  -       00:00:33    3              Serial0/0/0
R2# show ipv6 route ospf
IPv6 Routing Table - 11 entries
Codes: C - Connected, L - Local, S - Static, R - RIP, B - BGP
       U - Per-user Static route, M - MIPv6
       I1 - ISIS L1, I2 - ISIS L2, IA - ISIS interarea, IS - ISIS summary
       O - OSPF intra, OI - OSPF inter, OE1 - OSPF ext 1, OE2 - OSPF ext 2
       ON1 - OSPF NSSA ext 1, ON2 - OSPF NSSA ext 2
       D - EIGRP, EX - EIGRP external
O    2001:DB8:CAFE:1::/64 [110/65]
      via FE80::1, Serial0/0/0
O    2001:DB8:CAFE:3::/64 [110/65]
      via FE80::3, Serial0/0/1
R2#
```

The two commands **show ipv6 ospf neighbors** and **show ipv6 route ospf** verify that R2 has established adjacencies with R1 and R3 and learned the necessary routes. You configure the link to the Internet in the next section.

Modifying OSPFv3

As with OSPFv2, you can configure OSPFv3 to propagate a default route and fine-tune the interfaces.

Propagating a Default Route

The process to propagate a default route in OSPFv3 is the same as for OSPFv2. As you can see in the configuration for R2 in Example 17-9, you configure the default route and then use the command **default-information originate** in router configuration mode to propagate the route to OSPF neighbors.

Example 17-9   Propagating a Default Route in OSPFv3

```
R2(config)# ipv6 route ::/0 serial 0/1/0
R2(config)# ipv6 router ospf 10
R2(config-rtr)# default-information originate
R2(config-rtr)# end
R2#
```

As Example 17-10 shows, R1 and R3 both have a default route indicated by the OE2 in the routing table.

Example 17-10   Default Route Propagated to R1 and R3

```
R1# show ipv6 route ospf | begin OE2 :
OE2 ::/0 [110/1], tag 1
      via FE80::2, Serial0/0/0
O    2001:DB8:CAFE:2::/64 [110/65]
       via FE80::2, Serial0/0/0
O    2001:DB8:CAFE:3::/64 [110/129]
       via FE80::2, Serial0/0/0
O    2001:DB8:CAFE:A002::/64 [110/128]
       via FE80::2, Serial0/0/0
R1#
```

```
R3# show ipv6 route ospf | begin OE2 :
OE2 ::/0 [110/1], tag 1
      via FE80::2, Serial0/0/1
O    2001:DB8:CAFE:1::/64 [110/129]
       via FE80::2, Serial0/0/1
O    2001:DB8:CAFE:2::/64 [110/65]
       via FE80::2, Serial0/0/1
O    2001:DB8:CAFE:A001::/64 [110/128]
       via FE80::2, Serial0/0/1
R3#
```

Modifying the Timers

To modify the OSPFv3 timers, use the same commands as for OSPFv2, but change **ip** to **ipv6**, as in Example 17-11.

Example 17-11   Configuring Hello and Dead Intervals in OSPFv3

```
R2(config)# interface s0/0/0
R2(config-if)# ipv6 ospf hello-interval 5
R2(config-if)# ipv6 ospf dead-interval 20
R2(config-if)# end
R2#
%OSPF-5-ADJCHG: Process 10, Nbr 1.1.1.1 on Serial0/0/0 from FULL to DOWN,
  Neighbor Down: Dead timer expired
%OSPFv3-5-ADJCHG: Process 10, Nbr 1.1.1.1 on Serial0/0/0 from FULL to DOWN,
  Neighbor Down: Interface down or detached
```

R2 loses adjacency with R1. To restore adjacency, you must configure R1 with the same timers, as in Example 17-12.

Example 17-12   Configuring the Timers on R1 to Match R2

```
R1(config)# interface s0/0/0
R1(config-if)# ipv6 ospf hello-interval 5
R1(config-if)# ipv6 ospf dead-interval 20
R1(config-if)# end
%OSPFv3-5-ADJCHG: Process 10, Nbr 2.2.2.2 on Serial0/0/0 from LOADING to FULL,
   Loading Done
R1#
```

 Packet Tracer Activity: Fine-Tuning Dual-Stack OSPF

Refer to the Digital Study Guide to access the PKA file for this activity. You must have Packet Tracer software to run this activity. See the Introduction for details.

Troubleshooting OSPF

Understanding how OSPF operates is fundamental to troubleshooting any OSPF issues. Key to this understanding is the concept of the states OSPF transitions through on its way to adjacency with a neighbor.

OSPF States

Figure 17-4 lists the OSPF states. When troubleshooting OSPF neighbors, be aware that the FULL and 2WAY states are normal. All other states are transitory.

Figure 17-4   Transitioning Through the OSPF States

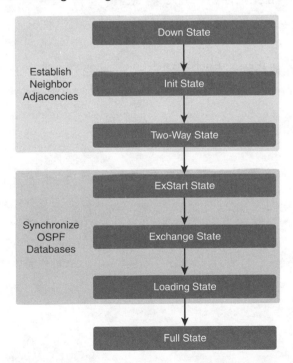

OSPF Adjacency

The lack of adjacency is a common issue in OSPF troubleshooting because the two OSPF neighbors must agree on several settings. OSPF adjacencies do not form if one or more of the following do not match:

- The interfaces are not on the same network.

- OSPF network types do not match.

- OSPF hello or dead timers do not match.

- The interface to the neighbor is incorrectly configured as passive.

- An OSPF **network** command is missing or incorrect.

- Authentication is misconfigured.

OSPF Troubleshooting Commands

When trying to isolate an OSPFv2 routing issue, the following commands are useful:

- **show ip protocols:** Verifies vital OSPF configuration information, including the OSPF process ID, the router ID, networks the router is advertising, neighbors the router is receiving updates from, and the default administrative distance, which is 110 for OSPF.

- **show ip ospf neighbor:** Verifies that the router has formed an adjacency with its neighboring routers.

- **show ip ospf interface:** Displays the OSPF parameters configured on an interface, such as the OSPF process ID, area, cost, and timer intervals.

- **show ip ospf:** Examines the OSPF process ID and router ID. This command also displays the OSPF area information and the last time the SPF algorithm was calculated.

- **show ip route ospf:** Displays only the OSPF learned routes in the routing table.

- **clear ip ospf process:** Resets the OSPFv2 neighbor adjacencies.

Figure 17-5 illustrates a method for using these commands in a systematic way.

Figure 17-5   Systematic Method for Troubleshooting OSPFv2

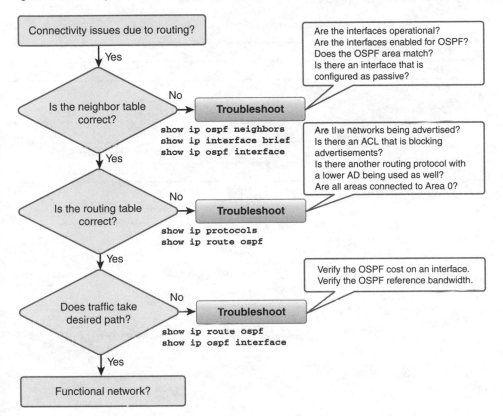

You can use the same process to troubleshoot OSPFv3 implementations. Simply replace the **ip** with **ipv6** in the list of OSPF-specific **show** commands:

- **show ipv6 protocols**

- **show ipv6 ospf neighbor**

- **show ipv6 ospf interface**

- **show ipv6 ospf**

- **show ipv6 route ospf**

- **clear ipv6 ospf process**

Packet Tracer Activity: Troubleshooting Dual-Stack OSPF

Refer to the Digital Study Guide to access the PKA file for this activity. You must have Packet Tracer software to run this activity. See the Introduction for details.

Study Resources

For today's exam topics, refer to the following resources for more study.

Resource	Location	Topic
Primary Resources		
Scaling Networks v6	10	All
ICND2 Official Cert Guide	8	Additional OSPF Features
	11	All
	23	OSPFv3 Verification and Troubleshooting
Supplemental Resources		
CCNA Portable Command Guide	15	DR/BDR Elections
		Timers
		Propagating a Default Route
		Troubleshooting OSPFv2 and OSPFv3
CCNA Video Series	3	Lesson 6: Designated and Backup Designated Routers
		Lesson 6: Network Types
		Lesson 6: Timers
		Lesson 6: OSPF Troubleshooting Exercise #1
		Lesson 6: OSPF Troubleshooting Exercise #2
CCNA Network Simulator	ICND 2	Chapter 8: OSPF Metric Tuning I
		Chapter 8: OSPF Metric Tuning II
		Chapter 8: OSPF Metric Tuning III
		Chapter 11: OSPF Troubleshooting I
		Chapter 11: OSPF Multiarea Troubleshooting
		Chapter 23: OSPF for IPv6 Metric Tuning I
		Chapter 23: OSPF for IPv6 Metric Tuning II
		Chapter 23: OSPF for IPv6 Metric Tuning III
		Chapter 23: OSPF for IPv6 Troubleshooting I
		Chapter 23: OSPF for IPv6 Troubleshooting II

Check Your Understanding

Refer to the Digital Study Guide to take a short quiz covering the content of this day.

EIGRP Operation

CCNA 200-125 Exam Topics

- Configure, verify, and troubleshoot EIGRP for IPv4

- Configure, verify, and troubleshoot EIGRP for IPv6

Key Topics

Enhanced Interior Gateway Routing Protocol (EIGRP) is a distance vector, classless routing protocol that was released in 1992 with Cisco IOS Software Release 9.21. As its name suggests, EIGRP is an enhancement of the Interior Gateway Routing Protocol (IGRP). Today's review covers the operation of EIGRP.

EIGRP Overview

EIGRP includes several features that are not commonly found in other distance vector routing protocols, including the following:

- Reliable Transport Protocol (RTP)

- Bounded updates

- Diffusing Update Algorithm (DUAL)

- Capability to establish adjacencies

- Neighbor and topology tables

Although EIGRP might act like a link-state routing protocol, it is still a distance vector routing protocol. Table 16-1 summarizes the main differences between a traditional distance vector routing protocol, such as RIP, and the enhanced distance vector routing protocol EIGRP.

Table 16-1   Comparing Traditional Distance Vector and EIGRP

Traditional Distance Vector Routing Protocols	Enhanced Distance Vector Routing Protocol: EIGRP
Uses the Bellman-Ford or Ford-Fulkerson algorithm	Uses DUAL
Ages out routing entries and uses periodic updates	Does not age out routing entries or use periodic updates
Keeps track of only the best routes, the best path to a destination network	Maintains a topology table that is separate from the routing table, which includes the best path and any loop-free backup paths
When a route becomes unavailable, requires the router to wait for a new routing update	When a route becomes unavailable, uses a backup path, if one exists in the topology table
Achieves slower convergence because of hold-down timers	Achieves faster convergence because of the absence of hold-down timers and a system of coordinated route calculations

EIGRP Characteristics

EIGRP has some unique characteristics, including protocol–dependent modules (PDMs), the Reliable Transport Protocol (RTP), and five EIGRP-specific message types.

PDMs

EIGRP is capable of routing several different protocols, including IPv4 and IPv6, using protocol-dependent modules. PDMs are responsible for the specific routing tasks for each network layer protocol, including the following:

- Maintaining the neighbor and topology tables of EIGRP routers that belong to that protocol suite
- Building and translating protocol-specific packets for DUAL
- Interfacing DUAL to the protocol-specific routing table
- Computing the metric and passing this information to DUAL
- Implementing filtering and access lists
- Performing redistribution functions to and from other routing protocols
- Redistributing routes learned by other routing protocols

RTP

EIGRP's Reliable Transport Protocol (RTP) makes PDMs possible. Instead of relying on TCP, EIGRP uses RTP for the delivery and reception of EIGRP packets, as Figure 16-1 shows.

Figure 16-1   EIGRP Replaces TCP with RTP

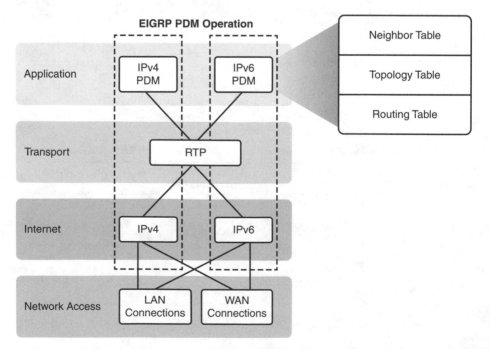

EIGRP was designed as a network layer-independent routing protocol; therefore, it cannot use the services of UDP or TCP because IPX and AppleTalk do not use protocols from the TCP/IP protocol suite.

Although *reliable* is part of its name, RTP includes both reliable delivery and unreliable delivery of EIGRP packets. Reliable RTP requires an acknowledgment to be returned, whereas an unreliable RTP packet does not require an acknowledgment.

EIGRP Packet Types

RTP can send EIGRP packets as unicast or multicast.

- Multicast EIGRP packets for IPv4 use the reserved IPv4 multicast address 224.0.0.10.

- Multicast EIGRP packets for IPv6 are sent to the reserved IPv6 multicast address FF02::A.

EIGRP uses five packet types:

- **Hello:** EIGRP uses hello packets to discover neighbors and to form adjacencies with those neighbors. EIGRP hello packets are multicasts and use unreliable delivery, so no response is required from the recipient. On most networks, EIGRP hello packets are sent every 5 seconds. On multipoint nonbroadcast multiaccess (NBMA) networks such as X.25, Frame Relay, and ATM interfaces with access links of T1 (1.544 Mbps) or slower, hellos are unicast every 60 seconds. By default, the hold time is three times the hello interval, or 15 seconds on most networks and 180 seconds on low-speed NBMA networks. If the hold time expires, EIGRP declares the route as down, and DUAL searches for a new path in the topology table or by sending out queries.

- **Update:** EIGRP does not send periodic updates. Update packets are sent only when necessary, contain only the routing information needed, and are sent only to the routers that require it. EIGRP update packets use reliable delivery. Update packets are sent as a multicast when required by multiple routers, or as a unicast when required by only a single router.

- **Acknowledgment:** EIGRP sends acknowledgment (ACK) packets unreliably even when reliable delivery is used. RTP uses reliable delivery for EIGRP update, query, and reply packets. EIGRP acknowledgment packets are always sent as an unreliable unicast.

- **Query:** DUAL uses a query packet when searching for networks. Queries use reliable delivery and can use multicast or unicast.

- **Reply:** A reply packet is sent in response to a query packet regardless of whether the replying router has information about the queried route. Replies use reliable delivery and, unlike queries, are always sent as unicast (never as multicast).

EIGRP Message Format

Figure 16-2 shows an example of an encapsulated EIGRP message.

Figure 16-2   Encapsulated EIGRP Message

Data Link Frame Header	IP Packet Header	EIGRP Packet Header	Type/Length/Value Types

Data Link Frame

MAC Source Address = Address of Sending Interface
MAC Destination Address = Multicast: 01-00-5E-00-00-0A

IP Packet

IP Source Address = Address of Sending Interface
IP Destination Address = Multicast: 224.0.0.10
Protocol Field = 88 for EIGRP

EIGRP Packet Header

Opcode for EIGRP Packet Type
AS Number

TLV Types
Some Types Include:

0x0001 EIGRP Parameters
0x0102 IP Internal Routes
0x0103 IP External Routes

Beginning from the right side of Figure 16-2, notice that the data field is called Type/Length/Value, or TLV. The types of TLVs relevant to the CCNA are EIGRP Parameters, IP Internal Routes, and IP External Routes. Figure 16-3 shows the details of the EIGRP packet header.

Figure 16-3   EIGRP Packet Header

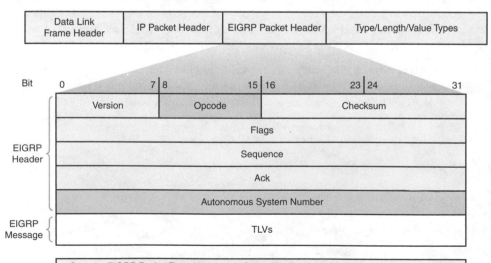

The EIGRP packet header is included with every EIGRP packet, regardless of its TLV. The EIGRP packet header and TLV are then encapsulated in an IP packet. In the IP packet header, the Protocol field is set to 88 to indicate EIGRP, and the Destination Address is set to either the unicast address of an EIGRP neighbor or the multicast address 224.0.0.10. If the EIGRP packet is encapsulated in an Ethernet frame, the destination MAC address is also a multicast address: 01-00-5E-00-00-0A.

Important fields for our discussion include the Opcode field and the Autonomous System Number field. Opcode specifies the EIGRP packet type. The autonomous system number specifies the EIGRP routing process. Cisco routers can run multiple instances of EIGRP. The autonomous system number is used to track multiple instances of EIGRP.

Activity: Identify the EIGRP Packet Type

Refer to the Digital Study Guide to complete this activity.

EIGRP Processes

EIGRP has a unique method of convergence that includes a composite metric and the Diffusing Update Algorithm (DUAL).

EIGRP Convergence

Figure 16-4 summarizes the process EIGRP uses to reach convergence and respond to network changes.

Figure 16-4   EIGRP Convergence

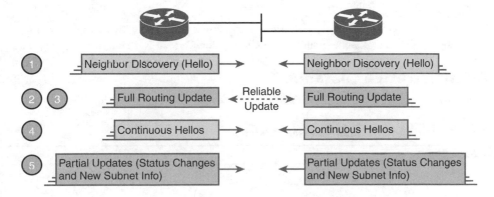

1. The routers exchange hellos to establish adjacency and update their neighbor tables.

2. The routers exchange full routing information and update their topology tables.

3. The routers choose the best routes and update the routing table.

4. The routers maintain adjacency with hello messages.

5. When a topology change occurs, the routers respond with partial updates and reconverge on the new information.

EIGRP Composite Metric

EIGRP uses the values bandwidth, delay, reliability, and load in its composite metric to calculate the preferred path to a network. By default, EIGRP uses only bandwidth and delay in its metric calculation, as Figure 16-5 shows.

Figure 16-5   Calculating the EIGRP Default Metric

```
Default metric = [K1*bandwidth + K3*delay] * 256

Because both K1 and K3 equal 1, the formula simplifies to: bandwidth + delay

bandwidth = speed of slowest link in route to the destination
    delay = sum of delays of each link in route to the destination
```

```
Slowest bandwidth:              (10,000,000/bandwidth kbps) * 256
Plus the sum of the delays: +   (sum of delay/10) * 256
                            =   EIGRP metric
```

```
R2#show ip route
<output omitted>

D   192.168.1.0/24 [90/3014400] via 192.168.10.10, 00:02:14, Serial0/0/1
```

The bandwidth metric is a static value that Cisco IOS assigns to interface types. For example, most serial interfaces are assigned the default value 1544 kbps, the bandwidth of a T1 connection. This value might or might not reflect the actual bandwidth of the interface and can be adjusted using the **bandwidth** command in interface configuration mode.

Delay is the measure of time it takes for a packet to traverse a route. The delay metric is a static value based on the type of link to which the interface is connected; it is measured in microseconds.

Administrative Distance

Table 16-2 lists the Cisco IOS default administrative distances for routing protocols.

Table 16-2   Default Administrative Distance

Route Source	AD
Connected	0
Static	1
EIGRP summary route	5
External BGP	20
Internal EIGRP	90
IGRP	100

Route Source	AD
OSPF	110
IS-IS	115
RIP	120
External EIGRP	170
Internal BGP	200

EIGRP has a default AD of 5 for summary routes, 90 for internal routes, and 170 for routes imported from an external source, such as default routes. When compared to other interior gateway protocols, EIGRP is the most preferred by Cisco IOS Software because it has the lowest AD.

DUAL

Distance vector routing protocols such as RIP prevent routing loops with hold-down timers. The primary way EIGRP prevents routing loops is with the DUAL algorithm. DUAL is used to obtain loop freedom at every instant throughout a route computation. This allows all routers involved in a topology change to synchronize at the same time. Routers that are not affected by the topology changes are not involved in the recomputation because queries and replies are bounded to only the routers that need or have the route-specific information. This method gives EIGRP faster convergence times than other routing protocols.

Because recomputation of DUAL can be processor intensive, it is best to avoid recomputation whenever possible. Therefore, DUAL maintains a list of backup routes it has already determined to be loop free. If the primary route in the routing table fails, the best backup route is immediately added to the routing table.

DUAL Concepts

The following terms and concepts are at the center of the loop avoidance mechanism of DUAL.

- **Successor:** A neighboring router that is used for packet forwarding and is the least-cost route to the destination network.

- **Feasible distance (FD):** The lowest calculated metric to reach the destination network.

- **Feasible successor (FS):** A neighbor that has a loop-free backup path to the same network as the successor. It satisfies the feasibility condition

- **Reported distance (RD) or advertised distance (AD):** The feasible distance as reported by the neighbor.

- **Feasible condition or feasibility condition (FC):** Condition met when a neighbor's reported distance (RD) to a network is less than the local router's feasible distance to the same destination network.

Tomorrow's review provides examples of these terms in its discussion about EIGRP verification commands.

DUAL FSM

Figure 16-6 graphically shows DUAL's finite state machine (FSM), or how the algorithm comes to a final decision.

Figure 16-6   DUAL Finite State Machine

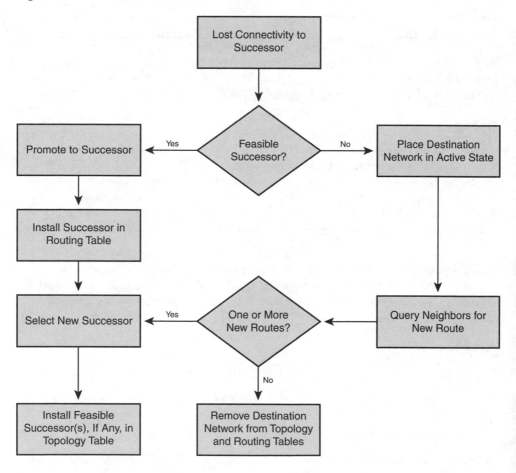

Activity: Identify the Administrative Distance

Refer to the Digital Study Guide to complete this activity.

Study Resources

For today's exam topics, refer to the following resources for more study.

Resource	Location	Topic
Primary Resources		
Scaling Networks v6	6	EIGRP Characteristics
		EIGRP Operation
ICND2 Official Cert Guide	9	All
Supplemental Resources		
CCNA Video Series	3	Lesson 7: EIGRP Overview
		Lesson 7: EIGRP Components
		Lesson 7: EIGRP Data Structures
		Lesson 7: EIGRP Metric Calculation
		Lesson 7: The EIGRP Feasibility Condition
		Lesson 7: EIGRP for IPv6 Overview

Check Your Understanding

Refer to the Digital Study Guide to take a short quiz covering the content of this day.

EIGRP Implementation

CCNA 200-125 Exam Topics

- Configure, verify, and troubleshoot EIGRP for IPv4
- Configure, verify, and troubleshoot EIGRP for IPv6

Key Topics

Enhanced IGRP (EIGRP) is easy to get up and running with a basic configuration. To take full advantage of EIGRP, however, you must complete a variety of configuration tasks to modify the basic configuration. Today's review covers basic EIGRP for IPv4 and IPv6 configuration and verification. Tomorrow's review focuses on modifying and troubleshooting EIGRP.

EIGRP for IPv4 Configuration

This section covers the basics of configuring EIGRP for IPv4, including the **network** and **router-id** commands.

EIGRP Topology and Addressing Scheme

This review of the EIGRP configuration commands uses the topology in Figure 15-1 and the addressing scheme in Table 15-1.

Table 15-1   Addressing Scheme for EIGRP

Device	Interface	IP Address	Subnet Mask
R1	G0/0	172.16.1.1	255.255.255.0
	S0/0/0	172.16.3.1	255.255.255.252
	S0/0/1	192.168.10.5	255.255.255.252
R2	G0/0	172.16.2.1	255.255.255.0
	S0/0/0	172.16.3.2	255.255.255.252
	S0/0/1	192.168.10.9	255.255.255.252
	S0/1/0	209.165.200.225	255.255.255.224
R3	G0/0	192.168.1.1	255.255.255.0
	S0/0/0	192.168.10.6	255.255.255.252
	S0/0/1	192.168.10.10	255.255.255.252

Figure 15-1   EIGRP Configuration Topology

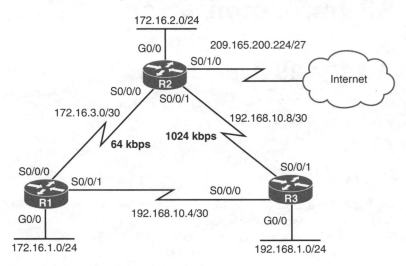

The network Command

Assuming that the interfaces of all the routers are configured and activated according to the IP addresses in Table 15-1, Example 15-1 shows the EIGRP configuration using the **network** command.

Example 15-1   EIGRP Configuration

```
R1(config)# router eigrp 1
R1(config-router)# network 172.16.0.0
R1(config-router)# network 192.168.10.0


R2(config)# router eigrp 1
R2(config-router)# network 172.16.0.0
R2(config-router)# network 192.168.10.0


R3(config)# router eigrp 1
R3(config-router)# network 192.168.1.0
R3(config-router)# network 192.168.10.0
```

The Router ID

The router ID is used in both EIGRP and OSPF routing protocols, although the role of the router ID is more significant in OSPF.

Cisco routers derive the router ID based on three criteria, in the following precedence:

1. The router uses the IPv4 address configured with the **eigrp router-id** router configuration mode command.

2. If the router ID is not configured, the router chooses the highest IPv4 address of any of its loopback interfaces.

3. If no loopback interfaces are configured, the router chooses the highest active IPv4 address of any of its physical interfaces.

For this topology example, you can explicitly configure the router ID, as in Example 15-2.

Example 15-2   Configuring Router IDs for EIGRP

```
R1(config)# router eigrp 1
R1(config-router)# eigrp router-id 1.1.1.1

R2(config)# router eigrp 1
R2(config-router)# eigrp router-id 2.2.2.2

R3(config)# router eigrp 1
R3(config-router)# eigrp router-id 3.3.3.3
```

EIGRP for IPv4 Verification

This section looks at the contents of four important EIGRP for IPv4 verification commands: **show ip protocols**, **show ip eigrp neighbors**, **show ip eigrp topology**, and **show ip route eigrp**.

Examining the Protocol Details

Example 15-3 shows the output for the **show ip protocols** command on R1.

Example 15-3   The Protocol Details for R1

```
R1# show ip protocols
*** IP Routing is NSF aware ***

Routing Protocol is "eigrp 1"
  Outgoing update filter list for all interfaces is not set
  Incoming update filter list for all interfaces is not set
  Default networks flagged in outgoing updates
  Default networks accepted from incoming updates
  EIGRP-IPv4 Protocol for AS(1)
    Metric weight K1=1, K2=0, K3=1, K4=0, K5=0
    NSF-aware route hold timer is 240
    Router-ID: 1.1.1.1
    Topology : 0 (base)
      Active Timer: 3 min
      Distance: internal 90 external 170
      Maximum path: 4
      Maximum hopcount 100
      Maximum metric variance 1
Automatic Summarization: disabled
```

```
Maximum path: 4
 Routing for Networks:
    172.16.0.0
    192.168.10.0
 Routing Information Sources:
     Gateway           Distance        Last Update
     192.168.10.6          90          00:40:20
     172.16.3.2            90          00:40:20
 Distance: internal 90 external 170
```

The output in Example 15-3 shows the verification of several important EIGRP protocol details, including the following:

- EIGRP is an active dynamic routing protocol on R1 configured with the autonomous system number 1.

- The EIGRP router ID of R1 is 1.1.1.1.

- The EIGRP administrative distances on R1 are internal AD of 90 and external of 170 (default values).

- By default, EIGRP does not automatically summarize networks. Subnets are included in the routing updates.

- The EIGRP neighbor adjacencies R1 has with other routers that are used to receive EIGRP routing updates.

Examining Neighbor Tables

Figure 15-2 shows the output for the **show ip eigrp neighbors** command on R1.

Figure 15-2   The Neighbor Table on R1

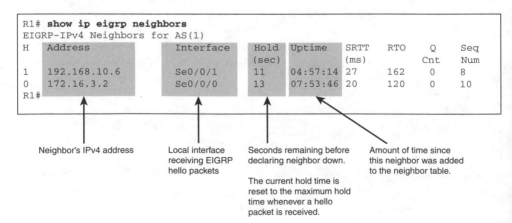

The **show ip eigrp neighbors** command output includes the following:

- **H column:** Lists the neighbors in the order they were learned.

- **Address:** Gives the IPv4 address of the neighbor.

- **Interface:** States the local interface on which this hello packet was received.

- **Hold:** Gives the current hold time. When a hello packet is received, this value is reset to the maximum hold time for that interface and then counts down to zero. If zero is reached, the neighbor is considered down.

- **Uptime:** Shows the amount of time since this neighbor was added to the neighbor table.

- **Smooth round trip timer (SRTT) and retransmission timeout (RTO):** Used by RTP to manage reliable EIGRP packets.

- **Queue count:** Should always be zero. If it is more than zero, EIGRP packets are waiting to be sent.

- **Sequence number:** Tracks updates, queries, and reply packets.

Examining the Topology Tables

EIGRP maintains a topology database with full route information, including all successors and feasible successors, as Example 15-4 shows for R2.

Example 15-4   The Topology Table on R2

```
R2# show ip eigrp topology
EIGRP-IPv4 Topology Table for AS(1)/ID(2.2.2.2)
Codes: P - Passive, A - Active, U - Update, Q - Query, R - Reply,
       r - reply Status, s - sia Status
P 172.16.2.0/24, 1 successors, FD is 2816
        via Connected, GigabitEthernet0/0
P 192.168.10.4/30, 1 successors, FD is 3523840
        via 192.168.10.10 (3523840/2169856), Serial0/0/1
        via 172.16.3.1 (41024000/2169856), Serial0/0/0
P 192.168.1.0/24, 1 successors, FD is 3012096
        via 192.168.10.10 (3012096/2816), Serial0/0/1
        via 172.16.3.1 (41024256/2170112), Serial0/0/0
P 172.16.3.0/30, 1 successors, FD is 40512000
        via Connected, Serial0/0/0
P 172.16.1.0/24, 1 successors, FD is 3524096
        via 192.168.10.10 (3524096/2170112), Serial0/0/1
        via 172.16.3.1 (40512256/2816), Serial0/0/0
P 192.168.10.8/30, 1 successors, FD is 3011840
        via Connected, Serial0/0/1
R2#
```

NOTE: For the output in Example 15-2 and the following discussion, assume that the **bandwidth** command has been configured according to the bandwidth values labeled on the topology in Figure 15-1. Tomorrow's review covers the **bandwidth** command specifically.

To review the specifics of EIGRP successors, feasible successors, feasible distance, reported distance, and feasible condition, let's focus on the highlighted entry for 192.168.1.0/24 (see Figure 15-3).

Figure 15-3   192.168.1.0/24: Successor and Feasible Successor

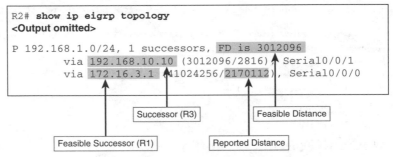

R2 has two routes for 192.168.1.0/24. The first subentry is a route through R3. It is the successor and is installed in the routing table because it has the lowest feasible distance. The second subentry is a route through R1. It is a feasible successor because it meets the feasibility condition, which states that the reported distance of the feasible successor must be less than the feasible distance of the successor. The reported distance from R1 is less than the feasible distance of the successor from R3. Therefore, if the successor becomes unavailable, DUAL can immediately install the feasible successor without running any computations.

The **show ip eigrp topology all-links** command displays all topology table entries, including routes that are not feasible successors (see Figure 15-4).

Figure 15-4   192.168.1.0/24: Successor, No Feasible Successor

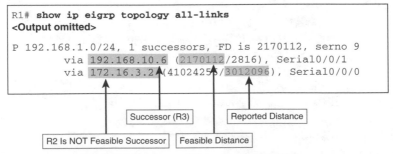

As with R2, R1 has a successor to 192.168.1.0/24; however, R1 does not have a feasible successor because the route from R2 does not meet the feasibility condition. The reported distance for the route from R2 is greater than the feasible distance of the successor route. Therefore, if the successor becomes unavailable, DUAL must run its algorithm to query neighbors for a potentially better route before it can install the route from R2.

Examining the Routing Table

Verifying that all expected routes are installed in the routing tables is one of the quickest ways to check that EIGRP is correctly implemented across all routers. Example 15-5 shows the EIGRP routing tables for all three routers.

Example 15-5   EIGRP Routes in the Routing Tables for R1, R2, and R3

```
R1# show ip route eigrp
     172.16.0.0/16 is variably subnetted, 5 subnets, 3 masks
D       172.16.2.0/24 [90/3524096] via 192.168.10.6, 00:24:34, Serial0/0/1
D    192.168.1.0/24 [90/2170112] via 192.168.10.6, 00:24:34, Serial0/0/1
     192.168.10.0/24 is variably subnetted, 3 subnets, 2 masks
D       192.168.10.8/30 [90/3523840] via 192.168.10.6, 00:24:34, Serial0/0/1
R1#


R2# show ip route eigrp
     172.16.0.0/16 is variably subnetted, 5 subnets, 3 masks
D       172.16.1.0/24 [90/3524096] via 192.168.10.10, 00:25:13, Serial0/0/1
D    192.168.1.0/24 [90/3012096] via 192.168.10.10, 01:02:22, Serial0/0/1
     192.168.10.0/24 is variably subnetted, 3 subnets, 2 masks
D       192.168.10.4/30 [90/3523840] via 192.168.10.10, 00:25:19, Serial0/0/1


R2#
R3# show ip route eigrp
     172.16.0.0/16 is variably subnetted, 3 subnets, 2 masks
D       172.16.1.0/24 [90/2170112] via 192.168.10.5, 00:25:41, Serial0/0/0
D       172.16.2.0/24 [90/3012096] via 192.168.10.9, 01:02:44, Serial0/0/1
D       172.16.3.0/30 [90/41024000] via 192.168.10.9, 01:02:44, Serial0/0/1
                      [90/41024000] via 192.168.10.5, 00:25:41, Serial0/0/0
R3#
```

EIGRP for IPv6 Concepts

EIGRP for IPv6 has the same functionality as EIGRP for IPv4, but it uses IPv6 as the network layer transport, communicating with EIGRP for IPv6 peers and advertising IPv6 routes. Table 15-2 summarizes the similarities and differences between the IPv4 and IPv6 versions of EIGRP.

Table 15-2   Comparing EIGRP for IPv4 and IPv6

Characteristic	EIGRP for IPv4	EIGRP for IPv6
Advertised routes	IPv4 networks	IPv6 prefixes
Distance vector	Yes	Yes
Convergence technology	DUAL	DUAL
Metric	Bandwidth and delay by default, reliability and load optional	Bandwidth and delay by default, reliability and load optional
Transport protocol	Reliable Transport Protocol (RTP)	RTP
Update messages	Incremental, partial, and bounded updates	Incremental, partial, and bounded updates
Neighbor discovery	Hello packets	Hello packets
Source and destination addresses	IPv4 source address and 224.0.0.10 IPv4 multicast destination address	IPv6 link-local source address and FF02::10 IPv6 multicast destination address
Authentication	Plain text and MD5 (message digest algorithm 5)	MD5
Router ID	32-bit router ID	32-bit router ID

EIGRP for IPv6 Configuration

The EIGRP for IPv6 configuration commands are similar to those used in EIGRP for IPv4. This review of the EIGRP for IPv6 configuration commands uses the topology in Figure 15-5 and the addressing scheme in Table 15-3.

Figure 15-5   EIGRP for IPv6 Configuration Topology

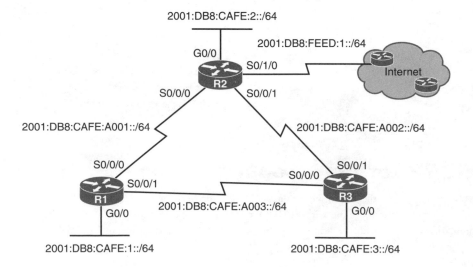

Table 15-3   Addressing Scheme for OSPFv3

Device	Interface	IPv6 Address/Prefix
R1	G0/0	2001:DB8:CAFE:1::1/64
	S0/0/0	2001:DB8:CAFE:A001::2/64
	S0/0/1	2001:DB8:CAFE:A003::1/64
	Link-local	FE80::1
	Router ID	1.1.1.1
R2	G0/0	2001:DB8:CAFE:2::1/64
	S0/0/0	2001:DB8:CAFE:A001::1/64
	S0/0/1	2001:DB8:CAFE:A002::1/64
	S0/1/0	2001:DB8:FEED:1::2/64
	Link-local	FE80::2
	Router ID	2.2.2.2
R3	G0/0	2001:DB8:CAFE:3::1/64
	S0/0/0	2001:DB8:CAFE:A003::2/64
	S0/0/1	2001:DB8:CAFE:A002::2/64
	Link-local	FE80::3
	Router ID	3.3.3.3

To configure EIGRP for IPv6, complete the following steps:

Step 1.   Enable IPv6 routing with the **ipv6 unicast-routing** command in global configuration mode.

Step 2.   Enter EIGRP for IPv6 routing configuration mode with the **ipv6 router eigrp** *AS-number* global configuration command.

Step 3.   Configure the 32-bit router ID with the **eigrp router-id** *IPv4-address* router configuration command.

Step 4.   The EIGRP for IPv6 process will start running after you enter the router ID. However, EIGRP for IPv6 has a shutdown feature. Therefore, it is a best practice to enter the **no shutdown** command to ensure that the process is running.

Step 5.   Enable EIGRP for IPv6 on each desired interface with the **ipv6 eigrp** *AS-number* interface configuration command.

Example 15-6 shows the configuration commands for R2 to enable EIGRP for IPv6 on all interfaces. The commands are the same for R1 and R3.

Example 15-6   Enabling EIGRP for IPv6 on R2

```
R2(config)# ipv6 unicast-routing
R2(config)# ipv6 router eigrp 100
R2(config-rtr)# eigrp router-id 2.2.2.2
R2(config-rtr)# no shutdown
R2(config-rtr)# interface g0/0
R2(config-if)# ipv6 eigrp 100
R2(config-if)# interface s0/0/0
R2(config-if)# ipv6 eigrp 100
R2(config-if)# interface s0/0/1
R2(config-if)# ipv6 eigrp 100
R2(config-if)# end
R2#
```

EIGRP for IPv6 Verification

The EIGRP for IPv6 verification commands are similar to those used in EIGRP for IPv4. Just replace the keyword **ip** with **ipv6**. This section looks at the contents of three important EIGRP for IPv6 verification commands: **show ipv6 protocols**, **show ipv6 eigrp neighbors**, and **show ipv6 route eigrp**.

Examining the Protocol Details

Example 15-7 shows the output for the **show ipv6 protocols** command on R1.

Example 15-7   The Protocol Details for R1

```
R1# show ipv6 protocols
IPv6 Routing Protocol is "connected"
IPv6 Routing Protocol is "ND"
IPv6 Routing Protocol is "eigrp 100"
EIGRP-IPv6 Protocol for AS(100)
  Metric weight K1=1, K2=0, K3=1, K4=0, K5=0
  NSF-aware route hold timer is 240
  Router-ID: 1.1.1.1
  Topology : 0 (base)
    Active Timer: 3 min
    Distance: internal 90 external 170
    Maximum path: 16
    Maximum hopcount 100
    Maximum metric variance 1
```

```
Interfaces:
    GigabitEthernet0/0
    Serial0/0/0
    Serial0/0/1
  Redistribution:
    None
R1#
```

The output in Example 15-2 shows the verification of several important EIGRP protocol details, including the following:

- EIGRP for IPv6 is an active dynamic routing protocol on R1 configured with the autonomous system number 100.

- The k values used to calculate the composite metric are the same as in EIGRP for IPv4.

- The EIGRP router ID of R1 is 1.1.1.1.

- As with EIGRP for IPv4, the administrative distances on R1 are internal AD of 90 and external of 170 (default values).

- The interfaces enabled for EIGRP for IPv6.

Examining the Neighbor Table

Figure 15-6 shows the output for the **show ipv6 eigrp neighbors** command on R1.

Figure 15-6   The Neighbor Table on R1

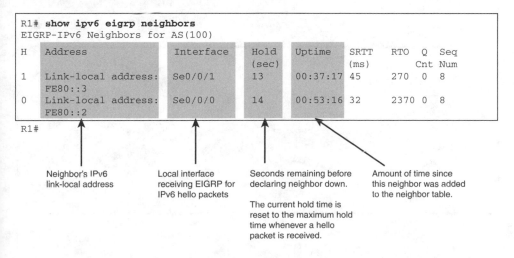

The **show ipv6 eigrp neighbors** command output includes the following:

- **H column:** Lists the neighbors in the order they were learned.

- **Address:** Gives the IPv6 link-local address of the neighbor.

- **Interface:** States the local interface on which this hello packet was received.

- **Hold:** Gives the current hold time. When a hello packet is received, this value is reset to the maximum hold time for that interface and then counts down to zero. If zero is reached, the neighbor is considered down.

- **Uptime:** Specifies the amount of time since this neighbor was added to the neighbor table.

- **SRTT and RTO:** Used by RTP to manage reliable EIGRP packets.

- **Queue count:** Should always be zero. If it is more than zero, EIGRP packets are waiting to be sent.

- **Sequence number:** Tracks updates, queries, and reply packets.

Examining the Routing Table

Verifying that all expected routes are installed in the routing tables is one of the quickest ways to check that EIGRP for IPv6 is correctly implemented across all routers. Example 15-8 shows the EIGRP routing tables for all three routers.

Example 15-8   EIGRP for IPv6 Routes in the Routing Tables for R1, R2, and R3

```
R1# show ipv6 route eigrp
D    2001:DB8:CAFE:2::/64 [90/2170112]
       via FE80::2, Serial0/0/0, receive
D    2001:DB8:CAFE:3::/64 [90/2170112]
       via FE80::3, Serial0/0/1, receive
D    2001:DB8:CAFE:A002::/64 [90/2681856]
       via FE80::2, Serial0/0/0, receive
       via FE80::3, Serial0/0/1, receive
R1#


R2# show ipv6 route eigrp
D    2001:DB8:CAFE:1::/64 [90/2170112]
       via FE80::1, Serial0/0/0, receive
D    2001:DB8:CAFE:3::/64 [90/2170112]
       via FE80::3, Serial0/0/1, receive
D    2001:DB8:CAFE:A003::/64 [90/2681856]
       via FE80::1, Serial0/0/0, receive
       via FE80::3, Serial0/0/1, receive
R2#


R3# show ipv6 route eigrp
D    2001:DB8:CAFE:1::/64 [90/2170112]
       via FE80::1, Serial0/0/0, receive
```

```
D    2001:DB8:CAFE:2::/64 [90/2170112]
       via FE80::2, Serial0/0/1, receive
D    2001:DB8:CAFE:A001::/64 [90/2681856]
       via FE80::1, Serial0/0/0, receive
       via FE80::2, Serial0/0/1, receive
R3#
```

 Packet Tracer Activity: Dual-Stack EIGRP Configuration

Refer to the Digital Study Guide to access the PKA file for this activity. You must have Packet Tracer software to run this activity. See the Introduction for details.

Study Resources

For today's exam topics, refer to the following resources for more study.

Resource	Location	Topic
Primary Resources		
Scaling Networks v6	6	Implement EIGRP for IPv4
		Implement EIGRP for IPv6
ICND2 Official Cert Guide	10	Core EIGRP Configuration and Verification
		EIGRP Metrics, Successors, and Feasible Successors
	24	EIGRP for IPv6 Configuration Basics
		EIGRP for IPv6 Configuration Example
		EIGRP for IPv6 Verification and Troubleshooting
Supplemental Resources		
CCNA Portable Command Guide	14	Configuring Enhanced Interior Gateway Routing Protocol (EIGRP) for IPv4
		EIGRP Router ID
		Configuration Example: EIGRP
		Configuration Example: EIGRPv6
CCNA Video Series	3	Lesson 7: EIGRP for IPv4 Configuration and Verification
		Lesson 7: EIGRP for IPv6 Configuration
		Lesson 7: EIGRP for IPv6 Verification

Resource	Location	Topic
Supplemental Resources		
CCNA Network Simulator	ICND2	Chapter 10: EIGRP Configuration I–II
		Chapter 10: EIGRP Serial Configuration I–VI
		Chapter 10: EIGRP Neighbors I–II
		Chapter 24: EIGRP for IPv6 Configuration
		Chapter 24: EIGRP for IPv6 Serial Configuration I–IV
		Chapter 24: EIGRP for IPv6 Neighbors I–II

Check Your Understanding

Refer to the Digital Study Guide to take a short quiz covering the content of this day.

Fine-Tuning and Troubleshooting EIGRP

CCNA 200-125 Exam Topics

- Configure, verify, and troubleshoot EIGRP for IPv4
- Configure, verify, and troubleshoot EIGRP for IPv6

Key Topics

Today we review the commands for fine-tuning and troubleshooting an EIGRP implementation. We look at using automatic summarization, modifying the cost, propagating a default route, and modifying the timers. We finish the day with EIGRP troubleshooting commands and methodology.

Modifying the EIGRP for IPv4 Configuration

As with OSPF, the EIGRP configuration can be modified in several ways, including enabling automatic summarization, propagating a default route, modifying the bandwidth value, and fine-tuning the timers.

Automatic Summarization

By default, EIGRP automatic route summarization is disabled. Route summarization allows a router to group networks together and advertise them as one large group using a single summarized route. Figure 14-1 shows an example of how automatic summarization works.

Figure 14-1   Automatic Summarization in EIGRP

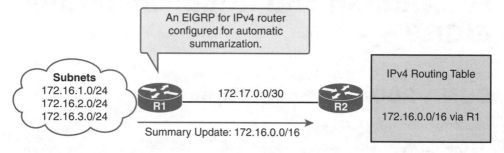

Classful Networks	
Class A: 0.0.0.0 to 127.255.255.255	Default Mask: 255.0.0.0 or /8
Class B: 128.0.0.0 to 191.255.255.255	Default Mask: 255.255.0.0 or /16
Class C: 192.0.0.0 to 223.255.255.255	Default Mask: 255.255.255.0 or /24

R1 and R2 are both configured using EIGRP for IPv4, with automatic summarization enabled. R1 has three subnets in its routing table: 172.16.1.0/24, 172.16.2.0/24, and 172.16.3.0/24. In the classful network addressing architecture, these subnets are all considered part of a larger Class B network, 172.16.0.0/16. Because EIGRP on R1 is configured for automatic summarization, when it sends its routing update to R2, it summarizes the three /24 subnets as a single network of 172.16.0.0/16; this reduces the number of routing updates sent and the number of entries in R2's IPv4 routing table.

To enable automatic summarization, configure the command **auto-summary** in router configuration mode, as in Example 14-1.

Example 14-1   Enabling Automatic Summarization

```
R1(config)# router eigrp 1
R1(config-router)# auto-summary


R2(config)# router eigrp 1
R2(config-router)# auto-summary


R3(config)# router eigrp 1
R3(config-router)# auto-summary
```

NOTE: It is probably best to leave automatic summarization disabled because this ensures that, even when subnets are assigned discontiguously, routing information will still propagate throughout the EIGRP routing domain.

EIGRP for IPv4 Topology

Our review of fine-tuning EIGRP for IPv4 uses the topology in Figure 14-2.

Figure 14-2   EIGRP for IPv4 Topology

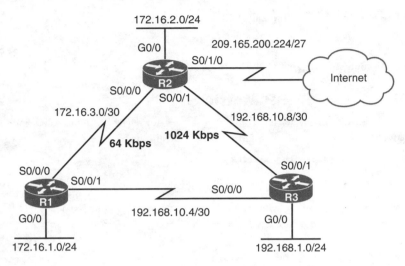

Propagating an IPv4 Default Route

The quad zero default static route can be used with any currently supported routing protocols. In this example, we configure the static default route on R2 because it is connected to the Internet. Example 14-2 shows the default static route configuration on R2.

Example 14-2   Configuring and Redistributing a Default Route in EIGRP

```
R2(config)# ip route 0.0.0.0 0.0.0.0 Serial0/1/0
R2(config)# router eigrp 1
R2(config-router)# redistribute static
```

The **redistribute static** command tells EIGRP to include this static route in its EIGRP updates to other routers. Example 14-3 shows the routing table for R1, with the default route highlighted.

Example 14-3   R1 Routing Table with Default Route Installed

```
R1# show ip route eigrp
     172.16.0.0/16 is variably subnetted, 5 subnets, 3 masks
D       172.16.2.0/24 [90/3524096] via 192.168.10.6, 00:06:27, Serial0/0/1
D    192.168.0.0/22 [90/2170112] via 192.168.10.6, 00:06:28, Serial0/0/1
     192.168.10.0/24 is variably subnetted, 3 subnets, 2 masks
D       192.168.10.8/30 [90/3523840] via 192.168.10.6, 00:06:28, Serial0/0/1
D*EX 0.0.0.0/0 [170/8643840] via 192.168.10.6, 00:00:14, Serial0/0/1
R1#
```

The code D*EX is interpreted as follows:

- **D:** This route was learned through EIGRP.

- ***:** This route is currently the candidate default route.

- **EX:** This route is an external route. Note the administrative distance of 170.

Modifying the EIGRP Metric

Because the bandwidth might default to a value that does not reflect the actual value, you can use the **bandwidth** interface command to modify the bandwidth metric:

```
Router(config-if)# bandwidth kilobits
```

In the topology in Figure 14-1, notice that the link between R1 and R2 has a bandwidth of 64 kbps, and the link between R2 and R3 has a bandwidth of 1024 kbps. Example 14-4 shows the configurations used on all three routers to modify the bandwidth.

Example 14-4   Modifying the Bandwidth

```
R1(config)# interface serial 0/0/0
R1(config-if)# bandwidth 64

R2(config)# interface serial 0/0/0
R2(config-if)# bandwidth 64
R2(config-if)# interface serial 0/0/1
R2(config-if)# bandwidth 1024

R3(config)# interface serial 0/0/1
R3(config-if)# bandwidth 1024
```

NOTE: The process to modify the bandwidth is the same whether the interface is configured with IPv4 or IPv6 addressing.

Modifying Hello Intervals and Hold Times

Hello intervals and hold times are configurable on a per-interface basis and do not have to match with other EIGRP routers to establish adjacencies. The syntax for the command to modify the hello interval follows:

```
Router(config-if)# ip hello-interval eigrp as-number seconds
```

If you change the hello interval, make sure that you also change the hold time to a value equal to or greater than the hello interval. Otherwise, neighbor adjacency will go down after the hold time expires and before the next hello interval. The command to configure a different hold time follows:

```
Router(config-if)# ip hold-time eigrp as-number seconds
```

The *seconds* value for both hello and holdtime intervals can range from 1 to 65,535. In Example 14-5, R1 and R2 are configured to use a 60-second hello interval and 180-second hold time.

Example 14-5   Modifying the Hello Intervals and Hold Times

```
R1(config)# interface s0/0/0
R1(config-if)# ip hello-interval eigrp 1 60
R1(config-if)# ip hold-time eigrp 1 180

R2(config)# interface s0/0/0
R2(config-if)# ip hello-interval eigrp 1 60
R2(config-if)# ip hold-time eigrp 1 180
```

Modifying EIGRP for IPv6

Modifying the EIGRP for IPv6 implementation includes propagating a default route, modifying the bandwidth value, and fine-tuning the timers.

EIGRP for IPv6 Topology

We use the topology in Figure 14-3 in our review of EIGRP for IPv6 modification.

Figure 14-3   EIGRP for IPv6 Topology

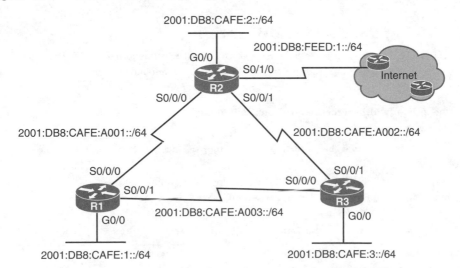

Propagating an IPv6 Default Route

Propagating a default route in EIGRP for IPv6 is exactly the same as in EIGRP for IPv4. Configure the static default route and enter the **redistribute static** command in router configuration mode, as in Example 14-6.

Example 14-6   Propagating a Default Route in EIGRP for IPv6

```
R2(config)# ipv6 route ::/0 serial 0/1/0
R2(config)# ipv6 router eigrp 100
R2(config-rtr)# redistribute static
R2(config-rtr)# end
R2#
```

R1 and R3 now have a default route, as verified with the **show ipv6 route** command in Example 14-7.

Example 14-7   Default Routes in R1 and R3 Routing Tables

```
R1# show ipv6 route
<output omitted>
EX   ::/0 [170/7289856]
     via FE80::2, Serial0/0/0, receive
R1#
```

```
R3# show ipv6 route
<output omitted>
EX   ::/0 [170/7289856]
     via FE80::2, Serial0/0/1, receive
R3#
```

Modifying Bandwidth Utilization

By default, EIGRP uses only up to 50 percent of an interface's bandwidth for EIGRP information. This prevents the EIGRP process from overutilizing a link and not allowing enough bandwidth for the routing of normal traffic.

Use the **ip bandwidth-percent eigrp** command to modify the percentage of bandwidth that EIGRP can use on an interface:

```
Router(config-if)# ipv6 bandwidth-percent eigrp as-number percent
```

For example, assume that R1 and R2 share a very slow 64 kbps link. Example 14-8 shows how to configure EIGRP to reduce the default usage to 40 percent.

Example 14-8   Modifying the Bandwidth Utilization

```
R1(config)# interface serial 0/0/0
R1(config-if)# ipv6 bandwidth-percent eigrp 100 40
```

```
R2(config)# interface serial 0/0/0
R2(config-if)# ipv6 bandwidth-percent eigrp 100 40
```

NOTE: The process to modify the bandwidth utilization is the same as for IPv4, except that the command uses **ipv6** instead of **ip**.

Modifying Hello Intervals and Hold Times

EIGRP for IPv6 uses the same hello interval and hold times as EIGRP for IPv4. The interface configuration mode commands are similar to those for IPv4:

```
Router(config-if)# ipv6 hello-interval eigrp as-number seconds
Router(config-if)# ipv6 hold-time eigrp as-number seconds
```

Example 14-9 shows the hello interval and hold times configurations for R1 and R2 with EIGRP for IPv6.

Example 14-9   Configuring EIGRP for IPv6 Hello and Hold Times

```
R1(config)# interface serial 0/0/0
R1(config-if)# ipv6 hello-interval eigrp 100 50
R1(config-if)# ipv6 hold-time eigrp 100 50

R2(config)# interface serial 0/0/0
R2(config-if)# ipv6 hello-interval eigrp 100 50
R2(config-if)# ipv6 hold-time eigrp 100 50
```

 Packet Tracer Activity: Fine-Tuning Dual-Stack EIGRP

Refer to the Digital Study Guide to access the PKA file for this activity. You must have Packet Tracer software to run this activity. See the Introduction for details.

EIGRP Troubleshooting Commands

Several commands are useful when troubleshooting an EIGRP network:

- **show ip eigrp interface:** Verifies which interfaces are enabled for EIGRP, the number of peers, and transmit queues

- **show ip protocols:** Verifies the currently configured EIGRP values for various properties of any enabled routing protocols

- **show ip eigrp neighbors:** Verifies that the router recognizes its neighbors

- **show ip route eigrp:** Verifies that the router learned the route to a remote network through EIGRP

Figure 14-4 illustrates a method for using these commands in a systematic way.

Figure 14-4   Systematic Method for Troubleshooting EIGRP for IPv4

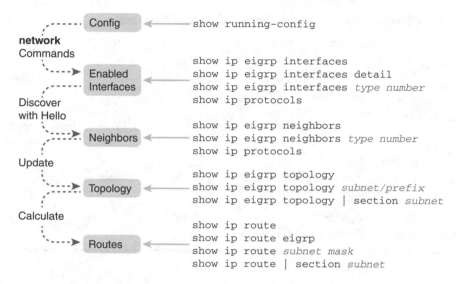

As with Open Shortest Path First (OSPF) protocol, neighbor adjacency is a prerequisite to EIGRP convergence and requires Layer 3 connectivity. By examining the output of the **show ip interface brief** command, you can verify that the status and protocol of connecting interfaces are up. Use **show ip protocols** (or some other EIGRP-related command) to verify that all routers are configured with the same autonomous system number. Use the **show ip eigrp interfaces** command to verify that all the necessary interfaces are participating in EIGRP.

You can use the same process to troubleshoot EIGRP for IPv6 implementations. Simply replace the **ip** with **ipv6** in the list of EIGRP-specific **show** commands:

- **show ipv6 eigrp neighbors**

- **show ipv6 route eigrp**

- **show ipv6 protocols**

- **show ipv6 eigrp interface**

Discontiguous Networks

EIGRP has a unique problem because you can configure EIGRP to automatically summarize at the classful boundary. Automatic summarization does not cause any problems, as long as the summarized network is contiguous instead of discontiguous. If automatic summarization is enabled in a discontiguous network, you will have a less-than-full convergence situation.

Even a contiguous network design can become discontiguous if one or more link failures divide a classful network into two or more parts. Figure 14-5 shows an internetwork with two contiguous classful networks: 10.0.0.0 and 172.16.0.0.

Figure 14-5   Contiguous Network Topology

172.16.3.0/24   R2   172.16.4.0/24

10.1.3.0/24   10.1.4.0/24

R1   172.16.1.0/24   172.16.2.0/24   R4

10.1.1.0/24   10.1.2.0/24

R3

In this figure, with all links up and working and automatic summarization in effect, all hosts can ping all other hosts. In this design, packets for network 172.16.0.0 flow over the high route, and packets for network 10.0.0.0 flow over the low route.

If any link between the routers fails, however, one of the two classful networks becomes discontiguous. For example, if the link between R3 and R4 fails, the route from R1 to R4 passes through subnets of network 172.16.0.0, so network 10.0.0.0 is discontiguous. The solution is either to design the network in a way that avoids the possibility of discontiguous subnets or to disable automatic summarization and manually configure summary routes.

Packet Tracer Activity: Troubleshooting EIGRP

Refer to the Digital Study Guide to access the PKA file for this activity. You must have Packet Tracer software to run this activity. See the Introduction for details.

Study Resources

For today's exam topics, refer to the following resources for more study.

Resource	Location	Topic
Primary Resources		
Scaling Networks v6	7	All
ICND2 Official Cert Guide	10	Other EIGRP Configuration Settings
	11	Interfaces Enabled with a Routing Protocol
		Neighbor Relationships
	24	Other EIGRP for IPv6 Configuration Settings
		EIGRP for IPv6 Verification and Troubleshooting
Supplemental Resources		
CCNA Portable Command Guide	14	Bandwidth Use
		Troubleshooting EIGRP and EIGRPv6

Resource	Location	Topic
Supplemental Resources		
CCNA Video Series	3	Lesson 7: EIGRP Timers
		Lesson 7: EIGRP Metric Calculation
		Lesson 7: EIGRP Troubleshooting Exercise #1
		Lesson 7: EIGRP Troubleshooting Exercise #2
CCNA Network Simulator	ICND2	Chapter 10: EIGRP Metric Manipulation
		Chapter 10: EIGRP Route Tuning I–IV
		Chapter 11: Path Troubleshooting III
		Chapter 11: EIGRP Troubleshooting
		Chapter 24: EIGRP for IPv6 Metric Manipulation
		Chapter 24: EIGRP for IPv6 Route Tuning I–IV

Check Your Understanding

Refer to the Digital Study Guide to take a short quiz covering the content of this day.

CDP and LLDP

CCNA 200-125 Exam Topics

- Configure and verify Layer 2 protocols

Key Topics

Cisco Discovery Protocol (CDP) is a Cisco proprietary Layer 2 protocol used to gather information about Cisco devices on the same data link. Cisco devices also support Link Layer Discovery Protocol (LLDP), which is a standards-based neighbor discovery protocol similar to CDP. Today we review the configuration and verification of CDP and LLDP.

CDP Overview

As Figure 13-1 shows, CDP sends advertisements to directly connected devices.

Figure 13-1   CDP Sends Advertisements Between Directly Connected Devices

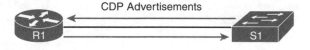

CDP runs on all Cisco-manufactured equipment. It gathers the protocol addresses of neighboring devices and discovers the platform of those devices. CDP runs over the data link layer only. This means that two systems that support different Layer 3 protocols can learn about each other. Table 13-1 summarizes the default CDP operation.

Table 13-1   CDP Defaults

Parameters	Default
CDP	Enabled globally and on all interfaces
CDP version	Version 2
CDP timer	60 seconds
CDP holdtime	180 seconds

CDP can assist in network discovery and troubleshooting. CDP advertises the following helpful information:

- **Device ID:** The hostname of the neighboring device
- **Addresses:** The IPv4 and IPv6 addresses used by the device
- **Port ID:** The name of the local and remote port

- **Capabilities:** Whether the device is a router or a switch, or has other capabilities

- **Version:** The version of CDP running on the device

- **Platform:** The hardware platform of the device, such as a Cisco 1941 router or 2960 switch

CDP Configuration

CDP is enabled on the device for all interfaces, as Example 13-1 shows.

Example 13-1   CDP Runs on All Interfaces+

```
Router# show cdp interface
Embedded-Service-Engine0/0 is administratively down, line protocol is down
   Encapsulation ARPA
   Sending CDP packets every 60 seconds
   Holdtime is 180 seconds
GigabitEthernet0/0 is administratively down, line protocol is down
   Encapsulation ARPA
   Sending CDP packets every 60 seconds
   Holdtime is 180 seconds
GigabitEthernet0/1 is up, line protocol is up
   Encapsulation ARPA
   Sending CDP packets every 60 seconds
   Holdtime is 180 seconds
Serial0/0/0 is administratively down, line protocol is down
   Encapsulation HDLC
   Sending CDP packets every 60 seconds
   Holdtime is 180 seconds
Serial0/0/1 is administratively down, line protocol is down
   Encapsulation HDLC
   Sending CDP packets every 60 seconds
   Holdtime is 180 seconds

 cdp enabled interfaces : 5
 interfaces up         : 1
 interfaces down       : 4
Router# show ip interface brief
Interface                  IP-Address    OK? Method Status                Protocol
Embedded-Service-Engine0/0 unassigned    YES unset  administratively down down
GigabitEthernet0/0         unassigned    YES unset  administratively down down
GigabitEthernet0/1         unassigned    YES unset  up                    up
Serial0/0/0                unassigned    YES unset  administratively down down
Serial0/0/1                unassigned    YES unset  administratively down down
Router#
```

Notice in the output that an interface does not have to be configured with a Layer 3 address to send or receive CDP advertisements. The interface only needs to be activated with the **no shutdown** command. In Example 13-2, the switch connected to the router in Example 13-1 has gathered CDP information about the router. The two devices are communicating across the Layer 2 link without any Layer 3 addressing.

Example 13-2   CDP Sends Layer 2 Messages

```
Switch# show cdp neighbors
Capability Codes: R - Router, T - Trans Bridge, B - Source Route Bridge
                  S - Switch, H - Host, I - IGMP, r - Repeater, P - Phone,
                  D - Remote, C - CVTA, M - Two-port Mac Relay


Device ID          Local Intrfce     Holdtme     Capability  Platform  Port ID
Router             Fas 0/5           155                     R B S I CISCO1941 Gig 0/1
Switch#
```

To disable CDP on the device, use the CDP global configuration command **no cdp run**.

```
Router(config)# no cdp run
```

Verify that the device is no longer running CDP with the **show cdp** command.

```
Router# show cdp
% CDP is not enabled
Router#
```

After waiting the for the 180-second holdtime to expire on the switch, we can verify that the switch is no longer receiving information about the router (see Example 13-3).

Example 13-3   The Switch Has No CDP Neighbors

```
Switch# show cdp neighbors
Capability Codes: R - Router, T - Trans Bridge, B - Source Route Bridge
                  S - Switch, H - Host, I - IGMP, r - Repeater, P - Phone,
                  D - Remote, C - CVTA, M - Two-port Mac Relay


Device ID          Local Intrfce    Holdtme     Capability  Platform  Port ID
Switch#
```

CDP can also be disabled on a per-interface basis. This configuration option is a security best practice for interfaces that are connected to untrusted networks. To disable CDP on an interface, use the **no cdp enable** command (see Example 13-4).

Example 13-4   Disabling CDP on an Interface

```
Router(config)# interface s0/0/0
Router(config-if)# no cdp enable
Router(config-if)# end
Router# show cdp interface
Embedded-Service-Engine0/0 is administratively down, line protocol is down
  Encapsulation ARPA
  Sending CDP packets every 60 seconds
  Holdtime is 180 seconds
GigabitEthernet0/0 is administratively down, line protocol is down
  Encapsulation ARPA
  Sending CDP packets every 60 seconds
  Holdtime is 180 seconds
GigabitEthernet0/1 is up, line protocol is up
  Encapsulation ARPA
  Sending CDP packets every 60 seconds
  Holdtime is 180 seconds
Serial0/0/1 is administratively down, line protocol is down
  Encapsulation HDLC
  Sending CDP packets every 60 seconds
  Holdtime is 180 seconds

 cdp enabled interfaces : 4
 interfaces up          : 1
 interfaces down        : 3
Router#
```

Notice in the output of the **show cdp interface** command that the Serial 0/0/0 interface is no longer listed, as it was in Example 13-1.

To adjust the time for CDP advertisements, use the **cdp timer** global configuration command.

```
Router(config)# cdp timer seconds
```

The range is 5 to 254 seconds. The default is 60 seconds. If you modify the CDP timer, you should also modify the holdtime with the **cdp holdtime** global configuration command.

```
Router(config)# cdp holdtime seconds
```

The range is from 10 to 255. The default is 180 seconds.

CDP Verification

You have already seen examples of **show cdp**, **show cdp neighbors**, and **show cdp interface**. The **show cdp neighbors detail** command lists all the information CDP gathers about directly connected neighbors. In Example 13-5, switch S3 knows a variety of information about R1, including the IP address and Cisco IOS version running on the router.

Example 13-5   CDP Detailed Information

```
S3# show cdp neighbors detail
-------------------------
Device ID: R3.31days.com
Entry address(es):
   IP address: 192.168.1.1
Platform: Cisco CISCO1941/K9,   Capabilities: Router Source-Route-Bridge Switch IGMP
Interface: FastEthernet0/5,   Port ID (outgoing port): GigabitEthernet0/1
Holdtime : 162 sec

Version :
Cisco IOS Software, C1900 Software (C1900-UNIVERSALK9-M), Version 15.4(3)M2,
RELEASE SOFTWARE (fc2)
Technical Support: http://www.cisco.com/techsupport
Copyright (c) 1986-2015 by Cisco Systems, Inc.
Compiled Fri 06-Feb-15 17:01 by prod_rel_team

advertisement version: 2
Duplex: full
Power Available TLV:

    Power request id: 0, Power management id: 0, Power available: 0, Power
management level: 0
Management address(es):
   IP address: 192.168.1.1

S3#
```

> **NOTE:**   The Device ID value shows R3.31days.com because R3 is configured with the **ip domain-name** command and SSH remote access.

When documentation is lacking or incomplete, a network administrator can use CDP to gather information about devices and discover the network topology. In Example 13-6, the network administrator remotely accesses R3 and discovers that R2 is connected to R3.

Example 13-6 Discovering More Devices

```
S3# ssh -l admin 192.168.1.1
Password:
R3> show cdp neighbors detail
-------------------------
Device ID: S3.31days.com
Entry address(es):
  IP address: 192.168.1.2
Platform: cisco WS-C2960-24TT-L,  Capabilities: Switch IGMP
Interface: GigabitEthernet0/1,  Port ID (outgoing port): FastEthernet0/5
Holdtime : 126 sec

Version :
Cisco IOS Software, C2960 Software (C2960-LANBASEK9-M), Version 15.0(2)SE7,
RELEASE SOFTWARE (fc1)
Technical Support: http://www.cisco.com/techsupport
Copyright (c) 1986-2014 by Cisco Systems, Inc.
Compiled Thu 23-Oct-14 14:49 by prod_rel_team

advertisement version: 2
Protocol Hello:  OUI=0x00000C, Protocol ID=0x0112; payload len=27, value=00000000
FFFFFFFF010221FF0000000000000CD996E87400FF0000
VTP Management Domain: ''
Native VLAN: 1
Duplex: full
Management address(es):
  IP address: 192.168.1.2


-------------------------
Device ID: R2.31days.com
Entry address(es):
  IP address: 192.168.10.1
Platform: Cisco CISCO1941/K9,  Capabilities: Router Source-Route-Bridge Switch IGMP
Interface: Serial0/0/1,  Port ID (outgoing port): Serial0/0/1
Holdtime : 148 sec

Version :
Cisco IOS Software, C1900 Software (C1900-UNIVERSALK9-M), Version 15.4(3)M2,
RELEASE SOFTWARE (fc2)
Technical Support: http://www.cisco.com/techsupport
Copyright (c) 1986-2015 by Cisco Systems, Inc.
```

```
Compiled Fri 06-Feb-15 17:01 by prod_rel_team


advertisement version: 2
Management address(es):
  IP address: 192.168.10.1



Total cdp entries displayed : 2
R3>
```

The network administrator can now access router R2, with authentication, and continue discovering the network.

As Example 13-7 shows, you use the **show cdp traffic** command to verify how many CDP packets the device has sent and received.

Example 13-7   Verifying the Number of CDP Packets

```
R3# show cdp traffic
CDP counters :
    Total packets output: 758, Input: 724
    Hdr syntax: 0, Chksum error: 0, Encaps failed: 1
    No memory: 0, Invalid packet: 0,
    CDP version 1 advertisements output: 0, Input: 0
    CDP version 2 advertisements output: 758, Input: 724
R3#
```

Packet Tracer Activity: Use CDP to Discover a Network

Refer to the Digital Study Guide to access the PKA file for this activity. You must have Packet Tracer software to run this activity. See the Introduction for details.

LLDP Overview

Cisco devices also support LLDP, which is a vendor-neutral open standard (IEEE 802.1AB). LLDP works with routers, switches, and wireless LAN access points. As with CDP, LLDP is a neighbor discovery protocol that is used for network devices to advertise information about themselves to other devices on the network. Also as with CDP, LLDP enables two systems running different network layer protocols to learn about each other.

Table 13-2 summarizes the default CDP operation.

Table 13-2   LLDP Defaults

Parameters	Default
LLDP	Disabled globally and on all interfaces
LLDP timer	30 seconds
LLDP holdtime	120 seconds
LLDP reinitialization delay	2 seconds

NOTE: The reinitialization delay is the number of seconds the device waits after LLDP is disabled on a port before it accepts a configuration to re-enable LLDP.

LLDP Configuration

To enable LLDP globally, enter the **lldp run** command.

```
Router(config)# lldp run
```

When enabled globally, LLDP is enabled on all interfaces. To disable LLDP on an interface, use the **no lldp transmit** and **no lldp receive** commands.

```
Router(config)# interface interface-id
Router(config-if)# no lldp transmit
Router(config-if)# no lldp receive
Router(config-if)# end
Router#
```

To adjust the time for CDP advertisements, use the **lldp timer** global configuration command.

```
Router(config)# lldp timer seconds
```

The range is 5 to 65534 seconds. The default is 30 seconds. If you modify the CDP timer, you should also modify the holdtime with the **cdp holdtime** global configuration command.

```
Router(config)# lldp holdtime seconds
```

The range is from 0 to 65535. The default is 120 seconds. You can also modify the delay time for LLDP to initialize on any interface with the **lldp reinit** global configuration command.

```
Router(config)# lldp reinit seconds
```

The range is 2 to 5 seconds. The default is 2 seconds.

For the topology in Figure 13-2, the policy is that LLDP should have the same timers as CDP. Routers should not transmit LLDP messages out LAN interfaces.

Figure 13-2   LLDP Configuration Topology

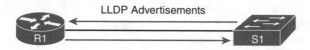

LLDP Advertisements

Example 13-8 shows the commands to implement the LLDP policy.

Example 13-8   LLDP Configuration

```
R1(config)# lldp run
R1(config)# lldp timer 60
R1(config)# lldp holdtime 180
R1(config)# interface g0/1
R1(config-if)# no lldp transmit
R1(config-if)# end
R1#
```

```
S1(config)# lldp run
S1(config)# lldp timer 60
S1(config)# lldp holdtime 180
S1(config)# end
S1#
```

LLDP Verification

The LLDP verification commands are similar to those in CDP. Simply replace the keyword **cdp** with **llpd**. Example 13-9 shows output from the LLDP verification commands.

Example 13-9   LLDP Verification Commands

```
R1# show lldp

Global LLDP Information:
    Status: ACTIVE
    LLDP advertisements are sent every 60 seconds
    LLDP hold time advertised is 180 seconds
    LLDP interface reinitialization delay is 2 seconds
R1# show lldp interface
<output omitted>
GigabitEthernet0/0:
    Tx: enabled
    Rx: enabled
    Tx state: INIT
    Rx state: WAIT PORT OPER
```

```
GigabitEthernet0/1:
    Tx: disabled
    Rx: enabled
    Tx state: INIT
    Rx state: WAIT FOR FRAME
<output omitted>
R1# show lldp neighbors
Capability codes:
    (R) Router, (B) Bridge, (T) Telephone, (C) DOCSIS Cable Device
    (W) WLAN Access Point, (P) Repeater, (S) Station, (O) Other


Device ID           Local Intf     Hold-time  Capability      Port ID
S1                  Gi0/1          180        B               Fa0/5


Total entries displayed: 1


R1# show lldp neighbors detail
------------------------------------------------
Local Intf: Gi0/1
Chassis id: 0cd9.96e8.8a00
Port id: Fa0/5
Port Description: FastEthernet0/5
System Name: S1.31days.com


System Description:
Cisco IOS Software, C2960 Software (C2960-LANBASEK9-M), Version 15.0(2)SE7,
RELEASE SOFTWARE (fc1)
Technical Support: http://www.cisco.com/techsupport
Copyright (c) 1986-2014 by Cisco Systems, Inc.
Compiled Thu 23-Oct-14 14:49 by prod_rel_team


Time remaining: 127 seconds
System Capabilities: B
Enabled Capabilities: B
Management Addresses:
    IP: 172.16.1.2
Auto Negotiation - supported, enabled
Physical media capabilities:
    100base-TX(FD)
    100base-TX(HD)
    10base-T(FD)
    10base-T(HD)
Media Attachment Unit type: 16
Vlan ID: 1
```

```
Total entries displayed: 1

R1# show lldp traffic

LLDP traffic statistics:
    Total frames out: 171
    Total entries aged: 0
    Total frames in: 34
    Total frames received in error: 0
    Total frames discarded: 0
    Total TLVs discarded: 0
    Total TLVs unrecognized: 0
R1#
```

Activity: Compare CDP and LLDP

Refer to the Digital Study Guide to complete this activity.

Study Resources

For today's exam topics, refer to the following resources for more study.

Resource	Location	Topic
Primary Resources		
Routing and Switching Essentials v6	10	Device Discovery
ICND1 Official Cert Guide	33	Analyzing Topology Using CDP and LLDP
Supplemental Resources		
CCNA Portable Command Guide	28	All
CCNA Video Series	7	Lesson 1: Cisco Discovery Protocol (CDP)
		Lesson 1: Link Layer Discovery Protocol (LLDP)
		Lesson 1: Using CDP or LLDP to Map a Network
CCNA Network Simulator	ICND1	Chapter 33: CDP I–II
		Chapter 33: LLDP I–II

Check Your Understanding

Refer to the Digital Study Guide to take a short quiz covering the content of this day.

LAN Security and Device Hardening

CCNA 200-125 Exam Topics

- Configure, verify, and troubleshoot port security
- Describe common access layer threat mitigation techniques
- Configure, verify, and troubleshoot basic device hardening
- Describe device security using AAA with TACACS+ and RADIUS

Key Topics

Today's review is a whirlwind of topics that include port security, LAN threat mitigation techniques, and device hardening.

NOTE: The CCNA exam topics for today are not covered in order.

Port Security Configuration

If you know which devices should be cabled and connected to particular interfaces on a switch, you can use port security to restrict that interface so that only the expected devices can use it. This reduces exposure to some types of attacks in which the attacker connects a laptop to the wall socket or uses the cable attached to another end device to gain access to the network.

Port security configuration involves several steps. Basically, you need to make the port an access port, which means that the port is not doing any VLAN trunking. You then need to enable port security and configure the actual Media Access Control (MAC) addresses of the devices allowed to use that port. The following list outlines the steps, including the configuration commands used:

Step 1. Configure the interface for static access mode using the **switchport mode access** interface subcommand.

Step 2. Enable port security using the **switchport port-security** interface subcommand.

Step 3. (Optional) Override the maximum number of allowed MAC addresses associated with the interface (1) using the **switchport port-security maximum** *number* interface subcommand.

Step 4. (Optional) Override the default action when there is a security violation (shutdown) using the **switchport port-security violation {protect | restrict | shutdown}** interface subcommand.

Step 5.   (Optional) Predefine any allowed source MAC address(es) for this interface using the **switchport port-security mac-address** *mac-address* command. Use the command multiple times to define more than one MAC address.

Step 6.   (Optional) Instead of Step 5, configure the interface to dynamically learn and configure the MAC addresses of currently connected hosts by configuring the **switchport port-security mac-address sticky** interface subcommand.

When an unauthorized device attempts to send frames to the switch interface, the switch can issue informational messages, discard frames from that device, or even discard frames from all devices by effectively shutting down the interface. Exactly which action the switch port takes depends on the option you configure in the **switchport port-security violation** command. Table 12-1 lists actions that the switch will take based on whether you configure the option **protect**, **restrict**, or **shutdown** (default).

Table 12-1   Actions When Port Security Violation Occurs

Option on the switchport port-security violation Command	protect	restrict	shutdown
Discards offending traffic	Yes	Yes	Yes
Sends log and SNMP messages	No	Yes	Yes
Disables the interface, discarding all traffic	No	No	Yes

Example 12-1 shows a port security configuration in which each access interface is allowed a maximum of three MAC addresses. If a fourth MAC address is detected, only the offending device's traffic is discarded. If the violation option is not explicitly configured, the traffic for devices that are allowed on the port also is discarded because the port would be shut down by default.

Example 12-1   Port Security Configuration Example

```
S1(config)# interface range fa 0/5 - fa 0/24
S1(config-if-range)# switchport mode access
S1(config-if-range)# switchport port-security
S1(config-if-range)# switchport port-security maximum 3
S1(config-if-range)# switchport port-security violation restrict
S1(config-if-range)# switchport port-security mac-address sticky
```

To verify port security configuration, use the more general **show port-security** command or the more specific **show port-security interface** *type number* command. Example 12-2 demonstrates the use of both commands. In the examples, notice that only one device is currently attached to an access port on S1.

Example 12-2   Port Security Verification Command Output Examples

```
S1# show port-security
Secure Port   MaxSecureAddr    CurrentAddr   SecurityViolation   Security Action
              (Count)          (Count)       (Count)
Fa0/5         3                1             0                   Restrict
Fa0/6         3                0             0                   Restrict
Fa0/7         3                0             0                   Restrict
Fa0/8         3                0             0                   Restrict
Fa0/9         3                0             0                   Restrict
Fa0/10        3                0             0                   Restrict
Fa0/11        3                0             0                   Restrict
Fa0/12        3                0             0                   Restrict
Fa0/13        3                0             0                   Restrict
Fa0/14        3                0             0                   Restrict
Fa0/15        3                0             0                   Restrict
Fa0/16        3                0             0                   Restrict
Fa0/17        3                0             0                   Restrict
Fa0/18        3                0             0                   Restrict
Fa0/19        3                0             0                   Restrict
Fa0/20        3                0             0                   Restrict
Fa0/21        3                0             0                   Restrict
Fa0/22        3                0             0                   Restrict
Fa0/23        3                0             0                   Restrict
Fa0/24        3                0             0                   Restrict
Total Addresses in System (excluding one mac per port)     : 0
Max Addresses limit in System (excluding one mac per port) : 8320
S1# show port-security interface fastethernet 0/5
Port Security              : Enabled
Port Status                : Secure-down
Violation Mode             : Restrict
Aging Time                 : 0 mins
Aging Type                 : Absolute
SecureStatic Address Aging : Disabled
Maximum MAC Addresses      : 3
Total MAC Addresses        : 1
Configured MAC Addresses   : 0
Sticky MAC Addresses       : 1
Last Source Address:Vlan   : 0014.22dd.37a3:1
Security Violation Count   : 0
```

 Activity: Determine Port Security Action

Refer to the Digital Study Guide to complete this activity.

Port Restoration After a Violation

When port security is activated on an interface, the default action when a violation occurs is to shut down the port. A security violation can occur in one of two ways:

- The maximum number of secure MAC addresses has been added to the address table for that interface, and a station whose MAC address is not in the address table attempts to access the interface.

- An address learned or configured on one secure interface is seen on another secure interface in the same VLAN.

When a violation occurs, a syslog message is sent to the console stating that the interface is now in the **err-disable** state. The console messages include the port number and the MAC address that caused the violation, as Example 12-3 shows.

Example 12-3   Port Security Violation Verification and Restoration

```
S1#
Sep 20 06:44:54.966: %PM-4-ERR_DISABLE: psecure-violation error detected on
   Fa0/18,
   putting Fa0/18 in err-disable state
Sep 20 06:44:54.966: %PORT_SECURITY-2-PSECURE_VIOLATION: Security violation
   occurred, caused by MAC address 000c.292b.4c75 on port FastEthernet0/18.
Sep 20 06:44:55.973: %LINEPROTO-5-PPDOWN: Line protocol on Interface
FastEthernet0/18, changed state to down
Sep 20 06:44:56.971: %LINK-3-UPDOWN: Interface FastEthernet0/18, changed state to
   down
!The two following commands can be used to verify the port status.
S1# show interface fa0/18 status
Port     Name   Status          Vlan   Duplex   Speed     Type
Fa0/18          err-disabled    5      auto     auto      10/100BaseTX
S1# show port-security interface fastethernet 0/18
Port Security                  : Enabled
Port Status                    : Secure-shutdown
Violation Mode                 : Shutdown
Aging Time                     : 0 mins
Aging Type                     : Absolute
SecureStatic Address Aging     : Disabled
Maximum MAC Addresses          : 1
Total MAC Addresses            : 0
Configured MAC Addresses       : 0
Sticky MAC Addresses           : 0
Last Source Address:Vlan       : 000c.292b.4c75:1
Security Violation Count       : 1
!To restore a port, manually shut it down and then reactivate it.
S1(config)# interface FastEthernet 0/18
```

```
S1(config-if)# shutdown
Sep 20 06:57:28.532: %LINK-5-CHANGED: Interface FastEthernet0/18, changed state to
    administratively down
S1(config-if)# no shutdown
Sep 20 06:57:48.186: %LINK-3-UPDOWN: Interface FastEthernet0/18, changed state to
    up
Sep 20 06:57:49.193: %LINEPROTO-5-UPDOWN: Line protocol on Interface
FastEthernet0/18, changed state to up
```

You can use the **show interface** *type number* **status** or **show port-security interface** *type number* command to verify the current state of the port. To restore the port, you must first manually shut down the interface and then reactivate it, as in Example 12-3.

LAN Threat Mitigation

Mitigating security threats on LANs is a huge topic that is mostly reserved for the CCNA Security (210-260 IINS) Certification Exam. However, the CCNA exam does require you to describe some command access layer threat mitigation techniques. In this section, we review DHCP snooping, changes to the native VLAN, shutdown of unused switch ports, AAA, and 802.1X.

DHCP Snooping

DHCP snooping is a switch-based security configuration that is meant to prevent a man-in-the-middle attack from a rogue DHCP server. For example, in Figure 12-1, R1 is configured to relay DHCP requests to the DHCP server attached to R2.

Figure 12-1   Rogue DHCP Server Intercepts DHCP Requests

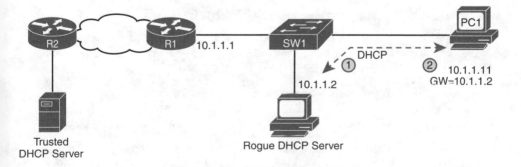

However, the rogue DHCP server attached to SW1 responds to the DHCP request from PC1 first. PC1 accepts the DHCP offer, setting the rogue DHCP server as the default gateway.

To protect against this type of attack, DHCP snooping uses the concept of trusted and untrusted ports. As Figure 12-2 shows, SW2, R1, and the DHCP server are attached to trusted ports on SW1. The other devices, including the wireless access point, are connected to untrusted ports.

Figure 12-2   Trusted and Untrusted Ports

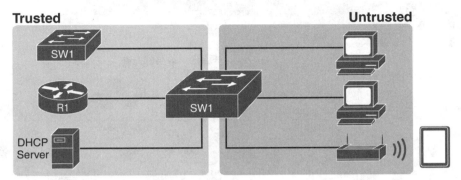

Some critical features of a DHCP snooping configuration include these:

- **Trusted ports:** Trusted ports allow all incoming DHCP messages.

- **Untrusted ports, server messages:** Untrusted ports discard all incoming messages that are considered server messages.

- **Untrusted ports, client messages:** Untrusted ports apply more complex logic for messages considered client messages. They check whether each incoming DHCP message conflicts with existing DHCP binding table information; if so, they discard the DHCP message. If the message has no conflicts, the switch allows the message through, which typically results in the addition of new DHCP binding table entries.

- **Rate limiting:** This feature optionally limits the number of received DHCP messages per second, per port.

NOTE: The configuration commands are beyond the scope of the CCNA. However, the configuration is rather straightforward. To find a Cisco configuration guide, search the Internet for the command **ip dhcp snooping**.

Native and Management VLAN Modification

The IEEE 802.1Q specification defines a native VLAN to maintain backward compatibility with untagged traffic common to legacy LAN scenarios. A native VLAN serves as a common identifier on opposite ends of a trunk link. VLAN 1 is the native VLAN by default.

A management VLAN is any VLAN configured to access the management capabilities of a switch. VLAN 1 is the management VLAN by default. The management VLAN is assigned an IP address and subnet mask, allowing the switch to be managed through HTTP, Telnet, SSH, or SNMP.

It is a best practice to configure the native VLAN as an unused VLAN distinct from VLAN 1 and other VLANs. In fact, it is not unusual to dedicate a fixed VLAN to serve the role of the native VLAN for all trunk ports in the switched domain. Likewise, the management VLAN should also be configured as something other than VLAN 1. The management and native VLANs can be configured as the same VLAN, as in Example 12-4.

Example 12-4   Configuring the Native and Management VLAN

```
S1(config)# vlan 86
S1(config-vlan)# name Management&Native
S1(config-vlan)# interface vlan 86
*Jul 13 14:14:04.840: %LINEPROTO-5-UPDOWN: Line protocol on Interface Vlan86,
   changed state to down
S1(config-if)# ip address 10.10.86.10 255.255.255.0
S1(config-if)# no shutdown
S1(config-if)# ip default-gateway 10.10.86.254
S1(config)# interface range fa0/1 - 2
S1(config-if-range)# switchport mode trunk
S1(config-if-range)# switchport trunk native vlan 86
S1(config-if-range)#
*Jul 13 14:15:55.499: %LINEPROTO-5-UPDOWN: Line protocol on Interface Vlan86,
   changed state to up
S1(config-if-range)#
```

First, a VLAN is created that will be used for the management and native VLAN. Next, by activating interface VLAN 86, the switch can be remotely managed. Finally, the trunk ports are statically configured and VLAN 86 is set as the native VLAN for all untagged traffic. After it is configured, the interface VLAN 86 comes up.

Switch Port Hardening

Router interfaces must be activated with the **no shutdown** command before they become operational. The exact opposite is true for the Cisco Catalyst switches. To provide out-of-the-box functionality, Cisco chose a default configuration that included interfaces that work without any configuration, including automatically negotiating speed and duplex. In addition, all interfaces are assigned to the default VLAN 1.

This default configuration exposes switches to some security threats. The security best practices for unused interfaces follow:

- Administratively disable the interface using the **shutdown** interface subcommand.

- Prevent VLAN trunking by making the port a nontrunking interface using the **switchport mode** access interface subcommand.

- Assign the port to an unused VLAN using the **switchport access vlan** *number* interface subcommand.

- Set the native VLAN to not be VLAN 1, but to instead be an unused VLAN, using the **switchport trunk native vlan** *vlan-id* interface subcommand.

Even though you shut down unused ports on the switches, if a device is connected to one of those ports and the interface is enabled, trunking can occur. In addition, all ports are in VLAN 1 by default. A good practice is to put all unused ports in a "black hole" VLAN. Example 12-5 demonstrates this best practice, assuming that ports 20–24 are unused.

Example 12-5   Assigning Unused Ports to a Black Hole VLAN

```
S1(config)# vlan 999
S1(config-vlan)# name BlackHole
S1(config-vlan)# interface range fa0/20 - 24
S1(config-if-range)# shutdown
S1(config-if-range)# switchport mode access
S1(config-if-range)# switchport access vlan 999
S1(config-if-range)#
```

AAA

Configuring usernames and passwords on all your network devices is not very scalable. A better option is to use an external server to centralize and secure all username/password pairs. To address this issue, Cisco devices support the Authentication, Authorization, and Accounting (AAA) framework to help secure device access.

Two AAA authentication protocols are supported on Cisco devices:

- Terminal Access Controller Access-Control System Plus (TACACS+, pronounced as "tack-axe plus")

- Remote Authentication Dial-In User Service (RADIUS)

Whether to select TACACS+ or RADIUS depends on the needs of the organization. For example, a large ISP might select RADIUS because it supports the detailed accounting required for billing users. An organization with various user groups might select TACACS+ because it requires authorization policies to be applied on a per-user or per-group basis. Table 12-2 compares TACACS+ and RADIUS.

Table 12-2   Comparison Between TACACS+ and RADIUS

Features	TACACS+	RADIUS
Most often used for	Network devices	Users
Transport protocol	TCP	UDP
Authentication port number(s)	49	1645, 1812
Protocol encrypts the password	Yes	Yes
Protocol encrypts entire packet	Yes	No
Supports function to authorize each user to a subset of CLI commands	Yes	No
Defined by	Cisco	RFC 2865

NOTE: AAA configuration is beyond the scope of the CCNA exam. However, refer to Wendell Odom's ICND2 certification guide for a simple explanation of AAA configuration.

802.1X

IEEE 802.1X is a standard port-based access control and authentication protocol. It is ideal for restricting unauthorized access through publicly available LAN devices, such as switches and wireless access points.

802.1X defines three roles for devices in the network, as Figure 12-3 shows.

Figure 12-3   802.1X Roles

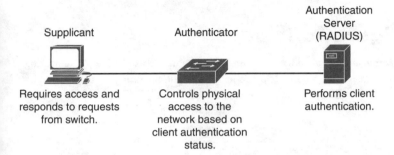

- **Client (supplicant):** This is usually the 802.1X-enabled port on the device that requests access to LAN and switch services and then responds to requests from the switch. In Figure 12-3, the device is a PC running 802.1X compliant client software.

- **Switch (authenticator):** The switch controls physical access to the network based on the authentication status of the client. The switch acts as a proxy between the client and the authentication server. It requests identifying information from the client, verifies that information with the authentication server, and relays a response to the client.

- **Authentication server:** The authentication server performs the actual authentication of the client. The authentication server validates the identity of the client and notifies the switch about whether the client is authorized to access the LAN and switch services. Because the switch acts as the proxy, the authentication service is transparent to the client. RADIUS is the only supported authentication server.

Figure 12-4 shows the authentication flows for a typical 802.1X process.

Figure 12-4   802.1X Authentication Flows

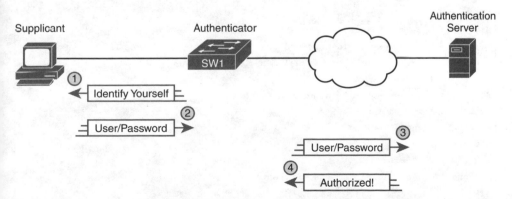

The 802.1X process is summarized as follows:

- The RADIUS authentication server is configured with usernames and passwords.

- LAN switches are enabled as 802.1X authenticators, are configured with the IP address of the authentication server, and have 802.1X enabled on all required ports.

- Users that connect devices to 802.1X-enabled ports must know the username/password before they can access the network.

SSH Configuration

Secure Shell (SSH) is recommended as the protocol to use for remote device management. Configuring SSH (port 22) is a security best practice because Telnet (port 23) uses insecure plain-text transmission of both the login and the data across the connection. Example 12-6 displays an SSH configuration.

Example 12-6   Configuring SSH Remote Access on a Switch

```
S1# show ip ssh
SSH Disabled-version 1.99
%Please create RSA keys to enable SSH (of at least 768 bits size) to enable SSH v2.
Authentication timeout: 120 secs; Authentication retries:3
S1# conf t
S1(config)# ip domain-name cisco.com
S1(config)# crypto key generate rsa
The name for the keys will be: S1.cisco.com
Choose the size of the key modulus in the range of 360 to 4096 for your
   General Purpose Keys. Choosing a key modulus greater than 512 may take
   a few minutes.

How many bits in the modulus [512]:1024
% Generating 1024 bit RSA keys, keys will be non-exportable...
[OK] (elapsed time was 4 seconds)

*Mar  1 02:20:18.529: %SSH-5-ENABLED: SSH 1.99 has been enabled
S1(config)# line vty 0 15
S1(config-line)# login local
S1(config-line)# transport input ssh
S1(config-line)# user admin password ccna
!The following commands are optional SSH configurations.
S1(config)# ip ssh version2
S1(config)# ip ssh authentication-retries 5
S1(config)# ip ssh time-out 60
S1(config)# end
S1# show ip ssh
SSH Enabled - version 2.0
Authentication timeout: 60 secs; Authentication retries: 5
S1#
```

The following description details the steps in Example 12-6:

Step 1.   Verify that the switch supports SSH using the **show ip ssh** command. If the command is not recognized, you know that SSH is not supported.

Step 2.   Configure a DNS domain name with the **ip domain-name** global configuration command.

Step 3.   Configure the switch using the **crypto key generate rsa** command to generate an RSA key pair and automatically enable SSH. When generating RSA keys, you are prompted to enter a modulus length. Cisco recommends a minimum modulus size of 1024 bits, as in Example 12-6.

NOTE: To remove the RSA key pair, use the **crypto key zeroize rsa** command. This disables the SSH service.

Step 4.   Change the vty lines to use usernames, with either locally configured usernames or an authentication, authorization, and accounting (AAA) server. In Example 12-6, the **login local** vty subcommand defines the use of local usernames, replacing the **login** vty subcommand.

Step 5.   Configure the switch to accept only SSH connections with the **transport input** ssh vty subcommand. (The default is **transport input telnet**.)

Step 6.   Add one or more **username password** global configuration commands to configure username/password pairs.

Step 7.   If desired, you can modify the default SSH configuration to change the SSH version to 2.0, the number of authentication tries, and the timeout, as in Example 12-6.

Step 8.   Verify your SSH parameters using the **show ip ssh** command.

 Activity: Order the Steps to Configure SSH

Refer to the Digital Study Guide to complete this activity.

 Packet Tracer Activity: Implement LAN Security and Device Hardening

Refer to the Digital Study Guide to access the PKA file for this activity. You must have Packet Tracer software to run this activity. See the Introduction for details.

Study Resources

For today's exam topics, refer to the following resources for more study.

Resource	Location	Topic
Primary Resources		
Introduction to Networks v6	11	Device Security
Routing and Switching Essentials v6	5	Switch Security
	6	VLAN Trunks
Connecting Networks v6	5	LAN Security
ICND1 Official Cert Guide	8	Securing Remote Access with Secure Shell
	9	Port Security
	34	Cisco Device Hardening
ICND2 Official Cert Guide	4	Mismatched Native VLAN on a Trunk
	6	Securing Access with IEEE 802.1X
		AAA Authentication
		DHCP Snooping
Supplemental Resources		
CCNA Portable Command Guide	23	All
	25	All
CCNA Video Series	2	Lesson 2: Enabling SSH Access
	6	Lesson 1: All
CCNA Network Simulator	ICND1	Chapter 8: SSH and Telnet
		Chapter 9: Switch Security I–IV
		Chapter 9: Port Security
		Chapter 17: Configuring SSH

? Check Your Understanding

Refer to the Digital Study Guide to take a short quiz covering the content of this day.

STP

CCNA 200-125 Exam Topics

- Configure, verify, and troubleshoot STP protocols

- Configure, verify and troubleshoot STP-related optional features

- Describe the benefits of switch stacking and chassis aggregation

Key Topics

Today's review covers the operation and configuration of the Spanning Tree Protocol (STP). The original STP IEEE 802.1D standard allowed for only one instance of STP to run for the entire switched network. Today's network administrators can implement Per-VLAN Spanning Tree (PVST) and Rapid STP (RSTP), both of which improve the original standard.

STP Concepts and Operation

A key characteristic of a well-built communications network is its resiliency. This means that the network needs to be capable of handling a device or link failure through redundancy. A redundant topology can eliminate a single point of failure by using multiple links, multiple devices, or both. STP helps prevent loops in a redundant switched network. Figure 11-1 shows an example of a three-layer topology (core, distribution, access) with redundant links.

Without STP, redundancy in the switched network can introduce the following issues:

- **Broadcast storms:** Each switch floods broadcasts endlessly.

- **Multiple frame transmission:** Multiple copies of unicast frames are delivered to the destination, causing unrecoverable errors.

- **MAC database instability:** Instability in the content of the MAC address table results from different ports of the switch receiving copies of the same frame.

Figure 11-1   Redundant Switched Topology

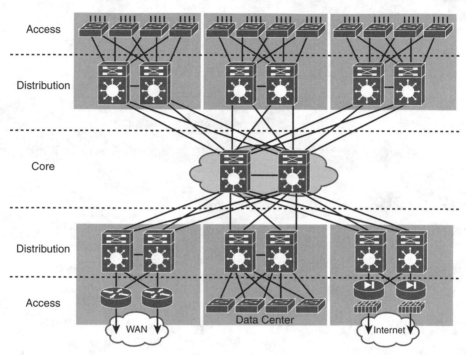

STP Algorithm

STP is an IEEE Committee standard defined as 802.1D. STP places certain ports in the blocking state so that they do not listen to, forward, or flood data frames. STP creates a tree that ensures that only one path exists for each network segment at any one time. If any segment experiences a disruption in connectivity, STP rebuilds a new tree by activating the previously inactive but redundant path.

The algorithm STP uses chooses the interfaces that should be placed into a forwarding state. For any interfaces not chosen to be in a forwarding state, STP places the interfaces in blocking state.

Switches exchange STP configuration messages every 2 seconds, by default, using a multicast frame called the bridge protocol data unit (BPDU). Blocked ports listen for these BPDUs to detect whether the other side of the link is down, thus requiring an STP recalculation. One piece of information included in the BPDU is the bridge ID (BID).

As Figure 11-2 shows, the BID is unique to each switch. It consists of a priority value (2 bytes) and the bridge MAC address (6 bytes).

Figure 11-2   Bridge ID

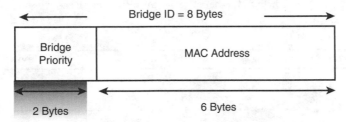

The default priority is 32,768. The root bridge is the bridge with the lowest BID. Therefore, if the default priority value is not changed, the switch with the lowest MAC address becomes the root.

STP Convergence

STP convergence is the process by which the switches collectively realize that something has changed in the LAN topology. The switches determine whether they need to change which ports block and which ports forward. The following steps summarize the STP algorithm used to achieve convergence:

Step 1. Elect a root bridge (switch with the lowest BID). Only one root bridge can exist per network. All ports on the root bridge are forwarding ports.

Step 2. Elect a root port for each nonroot switch, based on the lowest root path cost. Each nonroot switch has one root port. The root port is the port through which the nonroot bridge has its best path to the root bridge.

Step 3. Elect a designated port for each segment, based on the lowest root path cost. Each link has one designated port.

Step 4. The root ports and designated ports transition to the forwarding state, and the other ports stay in the blocking state.

Table 11-1 summarizes the reasons STP places a port in forwarding or blocking state.

Table 11-1   STP: Reasons for Forwarding or Blocking

Characterization of Port	STP State	Description
All the root switch's ports	Forwarding	The root switch is always the designated switch on all connected segments.
Each nonroot switch's root port	Forwarding	This is the port through which the switch has the least cost to reach the root switch.
Each LAN's designated port	Forwarding	The switch forwarding the lowest-cost BPDU onto the segment is the designated switch for that segment.
All other working ports	Blocking	The port is not used for forwarding frames, nor are any frames received on these interfaces considered for forwarding. BPDUs are still received.

Port bandwidth is used to determine the cost to reach the root bridge. Table 11-2 lists the default port costs defined by IEEE; these had to be revised with the advent of 10-Gbps ports.

Table 11-2   Default IEEE Port Costs

Ethernet Speed	Original IEEE Cost	Revised IEEE Cost
10 Mbps	100	100
100 Mbps	10	19
1 Gbps	1	4
10 Gbps	1	2

STP uses the four states in Figure 11-3 as port transitions from blocking to forwarding.

Figure 11-3   Spanning Tree Port States

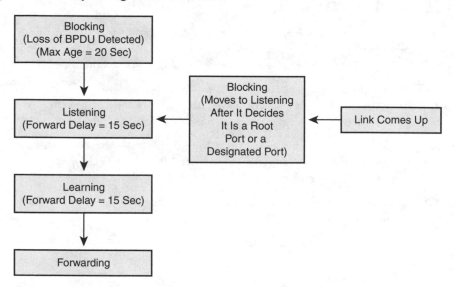

A fifth state, disabled, occurs either when a network administrator manually disables the port or when a security violation disables the port.

STP Varieties

Several varieties of STP emerged after the original IEEE 802.1D:

- **STP:** The original specification of STP, defined in 802.1D, provides a loop-free topology in a network with redundant links. STP is sometimes referred to as Common Spanning Tree (CST) because it assumes one spanning tree instance for the entire bridged network, regardless of the number of VLANs.

- **PVST+:** Per-VLAN Spanning Tree Plus is a Cisco enhancement of STP that provides a separate 802.1D spanning tree instance for each VLAN configured in the network.

- **RSTP:** Rapid STP, or IEEE 802.1w, is an evolution of STP that provides faster convergence than STP. However, RSTP still provides for only a single instance of STP.

- **Rapid PVST+:** Cisco enhancement of RSTP that uses PVST+. Rapid PVST+ provides a separate instance of 802.1w per VLAN.

- **Multiple Spanning Tree Protocol:** MSTP is an IEEE standard inspired by the earlier Cisco proprietary Multiple Instance STP (MISTP) implementation. MSTP maps multiple VLANs into the same spanning tree instance. The Cisco implementation of MSTP is MST, which provides up to 16 instances of RSTP and combines many VLANs with the same physical and logical topology into a common RSTP instance.

Part of your switch administration skill set is the ability to decide which type of STP to implement. Table 11-3 summarizes the features of each STP flavor.

Table 11-3   Features of STP Varieties

Protocol	Standard	Resources Needed	Convergence	Tree Calculation
STP	802.1D	Low	Slow	All VLANs
PVST+	Cisco	High	Slow	Per VLAN
RSTP	802.1w	Medium	Fast	All VLANs
Rapid PVST+	Cisco	Very high	Fast	Per VLAN
MSTP	802.1s, Cisco	Medium or high	Fast	Per instance

PVST Operation

PVST Plus (PVST+) is the default setting on all Cisco Catalyst switches. In a PVST+ environment, you can tune the spanning-tree parameters so that half the VLANs forward on each uplink trunk. You do this by configuring one switch to be elected the root bridge for half of the VLANs in the network and a second switch to be elected the root bridge for the other half of the VLANs. In the example in Figure 11-4, S1 is the root bridge for VLAN 10, and S3 is the root bridge for VLAN 20.

Figure 11-4   PVST+ Topology Example

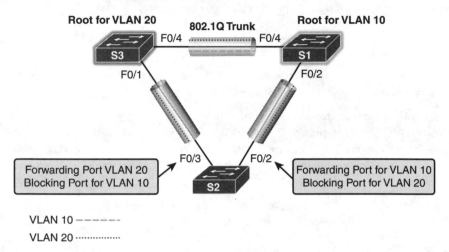

From the perspective of S2, a port is forwarding or blocking depending on the VLAN instance. After convergence, port F0/2 will be forwarding VLAN 10 frames and blocking VLAN 20 frames. Port F0/3 will be forwarding VLAN 20 frames and blocking VLAN 10 frames.

Switched networks running PVST+ have the following characteristics:

- Configured PVST per VLAN allows redundant links to be fully utilized.

- Each additional spanning tree instance for a VLAN adds more CPU cycles to all switches in the network.

Port States

The spanning tree is determined immediately after a switch is finished booting. If a switch port transitions directly from the blocking to the forwarding state without information about the full topology during the transition, the port can temporarily create a data loop. For this reason, STP introduces the five port states. Table 11-4 describes the port states that ensure that no loops are created during the creation of the logical spanning tree.

Table 11-4   PVST Port States

Operation Allowed	Blocking	Listening	Learning	Forwarding	Disabled
Can receive and process BPDUs	Yes	Yes	Yes	Yes	No
Can forward data frames received on interface	No	No	No	Yes	No
Can forward data frames switched from another interface	No	No	No	Yes	No
Can learn MAC addresses	No	No	Yes	Yes	No

Extended System ID

PVST+ requires a separate instance of spanning tree for each VLAN. The BID field in the BPDU must carry VLAN ID (VID) information, as Figure 11-5 shows.

Figure 11-5   Bridge ID for PVST+ with Extended System ID

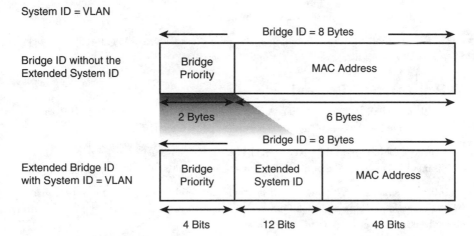

The BID includes the following fields:

- **Bridge Priority:** A 4-bit field is still used to carry bridge priority. However, the priority is conveyed in discrete values in increments of 4096 instead of discrete values in increments of 1 because only the first 4 most-significant bits are available from the 16-bit field.

- **Extended System ID:** A 12-bit field carrying the VID for PVST+.

- **MAC Address:** A 6-byte field with the MAC address of a single switch.

 Activity: Identify the STP Port States

Refer to the Digital Study Guide to complete this activity.

Rapid PVST+ Operation

In Rapid PVST+, a single instance of RSTP runs for each VLAN. This is why Rapid PVST+ has a very high demand for switch resources (CPU cycles and RAM).

NOTE: Rapid PVST+ is simply the Cisco implementation of RSTP on a per-VLAN basis. The rest of this review uses RSTP and Rapid PVST+ interchangeably.

With RSTP, IEEE improved the convergence performance of STP from 50 seconds to less than 10 seconds with its definition of Rapid STP (RSTP) in the standard 802.1w. RSTP is identical to STP in the following ways:

- It elects the root switch using the same parameters and tiebreakers.

- It elects the root port on nonroot switches with the same rules.

- It elects designated ports on each LAN segment with the same rules.

- It places each port in either forwarding or discarding state, although RSTP calls the blocking state the discarding state.

RSTP Interface Behavior

The main changes with RSTP can be seen when changes occur in the network. RSTP acts differently on some interfaces based on what is connected to the interface:

- **Edge-type behavior and PortFast:** RSTP improves convergence for edge-type connections by immediately placing the port in forwarding state when the link is physically active.

- **Link-type shared:** RSTP does not do anything differently from STP on link-type shared links. However, because most links between switches today are full duplex, point-to-point, and not shared, this does not matter.

- **Link-type point-to-point:** RSTP improves convergence over full-duplex links between switches. RSTP recognizes the loss of the path to the root bridge, through the root port, in 6 seconds based on 3 times the Hello timer value of 2 seconds. RSTP thus recognizes a lost path to the root much more quickly.

RSTP uses different terminology to describe port states. Table 11-5 lists the port states for RSTP and STP.

Table 11-5   RSTP and STP Port States

Operational State	STP State (802.1D)	RSTP State (802.1w)	Forwards Data Frames in This State?
Enabled	Blocking	Discarding	No
Enabled	Listening	Discarding	No
Enabled	Learning	Learning	No
Enabled	Forwarding	Forwarding	Yes
Disabled	Disabled	Discarding	No

RSTP removes the need for listening state and reduces the time required for learning state by actively discovering the network's new state. STP passively waits on new BPDUs and reacts to them during the listening and learning states. With RSTP, the switches negotiate with neighboring switches by sending RSTP messages. The messages enable the switches to quickly determine whether an interface can be immediately transitioned to a forwarding state. In many cases, the process takes only a second or two for the entire RSTP domain.

RSTP Port Roles

RSTP also adds three more port roles in addition to the root port and designated port roles defined in STP. Table 11-6 lists and defines the port roles.

Table 11-6   RSTP and STP Port Roles

RSTP Role	STP Role	Definition
Root port	Root port	A single port on each nonroot switch in which the switch hears the best BPDU out of all the received BPDUs
Designated port	Designated port	Of all switch ports on all switches attached to the same segment/collision domain, the port that advertises the "best" BPDU
Alternate port	—	A port on a switch that receives a suboptimal BPDU
Backup port	—	A nondesignated port on a switch that is attached to the same segment/collision domain as another port on the same switch
Disabled	—	A port that is administratively disabled or is not capable of working for other reasons

Figure 11-6 shows an example of these RSTP port roles.

Figure 11-6   RSTP Port Roles

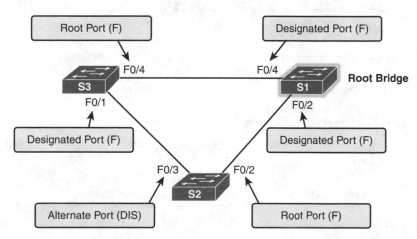

Edge Ports

In addition to these port roles, RSTP uses an edge port concept that corresponds to the PVST+ PortFast feature. An edge port connects directly to an end device. Therefore, the switch assumes that no other switch is connected to it. RSTP edge ports should immediately transition to the forwarding state, thereby skipping the time-consuming original 802.1D listening and learning port states. The only caveat is that the port must be a point-to-point link. If it is a shared link, then the port is nonedge and PortFast should not be configured. Why? Another switch could be added to a shared link, on purpose or inadvertently. Figure 11-7 shows examples of edge ports.

Figure 11-7   Edge Ports in RSTP

Activity: Identify the PVST+ and Rapid PVST+ Characteristics

Refer to the Digital Study Guide to complete this activity.

Configuring and Verifying Varieties of STP

By default, all Cisco switches use STP without any configuration by the network administrator. However, because STP runs on a per-VLAN basis, you can take advantage of several options to load-balance traffic across redundant links.

STP Configuration Overview

Before you configure or alter the behavior of STP, it is important to know the current default settings list in Table 11-7.

Table 11-7   Default STP Configuration on Cisco Catalyst 2960

Feature	Default Setting
Enable state	Enables STP on VLAN 1
Spanning tree mode	PVST+ (Rapid PVST+ and MSTP disabled)
Switch priority	32768
Spanning tree port priority (configurable on a per-interface basis)	128
Spanning tree port cost (configurable on a per-interface basis)	1000Mbps: 4 100Mbps: 19 10Mbps: 100
Spanning tree VLAN port priority (configurable on a per-VLAN basis)	128

Feature	Default Setting
Spanning tree VLAN port cost (configurable on a per-VLAN basis)	1000 Mbps: 4
	100 Mbps: 19
	10 Mbps: 100
Spanning tree timers	Hello time: 2 seconds
	Forward-delay time: 15 seconds
	Maximum-aging time: 20 seconds
	Transmit hold count: 6 BPDUs

Configuring and Verifying the BID

Regardless of which PVST you use, two main configuration options can help you achieve load balancing: the bridge ID and port cost manipulation. The bridge ID influences the choice of root switch and can be configured per VLAN. Each interface's (per-VLAN) STP cost to reach the root influences the choice of designated port on each LAN segment. Because PVST requires that a separate instance of spanning tree run for each VLAN, the BID field is required to carry VLAN ID (VID) information. This is accomplished by reusing a portion of the Priority field as the extended system ID to carry a VID.

To change the bridge ID, use one of the following commands:

```
Switch(config)# spanning-tree vlan vlan-id root {primary | secondary}
Switch(config)# spanning-tree vlan vlan-id priority priority
```

To change the interface cost, use the following command:

```
Switch(config-if)# spanning-tree vlan vlan-id cost cost
```

Figure 11-8 shows a simple three-switch STP topology without redundant links.

Figure 11-8   STP Topology

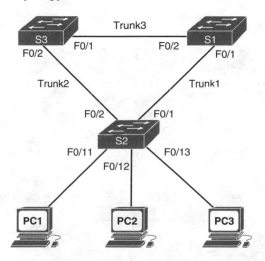

The network administrator wants to ensure that S1 is always the root bridge and S2 is the backup root bridge. The following commands achieve this objective:

```
S1(config)# spanning-tree vlan 1 root primary.
!---------
S2(config)# spanning-tree vlan 1 root secondary
```

The **primary** keyword automatically sets the priority to 24576 or to the next 4096 increment value below the lowest bridge priority detected on the network.

The **secondary** keyword automatically sets the priority to 28672, assuming that the rest of the network is set to the default priority of 32768.

Alternatively, the network administrator can explicitly configure the priority value in increments of 4096 between 0 and 65536 using the following command:

```
S1(config)# spanning-tree vlan 1 priority 24576
!---------
S2(config)# spanning-tree vlan 1 priority 28672
```

NOTE: These commands changed the priority values only for VLAN 1. Additional commands must be entered for each VLAN to take advantage of load balancing.

To verify the current spanning tree instances and root bridges, use the **show spanning-tree** command (see Example 11-1).

Example 11-1   Verifying Spanning Tree Configurations

```
S1# show spanning-tree


VLAN0001
  Spanning tree enabled protocol ieee
  Root ID    Priority    24577
             Address     001b.5302.4e80
             This bridge is the root
             Hello Time   2 sec  Max Age 20 sec  Forward Delay 15 sec

  Bridge ID  Priority    24577  (priority 24576 sys-id-ext 1)
             Address     001b.5302.4e80
             Hello Time   2 sec  Max Age 20 sec  Forward Delay 15 sec
             Aging Time  300


Interface         Role Sts Cost      Prio.Nbr Type
----------------- ---- --- --------- -------- -------------------------------
Fa0/1             Desg FWD 19        128.1    P2p
Fa0/2             Desg FWD 19        128.2    P2p
```

Because an extended system ID is used in the BID, the value of the priority includes the addition of the VLAN ID. Therefore, a priority of 24576 plus a VLAN of 1 results in a priority output of 24577.

Configuring PortFast and BPDU Guard

To speed convergence for access ports when they become active, you can use Cisco's proprietary PortFast technology. After PortFast is configured and a port is activated, the port immediately transitions from the blocking state to the forwarding state.

In a valid PortFast configuration, BPDUs should never be received because that indicates that another bridge or switch is connected to the port, potentially causing a spanning tree loop. When it is enabled, BPDU guard puts the port in an errdisabled (error-disabled) state upon receipt of a BPDU. This effectively shuts down the port. The BPDU guard feature provides a secure response to invalid configurations because you must manually put the interface back into service.

Example 11-2 shows the interface commands to configure PortFast and BPDU Guard on S2 in Figure 11-8.

Example 11-2   Configuring PortFast and BPDU Guard

```
S2# configure terminal
Enter configuration commands, one per line. End with CNTL/Z.
S2(config)# interface range f0/11 - f0/13
S2(config-if-range)# switchport mode access
S2(config-if-range)# spanning-tree portfast
S2(config-if-range)# spanning-tree bpduguard enable
```

Alternatively, you can configure the global commands **spanning-tree portfast default** and **spanning-tree bpduguard default**, which enable PortFast and BPDU Guard on all access ports.

Configuring Rapid PVST+

Remember, PVST+ is the default operation of Cisco switches. To change to Rapid PVST+, use a single global command on all switches: **spanning-tree mode rapid-pvst**.

Table 11-8 summarizes all the commands related to Rapid PVST+.

Table 11-8   Commands for Rapid PVST+

Description	Command
Configure Rapid PVST+ and the spanning tree mode	Switch(config)# **spanning-tree mode rapid-pvst**
Specify a link type as point-to-point (not normally necessary because the shared link type is unusual)	Switch(config-if)# **spanning-tree link-type point-to-point**
Force the renegotiation with neighboring switches on all interfaces or the specified interface	Switch# **clear spanning-tree detected protocols** [**interface** *interface-id*]

Verifying STP

Several commands enable you to verify the state of the current STP implementation. Table 11-9 summarizes commands most likely to appear on the CCNA exam.

Table 11-9   STP Verification Commands

Description	Command
Displays STP information	Switch# **show spanning-tree**
Displays STP information for active interfaces only	Switch# **show spanning-tree active**
Displays abbreviated information for all STP instances	Switch# **show spanning-tree brief**
Displays detailed information for all STP instances	Switch# **show spanning-tree detail**
Displays STP information for the specified interface	Switch# **show spanning-tree interface** *interface-id*
Displays STP information for the specified VLAN	Switch# **show spanning-tree vlan** *vlan-id*
Displays a summary of STP port states	Switch# **show spanning-tree summary**

NOTE: Ideally, you should review the output of these commands today on lab equipment or a simulator. At the very least, refer to the examples in your study resources.

 Packet Tracer Activity: Modify a Default STP Configuration

Refer to the Digital Study Guide to access the PKA file for this activity. You must have Packet Tracer software to run this activity. See the Introduction for details.

Switch Stacking

Stacking switches, such as the four 3750 switches in Figure 11-9, enables a network administrator to make a stack of switches act like one switch.

Figure 11-9   Cisco Catalyst 3750 Switch Stack

This improves management and protocol efficiency in the following ways:

- The stack has a single management IP address.

- One configuration file includes all interfaces in all four physical switches.

- STP, CDP, and VTP run on one switch, not multiple switches.

- The switch ports appear as if all are on the same switch.

- There is one MAC address table, and it references all ports on all physical switches.

The switches are connected through stacking ports. Every member is uniquely identified by its own stack member number. All members are eligible masters. If the master becomes unavailable, an automatic process takes place to elect a new master from the remaining stack members.

Switch stacking also reduces the STP diameter, which is the maximum number of switches data must cross between any two connected switches. For example, in Figure 11-10, the switch diameter between S1-4 and S3-4 is nine switches.

Figure 11-10   Switch Diameter Is 9

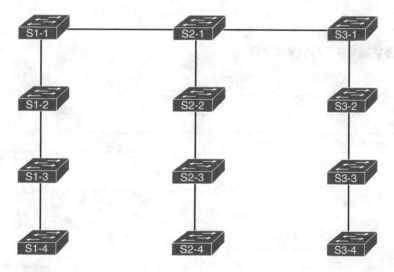

However, because of the default STP timers, IEEE recommends a maximum diameter of 7. Stacking the 12 switches in Figure 11-10 into three stacks reduces the maximum diameter from 9 to 3, as Figure 11-11 shows.

Figure 11-11   Switch Stacking Reduces STP Diameter

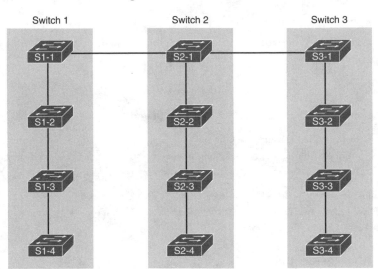

Study Resources

For today's exam topics, refer to the following resources for more study.

Resource	Location	Topic
Primary Resources		
Scaling Networks v6	3	All
ICND2 Official Cert Guide	2	All
	3	All
	6	Switch Stacking and Chassis Aggregation
Supplemental Resources		
CCNA Portable Command Guide	9	All
CCNA Video Series	2	Chapter 7: Spanning Tree Protocol (STP)
CCNA Network Simulator	ICND2	Chapter 3: STP Analysis
		Chapter 3: STP Configuration
		Chapter 3: STP Prediction Drills I–IV
		Chapter 3: STP Configuration I–III
		Chapter 3: PortFast Configuration I–II
		Chapter 3: BPDU Guard Configuration I–II
		Chapter 3: Path Analysis II–IV

 Check Your Understanding

Refer to the Digital Study Guide to take a short quiz covering the content of this day.

EtherChannel and HSRP

CCNA 200-125 Exam Topics

- Configure, verify, and troubleshoot (Layer 2/Layer 3) EtherChannel
- Configure, verify, and troubleshoot basic HSRP

Key Topics

EtherChannel technology enables you to bundle multiple physical interfaces into one logical channel to increase the bandwidth on point-to-point links. In addition, EtherChannel provides a way to prevent the need for Spanning Tree Protocol (STP) convergence when only a single port or cable failure occurs.

Most end devices do not store routes to reach remote networks. Instead, they are configured with a default gateway that handles routing for them. But what if that default gateway fails? To ensure that a device will still have access to remote networks, you should implement some type of default gateway redundancy in the network. That is the role of First Hop Redundancy Protocols (FHRPs). Hot Standby Router Protocol (HSRP) is the only FHRP that the CCNA exam covers.

EtherChannel Operation

EtherChannel, a technology that Cisco developed, can bundle up to eight equal-speed links between two switches, as you can see between the two distribution layer switches in Figure 10-1.

Figure 10-1   Sample EtherChannel Topology

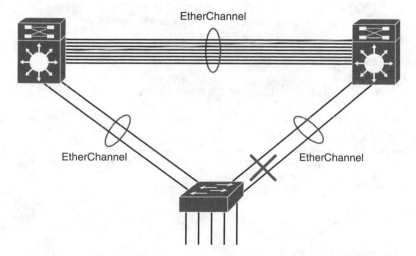

STP sees the bundle of links as a single interface. As a result, if at least one of the links is up, STP convergence does not have to occur. This makes much better use of available bandwidth while reducing the number of times STP must converge. Without using EtherChannel or modifying the STP configuration, STP would block all the links except one.

Benefits of EtherChannel

When an EtherChannel is configured, the resulting virtual interface is called a *port channel*. The physical interfaces are bundled together into a port channel interface. EtherChannel has the following benefits:

- Most configuration tasks can be done on the EtherChannel interface instead of on each individual port, thus ensuring configuration consistency throughout the links.

- EtherChannel relies on the existing switch ports to increase bandwidth. No hardware upgrades are needed.

- Load balancing is possible between links that are part of the same EtherChannel. (Load balancing configuration is beyond the scope of the CCNA exam.)

- EtherChannel creates an aggregation that STP recognizes as one logical link.

- EtherChannel provides redundancy. The loss of one physical link does not create a change in the topology.

Implementation Restrictions

Keep in mind a few limitations when implementing EtherChannel on Cisco 2960 Catalyst switches:

- Interface types, such as Fast Ethernet and Gigabit Ethernet, cannot mix within the same EtherChannel.

- Each EtherChannel can consist of up to eight compatibly configured Ethernet ports.

- Cisco IOS Software currently supports up to six EtherChannels.

- Some servers also support EtherChannel to the switch to increase bandwidth; however, the server then needs at least two EtherChannels to provide redundancy because it can send traffic to only one switch through the EtherChannel.

- The EtherChannel configuration must be consistent on both switches. The trunking configuration (native VLAN, allowed VLANs, and so on) must be the same. All ports also must be Layer 2 ports.

- All ports in the EtherChannel must be Layer 2 ports, or all ports within the EtherChannel must be Layer 3 ports.

NOTE: You can configure Layer 3 EtherChannels on multilayer switches; however, that is beyond the scope of the CCNA exam.

EtherChannel Protocols

You can configure EtherChannel as static or unconditional; however, you also can use two protocols to configure the negotiation process: Port Aggregation Protocol (PAgP—Cisco proprietary) and Link Aggregation Control Protocol (LACP—IEEE 802.3ad). These two protocols ensure that both sides of the link have compatible configurations—same speed, duplex setting, and VLAN information. The modes for each differ slightly.

Port Aggregation Protocol

PAgP is a Cisco proprietary protocol that aids in the automatic creation of EtherChannel links. PAgP checks for configuration consistency and manages link additions and failures between two switches. It ensures that when an EtherChannel is created, all ports have the same type of configuration. PAgP uses the following modes:

- **On:** This mode forces the interface to channel without PAgP.

- **Desirable:** The interface initiates negotiations with other interfaces by sending PAgP packets.

- **Auto:** The interface responds to the PAgP packets that it receives but does not initiate PAgP negotiation.

The modes must be compatible on each side of the EtherChannel. For example, Sw1 and Sw2 in Figure 10-2 must be configured with one of the combinations of settings in Table 10-1.

Figure 10-2   Two-Switch EtherChannel Topology

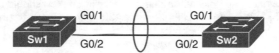

Table 10-1   PAgP Mode Settings

Sw1	Sw2	Channel Established?
On	On	Yes
Auto/Desirable	Desirable	Yes
On/Auto/Desirable	Not configured	No
On	Desirable	No
Auto/On	Auto	No

Link Aggregation Control Protocol

The Link Aggregation Control Protocol (LACP) is part of an IEEE specification (802.3ad) that allows a switch to negotiate an automatic bundle by sending LACP packets to the peer. It performs a function similar to PAgP with Cisco EtherChannel. Cisco devices support both PAgP and LACP. LACP uses the following modes:

- **On:** This mode forces the interface to channel without LACP.

- **Active:** The interface initiates negotiations with other interfaces by sending LACP packets.

- **Passive:** The interface responds to the LACP packets that it receives but does not initiate LACP negotiation.

As with PAgP, the LACP modes must be compatible on each side of the EtherChannel. For example, Sw1 and Sw2 in Figure 10-2 must be configured with one of the combinations of settings in Table 10-2.

Table 10-2   LACP Mode Settings

Sw1	Sw2	Channel Established?
On	On	Yes
Active/Passive	Active	Yes
On/Active/Passive	Not configured	No
On	Active	No
Passive/On	Passive	No

NOTE: For both protocols, the on mode creates the EtherChannel configuration unconditionally, without PAgP or LACP dynamic negotiation. You should probably memorize the mode settings for both PAgP and LACP in preparation for the CCNA exam.

Configuring EtherChannel

To implement EtherChannel, follow these steps:

Step 1.   Specify the interfaces that you want to bundle together in one link using the **interface range** *interfaces* command.

Step 2.   Create a port channel using the **channel-group** *identifier* **mode** *mode* command. The *identifier* can be any number between 1 and 6, inclusive, and does not have to match the other switch. The mode is either **on** or one of the PAgP or LACP modes.

Step 3.   Enter interface configuration mode for the new port channel with the **interface port-channel** *identifier* command. The *identifier* is the same number used in the **channel-group** command.

Step 4.   Configure the trunking and VLAN settings.

Using the topology in Figure 10-2, assume that Sw1 is already configured for EtherChannel with G0/1 and G0/2 trunking. The native VLAN is 86. The allowed VLANs are 1, 10, 20, and 86. EtherChannel is forced on. No PAgP or LACP is needed. Example 10-1 shows the configuration for Sw2.

Example 10-1 EtherChannel Configuration

```
Sw2(config)# interface range g0/1-2
Sw2(config-if-range)# channel-group 1 mode on
Creating a port-channel interface Port-channel 1
Sw2(config-if-range)# interface port-channel 1
Sw2(config-if)# switchport mode trunk
Sw2(config-if)# switchport trunk native vlan 86
Sw2(config-if)# switchport trunk allowed vlan 1,10,20,86
```

In configuring PAgP or LACP, use the appropriate mode keyword for the **channel-group** command. Just ensure that the commands on both sides of the channel are compatible according to Tables 10-1 and 10-2.

Verifying EtherChannel

If you configured management addressing, you can quickly verify both sides of an EtherChannel bundle by pinging across the trunk. The two switches should be able to ping each other. Devices configured as members of the various VLANs also should be able to ping each other.

To verify the configuration, use the **show run** command (see Example 10-2).

Example 10-2 Verifying the EtherChannel Configuration

```
Sw2# show run | begin interface Port
interface Port-channel1
 switchport trunk native vlan 86
 switchport trunk allowed vlan 1,10,20,86
 switchport mode trunk
!
<output omitted>
interface GigabitEthernet0/1
 switchport trunk native vlan 86
 switchport trunk allowed vlan 1,10,20,86
 switchport mode trunk
 channel-group 1 mode on
!
interface GigabitEthernet0/2
 switchport trunk native vlan 86
 switchport trunk allowed vlan 1,10,20,86
 switchport mode trunk
 channel-group 1 mode on
```

To get an overall summary of the EtherChannel configuration, use the **show etherchannel summary** command (see Example 10-3).

Example 10-3   Verifying EtherChannel Is Operational

```
Sw2# show etherchannel summary
Flags:  D - down        P - bundled in port-channel
        I - stand-alone  s - suspended
        H - Hot-standby (LACP only)
        R - Layer3       S - Layer2
        U - in use       f - failed to allocate aggregator

        M - not in use, minimum links not met
        u - unsuitable for bundling
        w - waiting to be aggregated
        d - default port

Number of channel-groups in use: 1
Number of aggregators:          1

Group  Port-channel  Protocol    Ports
------+-------------+-----------+-----------------------------------------------
1      Po1(SU)          -        Gig0/1(P)  Gig0/2(P)
```

To verify the operational status of a specific interface in the EtherChannel bundle, use the **show interface switchport** command (see Example 10-4).

Example 10-4   Verifying an Interface's Port Channel Settings

```
Sw2# show interface fa0/1 switchport
Name: Fa0/1
Switchport: Enabled
Administrative Mode: trunk
Operational Mode: trunk (member of bundle Po1)
Administrative Trunking Encapsulation: dot1q
Operational Trunking Encapsulation: dot1q
Negotiation of Trunking: On
Access Mode VLAN: 1 (default)
Trunking Native Mode VLAN: 86 (VLAN0086)
Administrative Native VLAN tagging: enabled
Voice VLAN: none
Administrative private-vlan host-association: none
Administrative private-vlan mapping: none
Administrative private-vlan trunk native VLAN: none
Administrative private-vlan trunk Native VLAN tagging: enabled
```

```
Administrative private-vlan trunk encapsulation: dot1q
Administrative private-vlan trunk normal VLANs: none
Administrative private-vlan trunk associations: none
Administrative private-vlan trunk mappings: none
Operational private-vlan: none
Trunking VLANs Enabled: 1,10,20,86
Pruning VLANs Enabled: 2-1001
```

Troubleshooting EtherChannel

All interfaces within an EtherChannel must have the same configuration of speed and duplex mode, native and allowed VLANs on trunks, and access VLAN on access ports:

- Assign all ports in the EtherChannel to the same VLAN, or configure them as trunks. Ports with different native VLANs cannot form an EtherChannel.

- When configuring a trunk on an EtherChannel, verify the trunking mode on the EtherChannel. Configuring trunking mode on individual ports that make up the EtherChannel is not recommended. However, if it is done, verify that the trunking configuration is the same on all interfaces.

- An EtherChannel supports the same allowed range of VLANs on all the ports. If the allowed range of VLANs is not the same, the ports do not form an EtherChannel even when PAgP is set to **auto** or **desirable** mode.

- The dynamic negotiation options for PAgP and LACP must be compatibly configured on both ends of the EtherChannel.

Configuration issues with the **channel-group** command include the following:

- Configuring the **on** keyword on one switch, and **desirable**, **auto**, **active**, or **passive** on the other switch. The **on** keyword does not enable PAgP or LACP. Both switches should be configured on one of the acceptable PAgP or LACP modes.

- Configuring the **auto** keyword on both switches enables PAgP, but both wait on the other switch to begin negotiations.

- Configuring the **passive** keyword on both switches enables LACP, but both wait on the other switch to begin negotiations.

- Mixing keywords from PAgP and LACP, which are not compatible. For example, configuring **active** (LACP) on one switch and **desirable** or **auto** (PAgP) on the other switch.

First-Hop Redundancy Concepts

FHRPs enable you to install multiple routers in a subnet to collectively act as a single default router. These routers share a virtual IP address, as Figure 10-3 shows.

Figure 10-3   Redundant Default Gateway Example

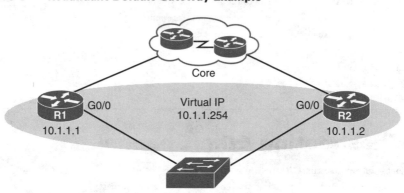

In the figure, the G0/0 interfaces on R1 and R2 are configured with the IP addresses shown. However, both routers are also configured with the virtual IP. This virtual IP address is the default gateway address configured on end devices. A redundancy protocol provides the mechanism for determining which router should take the active role in forwarding traffic. It also determines when a standby router must take over the forwarding role. The transition from one forwarding router to another is transparent to the end devices. This capability of a network to dynamically recover from the failure of a device acting as a default gateway is known as first-hop redundancy.

Regardless of which FHRP is implemented, the following steps take place when the active router fails:

Step 1.   The standby router stops seeing hello messages from the forwarding router.

Step 2.   The standby router assumes the role of the forwarding router.

Step 3.   Because the new forwarding router assumes both the IP and MAC addresses of the virtual router, the end stations do not recognize a disruption in service.

FHRPs

The following list defines the three options available for FHRPs:

- **Hot Standby Router Protocol (HSRP):** A Cisco proprietary FHRP designed to allow for transparent failover of a first-hop IPv4 device. The function of the HSRP standby router is to monitor the operational status of the HSRP group and to quickly assume packet-forwarding responsibility if the active router fails. HSRP for IPv6 provides support for IPv6 networks.

- **Virtual Router Redundancy Protocol (VRRP):** An IETF standard that dynamically assigns responsibility for one or more virtual routers to the VRRP routers on an IPv4 LAN. Operation is similar to HSRP. VRRPv3 supports IPv4 and IPv6.

- **Gateway Load Balancing Protocol (GLBP):** Cisco proprietary FHRP that protects data traffic from a failed router or circuit, as in HSRP and VRRP, while also allowing load balancing (also called load sharing) between a group of redundant routers. GLBP for IPv6 provides support for IPv6 networks.

The CCNA exam covers HSRP.

HSRP Operation

HSRP uses an active/standby model in which one router actively assumes the role of default gateway for devices on the subnet. One or more routers on the same subnet are then in standby mode. The HSRP active router implements a virtual IP address and matching virtual MAC address. This virtual IP address is part of the HSRP configuration and belongs to the same subnet as the physical interface IP address, but it is a different IP address. The router then automatically creates the virtual MAC address. All the cooperating HSRP routers know these virtual addresses, but only the HSRP active router uses these addresses at any one point in time.

Assume that you have two HSRP routers similar to R1 and R2 in Figure 10-3. These HSRP routers send each other messages to negotiate which router should be active. Then they continue to send each other messages so that the standby router can detect when the active router fails. If the active router fails, the standby router automatically assumes the virtual IP and MAC addresses, serving as the default gateway for the LAN. The new active router then sends out a gratuitous ARP so that the switches on the subnet will change their MAC address tables to reflect the correct port to reach the virtual MAC. This failover process is transparent to end devices, which are all configured with the virtual IP address as the default gateway.

So what about load balancing? Aren't we wasting the capacity of the standby router and the links connecting to it? Yes, if the routers are connected to only one subnet. However, if VLANs are configured, the routers can share the load by each serving as the active router for some of the VLANs. For example, in Figure 10-3, R1 is the active router for VLAN 10, and R2 is the active router for VLAN 20. Both routers are configured with subinterfaces for inter-VLAN routing and the two virtual IP addresses so that each can assume the role of active router if the other router fails.

HSRP Versions

Cisco IOS defaults to HSRP version 1. Table 10-3 compares HSRP version 1 and version 2.

Table 10-3   HSRP Version 1 and Version 2 Features

HSRP Feature	Version 1	Version 2
Group numbers supported	0–255	0–4095
Authentication	None	MD5
Multicast addresses	IPv4: 224.0.0.2	IPv4: 224.0.0.102 IPv6: FF02::66
Virtual MAC ranges	0000.0C07.AC00 to 0000.0C07.ACFF	IPv4: 0000.0C9F.F000 to 0000.0C9F.FFFF IPv6: 0005.73A0.0000 to 0005.73A0.0FFF

NOTE: The last three hexadecimal digits of the virtual MAC indicate the configured group number. Group numbers are important for more advanced HSRP configurations, which are beyond the scope of the CCNA.

HSRP Priority and Preemption

By default, the router with the numerically highest IPv4 address is elected as the active HSRP router. To configure a router to be the active router regardless of IPv4 addressing, use the **standby priority** interface configuration command. The default priority is 100. The router with the highest priority will be the active HSRP router, assuming that no election has already occurred.

To force a new HSRP election, preemption must be enabled with the **standby preempt** interface configuration command.

HSRP Configuration and Verification

Let's look at how to configure the topology in Figure 10-3. HSRP requires only one command on both routers:

```
Router(config-if)# standby group ip ip-address
```

The interface must be on the same subnet as the other HSRP router or routers. The *group* number and virtual *ip-address* must be the same on all HSRP routers.

Unless the **priority** command is used, the first router configured becomes the HSRP active router. Therefore, even though in Example 10-5 R1 is configured first, it includes a priority configuration to make sure that R1 is always the active router. Also, to make sure that R1 resumes the active router role after losing connectivity, the **standby preempt** command is configured.

Example 10-5   Configuring HSRP

```
R1(config)# interface g0/0
R1(config-if)# ip address 10.1.1.1 255.255.0.0
R1(config-if)# standby 1 ip 10.1.1.254
R1(config-if)# standby 1 priority 200
R1(config-if)# standby 1 preempt

R2(config)# interface g0/0
R2(config-if)# ip address 10.1.1.2 255.255.0.0
R2(config-if)# standby 1 ip 10.1.1.254
```

To verify that HSRP is up and running, use the **show standby** command or the **brief** version of the command, as in Example 10-6.

Example 10-6   Verifying HSRP

```
R1# show standby
GigabitEthernet0/0 - Group 1
  State is Active
    2 state changes, last state change 00:11:51
  Virtual IP address is 10.1.1.254
  Active virtual MAC address is 0000.0c07.ac01
    Local virtual MAC address is 0000.0c07.ac01 (v1 default)
```

```
    Hello time 3 sec, hold time 10 sec
      Next hello sent in 1.232 secs
    Preemption enabled
    Active router is local
    Standby router is 10.1.1.2, priority 100 (expires in 9.808 sec)
    Priority 200 (configured 200)
    Group name is "hsrp-Gi0/0-1" (default)
R1# show standby brief
                    P indicates configured to preempt.
                    |
Interface    Grp  Pri P State   Active        Standby       Virtual IP
Gi0/0         1   200   Active  local         10.1.1.2      10.1.1.254
```

```
R2# show standby
GigabitEthernet0/0 - Group 1
  State is Standby
    1 state change, last state change 00:15:23
  Virtual IP address is 10.1.1.254
  Active virtual MAC address is 0000.0c07.ac01
    Local virtual MAC address is 0000.0c07.ac01 (v1 default)
  Hello time 3 sec, hold time 10 sec
    Next hello sent in 1.008 secs
  Preemption disabled
  Active router is 10.1.1.1, priority 200 (expires in 8.624 sec)
  Standby router is local
  Priority 100 (default 100)
  Group name is "hsrp-Gi0/0-1" (default)
R2# show standby brief
                    P   indicates configured to preempt.
                    |
Interface    Grp  Pri P State   Active        Standby       Virtual IP
Gi0/0         1   100   Standby 10.1.1.1      local         10.1.1.254
```

The **show standby brief** command displays the most pertinent information you might need in a few lines of output. The more verbose **show standby** command provides additional information, such as the number of state changes, the virtual MAC address, hellos, and the group name.

HSRP Load Balancing

As with STP, you might want your HSRP routers to be configured in active/active state, with one router active for one set of VLANs and the other router active for the remaining VLANs. Figure 10-4 shows a topology with multiple VLANs.

Figure 10-4   HSRP Load Balancing Example

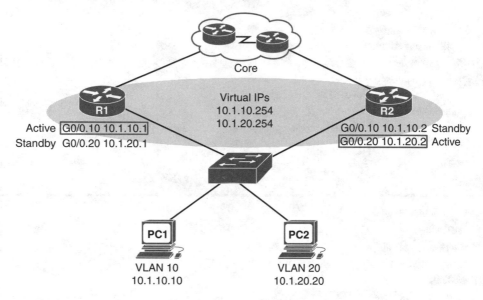

To implement HSRP load balancing for different VLANs, configure R1 as the active router for half the VLANs and R2 as the active router for the other half of the VLANs (see Example 10-7).

Example 10-7   Configuring HSRP Load Balancing

```
R1# show run | begin interface G

interface GigabitEthernet0/0
 no ip address
 duplex auto
 speed auto
!
interface GigabitEthernet0/0.10
 encapsulation dot1Q 10
 ip address 10.1.10.1 255.255.255.0
 standby version 2
 standby 1 ip 10.1.10.254
 standby 1 priority 150
 standby 1 preempt
!
interface GigabitEthernet0/0.20
 encapsulation dot1Q 20
 ip address 10.1.20.1 255.255.255.0
 standby version 2
 standby 1 ip 10.1.20.254
```

```
R2# show run | begin interface G

interface GigabitEthernet0/0
 no ip address
 duplex auto
 speed auto
!
interface GigabitEthernet0/0.10
 encapsulation dot1Q 10
 ip address 10.1.10.2 255.255.255.0
 standby version 2
 standby 1 ip 10.1.10.254
!
interface GigabitEthernet0/0.20
 encapsulation dot1Q 20
 ip address 10.1.20.2 255.255.255.0
 standby version 2
 standby 1 ip 10.1.20.254
 standby 1 priority 150
 standby 1 preempt
!
```

To verify that HSRP with load balancing is operational, use the **show standby** command or the **brief** version of the command (see Example 10-8).

Example 10-8 Verifying HSRP Load Balancing

```
R1# show standby brief
                     P indicates configured to preempt.
                     |
Interface   Grp  Pri  P State    Active       Standby      Virtual IP
            1    150    Active    local        10.1.10.2    10.1.10.254
            1    100    Standby   10.1.20.2    local        10.1.20.254


R2# show standby brief
                     P indicates configured to preempt.
                     |
Interface   Grp  Pri  P State    Active       Standby      Virtual IP
            1    100    Standby   10.1.10.1    local        10.1.20.254
            1    150    Active    local        10.1.20.1    10.1.20.254
```

Troubleshooting HSRP

Issues with HSRP most likely result from one or more of the following:

- The active router that controls the virtual IP for the group was not successfully elected.

- The standby router did not successfully keep track of the active router.

- No decision was made regarding when to hand another router control of the virtual IP for the group.

- End devices failed to successfully configure the virtual IP address as the default gateway.

HSRP common configuration issues include the following:

- The HSRP routers are not connected to the same network segment.

- The HSRP routers are not configured with IPv4 addresses from the same subnet.

- The HSRP routers are not configured with the same virtual IPv4 address.

- The HSRP routers are not configured with the same HSRP group number.

- End devices are not configured with the correct default gateway address.

Packet Tracer Activity: Configure EtherChannel and HSRP

Refer to the Digital Study Guide to access the PKA file for this activity. You must have Packet Tracer software to run this activity. See the Introduction for details.

Packet Tracer Activity: Troubleshoot EtherChannel and HSRP

Refer to the Digital Study Guide to access the PKA file for this activity. You must have Packet Tracer software to run this activity. See the Introduction for details.

Study Resources

For today's exam topics, refer to the following resources for more study.

Resource	Location	Topic
Primary Resources		
Scaling Networks v6	4	All
ICND2 Official Cert Guide	2	EtherChannel
	3	Configuring EtherChannel
	4	Troubleshooting Layer 2 EtherChannel
	20	All
Supplemental Resources		
CCNA Portable Command Guide	10	All
	21	All

Resource	Location	Topic
Supplemental Resources		
CCNA Video Series	2	Lesson 8: EtherChannel
	5	Lesson 2: Hot Standby Router Protocol (HSRP)
CCNA Network Simulator	INCD2	Chapter 3: Static EtherChannel
		Chapter 3: Dynamic EtherChannel I–IV
		Chapter 4: Path Troubleshooting I–II
		Chapter 20: HSRP Configuration I–IV

Check Your Understanding

Refer to the Digital Study Guide to take a short quiz covering the content of this day.

ACL Concepts

CCNA 200-125 Exam Topics

- Configure, verify, and troubleshoot IPv4 and IPv6 access list for traffic filtering

Key Topics

One of the most important skills a network administrator needs is mastery of access control lists (ACLs). Administrators use ACLs to stop traffic or permit only specified traffic on their networks. Standard and extended ACLs can apply a number of security features, including policy-based routing, quality of service (QoS), Network Address Translation (NAT), and Port Address Translation (PAT).

You can also configure standard and extended ACLs on router interfaces to control the type of traffic that is permitted through a given router. Today we review ACL concepts, including what they are, how a router uses them to filter traffic, and what types of ACLs are available.

ACL Operation

A router's default operation is to forward all packets, as long as a route exists for the packet and the link is up. ACLs can help implement a basic level of security. However, they are not the only security solution a large organization should implement. In fact, ACLs increase the latency of routers. If the organization is very large, with routers managing the traffic of hundreds or thousands of users, the administrator more than likely will use a combination of other security implementations that are beyond the scope of CCENT and CCNA.

Defining an ACL

An ACL is a router configuration script (a list of statements) that controls whether a router permits or denies packets to pass, based on criteria in the packet header. To determine whether a packet is permitted or denied, it is tested against the ACL statements in sequential order. When a statement matches, no more statements are evaluated; the packet is either permitted or denied. There is an implicit deny any statement at the end of the ACL. If a packet does not match any of the statements in the ACL, it is dropped.

Processing Interface ACLs

ACLs can be applied to an interface for inbound and outbound traffic. However, you need a separate ACL for each direction. The flow chart in Figure 9-1 details the steps a router takes when evaluating an ACL on inbound and outbound interfaces.

Figure 9-1   ACL Interface Processing for Inbound and Outbound Traffic

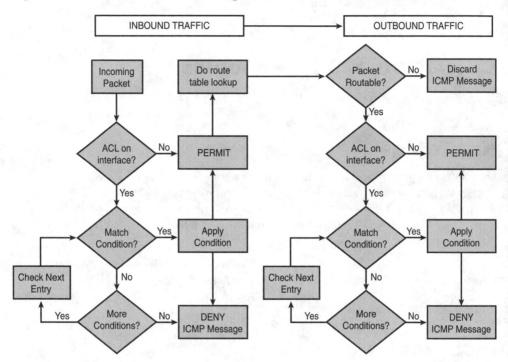

For inbound traffic, the router checks for an inbound ACL applied to the interface before doing a route table lookup. Then, for outbound traffic, the router makes sure that a route to the destination exists before checking for ACLs. Finally, if an ACL statement results in a dropped packet, the router sends an ICMP destination unreachable message.

The choice of using an inbound or outbound ACL is easy to make if, first, you place yourself inside the router—be the router. From such a stance, you can visualize processing a packet coming into a router interface (inbound), deciding what to do with the packet (Is there an inbound ACL? Is there a route to the destination?), and forwarding the packet (What is the outbound interface? Is there an ACL on the interface?).

List Logic with IP ACLs

An ACL is a list of commands that are processed in order, from the first statement in the list to the last statement. Each command has different matching logic that the router must apply to each packet when filtering is enabled. ACLs use first-match logic. If a packet matches one line in the ACL, the router takes the action listed in that line of the ACL and ignores the rest of the ACL statements.

For example, Figure 9-2 shows ACL 1 with three lines of pseudocode. The ACL is applied to R2's S0/0/1 interface, as the arrow indicates. Inbound traffic from R1 will be filtered using ACL 1.

Figure 9-2   Example of ACL Matching Logic

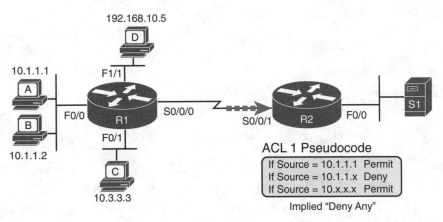

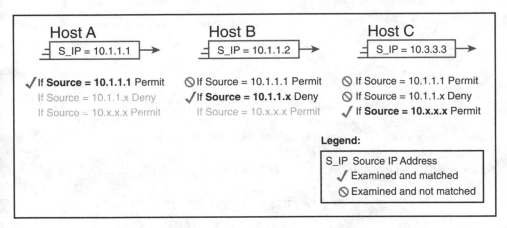

The box below the topology shows the logic for how packets from each host source address (labeled S_IP in the figure) are processed. Notice that when a match is made for Host A and Host B, the condition is applied (Host A is permitted and Host B is denied), and no further statements are evaluated. Host C matches the last statement in the list and is permitted.

Host D does not match any of the items in the ACL, so the packet is discarded. The reason is that every IP ACL has an implied deny any at the end of the ACL.

Planning to Use ACLs

Because an ACL can be used to filter traffic, it is important that you thoroughly plan the implementation of an ACL before actually configuring it.

Types of ACLs

ACLs can be configured to filter any type of protocol traffic, including other network layer protocols such as AppleTalk and IPX. For the CCNA exam, we focus on IPv4 and IPv6 ACLs, which come in the following types:

- **Standard IPv4 ACLs:** Filter traffic based on source address only

- **Extended IPv4 and IPv6 ACLs:** Can filter traffic based on source and destination address, specific protocols, and source and destination TCP and UDP ports

You can use two methods to identify both standard and extended ACLs:

- **Numbered IPv4 ACLs:** Use a number for identification

- **Named IPv4 and IPv6 ACLs:** Use a descriptive name or number for identification

Named ACLs must be used with some types of Cisco IOS configurations, including IPv6 ACLs. However, they provide two basic benefits for standard and extended IPv4 ACLs:

- By using a descriptive name (such as BLOCK-HTTP), a network administrator can more quickly determine the purpose of an ACL. This is particularly helpful in larger networks, where a router can have many ACLs with hundreds of statements.

- They reduce the amount of typing you must do to configure each statement in a named ACL, as you see in Day 8, "ACL Implementation."

Both numbered and named ACLs can be configured for standard as well as extended ACL implementations. Figure 9-3 summarizes the categories of IPv4 ACLs.

Figure 9-3   Comparisons of IPv4 ACL Types

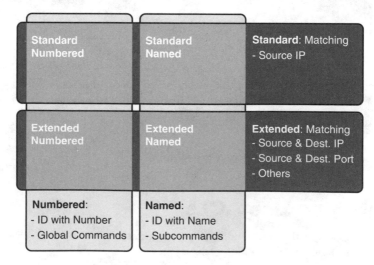

ACL Identification

Table 9-1 lists the different ACL number ranges for the IPv4 protocol. The table is not exhaustive. Other ACL numbers are available for other types of protocols that are either rarely used or beyond CCENT and CCNA scope. IPv6 uses only named ACLs.

Table 9-1   IPv4 ACL Numbers

Protocol	Range
IP	1–99
Extended IP	100–199
Standard IP (expanded)	1300–1999
Extended IP (expanded)	2000–2699

Named IP ACLs give you more flexibility in working with the ACL entries. In addition to using more memorable names, using named ACLs instead of numbered ACLs enables you to delete individual statements in a named IP access list.

Cisco IOS Software Release 12.3 introduced IP access list entry sequence numbering for both numbered and named ACLs. IP access list entry sequence numbering provides the following benefits:

- You can edit the order of ACL statements.

- You can remove individual statements from an ACL.

- You can use the sequence number to insert new statements into the middle of the ACL.

Sequence numbers are automatically added to the ACL if they are not entered explicitly at the time the ACL is created.

ACL Design Guidelines

Well-designed and –implemented ACLs add an important security component to your network. Follow these general principles to ensure that the ACLs you create have the intended results:

- Based on the test conditions, choose a standard or extended, numbered, or named ACL.

- Only one ACL is allowed per protocol, per direction, and per interface.

- Organize the ACL to enable processing from the top down. Organize your ACL so that more specific references to a network, subnet, or host appear before more general ones. Place conditions that occur more frequently before conditions that occur less frequently.

- All ACLs contain an implicit deny any statement at the end.

- Create the ACL before applying it to an interface.

- Depending on how you apply the ACL, the ACL filters traffic either going through the router or going to and from the router, such as traffic to or from the vty lines.

- You typically should place extended ACLs as close as possible to the source of the traffic that you want to deny. Because standard ACLs do not specify destination addresses, you must put the standard ACL as close as possible to the destination of the traffic you want to deny so that the source can reach intermediary networks.

Activity: Compare Standard Extended and Named ACLs

Refer to the Digital Study Guide to complete this activity.

Study Resources

For today's exam topics, refer to the following resources for more study.

Resource	Location	Topic
Primary Resources		
Routing and Switching Essentials v6	7	ACL Operation
Connecting Networks v6	4	IPv6 ACL Creation
ICND1 Official Cert Guide	25	IPv4 Access Control List Basics
ICND2 Official Cert Guide	16	IPv4 Access Control List Basics
Supplemental Resources		
CCNA Portable Command Guide	24	Access List Numbers
CCNA Video Series	6	Lesson 2: ACL Overview

Check Your Understanding

Refer to the Digital Study Guide to take a short quiz covering the content of this day.

ACL Implementation

CCNA 200-125 Exam Topics

- Configure, verify, and troubleshoot IPv4 and IPv6 access list for traffic filtering

Key Topics

Yesterday we reviewed ACL concepts. Today we focus on the configuration, verification, and troubleshooting of IPv4 and IPv6 ACLs.

Configuring Standard Numbered IPv4 ACLs

Standard IPv4 ACLs, which are numbered ACLs in the range of 1 to 99 and 1300 to 1999, or are named ACLs, filter packets based on a source address and mask. They permit or deny the entire TCP/IP protocol suite. Configuring an ACL requires two steps:

Step 1. Create the ACL.

Step 2. Apply the ACL.

Let's use the simple topology in Figure 8-1 to demonstrate how to configure both standard and extended IPv4 ACLs.

Figure 8-1 **IPv4 ACL Configuration Topology**

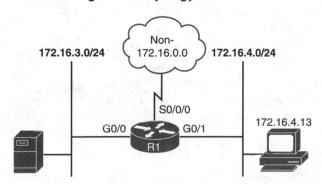

Standard Numbered IPv4 ACL: Permit Specific Network

Here we create an ACL to prevent traffic that is not part of the internal networks (172.16.0.0/16) from traveling out either of the Gigabit Ethernet interfaces.

Step 1.   Create the ACL.

Use the **access-list** global configuration command to create an entry in a standard IPv4 ACL:

```
R1(config)# access-list 1 permit 172.16.0.0 0.0.255.255
```

The sample statement matches any address that starts with 172.16.x.x. You can use the **remark** option to add a description to your ACL.

Step 2.   Apply the ACL.

Use the interface configuration command to select an interface to which to apply the ACL. Then use the **ip access-group** interface configuration command to activate the existing ACL on an interface for a specific direction (in or out):

```
R1(config)# interface gigabitethernet 0/0
R1(config-if)# ip access-group 1 out
R1(config-if)# interface gigabitethernet 0/1
R1(config-if)# ip access-group 1 out
```

This step activates the standard IPv4 ACL 1 on both the interfaces as an outbound filter.

This ACL allows only traffic from source network 172.16.0.0 to be forwarded out on G0/0 and G0/1. Traffic from networks other than 172.16.0.0 is blocked with the implied deny any.

Standard Numbered IPv4 ACL: Deny a Specific Host

Create an ACL to prevent traffic that originates from host 172.16.4.13 from traveling out G0/0. Create and apply the ACL with the commands in Example 8-1.

Example 8-1   ACL Preventing Traffic Originating from a Specific Host

```
R1(config)# access-list 1 deny 172.16.4.13 0.0.0.0
R1(config)# access-list 1 permit 0.0.0.0 255.255.255.255
R1(config)# interface gigabitethernet 0/0
R1(config-if)# ip access-group 1 out
```

This ACL is designed to block traffic from a specific address, 172.16.4.13, and to allow all other traffic to be forwarded on interface G0/0. The first statement can also be written with the keyword **host** replacing the 0.0.0.0 wildcard mask, as follows:

```
R1(config)# access-list 1 deny host 172.16.4.13
```

In fact, starting with Cisco IOS Software Release 12.3, you can enter the following:

```
R1(config)# access-list 1 deny 172.16.4.13
```

The second statement can be written with the keyword **any** replacing the source address 0.0.0.0 and wildcard mask 255.255.255.255, as follows:

```
R1(config)# access-list 1 permit any
```

Standard Numbered IPv4 ACL: Deny a Specific Subnet

Create an ACL to prevent traffic that originates from the subnet 172.16.4.0/24 from traveling out the G0/0 interface. Create and apply the ACL with the commands in Example 8-2.

Example 8-2   ACL Preventing Traffic Originating from a Specific Subnet

```
R1(config)# access-list 1 deny 172.16.4.0 0.0.0.255
R1(config)# access-list 1 permit any
R1(config)# interface g0/0
R1(config-if)# ip access-group 1 out
```

This ACL is designed to block traffic from a specific subnet, 172.16.4.0, and to allow all other traffic to be forwarded out G0/0.

Standard Numbered IPv4 ACL: Deny Telnet or SSH Access to the Router

For traffic into and out of the router (not through the router), filter Telnet or SSH access to the router by applying an ACL to the vty ports. Restricting vty access is primarily a technique for increasing network security and defining which addresses are allowed Telnet access to the router EXEC process. Create and apply the ACL with the commands in Example 8-3.

Example 8-3   Access List Allowing One Host Only Remote Access to R1

```
R1(config)# access-list 12 permit host 172.16.4.13
R1(config)# line vty 0 15
R1(config-line)# access-class 12 in
```

In this example, only host 172.16.4.13 is allowed to Telnet into R1. All other IP addresses are denied implicitly.

Configuring Extended Numbered IPv4 ACLs

For more precise traffic filtering control, use extended IPv4 ACLs. Extended IPv4 ACLS can be named or numbered in the range of 100 to 199 and 2000 to 2699. Extended ACLs check for source and destination IP addresses. In addition, at the end of the extended ACL statement, you can specify the protocol and optional TCP or UDP application to filter more precisely. To configure numbered extended IPv4 ACLs on a Cisco router, create an extended IP ACL and activate that ACL on an interface. For CCNA exam purposes, the extended IPv4 ACL command syntax is as follows:

```
Router(config)# access-list access-list-number {permit | deny} protocol source
source-wildcard [operator port] destination destination-wildcard [operator port]
[established] [log]
```

Table 8-1 explains the syntax of the command.

Table 8-1   Command Parameters for a Numbered Extended IPv4 ACL

Command Parameter	Description
`access-list-number`	Identifies the list using a number in the range of 100–199 or 2000–2699.
permit | **deny**	Indicates whether this entry allows or blocks the specified address.
`protocol`	If **ip** is specified, the entire TCP/IP protocol suite is filtered. Other protocols you can filter include TCP, UDP, ICMP, EIGRP, and OSPF. Use the **?** after the **permit** | **deny** argument to see all the available protocols.
`source` and `destination`	Identifies source and destination IP addresses.
`source-wildcard` and `destination-wildcard`	Wildcard mask. 0s indicate positions that must match, and 1s indicate "don't care" positions.
`operator [port |app_name]`	The operator can be **lt** (less than), **gt** (greater than), **eq** (equal to), or **neq** (not equal to). The port number referenced can be either the source port or the destination port, depending on where in the ACL the port number is configured. As an alternative to the port number, well-known application names can be used, such as Telnet, FTP, and SMTP.
established	For inbound TCP only. Allows TCP traffic to pass if the packet is a response to an outbound-initiated session. This type of traffic has the acknowledgment (ACK) bits set.
log	Sends a logging message to the console.

Extended Numbered IPv4 ACL: Deny FTP from Subnets

For the network in Figure 8-1, we now create an ACL to prevent FTP traffic originating from the subnet 172.16.4.0/24 and going to the 172.16.3.0/24 subnet from traveling out G0/0. Create and apply the ACL with the commands in Example 8-4.

Example 8-4   Access List Preventing FTP Traffic from Specific Subnets

```
R1(config)# access-list 101 deny tcp 172.16.4.0 0.0.0.255 172.16.3.0 0.0.0.255 eq 21
R1(config)# access-list 101 deny tcp 172.16.4.0 0.0.0.255 172.16.3.0 0.0.0.255 eq 20
R1(config)# access-list 101 permit ip any any
R1(config)# interface g0/0
R1(config-if)# ip access-group 101 out
```

The **deny** statements block FTP traffic originating from subnet 172.16.4.0 to subnet 172.16.3.0. The **permit** statement allows all other IP traffic out interface G0/0. Two statements must be entered for the FTP application because port 21 is used to establish, maintain, and terminate an FTP session, while port 20 is used for the actual file transfer task.

Extended Numbered IPv4 ACL: Deny Only Telnet from Subnet

Create an ACL to prevent Telnet traffic that originates from the subnet 172.16.4.0/24 from traveling out interface G0/0. Create and apply the ACL with the commands in Example 8-5.

Example 8-5   Access List Preventing Telnet Traffic from a Specific Subnet

```
R1(config)# access-list 101 deny tcp 172.16.4.0 0.0.0.255 any eq 23
R1(config)# access-list 101 permit ip any any
R1(config)# interface g0/0
R1(config-if)# ip access-group 101 out
```

This example denies Telnet traffic from 172.16.4.0 that is being sent out interface G0/0. All other
IP traffic from any other source to any destination is permitted out G0/0.

Activity: Evaluate an Extended ACL

Refer to the Digital Study Guide to complete this activity.

Configuring Named IPv4 ACLs

The named ACL feature enables you to identify standard and extended ACLs with an
alphanumeric string (name) instead of the current numeric representations.

Because you can delete individual entries with named ACLs, you can modify your ACL without
having to delete and then reconfigure the entire ACL. With Cisco IOS Software Release 12.3 and
later, you can insert individual entries using an appropriate sequence number.

Standard Named IPv4 ACL Steps and Syntax

The following steps and syntax are used to create a standard named ACL:

Step 1.   Name the ACL.

Starting from global configuration mode, use the **ip access-list standard** command to
name the standard ACL. ACL names are alphanumeric and must be unique:

```
Router(config)# ip access-list standard name
```

Step 2.   Create the ACL.

From standard named ACL configuration mode, use **permit** or **deny** statements to
specify one or more conditions for determining whether a packet is forwarded or
dropped. If you do not specify a sequence number, Cisco IOS increments the sequence
number by 10 for every statement you enter:

```
Router(config-std-nacl)# [sequence-number] {permit | deny} source
source-wildcard
```

Step 3.   Apply the ACL.

Activate the named ACL on an interface with the **ip access-group** name command:

```
Router(config-if)# ip access-group name [in | out]
```

Standard Named IPv4 ACL: Deny a Single Host from a Given Subnet

For the network shown previously in Figure 8-1, create a standard ACL named TROUBLEMAKER to prevent traffic that originates from the host 172.16.4.13 from traveling out interface G0/0. Create and apply the ACL with the commands in Example 8-6.

Example 8-6   Named ACL Preventing Traffic from a Specific Host

```
R1(config)# ip access-list standard TROUBLEMAKER
R1(config-std-nacl)# deny host 172.16.4.13
R1(config-std-nacl)# permit 172.16.4.0 0.0.0.255
R1(config-std-nacl)# interface g0/0
R1(config-if)# ip access-group TROUBLEMAKER out
```

Extended Named IPv4 ACL Steps and Syntax

The following steps and syntax are used to create an extended named ACL:

Step 1.   Name the ACL.

Starting from global configuration mode, use the **ip access-list extended** command to name the extended ACL:

```
Router(config)# ip access-list extended name
```

Step 2.   Create the ACL.

From extended named ACL configuration mode, use **permit** or **deny** statements to specify one or more conditions for determining whether a packet is forwarded or dropped:

```
Router(config-ext-nacl)# [sequence-number] {deny | permit} protocol
source source-wildcard [operator port] destination destination-wildcard
[operator port] [established] [log]
```

Step 3.   Apply the ACL.

Activate the named ACL on an interface with the **ip access-group** name command:

```
Router(config-if)# ip access-group name [in | out]
```

Adding Comments to Named or Numbered IPv4 ACLs

You can add comments to ACLs using the **remark** argument in place of the **permit** or **deny**. Remarks are descriptive statements that you can use to better understand and troubleshoot either named or numbered ACLs.

Example 8-7 shows how to add a comment to a numbered ACL.

Example 8-7   Adding Comments to a Numbered ACL

```
R1(config)# access-list 101 remark Permitting John to Telnet to Server
R1(config)# access-list 101 permit tcp host 172.16.4.13 host 172.16.3.10 eq telnet
```

Example 8-8 shows how to add a comment to a named ACL.

Example 8-8   Adding Comments to a Named ACL

```
R1(config)# ip access-list standard PREVENTION
R1(config-std-nacl)# remark Do not allow Jones subnet through
R1(config-std-nacl)# deny 172.16.4.0 0.0.0.255
```

Verifying IPv4 ACLs

When you finish configuring an ACL, use **show** commands to verify the configuration. Use the **show access-lists** command to display the contents of all ACLs, as in Example 8-9. By entering the ACL name or number as an option for this command, you can display a specific ACL.

Example 8-9   Verifying Access List Configuration

```
R1# show access-lists
Standard IP access list SALES
    10 permit 10.3.3.1
    20 permit 10.4.4.1
    30 permit 10.5.5.1
    40 deny   10.1.1.0, wildcard bits 0.0.0.255
    50 permit any
Extended IP access list ENG
    10 permit tcp host 10.22.22.1 any eq telnet (25 matches)
    20 permit tcp host 10.33.33.1 any eq ftp
    30 permit tcp host 10.33.33.1 any eq ftp-data
```

Notice in the output from the **show access-lists** command in Example 8-9 that sequence numbers are incremented by 10—most likely because the administrator did not enter a sequence number. Also notice that this command tells you how many times Cisco IOS has matched a packet to a statement—25 times, in the case of the first statement in the named ACL ENG.

The **show ip interface** command displays IP interface information and indicates whether any IP ACLs are set on the interface. In the **show ip interface g0/0** command output in Example 8-10, IP ACL 1 has been configured on the G0/0 interface as an inbound ACL. No outbound IP ACL has been configured on the G0/0 interface.

Example 8-10   Verifying Access List Configuration on a Specific Interface

```
R1# show ip interface g0/0
GigabitEthernet0/0 is up, line protocol is up
  Internet address is 10.1.1.11/24
  Broadcast address is 255.255.255.255
  Address determined by setup command
  MTU is 1500 bytes
  Helper address is not set
  Directed broadcast forwarding is disabled
  Outgoing access list is not set
  Inbound access list is 1
  Proxy ARP is enabled
  <output omitted>
```

Finally, you can also verify your ACL creation and application with the **show running-config** command (see Example 8-11).

Example 8-11   Verifying ACL Creation and Application in the Running Configuration

```
R1# show running-config
Building configuration...
!
<output omitted>
!
interface GigabitEthernet0/0
 ip address 10.44.44.1 255.255.255.0
 ip access-group ENG out
!
<output omitted>
!
interface Serial0/0/0
ip address 172.16.2.1 255.255.255.252
 ip access-group SALES in
!
<output omitted>
ip access-list standard SALES
 permit 10.3.3.1
 permit 10.4.4.1
 permit 10.5.5.1
 deny   10.1.1.0 0.0.0.255
 permit any
```

```
!
ip access-list extended ENG
 permit tcp host 10.22.22.1 any eq telnet
 permit tcp host 10.33.33.1 any eq ftp
 permit tcp host 10.33.33.1 any eq ftp-data
!
<output omitted>
```

Comparing IPv4 and IPv6 ACLs

IPv4 and IPv6 ACLs have some subtle differences (see Table 8-2).

Table 8-2   IPv4 and IPv6 ACLs

Feature	IPv4 Only	IPv6 Only	Both
Match source and/or destination address			X
Match host addresses or subnets/prefixes			X
Applied directionally on an interface			X
Match TCP or UDP source and/or destination ports			X
Match ICMP codes			X
Include implicit deny at end of ACL			X
Match IPv4 packets only	X		
Match IPv6 packets only		X	
Use numbers to identify the ACL	X		
Use names to identify the ACL			X
Include some implicit **permit** statements at end of ACL		X	

Configuring IPv6 ACLs

The basic steps to configure IPv6 ACLs are the same as for named IPv4 ACLs:

Step 1.   Name the ACL.

Step 2.   Create the ACL.

Step 3.   Apply the ACL.

Step 1: Name the IPv6 ACL

To name an IPv6 ACL, enter the **ipv6 access-list** command in global configuration mode:

```
Router(config)# ipv6 access-list name
```

Notice that the command syntax to name an IPv6 ACL is the same whether you are configuring standard or extended IPv6 ACLs. However, standard and extended IPv6 ACLs are different than standard and extended IPv4 ACLs.

Step 2: Create the IPv6 ACL

A standard IPv6 ACL includes both source and destination address information, but it does not include TCP, UDP, or ICMPv6 information. The syntax for a standard IPv6 ACL follows:

```
Router(config-ipv6-acl)# [permit | deny] ipv6 {source-ipv6-prefix/prefix-length |
any | host source-ipv6-address} {destination-ipv6-prefix/prefix-length | any | host
destination-ipv6-address} [log]
```

Extended IPv6 ACLs match on many more IPv6 packet header fields, as well as TCP, UDP, and ICMPv6 messages and IPv6 extension headers. The syntax for extended IPv6 ACLs follows:

```
Router(config-ipv6-acl)# [permit | deny] protocol {source-ipv6-prefix/prefix-length
| any | host source-ipv6-address} [operator [port-number]] {destination-ipv6-
prefix/prefix-length | any | host destination-ipv6-address} [operator [port-
number]] [dest-option-type [doh-number |doh-type]] [dscp value] [flow-label value]
[fragments] [log] [log-input] [mobility][mobility-type [mh-number | mh-type]]
[reflect name [timeout value]] [routing][routing-type routing-number] [sequence
value] [time-range name]
```

If you choose **icmp**, **tcp**, or **udp** as the *protocol*, additional filtering options are available to match those specific headers. For example, configuring **icmp** as the *protocol* enables you to filter the *icmp-type*. Configuring **tcp** as the *protocol* enables you to filter the six TCP flags, ACK, FIN, PSH, RST, SYN, and URG. Configuring **udp** as the *protocol* enables you to filter IPv6 extension headers, such as IPsec.

Step 3: Apply the IPv6 ACL

The syntax to apply an IPv6 ACL to an interface follows:

```
Router(config-if)# ipv6 traffic-filter access-list-name { in | out }
```

The syntax to apply an IPv6 ACL to VTY lines is similar to that of IPv4. Just replace **ip** with **ipv6**, as follows:

```
Router(config-line)# ipv6 access-class access-list-name
```

Standard IPv6 ACL: Allow SSH Remote Access

The topology in Figure 8-2 is used here for IPv6 ACL configuration scenarios.

Figure 8-2   IPv6 ACL Configuration Topology

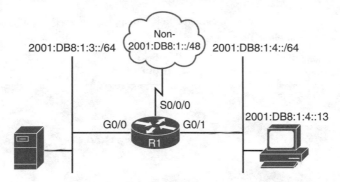

Example 8-12 demonstrates how to create and apply an IPv6 ACL to allow only 2001:DB8:1:4::13 to remotely connect to R1 VTY lines.

Example 8-12   Access List Allowing Only One Host to Access R1

```
R1(config)# ipv6 access-list SSH-HOST
R1(config-ipv6-acl)# permit ipv6 host 2001:db8:1:4::13 any
R1(config-ipv6-acl)# deny ipv6 any any
R1(config-ipv6-acl)# exit
R1(config)# line vty 0 4
R1(config-line)# ipv6 access-class SSH-HOST in
```

The **permit** statement allows only one host, 2001:DB8:1:4::13. All other IPv6 traffic is denied. The IPv6 ACL is then applied to the first five VTY lines with the **ipv6 access-class** command.

Extended IPv6 ACL: Allow Only Web Traffic

Example 8-13 demonstrates how to create and apply an IPv6 ACL to allow only web traffic originating from the subnet 2001:DB8:1:4::/64 and going to the 2001:DB8:1:3::/64 subnet.

Example 8-13   Access List Preventing Web Traffic from Specific Subnets

```
R1(config)# ipv6 access-list WEB-ONLY
R1(config-ipv6-acl)# permit tcp 2001:DB8:1:4::/64 2001:DB8:1:3::/64 eq www
R1(config-ipv6-acl)# deny ipv6 2001:DB8:1:4::/64 2001:DB8:1:3::/64
R1(config-ipv6-acl)# permit ipv6 2001:DB8:1:4::/64 any
R1(config-ipv6-acl)# exit
R1(config)# interface g0/0
R1(config-if)# ipv6 traffic-filter WEB-ONLY in
```

The first **permit** statement allows traffic from prefix 2001:DB8:1:4::/64 to access web services on any device in prefix 2001:DB8:1:3::/64. The **deny** statement makes sure that all other traffic from 2001:DB8:1:4::/64 to 2001:DB8:1:3::/64 is blocked. The last **permit** statement allows all other inbound traffic from 2001:DB8:1:4::/64 to any destination.

Verifying IPv6 ACLs

Similar to IPv4 ACLs, you can view the configuration and application of IPv6 ACLs with the **show run** command, as in Example 8-14.

Example 8-14 Examining ACLs in the Configuration

```
R1# show run
Building configuration...
<some output omitted>
!
interface GigabitEthernet0/1
 ipv6 traffic-filter WEB-ONLY in
 ipv6 address FE80::1 link-local
 ipv6 address 2001:DB8:1:4::1/64
!
ipv6 access-list WEB-ONLY
 permit tcp 2001:DB8:1:4::/64 2001:DB8:1:3::/64 eq www
 deny ipv6 2001:DB8:1:4::/64 2001:DB8:1:3::/64
 permit ipv6 2001:DB8:1:4::/64 any
ipv6 access-list SSH-HOST
 permit ipv6 host 2001:DB8:1:4::13 any
 deny ipv6 any any
!
line vty 0 4
 ipv6 access-class SSH-HOST in
 login local
 transport input ssh
!
R1#
```

However, the configuration of production routers is usually long and complex. For the simulation questions on the CCNA exam, you might not even have access to the **show run** command. Therefore, you should use verification commands that more precisely and efficiently provide the information you need.

For example, **show access-lists** quickly reveals all IPv4 and IPv6 ACLs configured on the device, as Example 8-15 shows.

Example 8-15 Verifying All ACLs Configured

```
R1# show access-lists
Standard IP access list SALES
    10 permit 10.3.3.1
    20 permit 10.4.4.1
    30 permit 10.5.5.1
    40 deny    10.1.1.0, wildcard bits 0.0.0.255
    50 permit any
```

```
Extended IP access list ENG
    10 permit tcp host 10.22.22.1 any eq telnet
    20 permit tcp host 10.33.33.1 any eq ftp
    30 permit tcp host 10.33.33.1 any eq ftp-data
IPv6 access list SSH-HOST
    permit ipv6 host 2001:DB8:1:4::13 any sequence 10
    deny ipv6 any any sequence 20
IPv6 access list WEB-ONLY
    permit tcp 2001:DB8:1:4::/64 2001:DB8:1:3::/64 eq www sequence 10
    deny ipv6 2001:DB8:1:4::/64 2001:DB8:1:3::/64 sequence 20
    permit ipv6 2001:DB8:1:4::/64 any sequence 30
R1#
```

Notice that Cisco IOS added sequence numbers to the end of the IPv6 ACLs instead of at the beginning, as it does for IPv4 ACLs.

In Example 8-16, only the IPv6 ACLs are shown. This output was generated after multiple packets matched each of the statements in the ACLs.

Example 8-16   Verifying IPv6 ACL Match Statistics

```
R1# show ipv6 access-list
IPv6 access list SSH-HOST
    permit ipv6 host 2001:DB8:1:4::13 any (1 match(es)) sequence 10
    deny ipv6 any any (5 match(es)) sequence 20
IPv6 access list WEB-ONLY
    permit tcp 2001:DB8:1:4::/64 2001:DB8:1:3::/64 eq www (5 match(es))
       sequence 10
    deny ipv6 2001:DB8:1:4::/64 2001:DB8:1:3::/64 (4 match(es)) sequence 20
    permit ipv6 2001:DB8:1:4::/64 any (75 match(es)) sequence 30
R1#
```

To verify the placement of IPv6 ACL on an interface, you can use the **show ipv6 interface** command. If an ACL is applied, the output will have a line entry, as highlighted in Example 8-17.

Example 8-17   Verifying an IPv6 ACL Applied to an Interface

```
R1# show ipv6 interface g0/1
GigabitEthernet0/1 is up, line protocol is up
  IPv6 is enabled, link-local address is FE80::1
  No Virtual link-local address(es):
  Global unicast address(es):
    2001:DB8:1:4::1, subnet is 2001:DB8:1:4::/64
  Joined group address(es):
```

```
    FF02::1
    FF02::2
    FF02::1:FF00:1
  MTU is 1500 bytes
  ICMP error messages limited to one every 100 milliseconds
  ICMP redirects are enabled
  ICMP unreachables are sent
  Input features: Access List
  Inbound access list WEB-ONLY
  ND DAD is enabled, number of DAD attempts: 1
  ND reachable time is 30000 milliseconds (using 30000)
  ND advertised reachable time is 0 (unspecified)
  ND advertised retransmit interval is 0 (unspecified)
  ND router advertisements are sent every 200 seconds
  ND router advertisements live for 1800 seconds
  ND advertised default router preference is Medium
  Hosts use stateless autoconfig for addresses.
R1#
```

Troubleshooting ACLs

Your network can be configured correctly with all hosts receiving DHCP addressing, fully populated routing tables, and a fully operating physical layer, but an ACL somewhere in the data path can still be causing a problem. Troubleshooting a problem caused by an ACL can make your job more difficult.

ACLs can block normal troubleshooting tools such as ping and traceroute while still allowing normal traffic. Therefore, the network administrator might need to rely on other tools to find a problem.

If you have determined that the problem is with the ACL configuration, the following three steps summarize a structured troubleshooting process you can use to track down the issue.

Step 1.   ACL configurations cannot cause a problem until they are applied. Therefore, determine what interfaces are impacted by ACLs with the **show run** or **show ip interfaces** commands.

Step 2.   Verify the ACL configuration with the **show access-lists**, **show ip access-lists**, or **show run** commands.

Step 3.   Analyze the ACLs to determine which packets will match. The **show access-lists** and **show ip access-lists** help by identifying the number of times packets have matched a statement.

Some common ACL configuration errors include the following:

- ACLs statements are out of order.
- The source and destination addresses and/or ports are reversed.

- The ACL is applied in the wrong direction.

- Syntax or spelling errors cause the ACL to have the wrong intended effect or no effect.

- Standard ACLs are close to the source instead of the destination.

Refer to your study resources for several excellent troubleshooting examples for both IPv4 and IPv6 ACLs.

Study Resources

For today's exam topics, refer to the following resources for more study.

Resource	Location	Topic
Primary Resources		
Routing and Switching Essentials v6	7	Standard IPv4 ACLs
		Troubleshoot ACLs
Connecting Networks v6	4	All
ICND1 Official Cert Guide	25	Standard Numbered IPv4 ACLs
		Practice Applying Standard IPv4 ACLs
	26	All
ICND2 Official Cert Guide	16	Standard Numbered IPv4 ACLs
		Practice Applying Standard IPv4 ACLs
	17	All
	25	All
Supplemental Resources		
CCNA Portable Command Guide	24	All
CCNA Video Series	6	Lesson 2: All
CCNA Network Simulator	ICND1	Chapter 25: Standard ACL
		Chapter 26: Extended ACL I–II
		Chapter 26: ACL I–VI
		Chapter 26: ACL Analysis I
		Chapter 26: Named ACL I–III
	ICND2	Advanced IPv6 ACL I–II
		IPv6 ACL I–VI
		IPv6 ACL Analysis I

Check Your Understanding

Refer to the Digital Study Guide to take a short quiz covering the content of this day.

DHCP and DNS

CCNA 200-125 Exam Topics

- Configure and verify DHCP on a router (excluding static reservations)
- Troubleshoot client- and router-based DHCP connectivity issues
- Describe DNS lookup operation
- Troubleshoot client connectivity issues involving DNS

Key Topics

Imagine that you have to manually configure the IP addressing for every device you want to connect to the network. Furthermore, imagine that you have to type in the IP address for every website you want to visit. Today we review the two protocols that automate this process: Dynamic Host Configuration Protocol (DHCP)and Domain Name System (DNS). DHCP and DNS make the life of Internet users easier.

DHCPv4

DHCPv4 allows a host to obtain an IP address dynamically when it connects to the network. The DHCPv4 client contacts the DHCPv4 server by sending a request for an IP address. The DHCPv4 server chooses an address from a configured range of addresses called a pool and assigns it to the host client for a set period. Figure 7-1 graphically shows the process for how a DHCPv4 server fulfills a request from a DHCPv4 client.

When a DHCPv4-configured device boots up or connects to the network, the client broadcasts a DHCPDISCOVER packet to identify any available DHCPv4 servers on the network. A DHCPv4 server replies with a DHCPOFFER, which is a lease offer message with an assigned IP address, subnet mask, DNS server, and default gateway information, as well as the duration of the lease.

The client can receive multiple DHCPOFFER packets if the local network has more than one DHCPv4 server. The client chooses the first offer and broadcasts a DHCPREQUEST packet that identifies the explicit server and lease offer that it is accepting.

Assuming that the IP address is still valid, the chosen server returns a DHCPACK (acknowledgment) message finalizing the lease. If the offer is no longer valid for some reason, the chosen server responds to the client with a DHCPNAK (negative acknowledgment) message. After it is leased, the client renews before the lease expiration through another DHCPREQUEST. If the client is powered down or taken off the network, the address is returned to the pool for reuse.

Figure 7-1   Allocating IP Addressing Information Using DHCPv4

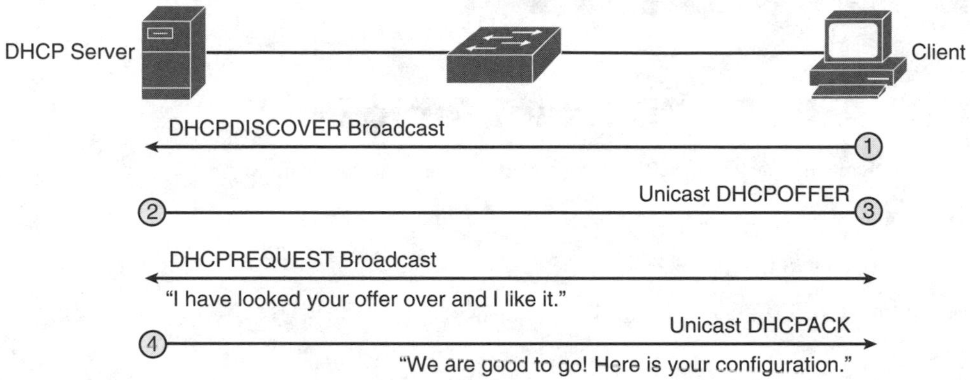

DHCPv4 Configuration Options

A Cisco router can be configured to handle DHCP requests in two ways: as a DHCP server or as a DHCP relay agent. A Cisco router can also be configured as a DHCP client, requesting an IPv4 address from a DHCP server for one or more of its interfaces. All these options can be configured at the same time on the same device. For example, a router might be the DHCP server for a directly connected LAN while at the same time forwarding DHCP server requests to another DHCP server for other LANs. In addition, the router could have one or more of its interfaces configured to request DHCP addressing from a remote server.

Configuring a Router as a DHCPv4 Server

A Cisco router running Cisco IOS Software can be configured to act as a DHCPv4 server. The Cisco IOS DHCPv4 server assigns and manages IPv4 addresses from specified address pools within the router to DHCPv4 clients.

The steps to configure a router as a DHCPv4 server follow:

Step 1.   Use the **ip dhcp excluded-address** *low-address* [*high-address*] command to identify an address or range of addresses to exclude from the DHCPv4 pool. For example:

```
R1(config)# ip dhcp excluded-address 192.168.10.1 192.168.10.9

R1(config)# ip dhcp excluded-address 192.168.10.254
```

Step 2.   Create the DHCPv4 pool using the **ip dhcp pool** *pool-name* command, which places you in DHCP config mode:

```
R1(config)# ip dhcp pool LAN-POOL-10

R1(dhcp-config)#
```

Step 3.   Configure the IP addressing parameter you need to automatically assign to requesting clients. Table 7-1 lists the required commands.

Table 7-1   Required DHCPv4 Configuration Commands

Required Task	Command
Define the address pool	**network** *network-number* *[mask	/prefix-length]*
Define the default router or gateway	**default-router** *address* *[address2...address8]*

Table 7-2 lists some of the more common optional DHCPv4 tasks.

Table 7-2   Optional DHCPv4 Configuration Commands

Optional Task	Command
Define a DNS server	**dns-server** *address* *[address2...address8]*
Define the domain name	**domain-name** *domain*
Define the duration of the DHCPv4 lease	**lease** *{days [hours] [minutes]*	**infinite**}
Define the NetBIOS WINS server	**netbios-name-server** *address* *[address2...address8]*

Figure 7-2 shows a sample DHCPv4 topology.

Figure 7-2   DHCPv4 Sample Topology

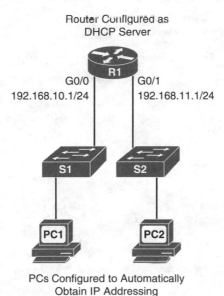

Router Configured as
DHCP Server

R1

G0/0   G0/1
192.168.10.1/24   192.168.11.1/24

S1   S2

PC1   PC2

PCs Configured to Automatically
Obtain IP Addressing

Example 7-1 shows DHCPv4 required and optional commands to configure R1 as the DHCPv4 server for both LANs.

Example 7-1   DHCPv4 Configuration Example

```
!Configure IP addresses that you want excluded from the DHCPv4 pool of addresses
R1(config)# ip dhcp excluded-address 192.168.10.1 192.168.10.9
R1(config)# ip dhcp excluded-address 192.168.10.254
R1(config)# ip dhcp excluded-address 192.168.11.1 192.168.11.9
R1(config)# ip dhcp excluded-address 192.168.11.254
!R1 needs two DHCPv4 pools for the two LANs. Each pool is configured with required
  and optional commands.
R1(config)# ip dhcp pool LAN-POOL-10
R1(dhcp-config)# network 192.168.10.0 255.255.255.0
R1(dhcp-config)# default-router 192.168.10.1
R1(dhcp-config)# dns-server 192.168.50.195 209.165.202.158
R1(dhcp-config)# domain-name cisco.com
R1(dhcp-config)# lease 2
R1(dhcp-config)# netbios-name-server 192.168.10.254
R1(dhcp-config)# ip dhcp pool LAN-POOL-11
R1(dhcp-config)# network 192.168.11.0 255.255.255.0
R1(dhcp-config)# default-router 192.168.11.1
R1(dhcp-config)# dns-server 192.168.50.195 209.165.202.158
R1(dhcp-config)# domain-name cisco.com
R1(dhcp-config)# lease 2
R1(dhcp-config)# netbios-name-server 192.168.11.254
R1(dhcp-config)# end
```

Cisco IOS Software supports DHCPv4 service by default. To disable it, use the global command
no service dhcp.

To verify DHCPv4 operations on the router, use the commands in Example 7-2.

Example 7-2   Verifying DHCPv4 Operation

```
R1# show ip dhcp binding
Bindings from all pools not associated with VRF:
IP address          Client-ID/              Lease expiration        Type
                    Hardware address/
                    User name
192.168.10.10       0100.1641.aea5.a7       Jul 18 2008 08:17 AM    Automatic
192.168.11.10       0100.e018.5bdd.35       Jul 18 2008 08:17 AM    Automatic

R1# show ip dhcp server statistics
Memory usage         26455
Address pools        2
Database agents       0
Automatic bindings    2
Manual bindings       0
Expired bindings      0
```

```
Malformed messages     0
Secure arp entries     0
Message                Received
BOOTREQUEST            0
DHCPDISCOVER           2
DHCPREQUEST            2
DHCPDECLINE            0
DHCPRELEASE            0
DHCPINFORM             0

Message                Sent
BOOTREPLY              0
DHCPOFFER              2
DHCPACK               2
DHCPNAK               0
R1#
```

Because PC1 and PC2 are connected to the LANs, each automatically receives its IP addressing information from the router's DHCPv4 server. Example 7-3 shows the output from the **ipconfig/all** command on PC1.

Example 7-3   DHCPv4 Client Configuration

```
C:\> ipconfig/all

Windows IP Configuration

         Host Name . . . . . . . . . . . . : ciscolab
         Primary Dns Suffix  . . . . . . . :
         Node Type . . . . . . . . . . . . : Hybrid
         IP Routing Enabled. . . . . . . . : No
         WINS Proxy Enabled. . . . . . . . : No

Ethernet adapter Local Area Connection:

         Connection-specific DNS Suffix  . : cisco.com
         Description . . . . . . . . . . . : Intel(R) PRO/1000 PL
         Physical Address. . . . . . . . . : 00-7-41-AE-A5-A7
         Dhcp Enabled. . . . . . . . . . . : Yes
         Autoconfiguration Enabled . . . . : Yes
         IP Address. . . . . . . . . . . . : 192.168.10.11
         Subnet Mask . . . . . . . . . . . : 255.255.255.0
         Default Gateway . . . . . . . . . : 192.168.10.1
```

```
        DHCP Server . . . . . . . . . . : 192.168.10.1
        DNS Servers . . . . . . . . . . : 192.168.50.195
                                          209.165.202.158
        Primary WINS Server . . . . . . : 192.168.10.254
        Lease Obtained. . . . . . . . . : Wednesday, July 16, 2008 8:16:59 AM
        Lease Expires . . . . . . . . . : Friday, July 18, 2008 8:16:59 AM

C:\>
```

To release the DHCPv4 configuration on a Windows-based client, enter the **ipconfig/release** command. To renew the DHCPv4 configuration, enter the **ipconfig/renew** command.

Configuring a Router to Relay DHCPv4 Requests

In a complex network, the DHCPv4 servers are usually contained in a server farm. Therefore, clients typically are not on the same subnet as the DHCPv4 server, as in the previous example. To ensure that broadcasted DHCPDISCOVER messages are sent to the remote DHCPv4 server, use the **ip helper-address** command.

For example, in Figure 7-3, the DHCPv4 server is located on the 192.168.11.0/24 LAN and is serving IP addressing information for both LANs.

Figure 7-3   DHCPv4 Relay Topology

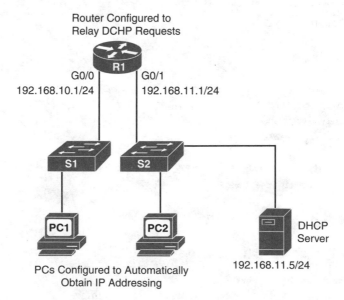

Without the **ip helper-address** command, R1 would discard any broadcasts from PC1 requesting DHCPv4 services. To configure R1 to relay DHCPDISCOVER messages, enter the following commands:

```
R1(config)# interface gigabitethernet 0/0
R1(config-if)# ip helper-address 192.168.11.5
```

Notice that the command is entered on the interface that will receive DHCPv4 broadcasts. R1 then forwards DHCPv4 broadcast messages as a unicast to 192.168.11.5. By default, the **ip helper-address** command forwards the following eight UDP services:

- **Port 37:** Time

- **Port 49:** TACACS

- **Port 53:** DNS

- **Port 67:** DHCP/BOOTP client

- **Port 68:** DHCP/BOOTP server

- **Port 69:** TFTP

- **Port 137:** NetBIOS name service

- **Port 138:** NetBIOS datagram service

To specify additional ports, use the global command **ip forward-protocol udp** [*port-number* | *protocol*]. To disable broadcasts of a particular protocol, use the **no** form of the command.

Configuring a Router as a DHCPv4 Client

Cisco routers in small offices or branch sites are often configured as DHCPv4 clients. The method used depends on the ISP. However, in its simplest configuration, the interface used to connect to a cable or DSL modem is configured with the **ip address dhcp** interface configuration command.

For example, in Figure 7-4, the BRANCH router's GigabitEthernet 0/1 interface can be configured to request addressing from the ISP router.

Figure 7-4   Router as a DHCP Client

G0/1

BRANCH   **ISP**

DHCP Client

Example 7-4 shows the configuration and verification of DHCP addressing on BRANCH.

Example 7-4   Configuring a Router as a DHCP Client

```
BRANCH(config)# interface g0/1
BRANCH(config-if)# ip address dhcp
BRANCH(config-if)# no shutdown
*Mar 15 08:45:34.632: %DHCP-6-ADDRESS_ASSIGN: Interface GigabitEthernet0/1
  assigned
   DHCP address 209.165.201.12, mask 255.255.255.224, hostname BRANCH
BRANCH(config-if)# end
```

```
BRANCH# show ip interface g0/1
GigabitEthernet0/1 is up, line protocol is up
  Internet address is 209.165.201.12/27
  Broadcast address is 255.255.255.255
  Address determined by DHCP
  <output omitted>
BRANCH#
```

Activity: Order the Steps in the DHCPv4 Operation

Refer to the Digital Study Guide to complete this activity.

Packet Tracer Activity: DHCPv4 Configuration

Refer to the Digital Study Guide to access the PKA file for this activity. You must have Packet Tracer software to run this activity. See the Introduction for details.

DHCPv6

IPv6 has two methods for automatically obtaining a global unicast address:

- Stateless address autoconfiguration (SLAAC)
- Stateful DHCPv6 (Dynamic Host Configuration Protocol for IPv6)

SLAAC

SLAAC uses ICMPv6 Router Solicitation (RS) and Router Advertisement (RA) messages to provide addressing and other configuration information. A client then uses the RA information to build an IPv6 address and verify it with a special type of Neighbor Solicitation (NS) known as Duplicate Address Detection (DAD). These three message types—RA, RS, and NS—belong to the Neighbor Discovery Protocol:

- **Router Solicitation (RS) message:** When a client is configured to obtain its addressing information automatically using SLAAC, the client sends an RS message to the router. The RS message is sent to the IPv6 all-routers multicast address, FF02::2.

- **Router Advertisement (RA) message:** A client uses this information to create its own IPv6 global unicast address. A router sends an RA message periodically or in response to an RS message. The RA message includes the prefix and prefix length of the local segment. By default, Cisco routers send RA messages every 200 seconds. RA messages are sent to the IPv6 all-nodes multicast address, FF02::1.

- **Neighbor Solicitation (NS) message:** An NS message is normally used to learn the data link layer address of a neighbor on the same network. In the SLAAC process, a host uses Duplicate Address Detection (DAD) by inserting its own IPv6 address as the destination address in an NS. The NS is sent out on the network to verify that a newly minted IPv6 address is unique. If a Neighbor Advertisement is received, the host knows that the IPv6 address is not unique.

Figure 7-5 shows the SLAAC process using three messages of the Neighbor Discovery Protocol (NDP).

Figure 7-5   Neighbor Discovery and the SLAAC Process

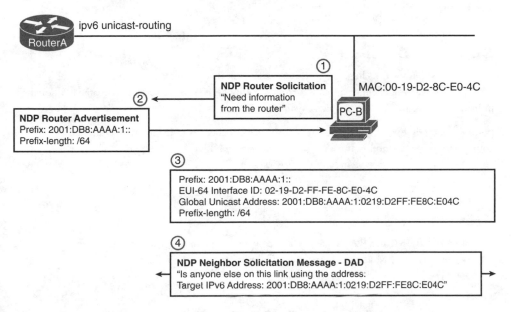

Let's briefly review the steps in Figure 7-5.

Step 1.   PC-B sends an RS message to the all–routers multicast address, FF02::2, to inform the local IPv6 router that it needs an RA.

Step 2.   RouterA receives the RS message and responds with an RA message. Included in the RA message are the prefix and prefix length of the network. The RA message is sent to the IPv6 all-nodes multicast address, FF02::1, with the link-local address of the router as the IPv6 source address.

Step 3.   PC-B uses this information to create its own IPv6 global unicast address. It appends the 64-bit prefix address to its own locally generated 64-bit interface ID, which it creates using either the EUI process (see Figure 7-5) or a random number generator. It uses RouterA's link-local address as the default gateway.

Step 4.   Before PC-B can use this newly created IPv6 address, it uses the DAD process, sending out an NS to verify that the address is unique.

> **NOTE:** A client's operating system can be configured to ignore RA messages, opting always to use the services of a DHCPv6 server.

An RA message informs a client how to obtain automatic IPv6 addressing: SLAAC, DHCPv6, or a combination of both. The RA message contains two flags to indicate the configuration option: the Managed Address Configuration flag (M flag) and the Other Configuration flag (O flag).

The default setting for these flags is 0, or both bits off. To the client, that means it is to use the SLAAC process exclusively to obtain all of its IPv6 addressing information. If either of these flags is set to 1 for some reason, you can use the **no** form of the following **ipv6 nd** commands in interface configuration mode to reset them to 0.

```
Router(config-if)# no ipv6 nd managed-config-flag
Router(config-if)# no ipv6 nd other-config-flag
```

Stateless DHCPv6

In stateless DHCPv6, the client uses the RA message from the router to generate its global unicast address. However, the client then sends a request to the DHCPv6 server to obtain any additional information that the RA has not already supplied.

For stateless DHCPv6, the O flag is set to 1 so that the client is informed that additional configuration information is available from a stateless DHCPv6 server. Use the following command on the interface to modify the RA message:

```
Router(config-if)# ipv6 nd other-config-flag
```

Stateful DHCPv6

For stateful DHCPv6, the RA message tells the client to obtain all its addressing information from a DHCPv6 server. The M flag must be set on the interface with the following command:

```
Router(config-if)# ipv6 nd managed-config-flag
```

Stateless and Stateful DHCPv6 Operation

Figure 7-6 shows the full operation of DHCPv6, regardless of the method used: SLAAC, stateless DHCPv6, or stateful DHCPv6.

Figure 7-6   DHCPv6 Operations

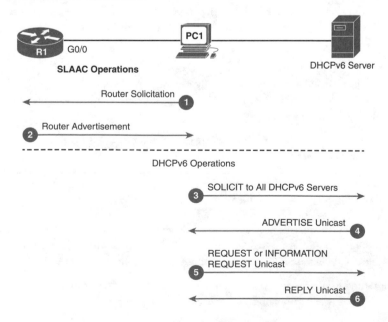

The following steps summarize Figure 7-6:

Step 1.   PC1 sends an RS on bootup to begin the process of obtaining IPv6 addressing.

Step 2.   R1 replies with an RA. If the M and O flags are not set, PC1 uses SLAAC. If either the M flag or the O flag is set, PC1 begins the DHCPv6 process.

Step 3.   PC1 sends a DHCPv6 SOLICIT message to the all-DHCPv6-servers address, FF02::1:2—a link-local multicast address that will not be forwarded by routers.

Step 4.   A DHCPv6 server responds with a DHCPv6 ADVERTISE unicast message informing the client of its presence.

Step 5.   The client then sends either a unicast DHCPv6 REQUEST (the M flag was set and the client is using stateful DHCPv6) or a unicast DHCPv6 INFORMATION-REQUEST (the O flag was set and the client is using stateless DHCPv6).

Step 6.   The server replies with the information requested.

DHCPv6 Configuration Options

A router can be configured as a stateless DHCPv6 server, a stateful DHCPv6 server, and a DHCPv6 client. As in DHCPv4, the router can be configured with all three, depending on what role it plays for its various interfaces.

Configuring a Router as a Stateless DHCPv6 Server

We use Figure 7-7 for all our examples in this section. R1 is the DHCPv6 server and R3 is the DHCPv6 client.

Figure 7-7   DHCPv6 Server and Client Topology

To configure R1 as a stateless DHCP server, you need to make sure that **ipv6 unicast-routing** is enabled. Then, in global configuration mode, configure the pool name, DNS server, and domain name. Finally, enable the DHCPv6 pool on the appropriate interface and set the O flag so that clients on that interface know to request DHCPv6 services from the router. Example 7-5 shows the configuration for R1.

Example 7-5   Configuring a Router as a Stateless DHCPv6 Server

```
R1(config)# ipv6 unicast-routing
R1(config)# ipv6 dhcp pool O-FLAG-SET
R1(config-dhcpv6)# dns-server 2001:db8:acad:1::5
R1(config-dhcpv6)# domain-name cisco.com
R1(config-dhcpv6)# exit
R1(config)# interface g0/1
R1(config-if)# ipv6 address 2001:db8:1:1::1/64
R1(config-if)# ipv6 dhcp server O-FLAG-SET
R1(config-if)# ipv6 nd other-config-flag
R1(config-if)# end
R1# show ipv6 dhcp pool
DHCPv6 pool: O-FLAG-SET
   DNS server: 2001:DB8:ACAD:1::5
   Domain name: cisco.com
   Active clients: 0
R1#
```

To configure a router interface as a DHCPv6 client, enable IPv6 on the interface and enter the **ipv6 address autoconfig** command, as in Example 7-6. Verify the configuration with the **show ipv6 interface** command.

Example 7-6   Configuring an Interface as a DHCPv6 Client

```
R3(config)# interface g0/1
R3(config-if)# ipv6 enable
R3(config-if)# ipv6 address autoconfig
R3(config-if)# end
R3# show ipv6 interface g0/1
GigabitEthernet0/1 is up, line protocol is up
   IPv6 is enabled, link-local address is FE80::32F7:DFF:FE25:2DE1
   No Virtual link-local address(es):
   Stateless address autoconfig enabled
   Global unicast address(es):
     2001:DB8:1:1:32F7:DFF:FE25:2DE1, subnet is 2001:DB8:1:1::/64 [EUI/CAL/PRE]
       valid lifetime 2591935 preferred lifetime 604735
   Joined group address(es):
     FF02::1
     FF02::1:FF25:2DE1
   MTU is 1500 bytes
   ICMP error messages limited to one every 100 milliseconds
   ICMP redirects are enabled
   ICMP unreachables are sent
   ND DAD is enabled, number of DAD attempts: 1
   ND reachable time is 30000 milliseconds (using 30000)
   ND NS retransmit interval is 1000 milliseconds
   Default router is FE80::D68C:B5FF:FECE:A0C1 on GigabitEthernet0/1
R3#
```

Configuring a Router as a Stateful DHCPv6 Server

The main difference between a stateless configuration and a stateful configuration is that a stateful server also includes IPv6 addressing information and keeps a record of the IPv6 addresses that are leased out. Also, for the client side, the **ipv6 address dhcp** command is used instead of the **ipv6 address autoconfig** command. Example 7-7 shows the stateful DHCPv6 server configuration with stateful address information added and the M bit set instead of the O bit.

Example 7-7   Configuring a Router as a Stateful DHCPv6 Server

```
R1(config)# ipv6 unicast-routing
R1(config)# ipv6 dhcp pool M-FLAG-SET
R1(config-dhcpv6)# address prefix 2001:db8:1:1::/64 lifetime infinite infinite
R1(config-dhcpv6)# dns-server 2001:db8:acad:1::5
R1(config-dhcpv6)# domain-name cisco.com
R1(config-dhcpv6)# exit
R1(config)# interface g0/1
R1(config-if)# ipv6 address 2001:db8:1:1::1/64
R1(config-if)# ipv6 nd managed-config-flag
R1(config-if)# end
!After R3 is configured as a DHCP client, verify DHCP with the following
  commands:
R1# show ipv6 dhcp pool
DHCPv6 pool: M-FLAG-SET
  Address allocation prefix: 2001:DB8:1:1::/64 valid 4294967295 preferred
    4294967295 (1 in use, 0 conflicts)
  DNS server: 2001:DB8:ACAD:1::5
  Domain name: cisco.com
  Active clients: 1
R1# show ipv6 dhcp binding
Client: FE80::32F7:DFF:FEA3:1640
  DUID: 0003000130F70DA31640
  Username: unassigned
  IA NA: IA ID 0x00060001, T1 43200, T2 69120
    Address: 2001:DB8:1:1:8902:60D6:E76:6C16
           preferred lifetime INFINITY, , valid lifetime INFINITY,
R1#
```

DHCP Troubleshooting

DHCP problems can arise for a multitude of reasons, such as software defects in operating systems, NIC drivers, or DHCP relay agents. However, the most common are configuration issues.

Resolve IPv4 Address Conflicts

An IPv4 address lease can expire on a client still connected to a network. If the client does not renew the lease, the DHCP server can reassign that IPv4 address to another client. When the client reboots, it requests an IPv4 address. If the DHCP server does not respond quickly, the client uses the last IPv4 address. Then two clients begin using the same IPv4 address, creating a conflict.

The **show ip dhcp conflict** command displays all address conflicts recorded by the DHCP server. The server uses the **ping** command to detect conflicts. The client uses Address Resolution Protocol (ARP) to detect clients. If an address conflict is detected, the address is removed from the pool and not assigned until an administrator resolves the conflict.

Test Connectivity Using a Static IP Address

When troubleshooting any DHCP issue, verify network connectivity by configuring static IPv4 address information on a client workstation. If the workstation cannot reach network resources with a statically configured IPv4 address, the root cause of the problem is not the DHCP server. At this point, network connectivity troubleshooting is required.

Verify Switch Port Configuration

If the DHCP client cannot obtain an IPv4 address from the DHCP server at startup, attempt to obtain an IPv4 address from the DHCP server by manually forcing the client to send a DHCP request. If a switch lies between the client and the DHCP server and the client cannot obtain the DHCP configuration, switch port configuration issues might be the cause. These causes can include issues from trunking and channeling to STP and RSTP. PortFast configuration and edge port configurations resolve the most common DHCPv4 client issues that occur with an initial installation of a Cisco switch.

Test DHCPv4 Operation on the Same Subnet or VLAN

Distinguishing whether DHCP is functioning correctly is important when the client is on the same subnet or VLAN as the DHCP server. If DHCP is working correctly when the client is on the same subnet or VLAN, the problem might be the DHCP relay agent. If the problem persists even with testing DHCP on the same subnet or VLAN as the DHCP server, the problem might be with the DHCP server.

DNS Operation

DNS is a distributed system of servers that resolve domain names to IP addresses. The domain name is part of the Uniform Resource Identifier (URI), as Figure 7-8 shows.

Figure 7-8   URI Structure

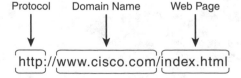

NOTE: Many people use the terms *web address* and *Universal Resource Locator (URL)*. However, *Uniform Resource Identifier (URI)* is the correct formal term.

When you type a new URI in your browser, your computer uses DNS to send out a request to resolve the URI into an IP address. Figure 7-9 summarizes the DNS process.

Figure 7-9   DNS Process

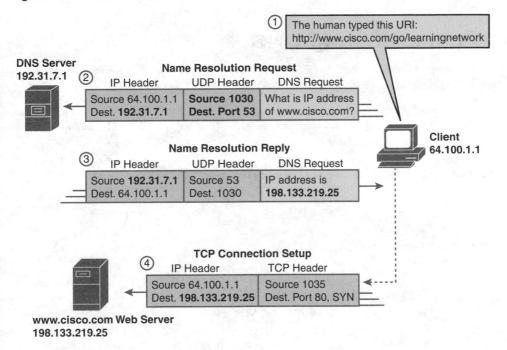

The DNS server stores different types of resource records used to resolve names. These records contain the name, address, and type of record. Some of these record types follow:

- **A:** An end device IPv4 address

- **NS:** An authoritative name server

- **AAAA:** An end device IPv6 address (pronounced "quad-A")

- **MX:** A mail exchange record

When a client makes a query, the server's DNS process first looks at its own records to resolve the name. If it cannot resolve the name using its stored records, it contacts other servers to resolve the name.

DNS root servers manage the top-domain suffixes, such as these:

- **.com:** Commercial businesses

- **.edu:** Educational organizations

- **.gov:** Government organizations

- **.mil:** Military organizations

- **.net:** Networking organizations, such as ISPs

- **.org:** Noncommercial organizations

Top-level DNS servers also exist for each country code, such as .ca (Canada), .de (Germany), .ru (Russia), and .cn (China).

Troubleshooting DNS

As a network administrator, your control over DNS issues is limited to two basic issues: DHCP server configurations and DNS server configurations.

In a small branch office, you are most likely using your ISP for all your DNS resolutions. Therefore, all the clients on your network will most likely have the IP address of the default gateway configured as the DNS server, as shown in the **ipconfig /all** output in Example 7-8.

Example 7-8   DNS Server As the Default Gateway

```
C:\> ipconfig /all


Windows IP Configuration
<output omitted>

   DHCP Enabled. . . . . . . . . . . : Yes
   Autoconfiguration Enabled . . . . : Yes
   IPv4 Address. . . . . . . . . . . : 10.10.10.2(Preferred)
   Subnet Mask . . . . . . . . . . . : 255.255.255.0
   Lease Obtained. . . . . . . . . . : Sunday, November 13, 2016 1:28:51 PM
   Lease Expires . . . . . . . . . . : Monday, November 14, 2016 1:28:50 PM
   Default Gateway . . . . . . . . . : 10.10.10.1
   DHCP Server . . . . . . . . . . . : 10.10.10.1
   DNS Servers . . . . . . . . . . . : 10.10.10.1
```

Therefore, issues with DNS are most likely due to issues with the default gateway router or the connection to your ISP. If you know the IP address of a publicly available server, you can verify that DNS is the issue if you can ping the IP address but not the URI.

In larger organizations, the network administrator is responsible for making sure the DHCP server is configured with accurate DNS IP addresses. Those DNS servers are most likely managed in-house to reduce the amount of outbound traffic to the public DNS servers. DNS server misconfiguration could be the cause if end user devices cannot resolve URIs. Therefore, the hierarchy of DNS servers within the organization should ensure that there are backup DNS servers and that, when a record doesn't exist, the DNS server can accurately forward the request to another DNS server.

Study Resources

For today's exam topics, refer to the following resources for more study.

Resource	Location	Topic
Primary Resources		
Introduction to Networks v6	10	IP Addressing Services
Routing and Switching Essentials v6	8	All
ICND1 Official Cert Guide	4	Using Names and the Domain Name System
	5	TCP/IP Applications
	20	All
	23	Using Ping with Names and with IP Addresses
Supplemental Resources		
CCNA Portable Command Guide	20	All
CCNA Video Series	5	Lesson 1: All
CCNA Network Simulator	ICND1	Chapter 20: Complete DHCP Server Configuration
		Chapter 20: DHCP Server Configuration I–V
		Chapter 20: DHCP Server Troubleshooting
		Chapter 23: Ping
		Chapter 23: Traceroute III

 Check Your Understanding

Refer to the Digital Study Guide to take a short quiz covering the content of this day.

NAT

CCNA 200-125 Exam Topics

- Configure, verify, and troubleshoot inside source NAT

Key Topics

To cope with the depletion of IPv4 addresses, several short-term solutions were developed. One short-term solution is to use private addresses and Network Address Translation (NAT). NAT enables inside network hosts to borrow a legitimate Internet IPv4 address while accessing Internet resources. When the requested traffic returns, the legitimate IPv4 address is repurposed and available for the next Internet request by an inside host. Using NAT, network administrators need only one or a few IPv4 addresses for the router to provide to the hosts, instead of one unique IPv4 address for every client joining the network. Although IPv6 ultimately solves the problem of IPv4 address space depletion that NAT was created to address, it is still in wide use in current network implementation strategies. Today we review the concepts, configuration, and troubleshooting of NAT.

NAT Concepts

NAT, defined in RFC 3022, has many uses. Its key use is to conserve IPv4 addresses by allowing networks to use private IPv4 addresses. NAT translates nonroutable, private, internal addresses into routable, public addresses. NAT also has the benefit of hiding internal IPv4 addresses from outside networks.

A NAT-enabled device typically operates at the border of a stub network. Figure 6-1 shows the master topology used during today's review. R2 is the border router and is the device used for today's example configurations.

Figure 6-1   NAT Topology

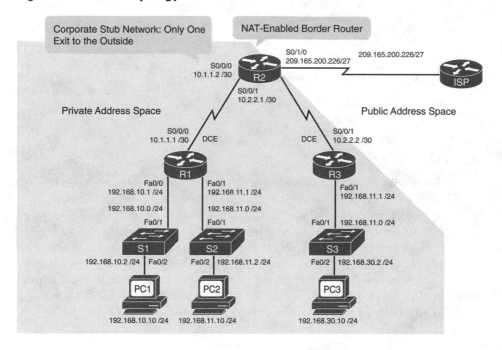

In NAT terminology, the inside network is the set of networks that are subject to translation (every network in the shaded region in Figure 6-1). The outside network refers to all other addresses. Figure 6-2 shows how to refer to the addresses when configuring NAT:

- **Inside local address:** Most likely a private address. In the figure, the IPv4 address 192.168.10.10 assigned to PC1 is an inside local address.

- **Inside global address:** A valid public address that the inside host is given when it exits the NAT router. When traffic from PC1 is destined for the web server at 209.165.201.1, R2 must translate the inside local address to an inside global address, which is 209.165.200.226, in this case.

- **Outside global address:** A reachable IPv4 address assigned to a host on the Internet. For example, the web server can be reached at IPv4 address 209.165.201.1.

- **Outside local address:** The local IPv4 address assigned to a host on the outside network. In most situations, this address is identical to the outside global address of that outside device. (Outside local addresses are beyond the scope of CCENT and CCNA.)

Figure 6-2   NAT Terminology

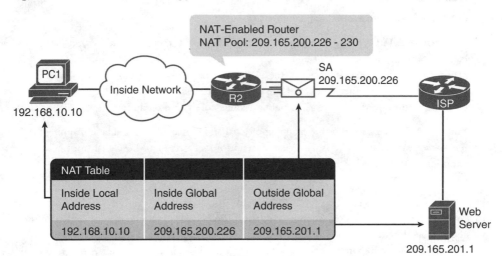

A NAT Example

Referring to Figure 6-1, the following steps illustrate the NAT process when PC1 sends traffic to the Internet:

1. PC1 sends a packet destined for the Internet to R1, the default gateway.

2. R1 forwards the packet to R2, as directed by its routing table.

3. R2 refers to its routing table and identifies the next hop as the ISP router. It then checks to see whether the packet matches the criteria specified for translation. R2 has an ACL that identifies the inside network as a valid host for translation. Therefore, it translates an inside local IPv4 address to an inside global IPv4 address, which, in this case, is 209.165.200.226. It stores this mapping of the local address to global address in the NAT table.

4. R2 modifies the packet with the new source IPv4 address (the inside global address) and sends it to the ISP router.

5. The packet eventually reaches its destination, which then sends its reply to the inside global address 209.165.200.226.

6. When replies from the destination arrive back at R2, it consults the NAT table to match the inside global address to the correct inside local address. R2 then modifies the packet, inserting the inside local address (192.168.10.10) as the destination address and sending it to R1.

7. R1 receives the packet and forwards it to PC1.

Dynamic and Static NAT

The two types of NAT translation are as follows:

- **Dynamic NAT:** Uses a pool of public addresses and assigns them on a first-come, first-served basis, or reuses an existing public address configured on an interface. When a host with a private IPv4 address requests access to the Internet, dynamic NAT chooses an IPv4 address from the pool that another host is not already using. Instead of using a pool, dynamic NAT can be configured to overload an existing public address configured on an interface.

- **Static NAT:** Uses a one-to-one mapping of local and global addresses. These mappings remain constant. Static NAT is particularly useful for web servers or hosts that must have a consistent address that is accessible from the Internet.

NAT Overload

NAT overloading (also called Port Address Translation [PAT]) maps multiple private IPv4 addresses to a single public IPv4 address or a few addresses. To do this, a port number also tracks each private address. When a response comes back from the outside, source port numbers determine the correct client for the NAT router to translate the packets.

Figure 6-3 and the following steps illustrate the NAT overload process.

Figure 6-3   NAT Overload Example

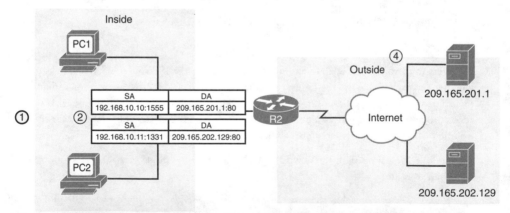

1. PC1 and PC2 send packets destined for the Internet.

2. When the packets arrive at R2, NAT overload changes the source address to the inside global IPv4 address and keeps a record of the assigned source port numbers (1555 and 1331, in this example) to identify the client from which the packets originated.

3. R2 updates its NAT table. Notice the assigned ports. R2 then routes the packets to the Internet.

4. When the web server replies, R2 uses the destination source port to translate the packet to the correct client.

NAT overload attempts to preserve the original source port. However, if this source port is already used, NAT overload assigns the first available port number, starting from the beginning of the appropriate port group 0–511, 512–1023, or 1024–65535.

NAT Benefits

Using NAT offers the following benefits:

- NAT conserves registered IPv4 address space because, with NAT overload, internal hosts can share a single public IPv4 address for all external communications.

- NAT increases the flexibility of connections to the public network. Multiple pools, backup pools, and load-balancing pools can be implemented to ensure reliable public network connections.

- NAT allows the existing scheme to remain while supporting a new public addressing scheme. This means that an organization can change ISPs and not need to change any of its inside clients.

- NAT provides a layer of network security because private networks do not advertise their inside local addresses outside the organization. However, the phrase *NAT firewall* is misleading; NAT does not replace firewalls.

NAT Limitations

The limitations of using NAT include the following:

- **Performance is degraded:** NAT increases switching delays because translating each IPv4 address within the packet headers takes time.

- **End-to-end functionality is degraded:** Many Internet protocols and applications depend on end-to-end functionality, with unmodified packets forwarded from the source to the destination.

- **End-to-end IP traceability is lost:** Tracing packets that undergo numerous packet address changes over multiple NAT hops becomes much more difficult, making troubleshooting challenging.

- **Tunneling is more complicated:** Using NAT also complicates tunneling protocols, such as IPsec, because NAT modifies values in the headers that interfere with the integrity checks that IPsec and other tunneling protocols do.

- **Services can be disrupted:** Services that require the initiation of TCP connections from the outside network, or stateless protocols such as those using UDP, can be disrupted.

Activity: Identify NAT Address Types

Refer to the Digital Study Guide to complete this activity.

Configuring Static NAT

Static NAT is a one-to-one mapping between an inside address and an outside address. Static NAT allows connections initiated by external devices to access inside devices. For example, you might want to map an inside global address to a specific inside local address that is assigned to your inside web server. The steps and syntax to configure static NAT follow:

Step 1.   Configure the static translation of an inside local address to an inside global address:

```
Router(config)# ip nat inside source static local-ip global-ip
```

Step 2.   Specify the inside interface:

```
Router(config)# interface type number
Router(config-if)# ip nat inside
```

Step 3.   Specify the outside interface:

```
Router(config)# interface type number
Router(config-if)# ip nat outside
```

Figure 6-4 shows a sample static NAT topology.

Figure 6-4   Static NAT Topology

Example 6-1 shows the static NAT configuration.

Example 6-1   Static NAT Configuration

```
R2(config)# ip nat inside source static 192.168.10.254 209.165.200.254
R2(config)# interface serial0/0/0
R2(config-if)# ip nat inside
R2(config-if)# interface serial 0/1/0
R2(config-if)# ip nat outside
```

This configuration statically maps the inside private IPv4 address of 192.168.10.254 to the outside public IPv4 address of 209.165.200.254. This allows outside hosts to access the internal web server using the public IPv4 address 209.165.200.254.

Configuring Dynamic NAT

Dynamic NAT maps private IPv4 addresses to public addresses drawn from a NAT pool. The steps and syntax to configure dynamic NAT are as follows:

Step 1.   Define a pool of global addresses to be allocated:

```
Router(config)# ip nat pool name start-ip end-ip {netmask | prefix-length
    prefix-length}
```

Step 2.   Define a standard access list permitting addresses that are to be translated:

```
Router(config)# access-list access-list-number source source-wildcard
```

Step 3.   Bind the pool of addresses to the access list:

```
Router(config)# ip nat inside source list access-list-number pool name
```

Step 4.   Specify the inside interface:

```
Router(config)# interface type number
Router(config-if)# ip nat inside
```

Step 5.   Specify the outside interface:

```
Router(config)# interface type number
Router(config-if)# ip nat outside
```

Figure 6-5 shows a sample dynamic NAT topology.

Figure 6-5   Dynamic NAT Topology

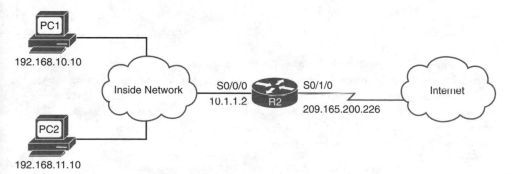

Example 6-2 shows the dynamic NAT configuration.

Example 6-2   Dynamic NAT Configuration

```
R2(config)# ip nat pool NAT-POOL1 209.165.200.226 209.165.200.240 netmask
  255.255.255.224
R2(config)# access-list 1 permit 192.168.0.0 0.0.255.255
R2(config)# ip nat inside source list 1 pool NAT-POOL1
R2(config)# interface serial 0/0/0
R2(config-if)# ip nat inside
R2(config-if)# interface serial s0/1/0
R2(config-if)# ip nat outside
```

Configuring NAT Overload

Commonly with home networks and small to medium-size businesses, the ISP assigns only one registered IPv4 address to your router. Therefore, it is necessary to overload that one IPv4 address so that multiple inside clients can use it simultaneously.

The configuration is similar to the use of dynamic NAT, except that instead of using a pool of addresses, the interface keyword is used to identify the outside IPv4 address. The **overload** keyword enables PAT so that source port numbers are tracked during translation.

Example 6-3 shows how R2 in Figure 6-5 is configured to overload its registered IPv4 address on the serial interface.

Example 6-3   Configuring NAT to Overload an Interface Address

```
R2(config)# access-list 1 permit 192.168.0.0 0.0.255.255
R2(config)# ip nat inside source list 1 interface serial 0/1/0 overload
R2(config)# interface serial 0/0/0
R2(config-if)# ip nat inside
R2(config-if)# interface serial s0/1/0
R2(config-if)# ip nat outside
```

You can also overload a NAT pool of addresses, which might be necessary in organizations that potentially have many clients that simultaneously need translations. In the previous Example 6-2, NAT is configured with a pool of 15 addresses (209.165.200.226–209.165.200.240). If R2 is translating all 15 addresses at any given moment, packets for the 16th client will be queued for processing and possibly time out. To avoid this problem, add the keyword **overload** to the command that binds the access list to the NAT pool, as follows:

```
R2(config)# ip nat inside source list 1 pool NAT-POOL1 overload
```

Interestingly, Cisco IOS uses the first IPv4 address in the pool until it runs out of available port numbers. Then it moves to the next IPv4 address in the pool.

Verifying NAT

Assume that both the static and dynamic NAT topologies in Figures 6-4 and 6-5 are configured on R2, with the inside server statically translated to 209.165.200.254 and the **NAT-POOL1** configured with the **overload** keyword. Furthermore, assume that two inside clients have connected to an outside host. You can use the **show ip nat translations** command to verify the current translations in the R2 NAT table, as Example 6-4 shows.

Example 6-4   Verifying NAT Operations with show ip nat translations

```
R2# show ip nat translations
Pro  Inside global       Inside local        Outside local      Outside global
---  209.165.200.254     192.168.10.254      ---                ---
tcp 209.165.200.226:47392 192.168.10.10:47392 209.165.201.30:80 209.165.201.30:80
tcp 209.165.200.226:50243 192.168.11.10:50243 209.165.201.30:80 209.165.201.30:80
```

The static entry is always in the table. Currently, the table has two dynamic entries. Notice that both inside clients received the same inside global address, but the source port numbers are different (47392 for PC1 and 50243 for PC2).

The **show ip nat statistics** command, in Example 6-5, displays information about the total number of active translations, NAT configuration parameters, the number of addresses in the pool, and how many have been allocated.

Example 6-5   Verifying NAT Operations with show ip nat statistics

```
R2# show ip nat statistics
Total translations: 3 (1 static, 2 dynamic, 2 extended)
Outside Interfaces: Serial0/1/0
Inside Interfaces: FastEthernet0/0 , Serial0/0/0 , Serial0/0/1
Hits: 29  Misses: 7
Expired translations: 5
Dynamic mappings:
-- Inside Source
access-list 1 pool NAT-POOL1 refCount 2
 pool NAT-POOL1: netmask 255.255.255.224
        start 209.165.200.226 end 209.165.200.240
        type generic, total addresses 3 , allocated 1 (7%), misses 0
```

Alternatively, use the **show run** command and look for NAT, access command list, interface, or pool-related commands with the required values. Carefully examine the output from these commands to discover any errors.

It is sometimes useful to clear the dynamic entries sooner than the default. This is especially true when testing the NAT configuration. To clear dynamic entries before the timeout has expired, use the **clear ip nat translation *** privileged EXEC command.

Troubleshooting NAT

When you have IP connectivity problems in a NAT environment, determining the cause of the problem is often difficult. The first step in solving your problem is to rule out NAT as the cause. Follow these steps to verify that NAT is operating as expected:

Step 1. Based on the configuration, clearly define what NAT is supposed to achieve. This might reveal a problem with the configuration.

Step 2. Verify that correct translations exist in the translation table using the **show ip nat translations** command.

Step 3. Use the **clear** and **debug** commands to verify that NAT is operating as expected. Check to see whether dynamic entries are re-created after they are cleared.

Step 4. Review in detail what is happening to the packet, and verify that routers have the correct routing information to forward the packet.

Use the **debug ip nat** command to verify the operation of the NAT feature by displaying information about every packet that the router translates, as in Example 6-6.

Example 6-6 Troubleshooting NAT with debug ip nat

```
R2# debug ip nat
IP NAT debugging is on
R2#
NAT: s=192.168.10.10->209.165.200.226, d=209.165.201.30[8]
NAT*: s=209.165.201.30, d=209.165.200.226->192.168.10.10[8]
NAT: s=192.168.10.10->209.165.200.226, d=209.165.201.30[8]
NAT: s=192.168.10.10->209.165.200.226, d=209.165.201.30[8]
NAT*: s=209.165.201.30, d=209.165.200.226->192.168.10.10[8]
NAT*: s=209.165.201.30, d=209.165.200.226->192.168.10.10[8]
NAT: s=192.168.10.10->209.165.200.226, d=209.165.201.30[8]
NAT: s=192.168.10.10->209.165.200.226, d=209.165.201.30[8]
NAT*: s=209.165.201.30, d=209.165.200.226->192.168.10.10[8]
NAT*: s=209.165.201.30, d=209.165.200.226->192.168.10.10[8]
NAT: s=192.168.10.10->209.165.200.226, d=209.165.201.30[8]
R2#
```

You can see that inside host 192.168.10.10 initiated traffic to outside host 209.165.201.30 and has been translated into address 209.165.200.226.

When decoding the debug output, note what the following symbols and values indicate:

- ***:** The asterisk next to NAT indicates that the translation is occurring in the fast-switched path. The first packet in a conversation is always process switched, which is slower. The remaining packets go through the fast-switched path if a cache entry exists.

- **s=:** This refers to the source IPv4 address.

- **a.b.c.d->w.x.y.z:** This indicates that source address **a.b.c.d** is translated into **w.x.y.z**.

- **d=:** This refers to the destination IPv4 address.

- **[xxxx]:** The value in brackets is the IP identification number. This information can be useful for debugging because it enables correlation with other packet traces from protocol analyzers.

 Packet Tracer Activity: Static and Dynamic NAT Configuration

Refer to the Digital Study Guide to access the PKA file for this activity. You must have Packet Tracer software to run this activity. See the Introduction for details.

NAT for IPv6

We finish our NAT review with a quick look at NAT for IPv6. IPv6 was developed with the intention of making NAT for IPv4 unnecessary. However, IPv6 includes its own IPv6 private address space and NAT, which are implemented differently than they are for IPv4.

IPv6 Private Address Space

IPv6 unique local addresses (ULA) are similar to RFC 1918 private addresses in IPv4, but they have significant differences as well. The intent of unique local addresses is to provide IPv6 address space for communications within a local site; ULAs are not meant to provide additional IPv6 address space or a level of security.

As Figure 6-6 shows, unique local addresses have the prefix FC00::/7, which results in a first hextet range of FC00–FDFF.

Figure 6-6   IPv6 Unique Local Address Format

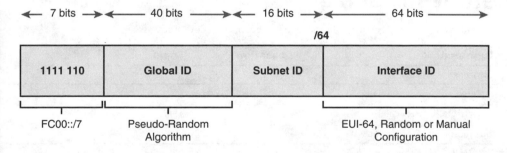

ULAs are also known as local IPv6 addresses (not to be confused with IPv6 link–local addresses). Unlike with private IPv4 addresses, it has not been the intention of the Internet Engineering Task Force (IETF) to use a form of NAT to translate between ULAs and IPv6 global unicast addresses. The Internet community is still examining the implementation and potential uses for IPv6 ULAs.

Purpose of NAT for IPv6

NAT for IPv6 is used in a much different context than NAT for IPv4. The varieties of NAT for IPv6 are used to transparently provide access between IPv6-only and IPv4-only networks, as Figure 6-7 shows. NAT for IPv6 is not used as a form of private IPv6-to–global IPv6 translation.

Figure 6-7   Overview of NAT64 Operation

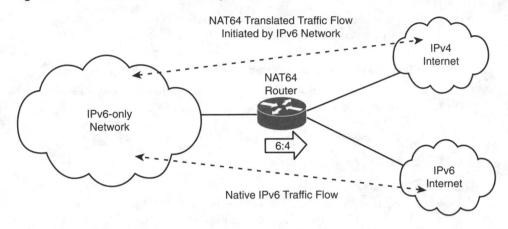

Over the years, several types of NAT for IPv6 have emerged, including Network Address Translation–Protocol Translation (NAT-PT). The IETF has deprecated NAT-PT in favor of its replacement, NAT64 (the 64 stands for IPv6–to–IPv4 translation). NAT64 is beyond the scope of the CCENT and CCNA; however, be prepared to answer questions about the major differences between NAT for IPv4 and NAT for IPv6.

NOTE: If you would like a detailed explanation of NAT64, see Rick Graziani's Cisco Press book *IPv6 Fundamentals* (ISBN: 9781587143137).

Study Resources

For today's exam topics, refer to the following resources for more study.

Resource	Location	Topic
Primary Resources		
Routing and Switching Essentials v6	9	All
ICND1 Official Cert Guide	27	All
Supplemental Resources		
CCNA Portable Command Guide	22	All
CCNA Video Series	5	Lesson 3: All
CCNA Network Simulator	ICND1	Chapter 27: Configuring NAT I–III
		Chapter 27: NAT Configuration I–VII
		Chapter 27: NAT

 Check Your Understanding

Refer to the Digital Study Guide to take a short quiz covering the content of this day.

WAN Overview

CCNA 200-125 Exam Topics

- Describe WAN topology options

- Describe WAN access connectivity options

- Describe DNS lookup operation

Key Topics

Today is a whirlwind review of WAN topologies, WAN connection options, and virtual private networks (VPNs). Because most of these exam topics are conceptual in nature and require no configuration skills, read through this review several times and refer to your study resources for more in-depth review.

WAN Topologies

Figure 5-1 shows the four basic WAN topology options that a business can select for its WAN infrastructure:

- **Point-to-point:** Typically uses a dedicated leased-line connection, such as T1/E1

- **Hub-and-spoke:** Offers a single-homed, point-to-multipoint topology in which a single interface on the hub router can be shared with multiple spoke routers through the use of virtual interfaces

- **Full mesh:** Gives each router a connection to every other router. Requires a large number of virtual interfaces.

- **Dual-homed:** Provides redundancy for a single-homed hub-and-spoke topology by providing a second hub to connect to spoke routers.

Figure 5-1   WAN Topology Options

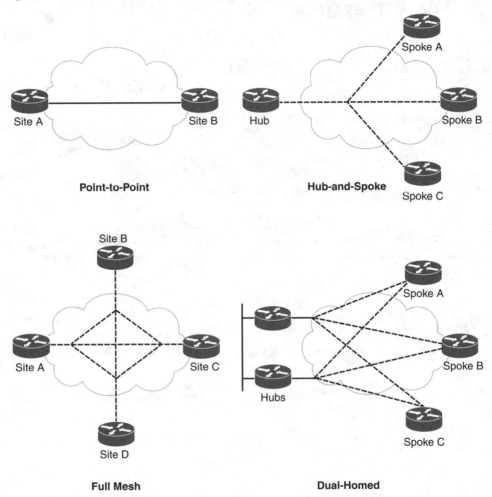

A business can choose to implement a variety of these topologies. For example, the enterprise might choose to implement a full mesh topology between its regional headquarters. It then might use a hub-and-spoke topology between regional headquarters and branch offices. If two of the branch offices communicate frequently, the network administrators might contract for a point-to-point link to lessen the traffic load on the hub routers. Using dual-homed connections to the Internet ensures that customers, partners, and teleworkers can always access the enterprise's resources.

WAN Connection Options

Many options for implementing WAN solutions are currently available. They differ in technology, speed, and cost. Figure 5-2 provides a high-level view of the various WAN link connection options. The following subsections describe these options in more detail.

Figure 5-2   WAN Link Connection Options

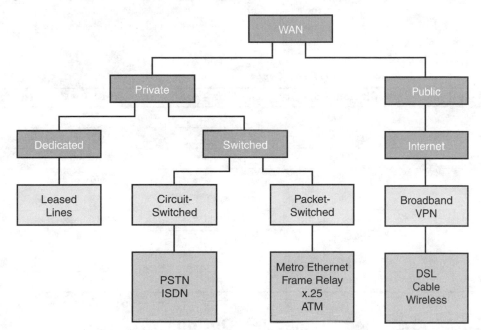

Dedicated Connection Options

Also called leased lines, dedicated connections are pre-established point-to-point WAN connections from the customer premises through the provider network to a remote destination (see Figure 5-3).

Figure 5-3   Leased Lines

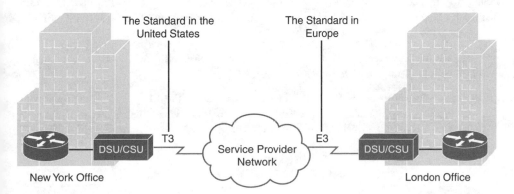

Leased lines are usually more expensive than switched services because of the dedicated, always-on cost of providing WAN service to the customer. The dedicated capacity removes latency and jitter and provides a layer of security because only the customer's traffic is allowed on the link. Table 5-1 lists the available leased line types and their bit-rate capacities.

Table 5-1   Leased Line Types and Capacities

Line Type	Bit-Rate Capacity	Line Type	Bit-Rate Capacity
56k	56 kbps	OC-9	466.56 Mbps
64k	64 kbps	OC-12	622.08 Mbps
T1	1.544 Mbps	OC-18	933.12 Mbps
E1	2.048 Mbps	OC-24	1244.16 Mbps
J1	2.048 Mbps	OC-36	1866.24 Mbps
E3	34.064 Mbps	OC-48	2488.32 Mbps
T3	44.736 Mbps	OC-96	4976.64 Mbps
OC-1	51.84 Mbps	OC-192	9953.28 Mbps
OC-3	155.54 Mbps	OC-768	39,813.12 Mbps

Circuit-Switched Connection Options

The two main types of circuit-switched connections are analog dialup and ISDN. Both technologies have a limited implementation base in today's networks. However, they both still are used in remote rural areas or other areas of the globe where more recent technologies are not yet available.

Analog dialup uses modems at very low-speed connections that might be adequate for the exchange of sales figures, prices, routine reports, and email, or as an emergency backup link.

ISDN turns the local loop into a TDM digital connection, which enables it to carry digital signals that result in higher-capacity switched connections than analog modems. Two types of ISDN interfaces exist:

- **Basic Rate Interface (BRI):** Provides two 64 kbps B-channels for voice or data transfer and a 16 kbps D-channel used for control signaling.

- **Primary Rate Interface (PRI):** Provides 23 B-channels with 64 kbps and 1 D-channel with 64 kbps in North America, for a total bit rate of up to 1.544 Mbps. Europe uses 30 B-channels and 1 D-channel, for a total bit rate of up to 2.048 Mbps.

Figure 5-4 illustrates the various differences between ISDN BRI and PRI lines.

Figure 5-4   ISDN Network Infrastructure and PRI/BRI Line Capacity

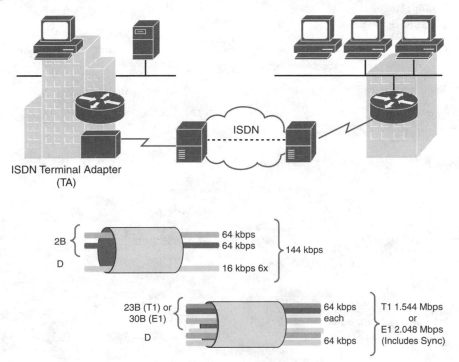

Packet-Switched Connection Options

The most common packet-switching technologies used in today's enterprise WANs include Metro Ethernet and MPLS. Legacy technologies include X.25 and ATM.

NOTE: Frame Relay is also a packet-switched technology that still has some market share. However, the CCNA exam no longer covers it.

Metro Ethernet

Metro Ethernet (MetroE) uses IP-aware Ethernet switches in the service provider's network cloud to offer enterprises converged voice, data, and video services at Ethernet speeds. Consider some benefits of Metro Ethernet:

- **Reduced expenses and administration:** Enables businesses to inexpensively connect numerous sites in a metropolitan area to each other and to the Internet without the need for expensive conversions to ATM or Frame Relay

- **Easy integration with existing networks:** Connects easily to existing Ethernet LANs

- **Enhanced business productivity:** Enables businesses to take advantage of productivity-enhancing IP applications that are difficult to implement on TDM or Frame Relay networks, such as hosted IP communications, VoIP, and streaming and broadcast video

MPLS

Multiprotocol Label Switching (MPLS) has the following characteristics:

- **Multiprotocol:** MPLS can carry any payload, including IPv4, IPv6, Ethernet, ATM, DSL, and Frame Relay traffic.

- **Labels:** MPLS uses labels inside the service provider's network to identify paths between distant routers instead of between endpoints.

- **Switching:** MPLS actually routes IPv4 and IPv6 packets, but everything else is switched.

As Figure 5-5 shows, MPLS supports a wide range of WAN technologies, including serial leased lines, Metro Ethernet, ATM, Frame Relay, and DSL (not shown).

Figure 5-5   Popular MPLS Connection Options

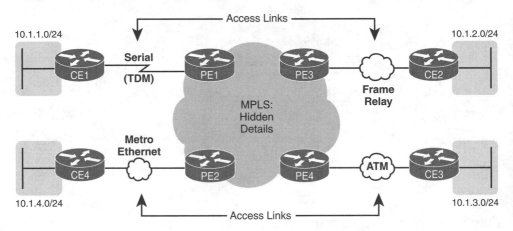

In Figure 5-5, CE refers to the customer edge routers. PE is the provider edge routers that add and remove labels.

NOTE: MPLS is primarily a service provider WAN technology.

Figure 5-5 shows a simplified Frame Relay network.

Internet Connection Options

Broadband connection options typically are used to connect telecommuting employees to a corporate site over the Internet. These options include digital subscriber line (DSL), cable, wireless, and Metro Ethernet.

DSL

DSL technology, shown in Figure 5-6, is an always-on connection technology that uses existing twisted-pair telephone lines to transport high-bandwidth data and provides IP services to subscribers.

Figure 5-6   Teleworker DSL Connection

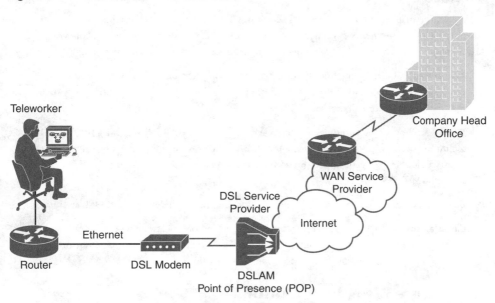

Current DSL technologies use sophisticated coding and modulation techniques to achieve data rates of up to 8.192 Mbps. A variety of DSL types, standards, and emerging technologies exist. DSL is a popular choice for enterprise IT departments to support home workers.

Cable Modem

Cable modems provide an always-on connection and simple installation. Figure 5-7 shows how a subscriber connects a computer or LAN router to the cable modem, which translates the digital signals into the broadband frequencies used for transmitting on a cable television network.

Figure 5-7   Teleworker Cable Modem Connection

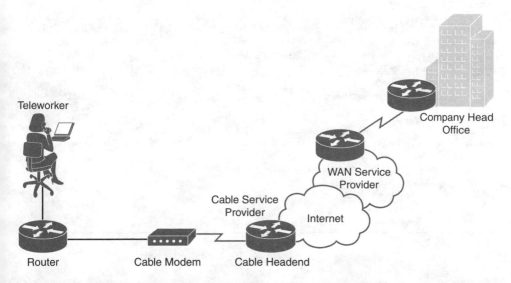

Wireless

In the past, the main limitation of wireless access was the need to be within range of a wireless router or a wireless modem with a wired connection to the Internet. However, the following wireless technology enable users to connect to the Internet from almost any location:

- **Municipal Wi-Fi:** Many cities have begun setting up municipal wireless networks. Some of these networks provide high-speed Internet access for free or for substantially less than the price of other broadband services.

- **WiMAX:** Worldwide Interoperability for Microwave Access (WiMAX) is an IEEE 802.16 technology that is just beginning to come into use. It provides high-speed broadband service with wireless access and provides broad coverage similar to a cell phone network instead of through small Wi-Fi hotspots.

- **Satellite Internet:** Technology typically used by rural users where cable and DSL are unavailable.

- **Cellular service:** Option for connecting users and remote locations where no other WAN access technology is available. Common cellular access methods include 3G/4G (third generation and fourth generation) and Long-Term Evolution (LTE) cellular access.

Choosing a WAN Link Option

Table 5-2 compares the advantages and disadvantages of the various WAN connection options reviewed.

Table 5-2   Choosing a WAN Link Connection

Option	Description	Advantages	Disadvantages	Sample Protocols
Leased line	Point-to-point connection between two LANs.	Most secure	Expensive	PPP, HDLC, SDLC
Circuit switching	Dedicated circuit path created between endpoints. The best example is dialup connections.	Less expensive	Call setup	PPP, ISDN
Packet switching	Devices transporting packets via a shared single point-to-point or point-to-multipoint link across a carrier internetwork. Variable-length packets are transmitted over PVCs or SVCs.	Highly efficient use of bandwidth	Shared media across link	Frame Relay, MetroE
Internet	Connectionless packet switching using the Internet as the WAN infrastructure. Uses network addressing to deliver packets. Because of security issues, VPN technology must be used.	Least expensive, globally available	Least secure	DSL, cable modem, wireless

VPN Technology

A virtual private network (VPN) is an encrypted connection between private networks over a public network such as the Internet. Instead of using a dedicated Layer 2 connection such as a leased line, a VPN uses virtual connections called VPN tunnels, which are routed through the Internet from the company's private network to the remote site or employee host.

VPN Benefits

Benefits of VPN include the following:

- **Cost savings:** Eliminates the need for expensive dedicated WAN links and modem banks

- **Security:** Uses advanced encryption and authentication protocols that protect data from unauthorized access

- **Scalability:** Can add large amounts of capacity without adding significant infrastructure

- **Compatibility with broadband technology:** Supported by broadband service providers, so mobile workers and telecommuters can take advantage of their home high-speed Internet service to access their corporate networks

Types of VPN Access

Three types of VPNs exist:

- **Site-to-site VPNs:** Site-to-site VPNs connect entire networks to each other. For example, they can connect a branch office network to a company headquarters network, as in Figure 5-8. Each site is equipped with a VPN gateway, such as a router, firewall, VPN concentrator, or security appliance. In the figure, a remote branch office uses a site-to-site VPN to connect with the corporate head office.

Figure 5-8   Site-to-Site VPNs

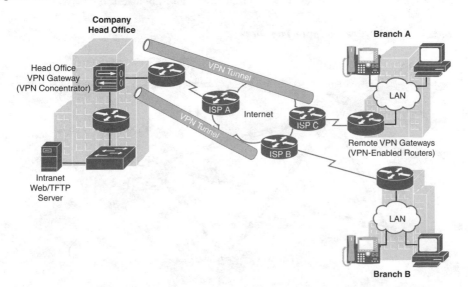

- **Remote-access VPNs:** Remote-access VPNs enable individual hosts, such as telecommuters, mobile users, and extranet consumers, to access a company network securely over the Internet, as in Figure 5-9. Each host typically has VPN client software loaded or uses a web-based client.

Figure 5-9   Remote-Access VPNs

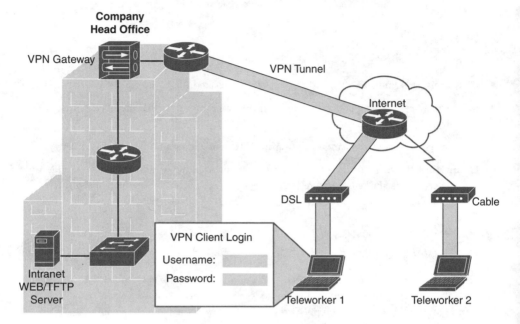

- **Dynamic Multipoint VPN:** DMVPN is a Cisco proprietary solution for building many VPNs in an easy, dynamic, and scalable manner. DMVPNs allow the network administrator to dynamically form hub-to-spoke tunnels and spoke-to-spoke tunnels, as in Figure 5-10.

Figure 5-10   DMVPN Example Topology

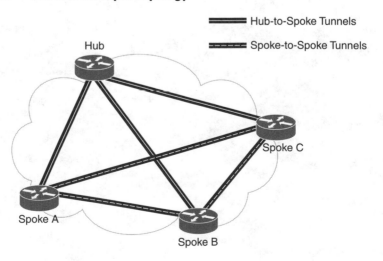

DMVPN uses the following technologies:

- **Next Hop Resolution Protocol (NHRP):** Maps public IP address for all tunnel spokes

- **IP Security (IPsec) encryption:** Provides the security to transport private information over public networks

- **Multipoint Generic Routing Encapsulation (mGRE):** Allows a single interface to support multiple IPsec tunnels

Activity: Identify the WAN Terminology

Refer to the Digital Study Guide to complete this activity.

Study Resources

For today's exam topics, refer to the following resources for more study.

Resource	Location	Topic
Primary Resources		
Connecting Networks v6	1	All
	3	VPNs
ICND2 Official Cert Guide	14	All
	15	Internet Access and Internet VPN Fundamentals
		Multipoint Internet VPNs Using DMVPN
Supplemental Resources		
CCNA Video Series	4	Lesson 2: Options for WAN Connectivity
		Lesson 3: WAN Topologies

Check Your Understanding

Refer to the Digital Study Guide to take a short quiz covering the content of this day.

Day 4

WAN Implementation

CCNA 200-125 Exam Topics

- Configure and verify PPP and MLPPP on WAN interfaces using local authentication
- Configure, verify, and troubleshoot PPPoE client-side interfaces using local authentication
- Configure, verify, and troubleshoot GRE tunnel connectivity
- Configure and verify single-homed branch connectivity using eBGP IPv4 (limited to peering and route advertisement using Network command only)

Key Topics

WAN implementation for the CCNA exam focuses on PPP, PPPoE, GRE, and eBGP. Today we review the commands to configure, verify, and troubleshoot these technologies.

PPP Concepts

PPP provides several basic but important functions that are useful on a leased line that connects two devices:

- Definition of a header and trailer that allows delivery of a data frame over the link
- Support for both synchronous and asynchronous links
- A Protocol Type field in the header, allowing multiple Layer 3 protocols to pass over the same link
- Built-in authentication tools, such as Password Authentication Protocol (PAP) and Challenge Handshake Authentication Protocol (CHAP)
- Control protocols for each higher-layer protocol that rides over PPP, allowing easier integration and support of those protocols

The PPP Frame Format

One of the more important features included in the PPP standard is the standardized Protocol field, which identifies the type of packet inside the frame. Notice in Figure 4-1 that PPP was built upon the HDLC frame. The HDLC frame shown is the Cisco format, which is the default encapsulation type for serial interfaces on Cisco routers.

Figure 4-1   Comparing the Cisco HDLC and PPP Frames

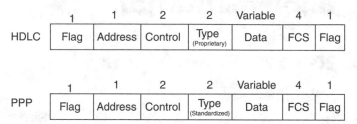

PPP defines a set of Layer 2 control messages that perform various link control functions. These control functions fall into two main categories:

- Functions needed regardless of the Layer 3 protocol sent across the link

- Functions specific to each Layer 3 protocol

The PPP Link Control Protocol (LCP) implements the control functions that work the same regardless of the Layer 3 protocol.

For features related to any higher-layer protocols (typically Layer 3 protocols), PPP uses a series of PPP control protocols (CP), such as IP Control Protocol (IPCP). PPP uses one instance of LCP per link and one CP for each Layer 3 protocol defined on the link. For example, on a PPP link using IPv4, IPv6, and Cisco Discovery Protocol (CDP), the link uses one instance of LCP, plus IPCP (for IPv4), IPv6CP (for IPv6), and CDPCP (for CDP). In the literature, you often see these referred to collectively as network control protocols (NCP).

PPP Link Control Protocol (LCP)

LCP provides four notable features (see Table 4-1).

Table 4-1   LCP Features

Function	LCP Feature	Description
Looped-link detection	Magic number	Detects whether the link is looped and disables the interface, allowing rerouting over a working route
Error detection	Link Quality Monitoring (LQM)	Disables an interface that exceeds an error percentage threshold, allowing rerouting over better routes
Multilink support	Multilink PPP	Load-balances traffic over multiple parallel links
Authentication	PAP and CHAP	Exchanges names and passwords so that each device can verify the identity of the device on the other end of the link

Looped-Link Detection

LCP quickly notices looped links using a feature called magic numbers. PPP LCP messages include a magic number, which differs on each router. If a line is looped (such as during testing by a telco technician), the router receives an LCP message with its own magic number instead of getting a message with the other router's magic number. PPP helps the router recognize a looped link quickly so that it can bring down the interface and possibly use an alternative route. If the router can immediately notice that the link is looped, it can put the interface in a down and down status, and the routing protocols can change their routing updates based on the fact that the link is down.

Enhanced Error Detection

When a network has redundant links, you can use PPP to monitor the frequency with which frames are received in error. After the configured error rate has been exceeded, PPP can take down the interface, allowing routing protocols to install a better backup route. PPP LCP analyzes the error rates on a link using a PPP feature called Link Quality Monitoring (LQM).

PPP Multilink

In a redundant configuration between two routers, the routers use Layer 3 load balancing, alternating traffic between the two links, which does not always result in truly balanced sharing of the traffic. Multilink PPP load-balances the traffic equally over the links while allowing the Layer 3 logic in each router to treat the parallel links as a single link. When encapsulating a packet, PPP fragments the packet into smaller frames, sending one fragment over each link. Multilink PPP allows the Layer 3 routing tables to use a single route that refers to the combined links, keeping the routing table smaller.

PPP Authentication

PAP and CHAP authenticate the endpoints on either end of a point-to-point serial link. CHAP is the preferred method today because the identification process uses values hidden with a message digest algorithm 5 (MD5) one-way hash, which is more secure than the clear-text passwords sent by PAP.

Figure 4-2 shows the different processes PAP and CHAP use. With PAP, the username and password are sent in the first message. With CHAP, the protocol begins with a message called a challenge, which asks the other router to send its username and password.

Figure 4-2   PPP Authentication Protocols

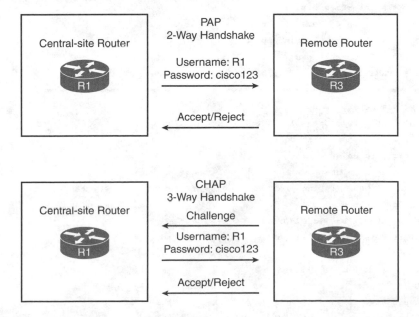

PAP is much less secure than CHAP because PAP sends the hostname and password in clear text in the message. CHAP instead uses a one-way hash algorithm, with input to the algorithm being a password that never crosses the link, plus a shared random number. The CHAP challenge states the random number; both routers are preconfigured with the password. The challenged router runs the hash algorithm using the just-learned random number and the secret password and sends the results back to the router that sent the challenge. The router that sent the challenge runs the same algorithm using the random number (sent across the link) and the password (not sent across the link). If the results match, the passwords must match. With the random number, the hash value is different every time.

PPP Configuration and Verification

This section references the topology in Figure 4-3.

Figure 4-3   PPP Topology

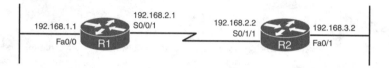

Basic PPP

Configuring PPP requires only the **encapsulation ppp** command on both ends of the link. Example 4-1 shows a simple configuration using the two routers in Figure 4-3.

Example 4-1   Configuring and Verifying PPP

```
R1(config)# interface serial 0/0/1
R1(config-if)# ip address 192.168.2.1 255.255.255.0
R1(config-if)# encapsulation ppp
R1(config-if)# no shutdown
%LINK-5-CHANGED: Interface Serial0/0/1, changed state to down

R2(config)# interface serial 0/1/1
R2(config-if)# ip address 192.168.2.2 255.255.255.0
R2(config-if)# encapsulation ppp
R2(config-if)# no shutdown
%LINK-5-CHANGED: Interface Serial0/1/1, changed state to up
%LINEPROTO-5-UPDOWN: Line protocol on Interface Serial0/1/1, changed state to up
R2(config-if)# end
R2# show interfaces serial 0/1/1
Serial0/1/1 is up, line protocol is up (connected)
   Hardware is HD64570
   Internet address is 192.168.2.2/24
   MTU 1500 bytes, BW 1544 Kbit, DLY 20000 usec, rely 255/255, load 1/255
   Encapsulation PPP, loopback not set, keepalive set (10 sec)
   LCP Open
   Open: IPCP, CDPCP
<output omitted>
```

The **show interfaces** command at the bottom of the example shows the normal output when the link is up and working. A few lines into the output, the highlighted phrases show that PPP is indeed configured and that LCP has completed its work successfully, as noted with the "LCP Open" phrase. In addition, the output lists the fact that two CPs, CDPCP and IPCP, have successfully been enabled (all good indications that PPP is working properly).

CHAP

Although CHAP is optional, it should be configured to provide a secure point-to-point link. The simplest version of CHAP configuration requires only a few commands. The configuration uses a password configured on each router. As an alternative, the password could be configured on an external authentication, authorization, and accounting (AAA) server outside the router. The configuration steps follow:

Step 1.   Configure the routers' hostnames using the **hostname** *name* global configuration command.

Step 2.   Configure the name of the other router and the shared secret password using the **username** *name* **password** *password* global configuration command.

Step 3.   Enable CHAP on the interface on each router using the **ppp authentication chap** interface subcommand.

Example 4-2 shows a sample configuration using the routers in Figure 4-3. Because the hostnames are already configured, that step is not shown.

Example 4-2   Configuring CHAP

```
R1(config)# username R2 password itsasecret
R1(config)# interface serial 0/0/1
R1(config-if)# ppp authentication chap
%LINEPROTO-5-UPDOWN: Line protocol on Interface Serial0/0/1, changed state to down

R2(config)# username R1 password itsasecret
%LINEPROTO-5-UPDOWN: Line protocol on Interface Serial0/1/1, changed state to up
R2(config)# interface serial 0/1/1
R2(config-if)# ppp authentication chap
%LINEPROTO-5-UPDOWN: Line protocol on Interface Serial0/1/1, changed state to down
%LINEPROTO-5-UPDOWN: Line protocol on Interface Serial0/1/1, changed state to up
```

Notice that as soon as CHAP is configured on R1, the interface goes down. Then on R2, after the password is configured correctly, the interface comes back up. Finally, it goes down briefly before coming back up when CHAP is configured on R2.

The commands themselves are not complicated, but it is easy to misconfigure the hostnames and passwords. Notice that each router refers to the other router's hostname in the **username** command, but both routers must configure the same password value. Also, not only are the passwords (itsasecret, in this case) case sensitive, but the hostnames, as referenced in the **username** command, also are case sensitive.

Because CHAP is a function of LCP, if the authentication process fails, LCP does not complete, and the interface falls to an up and down interface state.

PAP

As with CHAP, PAP is optional. You use it only if one of the devices does not support CHAP. PAP uses the same configuration commands as CHAP, except that the **ppp authentication pap** command is used instead of **ppp authentication chap**. The rest of the verification commands work the same, regardless of which of the two types of authentication are used. For example, if PAP authentication fails, then LCP fails and the link settles into an up and down state.

Cisco IOS Software also supports the capability to configure the router to first try one authentication method and then, if the other side does not respond, try the other option. The full command syntax for the **ppp authentication** command follows:

```
Router(config-if)# ppp authentication {pap | chap | pap chap | chap pap}
```

For example, the **ppp authentication chap pap** interface subcommand tells the router to send CHAP messages and, if no reply is received, to try PAP. Note that the second option is not tried if the CHAP messages flow between the two devices; as a result, authentication fails. It uses the other option only if the other device does not send back any messages.

PPP Troubleshooting

Use the **debug ppp** command to troubleshoot PPP issues.

```
Router# debug ppp {packet | negotiation | error | authentication | compression | cbcp}
```

PPP issues are most commonly related to authentication configuration errors. In Example 4-3, we know that either the username or the password is misconfigured on one or both sides of the link.

Example 4-3 PPP CHAP Authentication Failure in debug ppp authentication Output

```
R1# debug ppp authentication
PPP authentication debugging is on
Se0/0/0 PPP: Authorization required
Se0/0/0 CHAP: O CHALLENGE id 57 len 23 from "R1"
Se0/0/0 CHAP: I CHALLENGE id 66 len 23 from "R2"
Se0/0/0 CHAP: Using hostname from unknown source
Se0/0/0 CHAP: Using password from AAA
Se0/0/0 CHAP: O RESPONSE id 66 len 23 from "R1"
Se0/0/0 CHAP: I RESPONSE id 57 len 23 from "R2"
Se0/0/0 PPP: Sent CHAP LOGIN Request
Se0/0/0 PPP: Received LOGIN Response FAIL
Se0/0/0 CHAP: O FAILURE id 57 len 25 msg is "Authentication failed"
```

PPPoE Concepts

PPP can be used on all serial links, including links created with dialup analog and ISDN modems. To this day, the link from a dialup user to an ISP, using analog modems, likely uses PPP (see Figure 4-4).

Figure 4-4   Typical PPP Connection to ISP

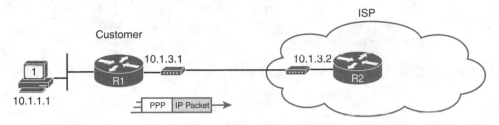

In addition, ISPs often use PPP as the data-link protocol over broadband connections for the following reasons:

- The capability to assign IP addresses to remote ends of a PPP link

- Support for CHAP to authenticate customers, allowing ISPs to also check accounting records before authorizing access

Technologies came to market in the following order, with varying support for PPP:

1. Analog modems for dialup that could use PPP and CHAP

2. ISDN for dialup that could use PPP and CHAP

3. DSL, which did not create a point-to-point link and could not support PPP and CHAP

PPPoE was developed because Ethernet links do not natively support PPP. As Figure 4-5 shows, PPPoE allows the sending of PPP frames encapsulated inside Ethernet frames.

Figure 4-5   Tunneling PPP Inside Ethernet

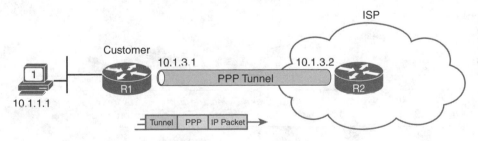

PPPoE Configuration

To implement PPPoE, complete the following steps:

Step 1.   Create a PPP tunnel using a dialer interface, which is a type of virtual interface. Configure PPP and addressing on the dialer interface. The ISP usually automatically assigns addressing.

Step 2.   Configure PPP CHAP to do authentication with the ISP.

Step 3.   Enable PPPoE on the physical interface with the **pppoe enable** command. The dialer interface is linked to the Ethernet interface with the **pppoe-client** command, followed by the number used to create the dialer pool in Step 2. The dialer interface number does not have to match the **dialer pool** number.

Step 4.   The maximum transmission unit (MTU) should be set down to 1492, versus the default of 1500, to accommodate the PPPoE headers. This prevents packet fragmentation, which causes delay in transmission.

PPPoE Configuration Example

Example 4-4 shows how to configure and verify PPPoE on R1.

Example 4-4   Configuring and Verifying PPPoE

```
R1(config)# interface dialer 5
R1(config-if)# encapsulation ppp
R1(config-if)# ip address negotiated
R1(config-if)# ip mtu 1492
R1(config-if)# dialer pool 5
R1(config-if)# ppp chap hostname customer2222
R1(config-if)# ppp chap password ConnectMe
R1(config-if)# no shutdown
R1(config-if)# interface GigabitEthernet 0/0
R1(config-if)# no ip address
R1(config-if)# pppoe enable
R1(config-if)# pppoe-client dial-pool-number 5
R1(config-if)# no shutdown
R1(config-if)# end
R1# show ip interface brief
Interface              IP-Address      OK? Method Status        Protocol
GigabitEthernet0/0     unassigned      YES NVRAM  up            up
GigabitEthernet0/1     172.16.1.1      YES manual up            up
Dialer5                64.100.10.1     YES manual up            up
Virtual-Access1        unassigned      YES unset  up            up
```

NOTE: Scott Empson's *CCNA Routing and Switching Portable Command Guide,* Third Edition (ISBN: 9781587204302), includes a different PPPoE configuration example.

PPPoE Troubleshooting

After ensuring that the client router and DSL modem are connected with the proper cables, one or more of the following are usually the cause of a PPPoE connection not functioning properly:

- Failure in the PPP negotiation process

- Failure in the PPP authentication process

- Failure to adjust the TCP maximum segment size

GRE Tunneling

Generic routing encapsulation (GRE) is one example of a basic, nonsecure, site-to-site VPN tunneling protocol. Typically, GRE is used to tunnel IP packets across the Internet, as in Figure 4-6. We briefly review GRE characteristics and configuration here.

Figure 4-6   Generic Routing Encapsulation

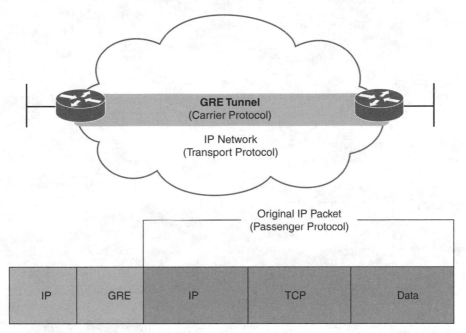

GRE Characteristics

GRE has these characteristics:

- GRE is defined as an IETF standard (RFC 2784).

- In the outer IP header, 47 is used in the Protocol field to indicate that a GRE header will follow.

- GRE encapsulation uses a Protocol Type field in the GRE header to support the encapsulation of any OSI Layer 3 protocol. RFC 1700 defines protocol types as EtherTypes.

- GRE itself is stateless; by default, it does not include any flow-control mechanisms.

- GRE does not include any strong security mechanisms to protect its payload.

- The GRE header, together with the tunneling IP header indicated in the figure, creates at least 24 bytes of additional overhead for tunneled packets.

GRE Configuration and Verification

In Figure 4-7, R1 is communicating with R2 through the Internet over a GRE tunnel.

Figure 4-7   GRE Tunnel Topology

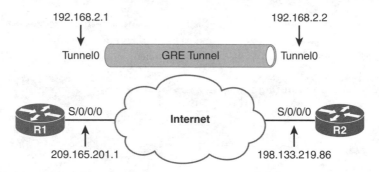

Notice that the addressing of the physical interfaces does not belong to the same subnet, but the addressing for the tunnel interface does belong to the same subnet.

To configure GRE, complete the following steps:

Step 1.   Create a tunnel interface using the **interface tunnel** *number* command.

Step 2.   Specify the tunnel source IP address. The source can also be the local interface name and number, such as Serial 0/0/0.

Step 3.   Specify the tunnel destination IP address.

Step 4.   Configure an IP address for the tunnel interface.

Step 5.   (Optional) Specify GRE tunnel mode as the tunnel interface mode with the **tunnel mode gre ip** command. GRE tunnel mode is the default tunnel interface mode for Cisco IOS Software.

Example 4-5 demonstrates the steps to configure GRE on R1 and R2. Notice that the OSPF configuration includes the tunnel subnet so that the routers can establish adjacency across the tunnel link.

Example 4-5   GRE Tunnel Configuration

```
R1(config)# interface Tunnel0
R1(config-if)# tunnel mode gre ip
R1(config-if)# ip address 192.168.2.1 255.255.255.0
R1(config-if)# tunnel source s0/0/0
R1(config-if)# tunnel destination 198.133.219.87
R1(config-if)# router ospf 1
R1(config-router)# network 192.168.2.0 0.0.0.255 area 0

R2(config)# interface Tunnel0
R2(config-if)# tunnel mode gre ip
R2(config-if)# ip address 192.168.2.2 255.255.255.0
R2(config-if)# tunnel source s0/0/0
R2(config-if)# tunnel destination 209.165.201.1
R2(config-if)# router ospf 1
R2(config-router)# network 192.168.2.0 0.0.0.255 area 0
```

NOTE: IPsec implementation is assumed in this example. However, IPsec configuration is beyond the scope of the CCNA/ICND2 exam.

To verify the GRE implementation, you should be able to ping R1 from R2 and also ping R2 from R1, and they should have converged routing tables. In addition, you can use the **show ip interface brief** and **show interface Tunnel** commands, as in Example 4-6.

Example 4-6   Verifying That the Tunnel Interface Is Up

```
R1# show ip interface brief | include Tunnel

Tunnel0             192.168.2.1     YES manual up              up
R1# show interface Tunnel 0
Tunnel0 is up, line protocol is up
  Hardware is Tunnel
  Internet address is 192.168.2.1/24
  MTU 17916 bytes, BW 100 Kbit/sec, DLY 50000 usec,
     reliability 255/255, txload 1/255, rxload 1/255
  Encapsulation TUNNEL, loopback not set
  Keepalive not set
  Tunnel source 209.165.201.1, destination 198.133.219.87
  Tunnel protocol/transport GRE/IP

<output omitted>
```

GRE Troubleshooting

Issues with GRE usually result from one or more of the following misconfigurations:

- The tunnel interface IP addresses are not on the same network or the subnet masks do not match.

- The interfaces for the tunnel source and/or tunnel destination are not configured with the correct IP address or are in the down state.

- Static or dynamic routing is not properly configured.

BGP Concepts

BGP exchanges routing information with another router, called a BGP neighbor or BGP peer. These BGP neighbors are routers in other companies, not routers in the same company. This distinguishes BGP from interior gateway protocols (IGP) such as OSPF and EIGRP that exchange routing information with routers in the same company.

An enterprise edge router is configured to advertise a public IPv4 prefix with its ISP. In Figure 4-8, the enterprise router is advertising the IPv4 prefix 192.0.2.0/24 to ISP1. ISP1 then advertises the prefix to ISP2, and so on. In this way, Internet routers learn about the enterprise's public address space.

Figure 4-8   BGP Routes Propagate to ISPs

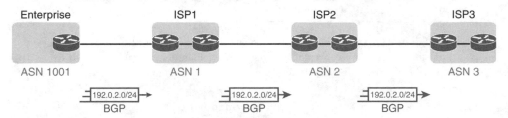

BGP uses TCP with well-known port number 179 to transport its messages between two BGP peers. When you configure BGP, it opens port 179, waiting for incoming connection requests from other routers. When a peer connects, the TCP connection is formed.

The autonomous system number (ASN in Figure 4-8) plays an important role in BGP by identifying networks that operate separately from other networks. For example, ISP1 in Figure 4-9 has three routers in ASN1. Routers in the same AS exchange interior BGP prefixes (iBGP) that most likely include prefixes learned from exterior BGP (eBGP) neighbors.

Figure 4-9   iBGP and eBGP

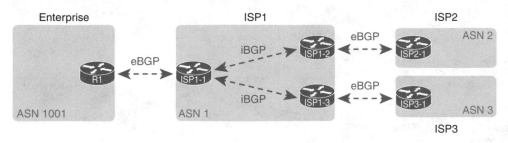

> **NOTE:**   For a more in-depth review of how BGP operates, see Chapter 12 in Wendell Odom's *CCNA Routing and Switching ICND2 200-105 Official Cert Guide* (ISBN: 9781587205798).

 Packet Tracer Activity: PPP and GRE Configuration

Refer to the Digital Study Guide to access the PKA file for this activity. You must have Packet Tracer software to run this activity. See the Introduction for details.

eBGP Configuration and Verification

For the CCNA exam, you are responsible for knowing how to configure and verify a single-homed eBGP connection. This typically is one location configured to advertise its public IPv4 prefixes to a local ISP, as shown in Figure 4-10.

Figure 4-10   eBGP Configuration Topology

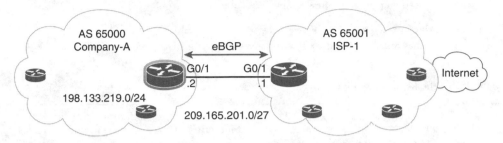

To implement eBGP for a single-homed connection, you complete the following tasks:

Step 1.   Enable BGP routing.

Step 2.   Configure BGP neighbor(s) (peering).

Step 3.   Advertise network(s) originating from this AS.

Table 4-2 lists the command syntax and describes basic eBGP configuration.

Table 4-2   BGP Configuration Commands

Command	Description
`Router(config)# router bgp as-number`	Enables a BGP routing process and places the router in router configuration mode.
`Router(config-router)# neighbor ip-address remote-as as-number`	Specifies a BGP neighbor. The *as-number* is the neighbor's AS number.
`Router(config-router)# network network-address [mask network-mask]`	Specifies a network as local to this AS, adds it to the BGP routing table, and advertises the network to BGP peers. The *network-mask* specifies how much of the *network-address* is advertised. If no mask is configured, the default classful mask is assumed.

Example 4-7 shows the BGP configuration for Company-A and ISP1.

Example 4-7   BGP Configuration Example

```
Company-A(config-if)# router bgp 65000
Company-A(config-router)# neighbor 209.165.201.1 remote-as 65001
Company-A(config-router)# network 198.133.219.0 mask 255.255.255.0

ISP-1(config-if)# router bgp 65001
ISP-1(config-router)# neighbor 209.165.201.2 remote-as 65000
%BGP-5-ADJCHANGE: neighbor 209.165.201.2 Up
ISP-1(config-router)# network 0.0.0.0
```

The **neighbor** command identifies the BGP peer and its AS number. Notice that the ISP AS number is different than the Company-A AS number. This informs the BGP process that the neighbor is in a different AS and is therefore an external BGP neighbor. Notice the adjacency message on ISP-1 after the **neighbor** command is entered.

The **network** command enters the *network-address* into the local BGP table. The BGP table contains all routes that are learned via BGP or advertised using BGP. eBGP then advertises the *network-address* to its eBGP neighbors.

On ISP-1, the **network 0.0.0.0** command advertises a default network to Company-A.

> **NOTE:** Although the **network 0.0.0.0** command is a valid BGP configuration option, there are better ways to advertise a default route in eBGP. However, these methods are beyond the scope of the CCNA exam.

Three commands can be used to verify eBGP (see Table 4-3).

Table 4-3 BGP Verification Commands

Command	Description
Router# **show ip route**	Verifies that routes advertised by the BGP neighbor are present in the IPv4 routing table
Router# **show ip bgp**	Verifies that received and advertised IPv4 networks are in the BGP table
Router# **show ip bgp summary**	Verifies IPv4 BGP neighbors and other BGP information

Example 4-8 displays the output for these three commands for Company-A.

Example 4-8 eBGP Verification for Company-A

```
Company-A# show ip route
Codes: L - local, C - connected, S - static, R - RIP, M - mobile, B - BGP
<rest of Codes table omitted>


Gateway of last resort is 209.165.201.1 to network 0.0.0.0


B*      0.0.0.0/0 [20/0] via 209.165.201.1, 00:00:47
        198.133.219.0/24 is variably subnetted, 2 subnets, 2 masks
C          198.133.219.0/24 is directly connected, GigabitEthernet0/0
L          198.133.219.1/32 is directly connected, GigabitEthernet0/0
        209.165.201.0/24 is variably subnetted, 2 subnets, 2 masks
C          209.165.201.0/27 is directly connected, GigabitEthernet0/1
L          209.165.201.2/32 is directly connected, GigabitEthernet0/1
Company-A# show ip bgp
BGP table version is 3, local router ID is 209.165.201.2
Status codes: s suppressed, d damped, h history, * valid, > best, i - internal,
              r RIB-failure, S Stale, m multipath, b backup-path, f RT-Filter,
              x best-external, a additional-path, c RIB-compressed,
Origin codes: i - IGP, e - EGP, ? - incomplete
RPKI validation codes: V valid, I invalid, N Not found
```

```
      Network              Next Hop              Metric LocPrf Weight Path
 *>   0.0.0.0              209.165.201.1              0            0 65001 i
 *>   198.133.219.0        0.0.0.0                    0        32768 i
Company-A# show ip bgp summary
BGP router identifier 209.165.201.2, local AS number 65000
BGP table version is 3, main routing table version 3
2 network entries using 288 bytes of memory
2 path entries using 160 bytes of memory
2/2 BGP path/bestpath attribute entries using 320 bytes of memory
1 BGP AS-PATH entries using 24 bytes of memory
0 BGP route-map cache entries using 0 bytes of memory
0 BGP filter-list cache entries using 0 bytes of memory
BGP using 792 total bytes of memory
BGP activity 2/0 prefixes, 2/0 paths, scan interval 60 secs


Neighbor        V    AS MsgRcvd MsgSent   TblVer  InQ OutQ  Up/Down   State/PfxRcd
209.165.201.1   4 65001       7       5        3    0    0  00:01:27             1
Company-A#
```

In the **show ip route** output, notice the B, which indicates that the route was learned through BGP. The **show ip bgp** command displays the BGP table. The next hop, 0.0.0.0 for 198.133.219.0, indicates that the network originates from this router. In the **show ip bgp summary** output, the first line displays the local IPv4 address used to peer with another BGP neighbor and this router's local AS number. The address and AS number of the remote BGP neighbor appear at the bottom of the output.

Study Resources

For today's exam topics, refer to the following resources for more study.

Resource	Location	Topic
Primary Resources		
Connecting Networks v6	2	PPP Operation
		PPP Implementation
		Troubleshoot WAN Connectivity
	3	PPPoE
		GRE
		eBGP

Resource	Location	Topic
ICND2 Official Cert Guide	12	All
	13	Leased-Line WANs with HDLC (includes PPP)
	15	GRE Tunnels and DMVPN
		PPP over Ethernet
Supplemental Resources		
CCNA Portable Command Guide	16	All mandatory configurations
	17	Configuring Border Gateway Protocol
		Configuration Example: eBGP
		Verifying BGP Connections
	18	All
CCNA Video Series	4	Lesson 1: Point-to-Point Protocol (PPP)
		Lesson 2: Options for WAN Connectivity (GRE videos only)
		Lesson 4: Border Gateway Protocol (BGP)
CCNA Network Simulator	12	eBGP Peering I–II
		eBGP Configuration I–II
	13	Serial Link Configuration I–IV
		Serial Configuration I–II
		Serial Authentication I–II
	15	GRE Tunnel Configuration I–IV
		GRE Tunnel Troubleshooting

Check Your Understanding

Refer to the Digital Study Guide to take a short quiz covering the content of this day.

QoS, Cloud, and SDN

CCNA 200-125 Exam Topics

- Describe basic QoS concepts
- Describe the effects of cloud resources on enterprise network architecture
- Describe network programmability in enterprise network architecture
- Verify ACLs using the APIC-EM ACL Analysis tool

Key Topics

Quality of Service (QoS) refers to the tools and techniques network administrators can use to prioritize traffic on the network.

Cloud computing is an increasingly important service that networks offer to end users. Enterprise networks can use any number of different cloud offerings to enhance productivity and lower costs.

Network programmability through Software Defined Networking (SDN) is becoming integral to enterprise networks because network administrators can quickly and efficiently manage thousands of networking devices.

Today we review the technologies behind QoS, Cloud, and SDN.

QoS

Normal default operation for switches and routers is to process frames and packets in the order in which they are received. This first-in, first-out (FIFO) queueing mechanism does not discriminate between traffic types.

QoS tools are used to classify traffic types based on the following four characteristics:

- **Latency (Delay):** Latency, or delay, is the amount of time it takes for data to be sent to the receiver. QoS tools can reduce the delay for time-sensitive packets, such as voice and video.
- **Jitter:** Jitter is the variance in the delay of packets. QoS tools can even out the delay of packets to improve end user experience.
- **Loss:** Loss refers to the number of lost messages, usually as a percentage of the packets sent. QoS tools reduce packet loss, especially for time-sensitive traffic.
- **Bandwidth:** Bandwidth is a measure of the amount of data an interface can send every second. QoS tools can manage which traffic type gets to use the bandwidth next and how much of the bandwidth each type of traffic gets over time.

Figure 3-1 list the three major traffic types. For voice and video, the minimum traffic characteristic values are shown.

Figure 3-1   Characteristics for Major Traffic Types

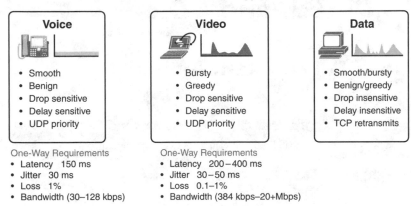

Voice	Video	Data
• Smooth	• Bursty	• Smooth/bursty
• Benign	• Greedy	• Benign/greedy
• Drop sensitive	• Drop sensitive	• Drop insensitive
• Delay sensitive	• Delay sensitive	• Delay insensitive
• UDP priority	• UDP priority	• TCP retransmits

One-Way Requirements
• Latency   150 ms
• Jitter   30 ms
• Loss   1%
• Bandwidth (30–128 kbps)

One-Way Requirements
• Latency   200–400 ms
• Jitter   30–50 ms
• Loss   0.1–1%
• Bandwidth (384 kbps–20+Mbps)

Figure 3-2 shows the sequence of QoS events as traffic is forwarded out an interface.

Figure 3-2   Overview of QoS Tools

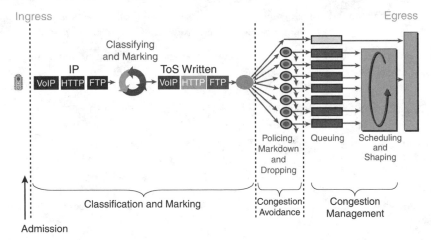

QoS tools shown in Figure 3-2 include the following:

- **Classification and marking:** QoS tools monitor traffic flows and classify packets based on the header contents. Messages are then marked by changing bits in the header.

- **Congestion avoidance:** When traffic exceeds available network resources, some traffic might be selectively dropped, delayed, or re-marked to avoid congestion.

- **Congestion management:** QoS tools manage the scheduling and shaping of traffic while packets wait their turn in a queue to exit the interface.

Classification and Marking

Classification refers to the process of matching fields in the headers in order to take some type of QoS action on the packet. These fields can include all the normal fields filtered by ACLs, as well as the Type of Service (ToS) field in an IPv4 packet or Traffic Class field in an IPv6 packet.

Marking refers to the process of changing bit values in the ToS or Traffic Class field. The contents of these two fields are identical, as Figure 3-3 shows.

Figure 3-3   The ToS and Traffic Class Fields in IPv4 and IPv6

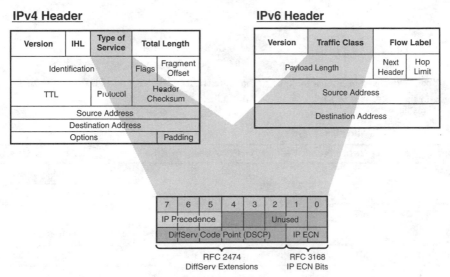

Figure 3-3 highlights the differentiated service code point (DSCP) bits, which is the core of the differentiated services (DiffServ) model for QoS. QoS tools can use the 2 bits allotted for IP explicit congestion notification (ECN) to inform downstream routers of congestion in the traffic flow.

DSCP and IPP

Standardized in RFC 2474, the 8 DSCP bits provide 64 different classifications that QoS can use. This is a vast improvement over the eight classifications allotted for the 3 bits in the previous IP precedence (IPP) field (RFC 791). For backward compatibility, the DSCP bits include the Class Selector (CS) values that are designated to match the IPP bits, as in Figure 3-4.

Figure 3-4   The Class Selector Values

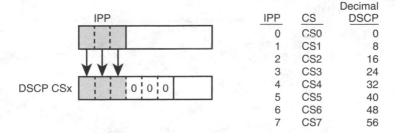

For Layer 2 trunk links, the third byte of the 4-byte 802.1Q header is reserved for Class of Service (CoS), and QoS tools can use it to mark frames. However, this field exists only as long as the frame is traversing trunk links, as Figure 3-5 shows. To continue the same level of service as traffic is routed on Layer 3, the ToS field must be marked.

Figure 3-5   CoS Marking Example

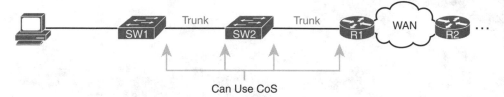

Can Use CoS

Additional fields that can be marked for QoS include the Traffic Identifier (TID) field in the 802.11 frame and the EXP field in MPLS. Table 3-1 lists all the QoS fields.

Table 3-1   QoS Marking Fields

Field	Name Header(s)	Length (bits)	Where Used
DSCP	IPv4, IPv6	6	End-to-end packet
IPP	IPv4, IPv6	3	End-to-end packet
CoS	802.1Q	3	Over VLAN trunk
TID	802.11	3	Over Wi-Fi
EXP	MPLS Label	3	Over MPLS WAN

NOTE: The MPLS EXP field was renamed the Traffic Class field in RFC 5462. However, EXP is still commonly used. The EXP name comes from the designation "experimental use."

EF and AF

Expedited Forwarding (EF) is a single DSCP decimal value of 46 that is suggested for use with packets that require low latency, low jitter, and low loss. QoS implementations typically use EF to mark voice packets.

Assured Forwarding (AF), specified in RFC 2597, defines a set of 12 DSCP values that are arranged in a matrix, as in Figure 3-6.

Figure 3-6   AF DSCP Values

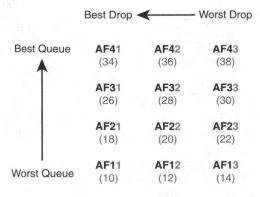

The four rows in Figure 3-6 show the queue priorities. The three columns show the drop priority. The AF names follow the format AFXY, where X refers to the queue and Y refers to the drop priority.

Congestion Management

Congestion management refers to the QoS tools used to manage queues as packets wait to exit an interface. Most networking devices can have a queuing system that can classify packets into multiple queues. A scheduler then decides which message to take next when the interface becomes available.

A popular tool is Class-Based Weighted Fair Queueing (CBWFQ), which assigns classes of traffic to queues and guarantees a minimum bandwidth for a queue. The scheduler then uses a round-robin algorithm to cycle through the queues in order, as in Figure 3-7.

Figure 3-7   CBWFQ Round-Robin Scheduling

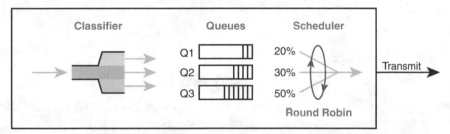

However, CBWFQ alone will not satisfy the needs of the most time-sensitive traffic type during periods of heavy bandwidth congestion. Each voice call needs between 30 and 320 kbps, maximum delay of 150 ms, maximum jitter of 30 ms, and less than 1 percent packet loss. The solution is to add Low Latency Queueing to CBWFQ. The scheduler always takes the next voice packet from the LLQ, as Figure 3-8 shows.

Figure 3-8   Low Latency Queuing

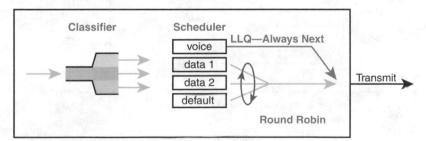

Policing, Shaping, and TCP Discards

Two tools that can help manage and avoid congestion on heavily utilized links include policing and shaping. Although these tools are not commonly used throughout the enterprise, they are particularly helpful at the WAN edge. Both tools attempt to keep the bit rate at or below a specified speed. Policers drop packets and shapers delay packets by placing them in a queue.

Policing makes sense at the WAN edge. For example, consider a Metro Ethernet WAN link that is contracted to allow no more than 200 Mbps, as in Figure 3-9.

Figure 3-9   WAN Edge with a CIR Below Link Speed

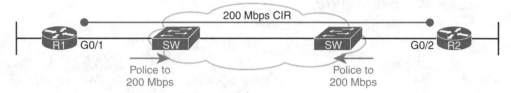

The service provider (SP) uses policing to match the Committed Information Rate (CIR). If the customer exceeds the 200 Mbps CIR, the SP can drop the excess packets or remark the excess packets but still allow them through. Later the excess packets can be discarded if the SP's network experiences congestion. Policing features include the following:

- Measure traffic over time and compare to a configured policing rate
- Allow for bursting traffic during slow times
- Discard excess messages or remark for discard later if congestion occurs downstream

On the customer side of the link in Figure 3-9, the network administrator can use a shaper to slow traffic to match the 200 Mbps CIR. The shaper slows traffic by queuing packets and then scheduling packets based on the shaping rate, as Figure 3-10 shows.

Figure 3-10   Shaping with LLQ and CBWFQ

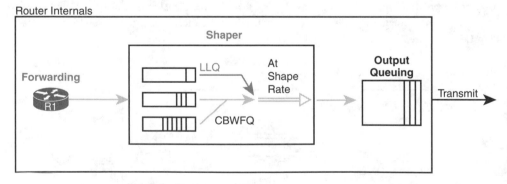

Shaping cannot slow the physical speed of an interface. Instead, it sends and waits. For example, with a 200 Mpbs CIR and a 1000 Mbps interface, the shaper sends traffic at 1000 Mbps 20 percent of the time. The other 80 percent of the time, the shaper is waiting.

This send–wait tactic can adversely impact time-sensitive voice and video traffic. Therefore, it is recommended that you set the time interval to 10 ms. Then the shaper will send 1000 Mbps for 2 ms and wait for 8 ms. This ensures that a voice packet will not have to wait more than 10 ms before being sent, which is well below the 150 ms maximum delay requirement.

The key features of shapers follow:

- Measure traffic over time and compare it to a configured shaping rate

- Allow for bursting traffic during slow times

- Slow packets by queuing them and, over time, releasing them from the queue at the shaping rate

QoS and TCP

Without congestion-avoidance tools, tail drop can occur (see Figure 3-11).

Figure 3-11   Tail Drop Example

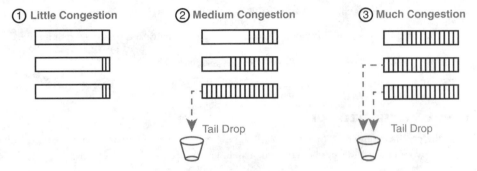

As the lower queues fill up, the packets received last are dropped.

TCP's connection-oriented services help QoS tools to minimize tail drop. Recall that TCP uses a windowing process between sender and receiver to dynamically change the amount of data that is sent before an acknowledgment must be received. QoS tools can exploit this windowing feature by discarding some TCP segments before the queues fill. This forces the TCP connections to slow, reduces congestion, and avoids tail drop.

QoS tools monitor the depth of the queues over time. Configured thresholds specify what percentage of TCP packets should be dropped as the queue fills, as in Figure 3-12.

Figure 3-12   Queue Thresholds for Discarding TCP Packets

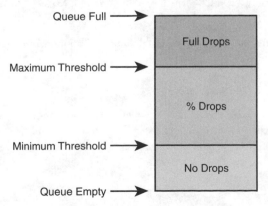

Activity: Identify the Assured Forwarding DSCP Value

Refer to the Digital Study Guide to complete this activity.

Cloud Computing

Cloud computing involves large numbers of computers connected through a network that can be physically located anywhere. Cloud computing provides the following benefits:

- Enables access to organizational data anywhere and at any time
- Streamlines IT operations by subscribing only to needed services
- Eliminates or reduces the need for onsite IT equipment, maintenance, and management
- Reduces cost for equipment, energy, physical plant requirements, and personnel training needs
- Enables rapid responses to increasing data volume requirements

Cloud providers rely heavily on virtualization to enable the solutions they offer to clients.

Server Virtualization

Historically, organizations bought multiple hardware servers and the server administrator installed one or more network applications on the server, such as an email server or file server (see Figure 3-13).

Figure 3-13   Dedicated Server with One OS

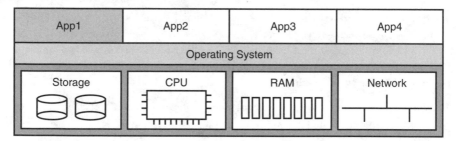

Each of these servers had its own CPU, memory, NIC, and disk space. However, this model faces several challenges:

- If a component fails, the service is unavailable until the component is repaired or replaced.
- Servers sometimes sit idle for long periods of time waiting for clients to use them.
- Servers take up space and waste energy.

Server virtualization takes advantage of idle resources and consolidates the number of required servers. Virtualization separates the operating system (OS) from the hardware. This also makes it possible for multiple OSs to exist on a single hardware platform. Each instance of an OS is called a virtual machine (VM).

A server with multiple VMs uses a hypervisor to manage access to the server's physical resources. The hypervisor sits between the VMs and the hardware, as in Figure 3-14.

Figure 3-14   Hypervisor Managing Four VMs

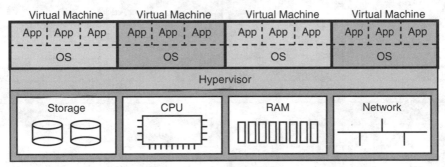

Another method for managing a set of VMs on a server, especially in a data center environment, is to use a virtual switch that connects the VMs to physical NICs, as in Figure 3-15. Instead of a hypervisor, an external controller (not shown) manages the server hardware.

Figure 3-15   Virtual Switch and VMs

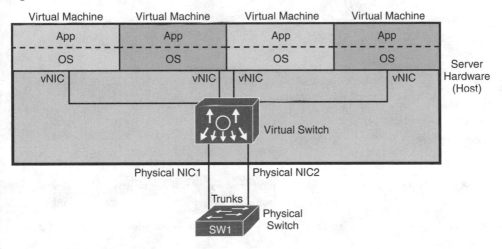

In a data center, multiple servers are placed in a rack. The two physical NICs in Figure 3-15 are attached to two redundant top of rack (ToR) switches. Racks are lined up in rows and managed by two redundant end of row (EoR) switches. Figure 3-16 shows this physical layout of a traditional data center.

Figure 3-16   Traditional Data Center Physical Topology

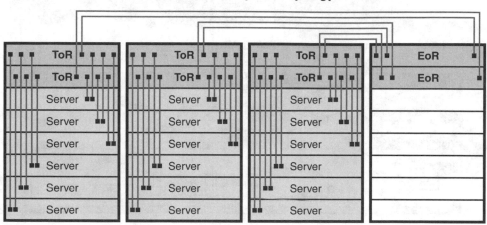

Cloud Computing Services

To understand the value of cloud computing, consider the effort it takes to manage VMs in a traditional data center. The workflow follows:

1. A customer requests a VM or a new set of VMs.

2. The data center engineer configures virtualization software.

3. Virtualization software creates VMs.

Although this process works, it does not have the characteristics of a cloud computing service as defined by the U.S. National Institute of Standards and Technology (NIST):

- **On-demand self-service:** The user can order, modify, and end service without human interaction.

- **Broad network access:** The service can be accessed from a variety of devices across any network.

- **Resource pooling:** The provider has a pool of resources that can be dynamically allocated to users. The user typically requires no awareness of the physical location of the resources.

- **Rapid elasticity:** To the user, the resource pool appears to be unlimited; it can expand and contract as needed.

- **Measured service:** The provider can measure the usage and then report that usage to the consumer, for both transparency and billing.

Cloud providers can offer a variety of services to meet the needs of their customers, including these:

- **Software as a Service (SaaS):** The cloud provider is responsible for access to services that are delivered over the Internet, such as email, communication, and Office 365. Users only need to provide their data.

- **Platform as a Service (PaaS):** The cloud provider is responsible for access to the development tools and services used to deliver the applications. Customers can customize the virtualized hardware.

- **Infrastructure as a Service (IaaS):** The cloud provider is responsible for access to the network equipment, virtualized network services, and network infrastructure support.

Four primary cloud models exist:

- **Public clouds:** Cloud-based applications and services offered in a public cloud are made available to the general population. The public cloud uses the Internet to provide services.

- **Private clouds:** Cloud-based applications and services offered in a private cloud are intended for a specific organization or entity, such as the government. A private cloud uses the organization's private network.

- **Hybrid clouds:** A hybrid cloud is made up of two or more clouds (example: part private, part public). Each part remains a distinct object, but both are connected using a single architecture.

- **Community clouds:** A community cloud is created for exclusive use by a specific community. The differences between public clouds and community clouds are the functional needs that have been customized for the community.

Virtual Network Infrastructure

A virtual network infrastructure consists of a collection of virtual network functions (VNFs), including virtual switches, virtual server load balancers (SLB), virtual routers, and virtual firewalls (see Figure 3-17).

Figure 3-17   Virtual Network Installed by a Cloud Provider's Tenant

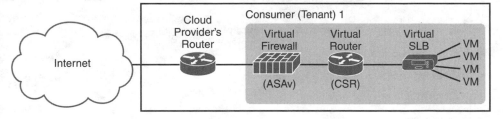

A cloud provider could offer an IaaS solution to a customer (tenant) that includes a virtual SLB. The customer could then install VNFs, such as a virtual version of the Cisco Adaptive Security Appliance (ASAv) and Cisco Cloud Services Router (CSR), to manage network traffic.

Software-Defined Networking

Network programmability refers to the trend toward software-defined networking (SDN). At its core, SDN decouples the data, control, and management planes from the physical device, virtualizes them, and defines the networking functions in software. This creates an architecture that can more efficiently and effectively be managed through programmatic control.

Data, Control, and Management Planes

A traditional networking device contains two planes. The data plane is responsible for forwarding data as quickly as possible. To do so, it relies on tables built by the control plane. Actions taken by the data plane include the following:

- Layer 2 and Layer 3 de-encapsulation/encapsulation

- Addition or removal of an 802.1Q trunking header

- MAC address table lookups

- IP routing table lookups

- Data encryption and addition of a new IP header (VPNs)

- Change to the source or destination IP address (NAT)

- Message discard due to a filter (ACLs, port security)

The control plane does all the calculations for populating tables used by the data plane and manages control messages between other networking devices. Figure 3-18 provides an example of OSPF operating on the control plane while the data plane is responsible for forwarding packets on the best route.

Figure 3-18   Control and Data Plane Example

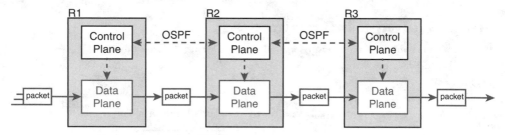

The following list includes the most common control plane protocols:

- Routing protocols (OSPF, EIGRP, RIP, BGP)

- IPv4 ARP

- IPv6 NDP

- Switch MAC learning

- STP

The management plane is responsible for all functions that are not directly related to controlling the data plane. Management protocols, such as the ones in Figure 3-19, are examples of management plane functions.

Figure 3-19   Management Plane Example

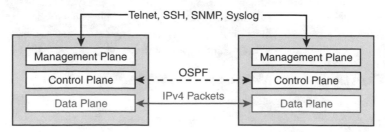

Controllers

Traditionally, the control plane has been part of the device OS and has been distributed across every device. That means every device must spend some resources calculating and maintaining Layer 2 and Layer 3 data structures (ARP tables, routing tables, and so on). When viewed as a whole, the network's control plane is distributed across all the networking devices.

In SDN, the functions of the control plane can be completely removed from the physical networking devices and placed in a centralized application called a controller. This frees up the devices to focus on data plane tasks.

The controller sits at the top of network topology diagrams. Therefore, the connections to the networking devices are called the southbound interface (SBI) (see Figure 3-20).

Figure 3-20   Centralized Controller and Distributed Data Plane

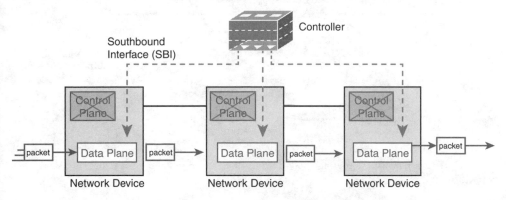

A northbound interface (NBI) also exists between the SDN controller and the applications that are installed on the controller. These applications are what enable network programmability.

SDN Examples

In his book *CCNA Routing and Switching ICND2 200-105 Official Cert Guide* (ISBN: 9781587205798), Wendell Odom covers three SDN solutions because they are all available in Cisco products.

Open SDN and OpenFlow

The Open Networking Foundation (ONF) model of SDN uses an SBI called OpenFlow. OpenFlow is a protocol used between the controller and the networking devices to manage traffic flows. ONF's controller, OpenDaylight, is the result of a collaborative effort among many vendors, including Cisco.

Figure 3-21 shows an OpenDaylight SDN controller with examples of NBI and SBI application programming interfaces (API).

Figure 3-21   ONF OpenDaylight Controller

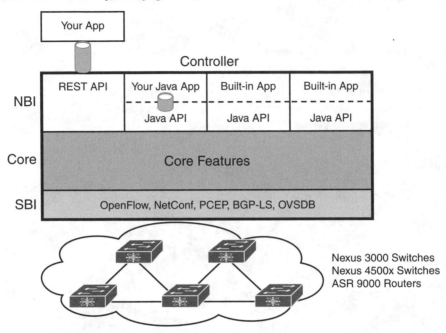

In addition to OpenFlow, the controller has SBIs for other activities, such as configuring network devices (NetConf), managing routing (BGP-LS and PCEP), and switching traffic between VMs (OVSDB).

NBIs typically include Java APIs for applications and the RESTful API. REST (Representational State Transfer) uses HTTP messages to transfer data to other applications that are not running on the controller.

The definition and operation of these SBI and NBI protocols is beyond the scope of the exam. Just know that the ONF is continuously researching better protocols to implement in the OpenDaylight project.

The Cisco commercial version of the OpenDaylight controller is the Cisco Open SDN Controller (OSC). OSC is available in a limited number of Cisco routers and switches.

The Cisco Application Centric Infrastructure

The Cisco in-house SDN solution for data centers is Application Centric Infrastructures (ACI). ACI uses the concept of endpoint groups and policies. Endpoint groups are a collection of similar VMs, such as a set of virtual switches for one of the data center's tenants. Policies define which endpoint groups can communicate with whom.

The Cisco Application Policy Infrastructure Controller (APIC) uses the endpoint topology and policies to direct the network regarding what needs to be in the forwarding tables and how to easily react to VM changes. ACI uses a partially centralized control plane, RESTful and native APIs, and OpFlex as an SBI, as in Figure 3-22.

Figure 3-22   Cisco ACI for Data Centers

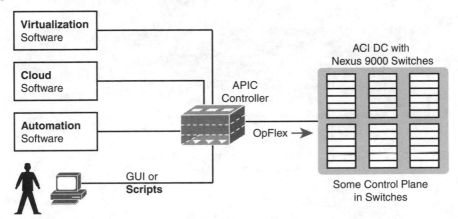

OpFlex is the Cisco solution for SBI communication with networking devices. Whereas OpenFlow centralizes the network control by pushing commands directly from the SDN controller, OpFlex uses policies to push command implementation down to a distributed network of controllers.

The Cisco APIC Enterprise Module (APIC-EM)

APIC-EM is the Cisco SDN offering for the enterprise. The APIC-EM solution uses a controller to manage existing network devices but also attempts to support new generations of Cisco enterprise routers and switches by using SBIs that are familiar to network administrators, such as remote access to the CLI (Telnet and SSH) and SNMP support.

Cisco also supplies a variety of applications that reside on the controller, some that use information gathered by the controller and some that control the operation of the network devices. A RESTful Northbound API makes it easy to collect information about the entire network.

To support the existing enterprise infrastructure of switches and routers, the control and data planes remain unchanged.

Figure 3-23 shows a general view of the APIC-EM controller architecture, with a few of the APIC-EM apps, the REST API, and a list of the SBIs.

Figure 3-23   APIC-EM Controller

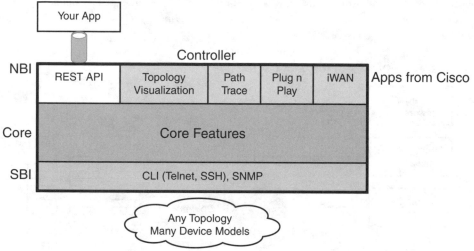

Table 3-2 compares the three examples of SDN.

Table 3-2   Comparing Characteristics of Three SDN Controllers

Characteristics	OpenDaylight, Cisco OSC	APIC	APIC-EM
Changes how the device control plane works versus traditional networking	Yes	Yes	No
Creates a centralized point from which humans and automation control the network	Yes	Yes	Yes
Determines the degree to which the architecture centralizes the control plane	Mostly	Partially	Not at all
Determines the SBIs used	OpenFlow	OpFlex	CLI, SNMP
Identifies the organization that is the primary definer/owner	ONF	Cisco	Cisco

APIC-EM and ACLs

One of the most important features of the APIC-EM controller is the capability to manage policies across the entire network. APIC-EM ACL Analysis and Path Trace provide tools to allow the administrator to analyze and understand ACL policies and configurations. Administrators are hesitant to change ACLs, for fear of breaking them and causing new problems. Together, ACL Analysis and Path Trace enable the administrator to easily visualize traffic flows and discover any conflicting, duplicate, or shadowed ACL entries.

ACL Analysis examines ACLs on devices, searching for redundant, conflicting, or shadowed entries. It enables ACL inspection and interrogation across the entire network, exposing any problems and conflicts. Figure 3-24 shows an example of the ACL Analysis tool.

Figure 3-24   APIC-EM ACL Analysis Tool

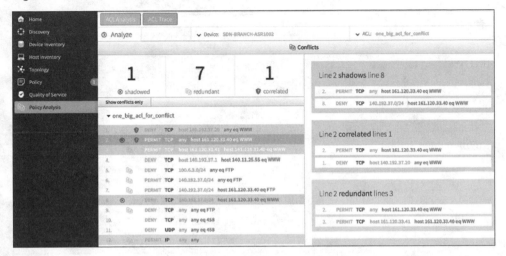

ACL Path Trace examines specific ACLs on the path between two end nodes, displaying any potential issues. Figure 3-25 shows an example of the ACL Path Trace tool.

Figure 3-25   APIC-EM ACL Path Trace Tool

NOTE: Search the Internet for "APIC-EM Demo" to watch some videos demonstrating the ACL Path Trace. In particular, look for Kevin Wallace's YouTube channel and his "APIC-EM Path Trace ACL Analysis Tool" video. This excellent video is also part of Kevin's *CCNA Routing and Switching 200-125 Premium Edition Complete Video Course.*

Study Resources

For today's exam topics, refer to the following resources for more study.

Resource	Location	Topic
Primary Resources		
Connecting Networks v6	6	All
	7	All
ICND2 Official Cert Guide	18	All
	27	All
	28	All
	Appendix B	The APIC-EM Path Trace ACL Analysis Tool
Supplemental Resources		
CCNA Portable Command Guide	19	Optional: This chapter covers QoS commands, which is beyond the scope of the CCNA exam.
CCNA Video Series	1	Lesson 3: Cloud Resources
	5	Lesson 5: Quality of Service (QoS)
	7	Lesson 4: Network Programmability
End-to-End QoS Network Design	1	All

NOTE: You can access the Cisco Press book *End-to-End QoS Network Design: Quality of Service for Rich-Media & Cloud Networks,* Second Edition (ISBN: 9781587143694) through your Safari Books Online account.

Check Your Understanding

Refer to the Digital Study Guide to take a short quiz covering the content of this day.

Device Monitoring, Management, and Maintenance

CCNA 200-125 Exam Topics

- Configure and verify device-monitoring protocols
- Configure and verify NTP operating in a client/server mode
- Configure and verify device management
- Perform device maintenance

Key Topics

The review today covers tools used to monitor, manage, and maintain routers and switches. For device monitoring, we review how to configure and verify the Simple Network Management Protocol (SNMP), syslog, and the Network Time Protocol (NTP). For device management, we review backing up and restoring your device configuration and Cisco IOS licensing. For device maintenance, we review file system management, Cisco IOS upgrades, and password recovery.

SNMP Operation

SNMP is an application layer protocol that provides a message format for communication between managers and agents.

SNMP Components

The SNMP system consists of three elements:

- SNMP manager
- SNMP agents (managed node)
- Management Information Base (MIB)

SNMP Messages

The SNMP manager is part of a network management system (NMS) and runs SNMP management software. SNMP agents are managed devices. The MIB stores SNMP variables. SNMP uses three basic messages between SNMP managers and agents. The SNMP manager uses get messages to poll a device for information and set messages to change a device parameter. An SNMP agent can independently notify the NMS when a problem occurs using SNMP traps.

For example, SNMP can monitor the CPU utilization on a Cisco router. The NMS can sample this value periodically and warn the network administrator when the value deviates from the baseline. An SNMP agent can also be configured to send a trap message when CPU utilization is driving away from normal values for the network. Table 2-1 summarizes the get and set actions.

Table 2-1   get and set SNMP Operations

Operation	Description
get-request	Retrieves a value from a specific variable.
get-next-request	Retrieves a value from a variable within a table. The SNMP manager does not need to know the exact variable name. A sequential search is performed to find the needed variable from within a table.
get-bulk-request	Retrieves large blocks of data, such as multiple rows in a table, that would otherwise require the transmission of many small blocks of data. (This works only with SNMPv2 or later.)
get-response	Replies to a **get-request**, **get-next-request**, or **set-request** sent by an NMS.
set-request	Stores a value in a specific variable.

SNMP Versions

Several versions of SNMP exist:

- **SNMPv1:** The Simple Network Management Protocol defined in RFC 1157.

- **SNMPv2c:** Defined in RFCs 1901 to 1908. Utilizes a community string–based administrative framework.

- **SNMPv3:** Interoperable standards-based protocol originally defined in RFCs 2273 to 2275. Provides secure access to devices by authenticating and encrypting packets over the network.

SNMPv1 and SNMPv2c use community strings that control access to the MIB. Community strings are plain-text passwords. Two types of community strings exist:

- **Read-only (ro):** Provides access to the MIB variables but does not allow these variables to be changed (only read)

- **Read-write (rw):** Provides read and write access to all objects in the MIB

The Management Information Base

The MIB organizes variables hierarchically. MIB variables enable the management software to monitor and control the network device. Formally, the MIB defines each variable as an object ID (OID). OIDs uniquely identify managed objects in the MIB hierarchy. The MIB organizes the OIDs based on RFC standards into a hierarchy of OIDs, usually shown as a tree.

RFCs define some common public variables. Figure 2-1 shows portions of the MIB structure defined by Cisco Systems.

Figure 2-1   Management Information Base Object IDs

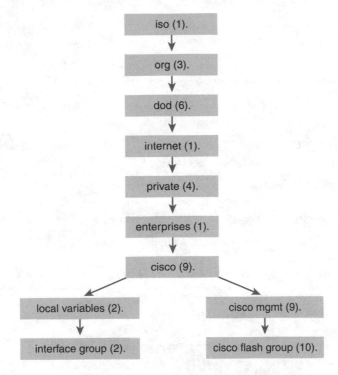

Note how the OID can be described in words or numbers to help locate a particular variable in the tree. For example, OIDs belonging to Cisco are numbered as follows: iso (1). org (3).dod (6).internet (1).private (4).enterprises (1).cisco (9). This is displayed or configured as 1.3.6.1.4.1.9.

One way to demonstrate using these OIDs is to look at how they can be implemented in the freeware SNMPGET utility. Example 2-1 shows how you might configure SNMPGET to obtain a 5-minute exponential moving average of the CPU busy percentage from a router.

Example 2-1   Obtaining a MIB Value with SNMPGET

```
[13:22][cisco@NMS~ ]$ snmpget -v2c -c community 10.250.250.14 1.3.6.1.4.1.9.2.1.58.0
SNMPv2-SMI::enterprises.9.2.1.58.0 = INTEGER: 11
```

The bold text shows a rather long command with several parameters highlighted:

- **-v2c:** The version of SNMP in use

- **-c community:** The SNMP password, called a community string

- **10.250.250.14:** The IP address of the monitored device

- **1.3.6.1.4.1.9.2.1.58.0:** The numeric OID of the MIB variable

The last line shows the response. The output shows a shortened version of the MIB variable. It then lists the actual value in the MIB location; in this example, it means that the CPU is at 11 percent utilization.

Configuring SNMP

Configuring SNMP Version 2c on a Cisco router or switch requires only one global configuration command: **snmp-server community**. The following steps include some optional commands:

Step 1.   (Required) Configure the community string and access level (read-only or read-write) with the **snmp-server community** *string* {**RO|RW**} global command.

Step 2.   (Optional) Document the location of the device using the **snmp-server location** *text-describing-location* global configuration command.

Step 3.   (Optional) Document the location of the device using the **snmp-server contact** *contact-name* global configuration command.

Step 4.   (Optional) Restrict SNMP access to NMS hosts that are permitted by an access control list (ACL) by defining an ACL and referencing the ACL on the **snmp-server community** *string acl* global configuration command.

Example 2-2 demonstrates using the required and optional commands.

Example 2-2   Configuring SNMP Version 2c for Read-Only Access

```
R1(config)# ip access-list standard SNMP_ACCESS
R1(config-std-nacl)# permit host 172.16.3.110
R1(config-std-nacl)# exit
R1(config)# snmp-server community 4md!n0n1y RO SNMP_ACCESS
R1(config)# snmp-server location Austin, TX
R1(config)# snmp-server contact Bob Smith
R1(config)# end
```

Verifying SNMP

To verify the SNMP configuration, use the **show snmp** command (see Example 2-3).

Example 2-3   Verifying SNMP

```
R1# show snmp
Chassis: FTX1636848Z
Contact: Bob Smith
Location: Lima, OH
0 SNMP packets input
    0 Bad SNMP version errors
    0 Unknown community name
    0 Illegal operation for community name supplied
    0 Encoding errors
    0 Number of requested variables
    0 Number of altered variables
```

```
     0 Get-request PDUs
     0 Get-next PDUs
     0 Set-request PDUs
     0 Input queue packet drops (Maximum queue size 1000)
359 SNMP packets output
     0 Too big errors (Maximum packet size 1500)
     0 No such name errors
     0 Bad values errors
     0 General errors
     0 Response PDUs
   359 Trap PDUs
SNMP Dispatcher:
   queue 0/75 (current/max), 0 dropped
SNMP Engine:
   queue 0/1000 (current/max), 0 dropped

SNMP logging: enabled
     Logging to 172.16.3.10, 0/10, 359 sent, 0 dropped.
```

The **show snmp** command output does not display information relating to the SNMP community string or the associated ACL (if applicable). Example 2-4 displays the SNMP community string and ACL information, using the **show snmp community** command.

Example 2-4   Verifying SNMP Community Strings

```
R1# show snmp community

Community name: ILMI
Community Index: cisco0
Community SecurityName: ILMI
storage-type: read-only   active

Community name: 4md!n0n1y
Community Index: cisco7
Community SecurityName: 4md!n0n1y
storage-type: nonvolatile    active      access-list: SNMP_ACCESS


Community name: 4md!n0n1y
Community Index: cisco8
Community SecurityName: 4md!n0n1y
storage-type: nonvolatile active
access-list: SNMP_ACCESS
```

Syslog

Syslog is a term used to describe a standard that the IETF first documented as RFC 3164 in 2001. It is a popular protocol that many networking devices use, including routers, switches, application servers, firewalls, and other network appliances. These devices can send their messages across the network to be stored on syslog servers for later access by network administrators.

Syslog Operation

Syslog uses UDP port 514 to send event notification messages across IP networks to event message collectors, as Figure 2-2 illustrates.

Figure 2-2   Syslog Server Example

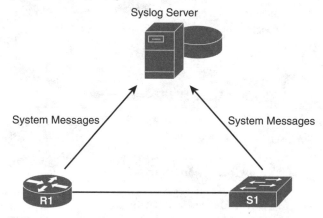

The syslog logging service provides three primary capabilities:

- Gathering logging information for monitoring and troubleshooting

- Selecting the type of logging information that is captured

- Specifying the destinations of captured syslog messages

On Cisco network devices, the syslog protocol starts by sending system messages and debug output to a local logging process internal to the device. It is possible to remotely monitor system messages by viewing the logs on a syslog server, or by accessing the device through Telnet, Secure Shell (SSH), or through the console port.

Cisco devices produce syslog messages as a result of network events. Every syslog message contains a severity level and a facility. Table 2-2 shows the complete list of syslog severity levels.

Table 2-2   Syslog Severity Level

Severity Name	Severity Level	Explanation
Emergency	Level 0	System unusable
Alert	Level 1	Immediate action needed
Critical	Level 2	Critical condition

Severity Name	Severity Level	Explanation
Error	Level 3	Error condition
Warning	Level 4	Warning condition
Notification	Level 5	Normal but significant condition
Informational	Level 6	Informational message
Debugging	Level 7	Debugging message

In addition to specifying the severity, syslog messages contain information on the facility. Syslog facilities are service identifiers that identify and categorize system state data for error and event message reporting. The logging facility options that are available are specific to the networking device. Common syslog message facilities reported on Cisco IOS routers include the following:

- IP

- OSPF protocol

- SYS operating system

- IP Security (IPsec)

- Interface IP (IF)

The default format for syslog messages follows:

```
seq no: timestamp: %facility-severity-MNEMONIC: description
```

Table 2-3 summarizes each field of the syslog message.

Table 2-3   Syslog Message Format

Field	Explanation
seq no	Stamps log messages with a sequence number only if the **service sequence-numbers** global configuration command is configured.
timestamp	Date and time of the message or event. Appears only if the **service timestamps** global configuration command is configured.
facility	The facility to which the message refers.
severity	Single-digit code from 0 to 7 that is the severity of the message.
MNEMONIC	Text string that uniquely describes the message.
description	Text string containing detailed information about the event being reported.

Using the message format and Table 2-3, you can easily interpret the following message:

```
00:00:46: %LINK-3-UPDOWN: Interface Port-channel, changed state to up
```

The **service sequence-numbers** command was not configured, but the **service timestamps** command was configured. The facility is LINK, the severity is 3, and the MNEMONIC is UPDOWN. The rest of the message provides a description of the event.

Syslog Configuration and Verification

By default, Cisco routers and switches send log messages for all severity levels to the console. On some Cisco IOS versions, the device also buffers log messages by default. To enable these two settings, use the **logging console** and **logging buffered** global configuration commands, respectively.

The **show logging** command displays the default logging service settings on a Cisco router, as Example 2-5 shows.

Example 2-5 Default Logging Service Settings

```
R1# show logging
Syslog logging: enabled (0 messages dropped, 2 messages rate-limited, 0 flushes,
  0 overruns, xml disabled, filtering disabled)


No Active Message Discriminator.


No Inactive Message Discriminator.


    Console logging: level debugging, 32 messages logged, xml disabled,
                     filtering disabled
    Monitor logging: level debugging, 0 messages logged, xml disabled,
                     filtering disabled
    Buffer logging:  level debugging, 32 messages logged, xml disabled,
                     filtering disabled
    Exception Logging: size (4096 bytes)
    Count and timestamp logging messages: disabled
    Persistent logging: disabled


No active filter modules.


    Trap logging: level informational, 34 message lines logged
          Logging Source-Interface:       VRF Name:


Log Buffer (8192 bytes):

*Jan  2 00:00:02.527: %LICENSE-6-EULA_ACCEPT_ALL: The Right to Use End User
License Agreement is accepted
*Jan  2 00:00:02.631: %IOS_LICENSE_IMAGE_APPLICATION-6-LICENSE_LEVEL: Module name
  = c1900 Next reboot level = ipbasek9 and License = ipbasek9
*Jan  2 00:00:02.851: %IOS_LICENSE_IMAGE_APPLICATION-6-LICENSE_LEVEL: Module name
  = c1900 Next reboot level = securityk9 and License = securityk9
*Jan  2 00:01:01.619: %IFMGR-7-NO_IFINDEX_FILE: Unable to open nvram:/ifIndex-
  table No such file or directory
<output omitted>
```

To configure the router to send system messages to a syslog server, complete the following three steps:

Step 1.   Configure the IP address of the syslog server in global configuration mode:

```
R1(config)# logging 192.168.1.3
```

Step 2.   Control the messages that will be sent to the syslog server with the **logging trap** *level* global configuration mode command. For example, to limit the messages to levels 4 and lower (0 to 4), use one of the two equivalent commands:

```
R1(config)# logging trap 4
```

or

```
R1(config)# logging trap warning
```

Step 3.   Optionally, configure the source interface with the **logging source-interface** *interface-type interface-number* global configuration mode command. This specifies that syslog packets contain the address of a specific interface, regardless of which interface the packet uses to exit the router. For example, to set the source interface to g0/0, use the following command:

```
R1(config)# logging source-interface g0/0
```

Example 2-6 shows the output from the **show logging** command. The default settings have been changed, as noted by the highlights.

Example 2-6   Verify the Logging Service After Configuration Check

```
R1# show logging
Syslog logging: enabled (0 messages dropped, 2 messages rate-limited, 0 flushes,
  0 overruns, xml disabled, filtering disabled)


No Active Message Discriminator.




No Inactive Message Discriminator.



    Console logging: level debugging, 41 messages logged, xml disabled,
                     filtering disabled
    Monitor logging: level debugging, 0 messages logged, xml disabled,
                     filtering disabled
    Buffer logging:  level debugging, 41 messages logged, xml disabled,
                     filtering disabled
    Exception Logging: size (4096 bytes)
    Count and timestamp logging messages: disabled
    Persistent logging: disabled
```

```
No active filter modules.

   Trap logging: level warnings, 43 message lines logged
        Logging to 192.168.1.3   (udp port 514, audit disabled,
            link up),
            4 message lines logged,
            0 message lines rate-limited,
            0 message lines dropped-by-MD,
            xml disabled, sequence number disabled
            filtering disabled
        Logging Source-Interface:      VRF Name:
        GigabitEthernet0/0
<output omitted>
```

Network Time Protocol

As you know, routers and switches issue log messages in response to different events. For example, when an interface fails, the device creates log messages. With default settings, Cisco IOS sends these messages to the console port. But Cisco IOS can be configured to also send messages to a syslog server, where they can be stored for administration review and troubleshooting. Figure 2-3 shows a topology with a syslog server.

Figure 2-3   Sample Network with a Syslog Server

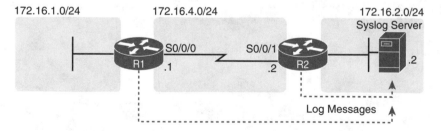

Most log messages list the date and time as part of the message so that when a network engineer looks back at the message, the engineer knows exactly when that message occurred.

The Network Time Protocol (NTP) provides a way to synchronize the time-of-day clock so that time stamps are consistent across devices, making troubleshooting easier.

To configure a router or switch to synchronize its time with an existing NTP server, use the **ntp server** command, as in Example 2-7.

Example 2-7   Configuration and Verification of an NTP Client

```
R1(config)# ntp server 172.16.2.2
R1(config)# ^Z
R1#
R1# show ntp status
Clock is synchronized, stratum 8, reference is 172.16.2.2
nominal freq is 250.0000 Hz, actual freq is 250.0000 Hz, precision is 2**21
ntp uptime is 4700 (1/100 of seconds), resolution is 4000
reference time is D42BD899.5FFCE014 (13:48:09.374 UTC Fri Oct 19 2016)
clock offset is -0.0033 msec, root delay is 1.28 msec
root dispersion is 3938.51 msec, peer dispersion is 187.59 msec
loopfilter state is 'CTRL' (Normal Controlled Loop), drift is 0.000000000 s/s
system poll interval is 64, last update was 42 sec ago.
R1# show ntp associations
address ref clock st when poll reach delay offset disp
*172.16.2.2 127.127.1.1 7 36 64 1 1.261 -0.001 7937.5
 * sys.peer, # selected, + candidate, - outlyer, x falseticker, configured
```

The output of the **show ntp status** command gives the NTP status in the very first line—R1 is synchronized with the NTP server at 172.16.2.2. The **show ntp associations** command lists a single line of output for every other NTP device with which the router has associated.

Routers and switches can actually be the NTP server with just one command (**ntp master**) as well. In addition, NTP can use authentication so that a router or switch does not get fooled into changing its time stamp.

Cisco IOS File System and Devices

Cisco IOS devices provide a feature called the Cisco IOS Integrated File System (IFS). This system enables you to create, navigate, and manipulate directories on a Cisco device. The directories available depend on the platform.

IFS Commands

Example 2-8 shows output from the **show file systems** command.

Example 2-8   Router Default File System Router

```
Router# show file systems
File Systems:

        Size(b)        Free(b)        Type    Flags    Prefixes
           -              -           opaque     rw      archive:
           -              -           opaque     rw      system:
           -              -           opaque     rw      tmpsys:
           -              -           opaque     rw      null:
           -              -           network    rw      tftp:
```

```
        262136          251594      nvram      rw    nvram:
            -               -        opaque     wo    syslog:
            -               -        opaque     rw    xmodem:
            -               -        opaque     rw    ymodem:
            -               -        network    rw    rcp:
            -               -        network    rw    http:
            -               -        network    rw    ftp:
            -               -        network    rw    scp:
            -               -        opaque     ro    tar:
            -               -        network    rw    https:
            -               -        opaque     ro    cns:
     1002143744       683163648      usbflash   rw    usbflash1:
*     255537152       183939072      usbflash   rw    usbflash0: flash:
Router#
```

The columns show the amount of available and free memory in bytes and the type of file system and its permissions. Permissions include read-only (ro), write-only (wo), and read and write (rw). Although several file systems are listed, of interest to us are the TFTP, Flash, and NVRAM file systems.

Notice that the Flash file system has an asterisk (*) preceding it, which indicates that this is the current default file system. For the 1900 router in Example 2-8, the file system is booted from USB Flash. The alias **flash:** is associated with usbflash0 so that you can use **flash:** in your commands (such as in **show flash:**).

As Example 2-9 shows, the **dir** command lists the main directory of the default file systems, whereas **show flash:** lists the entire contents of the default file system.

Example 2-9   Default File System Directories and Files in Flash

```
Router# dir
Directory of usbflash0:/

    1  -rw-    68831808    Jun 5 2013 18:43:02 +00:00  c1900-universalk9-mz.
SPA.152-4.M3.bin
    2  -rw-        3064    Jun 5 2013 18:54:10 +00:00  cpconfig-19xx.cfg
    3  drw-           0    Nov 6 2013 12:40:56 +00:00  ipsdir
   10  drw-           0    Jun 5 2013 18:54:32 +00:00  ccpexp
  246  -rw-        2464    Jun 5 2013 18:56:14 +00:00  home.shtml
  247  -rw-         813    Nov 6 2013 12:44:22 +00:00  realm-cisco.pub.key
  248  -rw-        2465    Nov 7 2013 11:22:20 +00:00  pre_autosec.cfg
255537152 bytes total (183939072 bytes free)
Router# show flash
-#- --length-- -----date/time------ path
1      68831808 Jun 5 2013 18:43:02 +00:00 c1900-universalk9-mz.SPA.152-4.M3.bin
2          3064 Jun 5 2013 18:54:10 +00:00 cpconfig-19xx.cfg
```

```
3                  0 Nov 6 2013 12:40:56 +00:00 ipsdir
4                462 Nov 6 2013 13:14:52 +00:00 ipsdir/iosips-sig-delta.xmz
5              14978 Nov 6 2013 12:55:56 +00:00 ipsdir/iosips-sig-typedef.xmz
6              38523 Nov 6 2013 12:55:58 +00:00 ipsdir/iosips-sig-category.xmz
7                304 Nov 6 2013 12:53:40 +00:00 ipsdir/iosips-seap-delta.xmz
8                835 Nov 6 2013 12:53:40 +00:00 ipsdir/iosips-seap-typedef.xmz
9             500751 Nov 6 2013 12:56:28 +00:00 ipsdir/iosips-sig-default.xmz
10                 0 Jun 5 2013 18:54:32 +00:00 ccpexp
11                 0 Jun 5 2013 18:54:32 +00:00 ccpexp/external
<output omitted>
245               72 Jun 5 2013 18:56:12 +00:00 ccpexp/version.txt
246             2464 Jun 5 2013 18:56:14 +00:00 home.shtml
247              813 Nov 6 2013 12:44:22 +00:00 realm-cisco.pub.key
248             2465 Nov 7 2013 11:22:20 +00:00 pre_autosec.cfg

183939072 bytes available (71598080 bytes used)

Router#
```

Of particular interest is the first listing, which is the filename for the Cisco IOS image.

Notice that the output does not show the configuration files stored in NVRAM. To see these, first change directories (**cd**) to the NVRAM directory (**nvram:**). Then list the contents with the **dir** command, as in Example 2-10.

Example 2-10   Listing Directory Contents for NVRAM

```
Router# cd nvram:
Router# dir
Directory of nvram:/

  253  -rw-       1269               <no date>  startup-config
  254  ----          5               <no date>  private-config
  255  -rw-       1269               <no date>  underlying-config
    1  -rw-       2945               <no date>  cwmp_inventory
    4  ----          0               <no date>  rf_cold_starts
    5  ----         76               <no date>  persistent-data
    6  -rw-         17               <no date>  ecfm_ieee_mib
    7  -rw-        559               <no date>  IOS-Self-Sig#1.cer
    8  -rw-        559               <no date>  IOS-Self-Sig#2.cer
    9  -rw-          0               <no date>  ifIndex-table

262136 bytes total (251594 bytes free)
Router#
```

NOTE: You can also simply use the command **dir nvram:** to list the contents of the nvram: directory.

The file we are most interested in as CCNA exam candidates is the startup-config file.

URL Prefixes for Specifying File Locations

File locations are specified in Cisco IFS using the URL convention shown in the example in Figure 2-4.

Figure 2-4   Using a URL to Specify TFTP Location

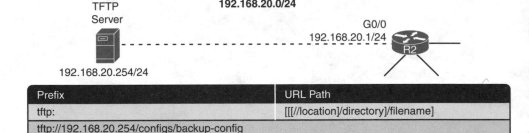

In Figure 2-4, the parts of the URL tftp://192.168.20.254/configs/backup-config can be dissected as follows:

- tftp: is the prefix specifying the protocol.

- Everything after the double slash (//) defines the file location.

- 192.168.20.254 is the location of the TFTP server.

- configs is the master directory on the TFTP server.

- backup-config is a sample filename.

The TFTP URL in Figure 2-4 is an example of a remote URL. Examples of URLs for accessing the local Cisco IFS include the following:

- flash:configs/backup-config

- system:running-config (this accesses RAM)

- nvram:startup-config

Commands for Managing Configuration Files

Knowing the URL structure is important because you use it when copying configuration files from one location to another. The Cisco IOS Software **copy** command enables you to move configuration files from one component or device to another, such as RAM, NVRAM, or a TFTP server. Figure 2-5 shows the command syntax.

Figure 2-5   copy Command Syntax

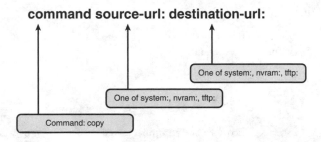

The source URL is where you are copying from. The destination URL is where you are copying to. For example, you are already familiar with the abbreviated command **copy run start**; however, in its most verbose form, this command specifies the file locations:

```
Router# copy system:running-config nvram:startup-config
```

The command states, "Copy the running configuration from the system's RAM to NVRAM and save it with the filename startup-config."

Example 2-11 demonstrates how to copy the current running configuration to a new local directory named configs that you would create.

Example 2-11   Copying Files to a Local Directory

```
Router# mkdir configs
Create directory filename [configs]? <Enter>
Created dir usbflash0:/configs
Router# copy system:running-config configs/backup-config
Destination filename [/configs/backup-config]? <Enter>
1269 bytes copied in 0.648 secs (1958 bytes/sec)
```

Other examples include copying from RAM to TFTP:

```
Router# copy system:running-config tftp:
```

Or simply:

```
Router# copy run tftp
```

Copying from TFTP to RAM:

```
Router# copy tftp: system:running-config
```

Or simply:

```
Router# copy tftp run
```

Copying from TFTP to the startup configuration file:

```
Router# copy tftp: nvram:startup-config
```

Or simply:

```
Router# copy tftp nvram
```

The **copy** commands using TFTP require more configurations (covered in the next section) after you enter them to carry out the instruction.

Manage Cisco IOS Images

As any network grows, storing Cisco IOS Software images and configuration files on the central TFTP server gives you control over the number and revision level of Cisco IOS images and configuration files that must be maintained. Use the **show version** command to verify the Cisco IOS image currently running on the device. Figure 2-6 shows a sample topology with a TFTP server.

Figure 2-6   TFTP Topology

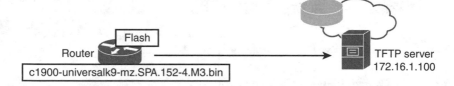

Backing Up a Cisco IOS Image

Make sure that a TFTP server is configured and running on the network. Then follow these steps to copy a Cisco IOS Software image from Flash memory to the network TFTP server:

Step 1.   ping the TFTP server to ensure that you have access to it:

```
R1# ping 172.16.1.100


Type escape sequence to abort.
Sending 5, 100-byte ICMP Echos to 172.16.1.100, timeout is 2 seconds:
!!!!!
Success rate is 100 percent (5/5), round-trip min/avg/max = 31/31/32 ms


R1#
```

Step 2.   Copy the current system image file from the router to the network TFTP server using the **copy flash: tftp:** command in privileged EXEC mode. You then are prompted. The command requires that you enter the IP address of the remote host and the name of the source and destination system image files:

```
R1# copy flash: tftp:

Source filename []? c1900-universalk9-mz.SPA.152-4.M3.bin

Address or name of remote host []? 172.16.1.100

Destination filename [c1900-universalk9-mz.SPA.152-4.M3.bin]? <Enter>

!!!!!!!!!!!!!!!!!!!!!!!!!!!!!!!!!!!!!!!!!!!!!!!!!!!!!!!!!

<Output omitted>

68831808 bytes copied in 113.061 secs (608802 bytes/sec)

R1#
```

During the copy process, exclamation points (!) indicate the progress. Each exclamation point signifies that one User Datagram Protocol (UDP) segment has successfully transferred.

Restoring a Cisco IOS Image

Verify with the **dir** or **show flash:** commands that the router has sufficient disk space to accommodate the new Cisco IOS Software image, as in Example 2-12.

Example 2-12   Output from the dir Command

```
R1# dir
Directory of usbflash0:/

    1  -rw-     68831808   Jun 5 2013 18:43:02 +00:00   c1900-universalk9-
                                                         mz.SPA.152-4.M3.bin
    2  -rw-         3064   Jun 5 2013 18:54:10 +00:00   cpconfig-19xx.cfg
    3  drw-            0   Nov 6 2013 12:40:56 +00:00   ipsdir
   10  drw-            0   Jun 5 2013 18:54:32 +00:00   ccpexp
  246  -rw-         2464   Jun 5 2013 18:56:14 +00:00   home.shtml
  247  -rw-          813   Nov 6 2013 12:44:22 +00:00   realm-cisco.pub.key
  248  -rw-         2465   Nov 7 2013 11:22:20 +00:00   pre_autosec.cfg
  249  drw-            0   Feb 8 2014 19:49:08 +00:00   configs

255537152 bytes total (183926784 bytes free)
R1#
```

The **show flash:** or **dir** commands help you determine the following:

- The total amount of Flash memory on the router

- The amount of Flash memory available

- The names of all the files stored in the Flash memory and the amount of Flash occupied

Example 2-13 shows the commands necessary to copy an image stored on the TFTP server to Flash.

Example 2-13   Upgrading the Cisco IOS Image from a TFTP Server

```
R1# copy tftp flash
Address or name of remote host []? 172.16.1.100
Source filename []? c1900-universalk9-mz.SPA.152-4.M3.bin
Destination filename [c1900-universalk9-mz.SPA.152-4.M3.bin]? <Enter>

Loading c1900-universalk9-mz.SPA.152-4.M3.bin from 172.16.1.100: !!!!!!!!!!!!!!!!!!
!!!!!!!!!!!!!!!!!!!!!!!!!!!!!!!!!!!!!!!!!!!!!!!!!!!!!!!!!!!!!!!!!!!!!!!!!!!!!!!!!!!!!
!!!!!!!!!!!!!!!!!!!!!!!!!!!!!!!!!!!!!!!!!!!!!!!!!!!!!!!!!!!!!!!!!!!!!!!!!!!!!!!!!!!!!!
!!!!!!!!!!!!!!!!!!!!!!!!!!!!!!!!!!!!!!!!!!!!!!!!!!!!!!!!!!!!!!!!!
[OK - 68831808 bytes]

68831808 bytes copied in 9.656 secs (7128397 bytes/sec)
R1#
```

The command asks for the IP address of the TFTP server and then the Cisco IOS image filename stored on the TFTP server that you want to copy over. When asked for the destination filename, you can change it, but this is not recommended because the name has specific meanings, as reviewed yesterday.

Managing Cisco IOS Licenses

Cisco IOS 15 uses a universal Cisco IOS image. Each device ships with the same universal image. Feature sets and technology packages are unlocked via licensing. The four technology packages follow:

- IP Base
- Data
- Unified Communications (UC)
- Security (SEC)

The IP Base license is a prerequisite to installing the other three technology packages. Use the **show license feature** privileged EXEC command to view the technology package currently installed. Figure 2-7 summarizes the licensing process.

Figure 2-7   Licensing Process

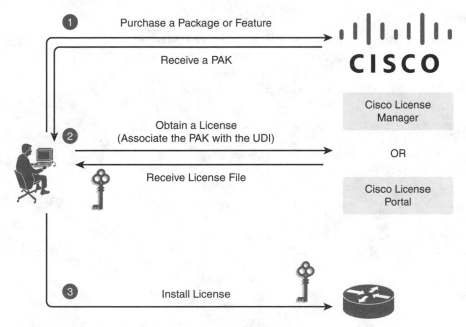

To permanently activate a new software or technology package on the router, complete the following three steps:

Step 1.   Purchase the software package or feature to install. You will receive a product activation key (PAK) to use during Step 2. A PAK is an 11-digit alphanumeric key created by Cisco manufacturing. It defines the feature set associated with the PAK. A PAK is not tied to a specific device until the license is created.

Step 2.   Obtain a license using one of the following methods:

- **Cisco License Manager (CLM)**—a freeware software application that you can download from CCO (http://www.cisco.com/go/clm)

- **Cisco License Registration Portal**—a web-based portal for getting and registering individual licenses (http://www.cisco.com/go/license)

    Regardless of which method you choose, each requires a PAK and a unique device identifier (UDI). The UDI is a combination of the product ID and serial number. Using the **show license udi** privileged EXEC command, you can obtain the UDI from the router on which you are installing the license. This information is also available on a pull-out label tray found on the device. The UDI is used to link your Cisco IOS to the hardware.

Step 3.   Use the XML license file received from Cisco to install the license.

    Use the **license install** *stored-location-url* privileged EXEC mode command to install the license.

    Reload the router to activate the license.

Example 2–14 demonstrates installing and verifying a license.

Example 2-14   Installing and Verifying a License

```
R1# license install flash0:seck9-C1900-SPE150_K9-FHH12250057.xml
Installing licenses from "seck9-c1900-SPE150_K9-FHH12250057.xml"
Installing...Feature:seck9...Successful:Supported
1/1 licenses were successfully installed
0/1 licenses were existing licenses
0/1 licenses were failed to install
R1#
%LICENSE-6-INSTALL: Feature seck9 1.0 was installed in this device.
UDI=1900-SPE150/K9:FHH12250057; StoreIndex=15:Primary License Storage
%IOS_LICENSE_IMAGE_APPLICATION-6-LICENSE_LEVEL: Module name = c1900
Next reboot level = seck9 and License = seck9
R1# reload
<output omitted>
R1# show version
<Output omitted>
License Info:
License UDI:
-------------------------------------------------
Device#    PID                    SN
-------------------------------------------------
*0         CISCO1941/K9       FTX1636848Z
Technology Package License Information for Module:'c1900'
----------------------------------------------------------------
Technology    Technology-package            Technology-package
              Current      Type             Next reboot
----------------------------------------------------------------
ipbase        ipbasek9     Permanent        ipbasek9
security      seck9        Permanent        seck9
uc            None         None             None
data          None         None             None
R1# show license
Index 1  Feature: ipbasek9
         Period left: Life time
         License Type: Permanent
         License State: Active, In Use
         License Count: Non-Counted
         License Priority: Medium
Index 2  Feature: securityk9
         Period left: Life time
         License Type: Permanent
         License State: Active, In Use
         License Count: Non-Counted
         License Priority: Medium
```

```
Index 3  Feature: datak9
         Period left: Not Activated
         Period Used: 0  minute  0  second
         License Type: EvalRightToUse
         License State: Not in Use, EULA not accepted
         License Count: Non-Counted
         License Priority: None
<Output omitted>
```

To back up a license, use the command **license save** *file-sys://lic-location* privileged EXEC command, as in Example 2-15.

Example 2-15   Backing Up a License

```
R1# license save flash0:R1_license_files
license lines saved ..... to flash0:R2_license_files

R1# show flash0:
-# - --length-- -----date/time------ path
1      68831808 Apr 2 2013 21:50:32  +00:00 c1900-universalk9-mz.SPA.152-4.M3.bin
2          1153 Apr 27 2013 01:34:32 +00:00 R1_license_files

182398976 bytes available (68832961 bytes used)

R1#
```

To uninstall a license, complete the following steps, as in Example 2-16:

Step 1.   Disable the technology package.

Step 2.   Clear the technology license package from storage.

A router reload is required after each step.

Example 2-16   Uninstalling a License

```
R1(config)# license boot module c1900 technology-package seck9 disable
R1(config)# do reload
<output omitted>
R1# license clear seck9
R1# configure terminal
R1(config)# no license boot module c1900 technology-package seck9 disable
R1(config)# do reload
<output omitted>
```

Password Recovery

Password recovery procedures for any Cisco router or switch are readily available online. For example, search for "1941 password recovery" and you will quickly find the procedures you need to follow to reset the password. This is why physical security is a must for all networking devices.

Routers and switches should be behind locked doors.

Step 1. Use the power switch to turn off the router, and then turn the router back on.

Step 2. Press the break key specified by your terminal software within 60 seconds of powerup to access the ROMmon prompt. For Tera Term, use the key combination Alt+b.

Step 3. Enter **confreg 0x2142** at the ROMmon prompt. This causes the router to bypass the startup configuration where the forgotten password is stored.

Step 4. Enter **reset** at the prompt. The router reboots, but it ignores the saved configuration. However, the file still exists in NVRAM.

Step 5. Press Ctrl-C to skip the initial setup procedure.

Step 6. Enter **enable** at the Router> prompt. This puts you into privileged EXEC mode, where you should be able to see the Router# prompt.

Step 7. Enter **copy startup-config running-config** to copy the backup NVRAM config file into memory.

Step 8. Enter **configure terminal**.

Step 9. Enter the **enable secret** *password* command to change the enable secret password.

Step 10. Issue the **no shutdown** command on every interface that you want to activate.

Step 11. From global configuration mode, enter **config-register 0x2102** to restore the original configuration registry setting.

Step 12. Press Ctrl-Z or enter **end** to leave configuration mode.

Step 13. Enter **copy running-config startup-config** to commit the changes. You can issue the **show ip interface brief** command to confirm that your interface configuration is correct. Every interface that you want to use should display up and up.

You have now completed password recovery. Entering the **show version** command confirms that the router will use the configured config register setting on the next reboot.

Packet Tracer Activity: Device Management and Maintenance

Refer to the Digital Study Guide to access the PKA file for this activity. You must have Packet Tracer software to run this activity. See the Introduction for details.

Study Resources

For today's exam topics, refer to the following resources for more study.

Resource	Location	Topic
Primary Resources		
Routing and Switching Essentials v6	10	Device Management
		Device Maintenance
Scaling Networks v6	5	SNMP
ICND1 Official Cert Guide	33	All
	35	All
	36	All
ICND2 Official Cert Guide	26	Simple Network Management Protocol
Supplemental Resources		
CCNA Portable Command Guide	26	All
	30	All
	31	All
CCNA Video Series	5	Lesson 4: Network Time Protocol (NTP)
	7	Lesson 1: Network Management Protocols
		Lesson 2: Device Management
CCNA Network Simulator	ICND1	Chapter 33: Syslog Configuration I–III
		Chapter 33: NTP Configuration I–III
		Chapter 35: Password Recovery
		Chapter 35: Booting a New Router IOS
		Chapter 35: Setting the Configuration Register
		Chapter 35: Comparing Configuration Files
		Chapter 35: Ignoring the Startup-config File
		Chapter 35: Migrating to a New IOS Image
		Chapter 35: IOS Verification
		Chapter 36: IOS Licensing Installation and Migration
		Chapter 36: IOS License Installation
		Chapter 36: IOS License Removal
		Chapter 36: IOS License Verification
	ICND2	Chapter 26: SNMP Configuration I–III
		Chapter 26: IP SLA Configuration I

? Check Your Understanding

Refer to the Digital Study Guide to take a short quiz covering the content of this day.

Troubleshooting Methodologies and Tools

CCNA 200-125 Exam Topics

- Apply troubleshooting methodologies to resolve problems
- Use Cisco IOS tools to troubleshoot and resolve problems
- Troubleshoot basic Layer 3 end-to-end connectivity issues
- Troubleshoot network connectivity issues using ICMP echo-based IP SLA

Key Topics

During the past 30 days, troubleshooting has been a part of many of the exam topics. Today we review the exam topics that specifically focus on troubleshooting. Then we wrap up our 31-day journey with a Packet Tracer activity that enables you to practice implementing many of the technologies that the CCNA exam covers.

Troubleshooting Documentation

To monitor and troubleshoot a network, network administrators must have a complete set of accurate and current network documentation. This documentation includes the following:

- Configuration files, including network configuration files and end system configuration files
- Physical and logical topology diagrams
- A baseline performance level

Configuration Files

The network configuration files should include detailed information for each network device, such as the following:

- Type of device and model designation
- IOS image name
- Device network hostname
- Location of the device (building, floor, room, rack, panel)
- All module types and the module slot where they are located (if a modular device)
- Data link layer addresses

- Network layer addresses
- Any additional important information about physical aspects of the device

The following information can be documented within the end system configuration files:

- Device name (purpose)
- Operating system and version
- IPv4 and IPv6 addresses
- Subnet mask and prefix length
- Default gateway, DNS server, and WINS server addresses
- Any high-bandwidth network applications that the end system runs

Topology Diagrams

Physical topologies typically include vital information to help network technicians locate and resolve issues. Figure 1-1 shows a simplified example of the type of information you might find on a physical topology.

Figure 1-1   Physical Topology

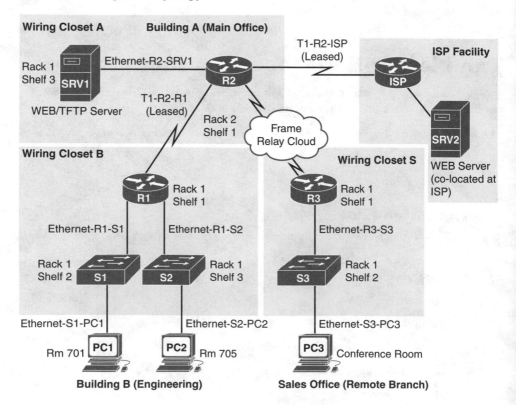

NOTE: A physical topology for an existing network generally is much more complex than the example shown here.

The physical and logical topology can be combined into one network topology. However, doing so might make the documentation complex and noisy with data. Therefore, organizations often have a separate logical topology, as in the example in Figure 1-2.

Figure 1-2   Logical Topology

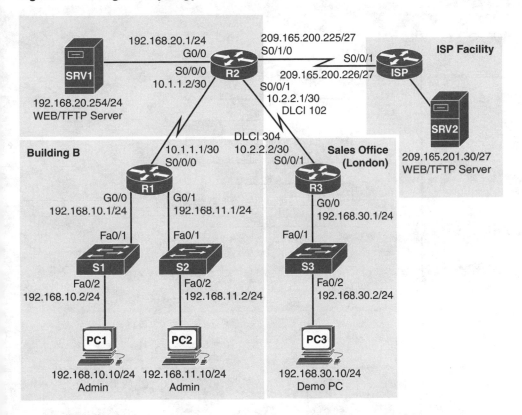

Baseline Date

The initial network performance baseline sets the stage for measuring the effects of network changes and subsequent troubleshooting efforts. Establishing this baseline requires three broad steps:

Step 1.   Determine the types of data to collect.

Step 2.   Identify devices and ports of interest.

Step 3.   Determine the baseline duration.

You can manually collect much of the data using many of the **show** commands that you have learned throughout your studies (**show ip route**, **show ip interface brief**, **show running-config**, and so on). However, establishing an initial baseline and conducting a performance-monitoring analysis both require many hours or days to accurately reflect network performance. Network management software or protocol inspectors and sniffers often run continuously over the course of the data collection process.

Troubleshooting Methods

Regardless of the method you use, troubleshooting any network problem involves three major stages, as Figure 1-3 shows.

Figure 1-3   The Troubleshooting Process

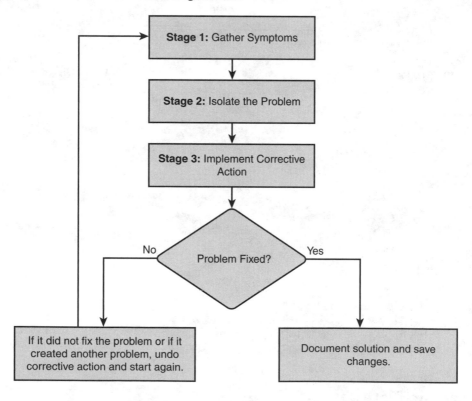

During the first stage, symptoms can appear in many different forms, including alerts from network management systems, console messages, and help desk tickets. The information gathered from these symptoms ultimately directs the network administrator's attention to an area of the network—a single device, a group of devices, or an entire subnet of devices.

During the second stage, the network administrator isolates the problem by using tools that most likely generate the data necessary to recommend a course of action for the next stage.

Finally, in the third stage, the network administrator implements the most likely solution and tests it. If the original problem is resolved, the administrator documents and saves the solution. If the problem is not resolved, the administrator removes the solution implemented and returns to the first stage (gathering symptoms).

One systematic way to implement the troubleshooting process is to use the OSI model and one of the following three methods:

- **Bottom–up:** Start at the physical layer and check all the physical components. Because many issues are related to Layer 1, this method often proves effective. The disadvantage is that this method involves physically checking every device in the affected area of the network.

- **Top–down:** Start with the end-user applications that are not working properly and move down through the layers. This method proves most effective when the issue is related to software. The disadvantage is that it requires checking every network application until the possible problem is found. Which application do you begin with?

- **Divide and conquer:** The network administrator uses experience and the nature of the symptoms to make an informed guess on which OSI layer to start the investigation. After verifying that a layer is functioning properly, the administrator can assume that the layers below it are functioning. The administrator can then work up the OSI layers. If an OSI layer is not functioning properly, the administrator can work down the OSI layer model. The disadvantage to this method is that it requires more expertise than the other methods.

To quickly resolve network problems, take the time to select the most effective network troubleshooting method (see Figure 1-4).

Figure 1-4   Guidelines for Selecting a Troubleshooting Method

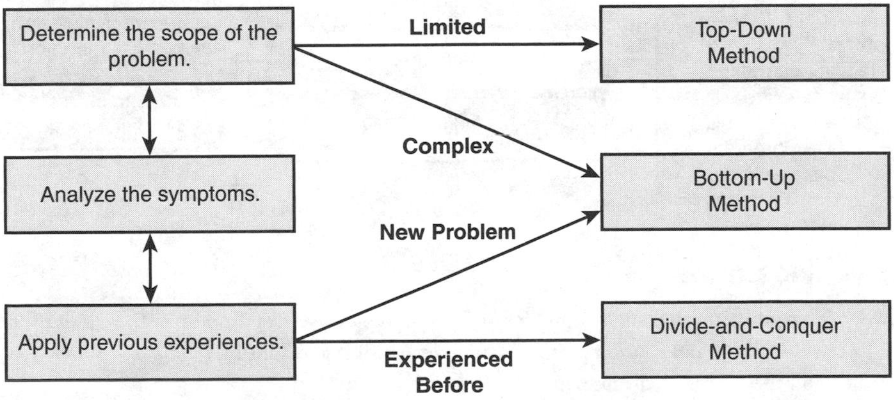

Troubleshooting at Each Layer

This section reviews some of the more common issues at each layer of the OSI model.

Physical Layer

Because the upper layers of the OSI model depend on the physical layer to function, a network administrator must know how to effectively isolate and correct problems at this layer. Figure 1-5 shows typical symptoms and their associated causes at the physical layer.

Figure 1-5   Physical Layer Symptoms and Causes

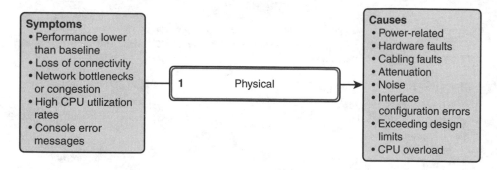

Data Link Layer

Layer 2 problems cause specific symptoms that, when recognized, help identify the problem quickly. Figure 1-6 shows typical symptoms and their associated causes at the data link layer.

Figure 1-6   Data Link Layer Symptoms and Causes

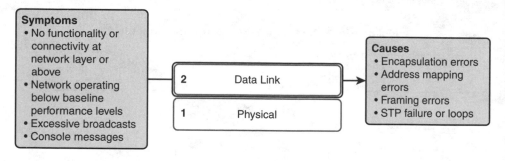

Network Layer

Network layer problems include any problem that involves a Layer 3 protocol, both routed protocols (such as IPv4 or IPv6) and routing protocols (such as EIGRP and OSPF). Figure 1-7 shows typical symptoms and their associated causes at the network layer.

Figure 1-7   Network Layer Symptoms and Causes

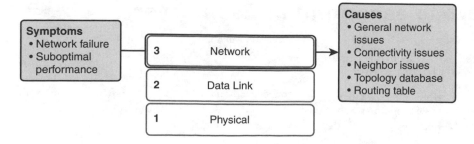

Transport Layer

Network problems can arise from transport layer problems on the router, particularly at the edge of the network where traffic is examined and modified. Two of the most commonly implemented transport layer technologies are access control lists (ACL) and network address translation (NAT), shown in Figure 1-8.

Figure 1-8   Transport Layer Symptoms and Causes

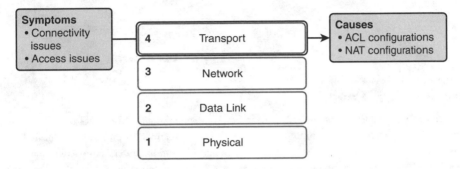

The most common issues with ACLs result from improper configuration, as Figure 1-9 illustrates.

Figure 1-9   Common ACL Misconfigurations

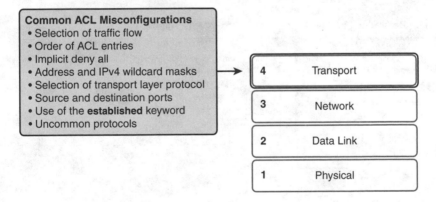

NAT can cause some unique issues, including misconfigured NAT inside or outside, or misconfigured access control lists (ACL). NAT can also cause issues when interoperating with other technologies, such as the ones in Figure 1-10.

Figure 1-10   Common Interoperability Issues with NAT

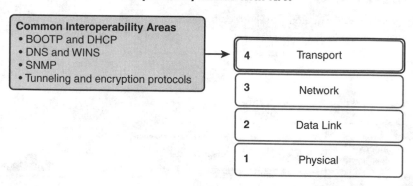

Application Layer

Application layer problems prevent services from being provided to application programs. A problem at the application layer can result in unreachable or unusable resources when the physical, data link, network, and transport layers are functional. It is possible to have full network connectivity, but the application simply cannot provide data. The types of symptoms and causes depend on the actual application itself. Figure 1-11 shows the most popular protocols that can cause issues at the application layer.

Figure 1-11   Application Layer Protocols

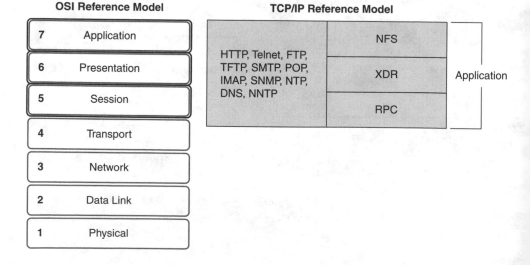

Bottom-Up Method and the Layers

When no end-to-end connectivity exists and you choose to use the bottom-up method, you can follow these sample steps:

Step 1. Check physical connectivity at the point where network communication stops.

Step 2. Check for duplex mismatches.

Step 3. Check data link and network layer addressing on the local network. This includes IPv4 ARP tables, IPv6 neighbor tables, MAC address tables, and VLAN assignments.

Step 4. Verify that default gateways are correctly configured on devices that need it.

Step 5. Ensure that devices are determining the correct path from the source to the destination. Manipulate the routing information, if necessary.

Step 6. Verify that the transport layer is functioning properly. You can also use Telnet to test transport layer connections from the command line.

Step 7. Verify that no access control lists are blocking traffic.

Step 8. Ensure that DNS settings are correct and that a DNS server is accessible.

Troubleshooting with IP Service Level Agreement

The IP service level agreement (SLA) feature on Cisco routers helps measure performance over a period of time to determine whether a link is meeting its service level agreement. This contributes to troubleshooting by immediately identifying that a problem exists. Multiple IP SLA operations can be running on the network or on a device at any time. IP SLA information is displayed using CLI commands or through SNMP.

A network engineer can use the IP SLA ICMP Echo operation to intermittently and automatically test the availability of network devices. For example, a device can be configured with an IP SLA that sends a ping every 30 seconds. This IP SLA ICMP Echo operation provides the following measurements:

- Availability monitoring (packet loss statistics)
- Performance monitoring (latency and response time)
- Network operation (end-to-end connectivity)

Consider the topology in Figure 1-12. The network administrator wants to measure the quality of the link between R1 and R3 over time.

Figure 1-12   IP SLA Configuration Topology

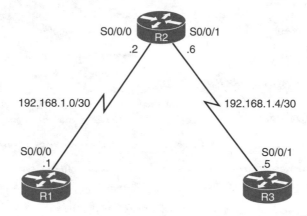

Example 1-1 shows the configuration for R1.

Example 1-1   IP SLA Configuration

```
R1(config)# ip sla 1
R1(config-ip-sla)# icmp-echo 192.168.1.5
R1(config-ip-sla-echo)# frequency 30
R1(config-ip-sla-echo)# exit
R1(config)# ip sla schedule 1 start-time now life forever
R1(config)# end
R1#
```

NOTE: To configure IP SLAs, make sure the security technology package is activated on the device.

The following steps explain the configuration:

Step 1.   The **ip sla** command configures a user-defined IP SLA number and enters IP SLA configuration mode.

Step 2.   The **icmp-echo** command configures the IP address to test the SLA.

Step 3.   The **frequency** command sets how often the ping is sent, in seconds.

Step 4.   The **ip sla schedule** command sets a schedule for a configured IP SLA. In the example, the IP SLA 1 is set to start immediately and to run forever or until the network administrator stops it.

Use the **show ip sla configuration** command to verify the IP SLA, as in Example 1-2.

Example 1-2 IP SLA Verification

```
R1# show ip sla configuration
IP SLAs Infrastructure Engine-III
Entry number: 1
Owner:
Tag:
Operation timeout (milliseconds): 5000
Type of operation to perform: icmp-echo
Target address/Source address: 192.168.1.5/0.0.0.0
Type Of Service parameter: 0x0
Request size (ARR data portion): 28
Verify data: No
Vrf Name:
Schedule:
   Operation frequency (seconds): 30   (not considered if randomly scheduled)
   Next Scheduled Start Time: Start Time already passed
   Group Scheduled : FALSE
   Randomly Scheduled : FALSE
   Life (seconds): Forever
   Entry Ageout (seconds): never
   Recurring (Starting Everyday): FALSE
   Status of entry (SNMP RowStatus): Active
Threshold (milliseconds): 5000
Distribution Statistics:
   Number of statistic hours kept: 2
   Number of statistic distribution buckets kept: 1
   Statistic distribution interval (milliseconds): 20
Enhanced History:
History Statistics:
   Number of history Lives kept: 0
   Number of history Buckets kept: 15
   History Filter Type: None
R1#
```

Use the **show ip sla statistics** command to display IP SLA operation monitoring statistics, as in Example 1-3.

Example 1-3   Display the IP SLA Statistics

```
R1# show ip sla statistics
IPSLAs Latest Operation Statistics

IPSLA operation id: 1
        Latest RTT: 1 milliseconds
Latest operation start time: 12:15:36 UTC Sat Dec 17 2016
Latest operation return code: OK
Number of successes: 10
Number of failures: 0
Operation time to live: Forever
R1#
```

 Packet Tracer Activity: CCNA Skills Practice

Refer to the Digital Study Guide to access the PKA file for this activity. You must have Packet Tracer software to run this activity. See the Introduction for details.

Study Resources

For today's exam topics, refer to the following resources for more study.

> **NOTE:** Troubleshooting topics are integrated throughout all the study resources that cover specific technology implementations. The following topic citations indicate areas in the resources that specifically address today's exam topics.

Resource	Location	Topic
Primary Resources		
Introduction to Networks v6	11	Network Troubleshooting
Connecting Networks v6	8	All
ICND1 Official Cert Guide	12	All
	23	Problem Isolation Using the **ping** Command
		Problem Isolation Using the **traceroute** Command
	24	All
	33	Sending Messages in Real Time to Current Users
ICND2 Official Cert Guide	19, 20, 21	Troubleshooting Topics
	26	IP Service Level Agreement

Resource	Location	Topic
Supplemental Resources		
CCNA Portable Command Guide	32	All
CCNA Video Series	1	Lesson 6: Basic Troubleshooting
	7	Lesson 1: Network Management Protocols (IP SLA content)
		Lesson 3: Troubleshooting with Cisco IOS Tools
CCNA Network Simulator	ICND1	Chapter 12: Topology Analysis
		Chapter 12: Switch Forwarding Troubleshooting
		Chapter 12: VLAN Troubleshooting
		Chapter 23: Ping
		Chapter 23: Traceroute III
		Chapter 33: Loopback Interfaces
		Chapter 33: Terminal Monitor
	ICND2	Chapter 19: MLS Troubleshooting
		Chapter 19: Router-on-a-Stick Troubleshooting
		Chapter 26: IP SLA Configuration I–II

 Check Your Understanding

Refer to the Digital Study Guide to take a short quiz covering the content of this day.

Exam Day

Today is your opportunity to prove that you have what it takes to manage a small enterprise branch network. Just 90 minutes and 50 to 60 questions stand between you and your CCNA certification. Use the following information to focus on the process details for the day of your CCNA exam.

What You Need for the Exam

Write down the exam location, date, exam time, exam center phone number, and proctor's name.

- You must have two forms of ID that include a photo and signature, such as a driver's license, passport, or military identification. In addition, the test center admission process requires the capture of a digital photo and digital signature.

- The test proctor will take you through the agreement and set up your testing station after you have signed the agreement.

- The test proctor will give you a sheet for scratch paper or a dry erase pad. Do not take these out of the room.

- The testing center will store any personal items while you take the exam. It is best to bring only what you need.

- You will be monitored during the entire exam.

What You Should Receive After Completion

When you complete the exam, you will see an immediate electronic response on whether you passed or failed. The proctor will give you a certified score report with the following important information:

- Your score report, including the minimum passing score and your score on the exam. The report also includes a breakout displaying your percentage for each general exam topic.

- Identification information required to track your certification. *Do not lose your certified examination score report.*

Summary

Your state of mind is a key factor in your success on the CCNA exam. If you know the details of the exam topics and the details of the exam process, you can begin the exam with confidence and focus. Arrive early to the exam. Bring earplugs just in case a testing neighbor has a bad cough or any loud nervous habits. Do not let an extremely difficult or specific question impede your progress. You cannot return to questions on the exam that you have already answered, so answer each question confidently and move on.

Post-Exam Information

Signing up for and actually taking the CCNA exam is no small accomplishment. Many network engineers have avoided certification exams for years. The following sections discuss your options after exam day.

Receiving Your Certificate

If you passed the exam, you will receive your official CCNA certificate in about 6 weeks (8 weeks internationally) after exam day. Your certificate will be mailed to the address you provided when you registered for the exam.

You need your examination score report to access the certification tracking system and set up a login to check your certification status. If you do not receive your certificate, you can open a case in the certificate online support located at the following web address:

https://ciscocert.secure.force.com/english/MainPage

When you receive your certificate, you might want to frame it and put it on a wall. A certificate on a wall is much harder to lose than a certificate in a filing cabinet or random folder. You never know when an employer or academic institution could request a copy.

Your CCNA is valid for 3 years. To keep your certificate valid, you must either pass the CCNA exam again or pass a more advanced certification before the end of the 3-year period.

Determining Career Options

After you pass the CCNA exam, be sure to add your CCNA certification to your resumé. Matthew Moran provides the following advice for adding certifications to a resumé in his book *Building Your I.T. Career: A Complete Toolkit for a Dynamic Career in Any Economy*, 2nd Edition (Pearson IT Certification, 2013, ISBN: 9780789749437):

> I don't believe you should place your certifications after your name. It is presumptuous to pretend that your latest certification is the equivalent to someone who has spent 4–7 years pursuing a Ph.D. or some other advanced degree. Instead, place your certifications or degrees in a section titled *Education and Certifications*. A master's degree might be the exception to this rule.

Moran also discusses good strategies for breaking into the IT industry after you have earned your CCNA:

> The most important factor is that you are moving toward a career goal. You might not get the title or job you want right out of school. If you can master those skills at your current position, while simultaneously building your network of contacts that lead to your dream position, you should be satisfied. You must build your career piece by piece. It won't happen all at once.

Moran outlines in his book that certifications such as the CCNA are part of an overall professional skill set that you must continually enhance to further your IT career.

Your CCNA certificate proves that you are disciplined enough to commit to a rigorous course of study and follow through with your professional goals. You won't likely be hired simply because you have a CCNA, but you will be placed ahead of other candidates. To supplement the CCNA certification on your resumé, be sure to highlight any networking skills that pertain to the CCNA in the job and skills descriptions on your resumé.

Examining Certification Options

Passing the CCNA exam is no easy task, but it is the starting point for more advanced Cisco certifications, such as the CCNA Security, CCNA Data Center, CCNA Cyber Ops, or even CCNP-level exams. When you log in to the online certification tracking tool (use the exam report to do this), be sure to view the Certification Progress link. This link provides specific information about certifications you can achieve with CCNA as the base.

If You Failed the Exam

If you fail your first attempt at the CCNA, you must wait at least 5 calendar days after the day of the exam to retest. Stay motivated and sign up to take the exam again within 30 days of your first attempt. The score report outlines your weaknesses. Find a study group and use The Cisco Learning Network (http://learningnetwork.cisco.com) online community to help you with those topics.

If you are familiar with the general concepts, focus on taking practice exams and memorizing the small details that make the exam so difficult. If you are a Cisco Networking Academy alumnus, you have access to the curriculum. Packet Tracer also provides an excellent network simulator. Consider your first attempt as a formal practice exam and excellent preparation to pass the second attempt.

Summary

Whether you display your certificate and update your resumé or prepare to conquer the exam on your second attempt, remember to marvel at the innovation and creativity behind each concept you learn. The ability of our society to continually improve communication will keep you learning, discovering, and employed for a lifetime.

Index

Symbols

* (asterisk), 165, 438
? command, 42–43
3-1-4 Rule, 92
3G connections, 388
3-tiered campus design, 24–26
4G connections, 388
10BASE-T, 21, 27, 34
10GBASE-LX4, 21
10GBASE-SX4, 21
10GBASE-T, 21
10GigE, 34
100BASE-FX, 21
100BASE-TX, 21
802.1D. *See* STP (Spanning Tree Protocol)
802.1x, 293–294
1000BASE-LX, 21
1000BASE-SX, 21
1000BASE-T, 21
1000BASE-TX, 21

A

A record (DNS), 365
AAA (Authentication, Authorization, and Accounting) framework, 292
AAAA record (DNS), 365
access control lists. *See* ACLs (access control lists)
access layer, 24
access layer switches, 14
access points, 17–19
access-list command, 336, 337–338, 375
ACI (Application Centric Infrastructures), 422–423
Acknowledgment field (TCP), 7–8
Acknowledgment packets (EIGRP), 241
ACL Analysis tool (APIC-EM), 424–425
ACL Path Trace tool (APIC-EM), 424–425
ACLs (access control lists), 337–339

APIC-EM (Application Policy Infrastructure Controller Enterprise Module) and, 424–425
defining, 329
design guidelines, 333–334
identification numbers, 333
interface processing ACLs, 329–330
IPv4 ACLs
    comments, 340–341
    compared to IPv6 ACLs, 343
    extended named IPv4 ACLs, 340
    extended numbered IPv4 ACLs, 337–339
    standard named IPv4 ACLs, 339–340
    standard numbered IPv4 ACLs, 335–337
    verification, 341–343
IPv6 ACLs
    applying, 344
    compared to IPv4 ACLs, 343
    creating, 344
    extended IPv6 ACLs, 345
    naming, 343 344
    standard IPv6 ACLs, 344–345
    troubleshooting, 348–349
    verification, 346–348
list logic with, 330–331
operation, 329
planning for, 331
types of, 332
Active mode (LACP), 316
AD (administrative distance), 113–115, 244–245
AD (advertised distance), 245
address conflicts, resolving, 363–364
Address Resolution Protocol (ARP), 4, 364
addresses, MAC, 11, 28
addressing, Ethernet, 36
addressing, IPv4, 77
    binary and alphanumeric representations, 90–91
    classes of addresses, 78–80
    conventions for writing, 100–102
    header format, 78
    IPv4-mapped IPv6 address, 97
    NAT (network address translation)
        benefits of, 373
        concepts, 369–371
        dynamic NAT, 371, 375–376

VTP (VLAN Trunking Protocol)
concepts, 169–171
configuration, 170–173
verification, 173–175

RS (Router Solicitation) message, 358

RSTP (Rapid STP)
definition of, 301
features of, 301

RTO (retransmission timeout), 253

RTP (Reliable Transport Protocol), 240–241

S

SaaS (Software as a Service), 418

satellite Internet, 388

SBI (southbound interface), 421

SDN (software-defined networking)
control planes, 419–420
controllers, 421
data planes, 419–420
examples, 421–424
Cisco ACI (Application Centric Infrastructures), 422–423
Cisco APIC-EM (Application Policy Infrastructure Controller Enterprise Module), 423–425
Open SDN and OpenFlow, 421–422
management planes, 420
overview of, 419

secondary keyword, 308

Secure Shell (SSH)
configuration, 294–295
remote access with, 134–135

security
ACLs (access control lists)
defining, 329
design guidelines, 333–334
identification numbers, 333
interface processing ACLs, 329–330
IP ACLs, list logic with, 330–331
operation, 329
planning for, 331
types of, 332
firewalls, 16
IDS (Intrusion Detection Systems), 16–17
IPS (Intrusion Prevention Systems), 16–17
password recovery, 448

ports
configuration, 285–287
switch port hardening, 291
violation verification and restoration, 287–289
SSH (Secure Shell) configuration, 294–295
threat mitigation
802.1x, 293–294
Authentication, Authorization, and Accounting (AAA) framework, 292
DHCP snooping, 289–290
native and management VLAN modification, 290–291
switch port hardening, 291

Sequence field (TCP), 7

servers
authentication servers, 293
DHCPv4 servers, 352–356
virtualization, 416–418

service password-encryption command, 47

service sequence-numbers command, 433

service timestamps command, 433

service-password encryption command, 123

services, cloud computing, 418–419

session layer (OSI model), 2

set-request, 428

severity levels (Syslog), 432

shaping, 413–415

shortcut keys, 43–44

Shortest Path First (SPF) algorithm, 117–118

show access-lists command, 341, 346–347

show cdp command, 275

show cdp interface command, 274

show cdp neighbors command, 275

show cdp neighbors detail command, 278–279

show cdp traffic command, 279

show command, 44–45

show etherchannel summary command, 318

T

W-X-Y-Z

REGISTER YOUR PRODUCT at CiscoPress.com/register
Access Additional Benefits and SAVE 35% on Your Next Purchase

- Download available product updates.
- Access bonus material when applicable.
- Receive exclusive offers on new editions and related products. (Just check the box to hear from us when setting up your account.)
- Get a coupon for 35% for your next purchase, valid for 30 days. Your code will be available in your Cisco Press cart. (You will also find it in the Manage Codes section of your account page.)

Registration benefits vary by product. Benefits will be listed on your account page under Registered Products.

CiscoPress.com – Learning Solutions for Self-Paced Study, Enterprise, and the Classroom
Cisco Press is the Cisco Systems authorized book publisher of Cisco networking technology, Cisco certification self-study, and Cisco Networking Academy Program materials.

At CiscoPress.com you can
- Shop our books, eBooks, software, and video training.
- Take advantage of our special offers and promotions (ciscopress.com/promotions).
- Sign up for special offers and content newsletters (ciscopress.com/newsletters).
- Read free articles, exam profiles, and blogs by information technology experts.
- Access thousands of free chapters and video lessons.

Connect with Cisco Press – Visit CiscoPress.com/community
Learn about Cisco Press community events and programs.

Cisco Press